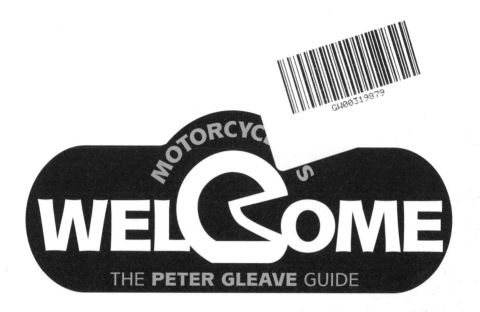

MOTORCYCLES

WELCOME

THE **PETER GLEAVE** GUIDE

Haynes

THE
BOOK

®

CONTENTS

Author: Peter Gleave

Maps: Customised Mapping

Database: Andrew Riseam

Cover photograph: Mac McDiarmid

© Peter Gleave 1999

First published 1999

Published by Haynes Publishing, Sparkford, nr Yeovil, Somerset, England BA22 7JJ. A catalogue record for this book is available from the British Library.

ISBN 1 85960 334 3

Printed in Great Britain by J. H. Haynes & Co. Ltd.

While every effort is taken to ensure the accuracy of the information given in this book, no liability can be accepted by the author or publishers for any loss, damage or injury caused by errors in, or omissions from, the information given.

FOREWORD

Motorcycling is a very big part of the leisure industry and is now more popular and socially acceptable than ever before. These days your bank manager, accountant or doctor could be bikers! With the help of this first edition of the Peter Gleave Motorcyclists Welcome Guide, the travelling motorcyclist can now plan his journey in advance.

The guide contains approximately 1200 entries of hotels, bed and breakfast establishments, pubs, restaurants and cafés, where motorcyclists can be assured of a warm welcome. All hotels and bed and breakfasts listed are quality establishments, and are particularly suited to the motorcyclist and his needs. For example, most are able to provide services such as secure parking and drying facilities for wet clothes.

There are sections on specific areas of motorcycling interest, which include a complete listing of all motorcycle dealers in the UK and their franchises, useful information on security, insurance and finance, and sections on tyre technology and oil which should provide all the information needed to ensure safe and efficient motorcycling.

This guide is the first of its kind to be published in the UK and we intend to produce a new and revised edition each year. If you have any suggestions or comments regarding any of the information you see in this guide, then please write to the publishers at the Home and Leisure Division, Haynes Publishing, Sparkford, nr Yeovil, Somerset BA22 7JJ.

HOW TO USE THIS GUIDE

The Peter Gleave Motorcyclists Welcome Guide is designed to be user friendly and is divided into twelve geographical regions as follows:-

South West
Central Southern
South East
London
Wales
Central Midlands
East Anglia
North Midlands
North of England
Scotland
Isle of Man
Ireland

Each town or city is listed in alphabetic order within those regions. For example if you want to travel to Brighton, then look in the South East section. There you will find a colour coded list of hotels, bed and breakfast establishments, guest houses, pubs, cafés and tea rooms. Each entry is numbered consecutively within each section and a colour is applied to each *number* to indicate the nature of the establishment, for example:

Hotels – Green
B&Bs – Orange
Guest Houses – Blue
Pubs – Red
Tea Rooms, Cafes, Restaurants and Bistros – Purple

Most entries have symbols to indicate the services they provide:

Å – camping	⬚ – TV in all rooms	▦ – Traditional 4-poster	⛺ –grnd floor bedrooms
⊤ – meeting facilities	● – games room	⅍ – restricted/no	⅋⊙⅃ – food served
ⅢⅢ – central heating	Ⅿ – lounge for residents	smoking	◖ – beer of excellence
⛓ – children welcome	⧉ – drying facilities	♩ – private fishing	⮚ – tea/coffee in rooms
⊜ – air conditioning	⬤ – packed lunch	⊏⊐ – radio in all rooms	S – secure parking
🛁 – sauna	provided	☆ – recommended	TV – colour tv in lounge
⮲ – outdoor swimming	⮹ – hairdryers in rooms	⅄ – quality wines	✽ – gardens
⮳ – indoor swimming	U – riding/pony trekking	⅄ – gym	
☎ – telephone in rooms	◗ – night porter		

1 AXMINSTER   FAIRWATER HEAD HOTEL Hawkchurch, Axminster, Devon EX13 5TX. Tel: 01297 678349.

Located in Hawkchurch, the "village of roses", the hotel has won the Ashley Catering Award for being one of the "Best Ten Hotel Gardens". The Hotel does not offer a set menu, rather a choice of home baked cream cakes, fruit cakes, scones and preserves along with a wide selection of teas. Lunchtime bar snacks.

2 AXMINSTER   THE MANOR HOUSE Combpyne, Axminster, Devon EX13 6SX. Contact Nicky Campbell Tel & Fax: 01297 445084.

LYME REGIS 4m. An ex-nunnery, The Manor House dates from before the 13th century. Set in 3 acres of woods in the tiny village of Combpyne, it is only a 10 minute walk from the sea. Good local restaurants and pubs. Well placed for exploring the beauty of east Devon. Closed Christmas. Pre-booking required December to February. Minimum stay: 2 nights. 2 DOUBLE, 1 TWIN, EN SUITE OR PRIVATE FACILITIES.

🔲 ✂   **Prices from £24 to £27**

3 BEER
ANCHOR INN, Beer, Near Seaton, Devon EX12 3ET. Tel: 01297 20386.

Located in a very picturesque fishing village with a garden that overlooks the bay. Each room has teas/coffee facilities, hairdryer, radio and television. Six rooms have a seaview. 8 DOUBLE (5 EN SUITE).

Prices from £40 to £65

4 BICKINGTON
DARTMOOR HALFWAY INN Bickington, Devon TQ12 4JW.
Contact Mr Huggins Tel: 01626 821 270.

Boddingtons, Bass 6x and Stella Murphys all served here. Food available 7 days a week except Christmas Day. Served Monday to Saturday 11am-11pm, Sunday; 12 noon-10.30pm. Bikers can expect to receive a friendly welcome. Motoguzzi Club GB meets here.

5 BIDEFORD   MAECROFT Acre Road, Horns Cross, Bideford, Devon EX39 5EB. Contact Mrs May Tel: 01237 451786.

CLOVELLY 6m. The endless view of open countryside towards Exmoor is where the modern bungalow of Maecroft is situated – 50 yards off the A39 opposite the Coach and Horses pub. Walk to the beach through a National Trust woodland to the South West Coast Path, visit the historic village of Clovelly, Rosemoor Gardens or take a trip to Lundy Island. Close to Dartmoor and Exmoor. Enclosed Parking. Reductions for longer stay. 2 DOUBLE, 1TWIN, PRIVATE FACILITIES AVAILABLE.

🔲 ✂ 🆂   **Prices from £16 to £18**

6 BODMIN
CROWN Lanlivery, Bodmin, Cornwall PL30 5BT.

Set within grounds of the local pub, the establishment offers an ideal base from which to explore the local area which includes the Bodmin Moor. SINGLE AND DOUBLE EN-SUITE ROOMS.

Prices from £27 to £45

7 BODMIN

TREMORVAH Rosehill, Lanivet, Bodmin, Cornwall PL30 5ES. Contact Mrs W. Wheeler Tel: 01208 831379.
Tremorvah, a former farmhouse with magnificent views is only a short distance from the stone at Lanivet Church that marks the centre of Cornwall. It is situated on the A389 near to Saints Way, Bodmin Moor and the Camel Trail. Walking, cycling, golf, horse riding and fishing facilities available nearby. Taxi service available. Closed Christmas. 2 DOUBLE, 1 TWIN/SINGLE, SOME EN SUITE. CHILDREN 4+.

Prices from £15 to £17

8 BODMIN

TREGELLIST FARM Tregellist, St. Kew, Bodmin, Cornwall PL30 3HG. Contact Mrs Jill Cleave Tel: 01208 880537.
WADEBRIDGE 5m. Built in 1989 Tregellist Farmhouse is attractive, comfortable accommodation situated on a 140 acre sheep farm. Lovely views and walks. Close to north Cornwall's beaches, the moors, Camel Trail, golf courses and Llanhydrock House. Traditional evening meals. Two pubs within 2 miles. Closed November to January inclusive. 1 TWIN, 1 DOUBLE, 1 FAMILY, EN SUITE AVAILABLE.

Prices from £20 to £22

9 BOSCASTLE
CARPENTERS KITCHEN The Harbour, Boscastle, Cornwall PL35 0HD. Contact Debbie and Geoff Beszant Tel: 01840 250595.
Carpenters Kitchen is a cosy stone building on the banks of the River Valency. Run by founder members of the Guild of Tea Shops in Cornwall. Coffee, lunches and afternoon teas available from 10.30-5.30pm. All rolls, desserts, cakes and scones etc are made on the premises. Local produce is used whenever possible.

10 BOSCASTLE

TREROSEWILL FARM Paradise, Boscastle, Cornwall PL35 0DL. Contact Mrs Cheryl Nicholls Tel & Fax: 01840 250545 E.mail: Nicholls@Trerosewill.TelMe.com.
A working farm where guests can take part in the farm activities is sited a short distance away from the village of Boscastle. The rooms are furnished to the highest standards, with amazing panoramic views of Lundy and the North Devon coast from many rooms. Traditional farmhouse cuisine. Special spring/autumn breaks. FHG Diploma. Closed Christmas and New Year.
1 TWIN, 3 DOUBLE, 2 FAMILY, ALL EN SUITE.

Prices from £19 to £29.50

11 BOVEY TRACEY

FRONT HOUSE LODGE East Street, Bovey Tracey, Devon TE13 9EL. Contact Gail & Ian Campbell Tel: 01626 832202.
Front House Lodge is a 16th century building furnished to a Victorian theme with bric-a-brac and china dolls. Provides delicious breakfasts and candlelit suppers. By the edge of Dartmoor with easy access to Exeter, Plymouth and coastal areas. Secluded garden and private car park. 2 TWIN, 3 DOUBLE, 1 FAMILY, ALL EN SUITE.

Prices from £20 to £24

12 BOVEY TRACEY
PINK'S PLACE 76 Fore Street, Bovey Tracey, Devon TQ13 9AE.
Contact Tina Richardson Tel: 01626 835363.
Pink's Place is set in Courtney House, a 19th century mission house run by nuns who looked after 'wayward' girls. Located near local attractions such as Dartmoor, Becky Falls and Bovey Mill, Pink's Place offers a range of teas and home made desserts and cakes.

13 BRIDGWATER

THE PRIORY Cannington, Bridgwater, Somerset TA5 2HQ.
Contact Stuart Briggs Tel: 01278 652079.
The Georgian residence of The Priory was built in 1760 and was home to the prioress of Cannington Court. The town of Bridgwater has shops, a post office and pubs that sell good food and local cider. The village of Nether Stowey was once home to the poets Samuel Taylor Coleridge and William Wordsworth and lies between the Quantock Hills and the Somerset coastline. SINGLE, TWIN AND DOUBLE ROOMS, EN SUITE OR PRIVATE FACILITIES.
⬜ ✂ Ⓢ   **Prices from £17 to £25**

14 BRIDGWATER
WOODLANDS 35 Durleigh Road, Bridgwater, Somerset TA6 7HX.
Contact Mr Palmer Tel: 01278 423 442.
An elegant listed house set in landscaped gardens. Situated in peaceful surroundings, it is ideally located for exploring the Quantock Hills and the beautiful Somerset countryside. Visit the nearby town centre where there is a good selection of pubs and restaurants. 4 BEDROOMS, 3 EN SUITE.
⬜ Ⓢ   **Prices from £22 to £50**

15 BRIDPORT

CAIRNHILL Shipton Gorge, Bridport, Dorset DT6 4LL. Contact Bob & Anne White Tel: 01308 898203.
An ideal place to explore the Dorset countryside, Cairnhill is situated in the village of Shipton Gorge. It is 2 miles from the coast and close to the beautiful village of Burton Bradstock. In easy reach of golf courses and fishing trips in West Bay. National Trust properties nearby. Indoor swimming pool and drying facilities. Closed November to March. 1 DOUBLE, 1 TWIN, 1 TWIN/SINGLE, ALL EN SUITE OR PRIVATE FACILITIES.
⬜ ✂   **Prices from £23 to £25**

16 BRIDPORT

THE BRAMLEYS Annings Lane, Burton Bradstock, Bridport, Dorset DT6 4QN. Contact Iris & Derek Jennings Tel: 01308 897954.
The Bramleys, situated in the peaceful village of Burton Bradstock, is a modern, spacious, family home. Fishing and golf are within 5 minutes and the beach is less than a mile away. Many attractions in this unspoilt area to be enjoyed. Continental breakfasts served every day, evening meals and Sunday lunches made by prior arrangement. Closed December and January.
2 DOUBLE, 1 TWIN, 1 SINGLE, 2 BATHROOMS.
✂   **Prices from £15 to £17**

17 BRISTOL
VALLEY FARM Sandy Lane, Stanton Drew, Bristol, BS18 4EL.
Contact Mr Keel Tel: 01275 332 723.
An attractively furnished modern farmhouse located in peaceful surroundings. All rooms are fully central heated, double glazed and there is a TV in each room. Take a trip into Bristol with its lively nightlife, restaurants and bars. Easy access to the historic town of Bath. 3 BEDROOMS, 2 EN SUITE.

🔲 🆂   **Prices from £20 to £45**

18 BRIXHAM

RICHMOND HOUSE Higher Manor Road, Brixham, Devon, TQ5 8HA. Contact Ian Hayhurst Tel & Fax: 01803 882391.
Richmond House Hotel is a detached Victorian villa is only a few minutes walk from restaurants, shops and harbour. Each room is well furnished, having a colour TV and hot drink facilities. Fishing trips, river cruises, coastal walks and visits to Dartmoor are some of the local attractions on offer. Exeter Cathedral and Plymouth ferries are in easy reach. Closed January and February. 6 VARIOUS ROOMS, ALL EN SUITE.

🔲 ✂ 🆂   **Prices from £16 to £20**

19 BRIXHAM
RADDICOMBE LODGE Kingswear Road, Brixham TQ5 0EX.
Contact Mrs Hoskins Tel: 01803 882 125.
A large country house set in a quiet leafy area overlooking National Trust land and the sea. Take a day trip to the picturesque harbour towns of Brixham and Dartmouth. Curl up next to the cosy open fires on chilly evenings. 9 BEDROOMS, ALL EN SUITE.

🔲 🆂   ▨ 𝘝𝘐𝘚𝘈   **Prices from £19 to £46**

20 BUDE
RECTORY FARM TEA ROOMS Crosstown, Morwenstow, Bude, Cornwall, EX23 9SR.
Tel: 01288 331251.
Set in a farmhouse dating back to the 13th century, the Tea Rooms are in a breathtaking situation, just yards from the cliff top. The building used to belong to the monks of St John of Bridgewater but now belongs to a family who has lived there for the last 50 years. Fresh local produce predominates in the traditional menu which includes home made cakes, biscuits and cookies. Cream Teas are also available served with a pot of tea from one of the many varieties available.

21 BUDE

CANN ORCHARD Howard Lane, Stratton, Bude, Cornwall EX23 9TD. Contact John & Joanne Crocker Tel & Fax: 01288 352098.
Cann Orchard, 3 acres of gardens, orchards and ponds is mentioned in the Doomsday Book. The listed farmhouse has been sympathetically restored and is in the perfect location for exploring the north Cornish coast line or the Dartmoor, Exmoor and Bodmin moors. Within a 10 minute journey surfing, sea fishing, horse riding and golf facilities are available. King Arthur's ruined castle at Tintagel is 30 minutes away. 2 DOUBLE EN SUITE, 1 TWIN PRIVATE BATHROOM. CHILDREN 7+.

🔲 ✂ 🆂   **Prices from £16 to £25**

22 BUDLEIGH SALTERTON
LONG RANGE Vales Road, Budleigh Salterton, Devon EX9 6HS.
Contact Mr Moreton Tel: 01395 443 321 Fax: 01395 445 220.
Long Range Hotel offers a comfortable and relaxing atmosphere in peaceful surroundings. Close to the sea and nature reserves, there is lots to see and do. En suite rooms have colour TV and coffee/tea facilities. 6 BEDROOMS, ALL EN SUITE.

Prices from £55

---

23 BURNHAM-ON-SEA

PRIORS MEAD 23 Rectory Road, Burnham-on-Sea, Somerset TA8 2BZ. Contact Peter and Fizz Alexander.
Telephone: 01278 782116.
The enchanting, Edwardian home of Priors Mead offers quality accommodation in picturesque grounds. Guests can make use of the swimming pool, croquet lawn and baby grand piano. Only 2 miles from junction 22 of the M5 it is ideally placed for touring Quantock Hills, Cheddar, Bath and Taunton. Reductions for stays of 3 nights. Closed Christmas. 3 KING-SIZE DOUBLE/TWIN, EN SUITE OR PRIVATE FACILITIES.

Prices from £17 to £18

---

24 BISH MILL
MILL INN Bish Mill, South Molton, Devon EX36 3QF. Tel: 01769 550944.
A friendly warm 17th century inn offering comfortable accommodation. Both rooms have tea/coffee facilities and television. Full English breakfast provided. 1 DOUBLE, 1 TWIN, SHARED BATHROOM.

Prices from £18

---

25 CALLINGTON

DOZMARY Tors View Close, Tavistock Road, Callington, Cornwall, PL17 7DY. Contact Mrs T.C Wills Tel: 01579 383677 E.mail: dozmarybb@aol.com.
This bungalow is very spacious and has excellent facilities, even special diets can be catered for. Callington has a good choice of eating establishments and is situated near the south Cornwall coast and the city of Plymouth. Reductions for longer stay. Closed Christmas and New Year. 1 DOUBLE EN SUITE, 1 FAMILY EN SUITE, 1 TWIN.

Prices from £17 to £20

---

26 CALSTOCK

TAMAR VALLEY B & B Kelly Cottage, Lower Kelly, Calstock, Cornwall, PL18 9RX. Contact Bill & Pat Parnell
Tel: 01822 832380 Fax: 01822 834678.
Tamar Valley B&B is a beautiful riverside home with a tranquil garden, where there is a health spa. The guests' bedrooms, lounge and balcony have rural views over the river. Close to National Trust sites, St. Mellion Golf & Country Club and Gunnislake. The coast and Dartmoor are not far away. Bus service to Tavistock and a train service to Plymouth nearby. Evening meals by arrangement.
2 DOUBLE, 1 TWIN/TRIPLE, ALL EN SUITE OR PRIVATE FACILITIES.

Prices from £20.50

27 CAMELFORD

HIGHER TREZION Tresinney, Advent, Camelford, Cornwall, PL32 9QW. Contact Mrs Janet Wood Tel: 01840 213761 Fax: 01840 212509.

A small sheep farm on the edge of Bodmin Moor is the setting for this peaceful accommodation. Offering marvellous views of the Camel Valley it is ideally situated for exploring Bodmin Moor and North Cornwall – Tintagel is only 7 miles away. Facilities for golf, fishing, walking, horses riding and cycling are nearby. Evening meals by arrangement. Real Farmhouse Breakfast. 1 DOUBLE/FAMILY EN SUITE, 1 DOUBLE/TWIN EN SUITE. CHILDREN 5+.

Prices from £18 to £20

28 CHAGFORD

PARFORD WELL Sandy Park, Chagford, Devon TQ13 8JW. Contact Tim Daniel Tel: 01647 433353.

Within Dartmoor National Park, Parford Well takes its name from the well in the walled garden of this tastefully decorated house. There are wonderful walks in this area; the wooded valley of the River Teign, around Castle Drogo or on the open moor. Traditional breakfasts are prepared with locally grown ingredients. Closed Christmas and New Year. 1 DOUBLE, 1 TWIN, 1 SINGLE, ALL EN SUITE OR PRIVATE FACILITIES. CHILDREN 8+.

Prices from £23 to £28

29 CHARD

WAMBROOK FARM Wambrook, Chard, Somerset TA20 3DF. Contact Mrs S. Eames Tel: 01460 62371.

A pleasing listed farmhouse, Wambrook Farm is situated in an attractive rural village 2 miles from Chard. Ideally located for visiting Devon and Somerset. Good pub food is available in the village. Closed December to March inclusive. 1 DOUBLE EN SUITE, 1 FAMILY EN SUITE.

Prices from £20

30 CHEDDAR

HILLTOPS Bradley Cross, Cheddar, Somerset BS27 3YR. Contact Mrs N. James Tel: 01934 742711.

Half a mile away from Cheddar Gorge and off the beaten track, the split-level bungalow of Hilltops offers a magnificent view of the Cheddar Valley and reservoir. Relaxed family atmosphere with beautiful rooms. Ideally located for the local tourist attractions. Closed Christmas and New Year. 1 TWIN, 2 DOUBLE (1 EN SUITE).

Prices from £16.50 to £19

31 CHEDDAR
HILLSIDE COTTAGE TEA ROOMS The Cliffs, Cheddar, Somerset BS27 3QH. Tel: 01934 743158.
The Tea Rooms were fulfilling their present function at the turn of the century and after a short break were re-established as such in 1984. Overlooking a large lake between Goughs and Coxs caves, they are ideally situated, being near a number of local attractions. Within reach are the Cheddar Caves, the Mendip Hills and the Cheddar Gorge Cheese Company. Cream tea is available as are home baked cakes and pastries, local dairy ice cream and speciality teas including herbal varieties.

32 COLYTON
THE WHITE COTTAGE Dolphin Street, Colyton, Devon EX13 6NA.
Contact Lawrence and Ann Parker Tel: 01297 552401.
Set in a 15th century Grade II listed building in the mediaeval town of Colyton, the Cottage is convenient for exploring the local Market Square and 15th century church. Cream teas are a speciality as are treacle tart and bread and butter pudding. All cakes are home made and a range of teas are available.

33 CRANTOCK

TREGENNA HOUSE West Pentire Road, Crantock, Cornwall, TR8 5RZ. Contact Sue & David Wrigley
Tel: 01637 830222 Fax: 01637 831267.
NEWQUAY 3m. Children are especially welcome at Tregenna House, making it ideal for the family. In this relaxed, friendly, family home you are allowed unrestricted access to the heated outdoor pool during the summer. The Coastal Footpath passes through the town of Crantock which itself has many beautiful surfing beaches and golf courses. Golfing breaks can be arranged. Evening meals by arrangement. Residential licence. 4 FAMILY ROOMS, 1 TWIN, 2 SINGLE, MOST EN SUITE.

🕯 🖻 ✂ Ⓢ   **Prices from £16 to £20**

34 CREWKERNE
CRUMMS Unit 9 George Centre, Crewkerne, Somerset TA18 7LU. Tel: 01460 76965.
Located in a small shopping arcade, Crumms is close to a selection of antiques shops. Sandwiches are a speciality, they are prepared fresh for eating on the premises or taking away. Also available are home made soups, light lunches, home made cakes and a range of teas and coffees.

35 DODDISCOMBSLEIGH
TOWN BARTON (The Old Manor House), Doddiscombsleigh, Devon EX6 7PS.
Tel: 01647 252394.
Each room has filter coffee, tea and fresh milk, television and radio. The breakfast consists of fresh fruit juice, toast and a selection of cereals. Cooked breakfasts are available at the Nobody Inn (featured in this guide) at a supplement of £3. 3 DOUBLE, ALL EN SUITE, 1 FOUR POSTER.

Prices from £70

36 DODDISCOMBSLEIGH
NOBODY INN Doddiscombsleigh, Devon EX6 7PS. Tel: 01647 252394.
A popular 15th century village pub with all rooms having tea/coffee facilities, television and radio.
2 DOUBLE EN SUITE, 1 TWIN WITH SHOWER & WASH BASIN, 1 SINGLE WITH WASH BASIN.

Prices from £23 to £70

37 DULVERTON

LOWER HOLWORTHY FARM Brompton Regis, Dulverton, Somerset TA22 9NY. Contact Mrs Payne Tel: 01398 371244.
Amongst the exquisite surroundings of Exmoor countryside sits this lovely farmhouse, on the shore of Wimbleball Lake. Bed and breakfast and optional evening meal. Open all year round. 4 BEDROOMS, ALL EN SUITE.
🖻 Ⓢ   **Prices from £21 to £42**

38 DULVERTON

RIDLERS PARK Dulverton, Somerset, TA22 9RZ.
Contact Mrs J. Davies Tel & Fax: 01398 341213.
A spacious modern house with hall panelling, intricately carved doors and under-floor heating, Ridlers Park offers marvellous views of the local countryside. The house has a very comfortable sitting room and sun lounge. Bedrooms have colour TV and tea/coffee making facilities. Situated on the Devon/Somerset border close to Exmoor, 3 miles off the B3227, 20 miles from junction 27 of the M5. Closed Christmas and New Year. 2 DOUBLE EN SUITE. NO CHILDREN.

Prices from £18 to £20

39 EXETER
COMFORT INN Kennford, Exeter, Devon, EX6 7UX.
Tel: 01392 832 121 Fax: 01392 833 590 E.mail: admin@gb056.u-net.com.
Located on the M5 which leads to A38. Situated in Exeter, the Comfort Inn offers a high standard of accommodation and service. Restaurant and bar serving drinks and food. Visit nearby Crealy Park and the National Marine Aquarium. Special package for bikers £26. per person inc. breakfast and dinner. Subject to availability. Must be booked through Central Reservations 0800 44 44 44. 63 BEDROOMS.

40 EXETER

HOLWAY BARTON Whimple, Exeter, Devon, EX5 2QY.
Contact David & Iris Brown Tel: 01404 822477.
Holway Barton is set in large attractive gardens, open farmland and bordered by a stream. The warm welcome offered by David & Iris Brown will add to the enjoyment of a relaxing break in the enchanting Devon village of Whimple. Exeter, the east Devon coastline, Dartmoor and Exmoor are all within easy reach. Closed Christmas and New Year. 1 DOUBLE, 2 TWIN, PRIVATE FACILITIES AVAILABLE.

Prices from £17.50 to £20

13

41 EXETER
THE GOLDEN LION Newton, Exeter, Devon, EX1 2BP.
Contact Mrs Green Tel: 01392 660069.
Every Thursday is Bikers night. We have lots and lots of fun. We have a skittle alley, a free pool table, quality juke box and plenty of parking opposite. We have a large function room where bikers meetings can be held. We have real ales, bottled and lager beers all with a friendly, warm and hospitable atmosphere.

42 EXETER

WOOD BARTON Farringdon, Exeter, Devon, EX5 2HY.
Contact Jackie Bolt Tel: 01395 233407 Fax: 01395 227226.
The 17th century farmhouse of Wood Barton is set in quiet countryside 3 miles from the M5, junction 30. Exeter, sandy beaches, National Trust houses, carp fishing, golf course and children's farm are within 6 miles. Good English breakfast cooked on an Aga. Closed Christmas. 1 TWIN, 1 DOUBLE, 1 FAMILY, ALL EN SUITE.

Prices from £21 to £25

43 EXETER

2 DEANERY PLACE Exeter, Devon, EX1 1HU.
Contact Heather Somers Tel: 01392 49081 Fax: 01392 490380.
In the heart of Exeter, 2 Deanery Place is only 50 yards away from the cathedral but is hidden away from the noise and traffic. In this renovated, 14th century home, guests may have breakfast on the private patio (weather permitting) and relax in the elegant drawing room. Open Chrstmas. 2 DOUBLE (1 X 4 POSTER), BOTH EN SUITE, 1 SINGLE. CHILDREN 10+.

Prices from £20 to £29.50

44 EXETER

WEYBROOK HOUSE Shillingford Abbot, Exeter, Devon,
EX2 9QE. Contact Jacquie Banks Tel & Fax: 01392 833079
E.mail: jab@weybrookho.freeserve.co.uk.
A warm welcome greets visitors to Weybrook House, 3 miles south west of Exeter. The accommodation is comfortable and the lounge has an open view of the Devon countryside. An excellent breakfast will kick-start your day. Easy access to Plymouth ferries and Exeter Airport. Closed Christmas and New Year. 2 DOUBLE EN SUITE, 1 TWIN PRIVATE. CHILDREN 15+.

Prices from £19 to £21

45 EXETER

DRAKE'S FARMHOUSE Drake's Farm, Ide, Exeter, Devon, EX2 9RQ. Contact Mrs N. Eastbrook Tel & Fax: 01392 256814.
Situated 2 miles from the M5 and near the cathedral city of Exeter, Drake's Farmhouse is a 15th century building in the centre of a quiet village. Conveniently placed for coast and moors and 5 minutes walk from two restaurants and pubs. Laundry facilities. TV, tea and coffee in all rooms. Ample secure parking. 2 DOUBLE (1 EN SUITE), 1 FAMILY EN SUITE.

Prices from £17.50 to £20

46 EXETER

**GRENDON Drewsteignton, Exeter, Devon, EX6 6RE.
Contact Mrs Robinson Tel: 01647 231486.**

EXETER 16m, OKHAMPTON 7m. Grendon is one mile from the A30 roundabout at Whiddon Down, which makes this family farmhouse very accessible. It is a thatched house of a medieval Tudor origin surrounded by farmland and wildlife on the edge of Dartmoor. Moorland and river walks nearby. Plymouth ferries and Exeter Airport within easy reach. Hard tennis court. Closed Christmas Day. 1 DOUBLE, 1 TWIN, 1 SINGLE. DOUBLE AND TWIN CAN BE USED AS FAMILY.

Prices from £18 to £20

**47 EXETER
TAWNEYS 86 Fore Street, Topsham, Exeter, Devon, EX3 0HQ.
Contact Dee McNeish Tel: 01392 877887.**

Set in the centre of Topsham, Tawneys offers a friendly atmosphere and the opportunity to buy from the range of local crafts on sale. Cream and afternoon teas, light lunches, daily specials and Wednesday roasts are all available as are a good selection of teas, including herbal varieties.

---

48 EXETER

**GLEDHILLS 32 Alphington Road, Exeter, Devon EX2 8HN.
Contact Mrs Greening Tel & Fax: 01392 430469.**

This is a licensed hotel close to the city, river and leisure centre which is family run. Bedrooms have full facilities and are modern and comfortable. Own car park. 12 BEDROOMS, 10 EN SUITE.

Prices from £20 to £45

---

49 FALMOUTH

**TREVIADES BARTON High Cross, Constantine, Falmouth, Cornwall, TR11 5RG. Contact Mrs Judy Ford
Tel & Fax: 01326 340524 E.mail: treviades.barton@btinternet.co.**

A picturesque courtyard and walled gardens are part of the historic surroundings of this small manor farmhouse that was 'modernised' in the 16th century. The friendly welcome is matched by the culinary skills of Judy, who uses only the finest ingredients from the garden. The magnificent gardens, Helford River, walking and boating add to the inviting nature of this location. Closed Christmas. 3 TWIN/DOUBLE/FAMILY, 2 EN SUITE, 1 PRIVATE.

Prices from £22 to £27

---

50 FALMOUTH

**TUDOR COURT 55 Melvill Road, Falmouth, Cornwall TR11 4DF.
Contact Mrs Bireley Tel & Fax: 01326 312807.**

This is a licensed, family owned, eleven bedroomed mock Tudor hotel. It is set within pleasant gardens and is ideally situated for Falmouth's three beaches, town and harbour. 11 BEDROOMS, 10 EN SUITE.

Prices from £21 to £39

51 GLASTONBURY

**HARTLAKE FARM Hartlake, Glastonbury, Somerset, BA6 9AB.
Contact Mrs Naomi Frost Tel: 01458 835406 Fax: 01749 670373.**
Hartllake Farm is a 17th century, self-contained accommodation where guests have the use of a small kitchen. With views of Glastonbury Tor and the Mendip Hills, this working dairy and beef farm sits on the banks of the river Hartlake. Situated on the A39 between Wells and Glastonbury it is ideally located for Bath, Bristol and Cheddar. 1 DOUBLE, 1 TWIN, BOTH EN SUITE.
CHILDREN 3 MONTHS +.

Prices from £19 to £22

52 GLASTONBURY

**COURT LODGE Butleigh, Glastonbury, Somerset, BA6 8SA.
Contact Mrs Atkinson Tel: 01458 850575.**
Set in picturesque garden, 3 miles from Glastonbury, this is a modernised 1850 lodge with homely atmosphere. Evening meals by arrangement or there are lovely meals available at the local pub. 4 BEDROOMS.

Prices from £15.50 to £29

**53 GURNEY SLADE
THE GEORGE INN Gurney Slade, Somerset, BA3 4TQ.
Contact Dave & Lynn Tel: 01749 840 554.**
Excellent choice of drinks and food. Choose from Ushers Real Ale, Budweiser, Fosters and Blackthorn. Food served Monday-Saturday 12 noon till 2pm, 6pm till 9pm. Sunday lunch time only. Bikers very welcome.

54 HELSTON

**COBBLERS COTTAGE Nantithet, Cury, Helston, Cornwall,
TR12 7RB. Contact Hilary & David Lugg Tel: 01326 241342.**
As the name suggests, this is a former shoemaker's shop and kiddlewink that has been modernised but still retains its 'olde worlde' personality. This house is situated in the middle of the Lizard Peninsula, 2 miles from the sea, in an area renowned for its scenery and coastal walks. Flambards Theme Park, Poldark Mine and many beautiful beaches are within the locality. Evening meals by arrangement. Closed Christmas. 2 DOUBLE EN SUITE, 1 TWIN EN SUITE.
CHILDREN 12+.

Prices from £20 to £23

55 HELSTON

**LITTLE PENGWEDNA FARM Helston, Cornwall, TR13 0AY.
Contact Mrs I. White Tel: 01736 850649.**
This charming 19th century farmhouse can be found on the B3302, just off the A30 and is in a perfect position to allow you to tour the Cornish east coast and many other places of interest. The farmhouse is wonderfully furnished and the hospitality is as warm and plentiful as their traditional farmhouse breakfasts, which makes a stay here a real treat. 4 DOUBLE EN SUITE, 2 TWIN EN SUITE.

Prices from £20 to £24

FRANK THOMAS

THE PERFECT COMBINATION

GORE-TEX®

Gore 22 Nevada Jacket

Gore 21 Arkansas Jacket

FRANK THOMAS
GORE-TEX®

Gore 21 Arkansas Jacket
Colours: Black/Yellow,
Black/Orange, Black/Red,
Black.
Sizes: Mens S - XXL
Ladies S - M
Retail Price: £249.99

Gore 22 Nevada Jacket
Colours: Black/Yellow,
Black/Blue, Black/Orange,
Black/Red, Black.
Sizes: Mens S - XXL
Ladies S - M
Retail Price: £249.99

For information on the Frank Thomas/GORE-TEX® collection contact:
Frank Thomas Ltd, Atlanta House, Midland Rd, Higham Ferrers,
Northants, NN10 8DN Tel: 01933 410272 Fax: 01933 319157

GORE-TEX®

100% Waterproof / Breathable / Windproof

56 HONITON

THE CREST Wilmington, Honiton, Devon, EX14 9JU. Contact Suzanne Kidwell Tel: 01404 831419.
SYDMOUTH/LYME REGIS 9m. In an area of outstanding natural beauty, The Crest is situated in the picturesque Umborne Valley. In over 2 acres of lawns there are camping facilities with showers & toilet and a residents sun lounge. Easy access to Dartmoor, Exmoor, Torbay and Dorset. Golf, health club, walking or horse riding breaks available. Approved disabled access. 1 DOUBLE, 1 TWIN, 1 FAMILY, ALL EN SUITE.

Prices from £18 to £19

57 IIFRACOMBE

WESTWELL HALL Torrs Park, Ilfracombe, Devon EX34 8AZ. Contact Mr Lomas Tel & Fax: 01271 862792.
Situated in grounds with glorious views over countryside and sea, this is a quiet secluded hotel. Adjacent to National Trust coastal walks. Ample secure parking. 10 BEDROOMS, ALL EN SUITE.

Prices from £20 to £46

58 ILFRACOMBE

CAIRN HOUSE 43 St Brantocks Road, Ilfracombe, Devon EX34 8EH. Contact Mr Tupper Tel: 01271 863911.
Set in its own grounds, this is a small comfortable hotel with superb views of the sea and surrounding hills. 10 BEDROOMS, ALL EN SUITE.

Prices from £18 to £40

59 ILFRACOMBE

SLOLEY FARM Castle Hill, Berrynarbor, Ilfracombe, Devon, EX34 9SX. Contact Mrs J. Mountain Tel & Fax: 01271 883032.
COMBE MARTIN 2m. A holiday complex offering bed & breakfast and good old fashioned home cooking in the hamlet of Berrynarbor. Sloley Farm offers a real taste of the countryside. There is abundant wildlife, farm animals and unspoilt views overlooking the Sterridge Valley. Located near Exmoor National Park, Rosemoor and Marwood Hill gardens. Evening meals by arrangement. Vegetarians catered for. 3 TWIN/DOUBLE, ALL EN SUITE. NO CHILDREN.

Prices from £18 to £25

60 ILFRACOMBE
FUCHSIA TEA ROOM AND GARDEN Fuchsia Valley, Lee, Ilfracombe, Devon EX34 8LW. Tel: 01271 863551.
A tea room has been sited in these building since around 1930. As the name suggests the prevailing theme is that of fuchsias, they are present in the decor, and the plants are available for sale. Cream Teas, Afternoon Teas and a selection of home made cakes, ice creams are available, toasties and light lunches. Food for takeaway. Clotted cream icecreams.

61 KINGSBRIDGE

SOUTH ALLINGTON HOUSE Chivelstone, Kingsbridge, Devon, TQ7 2NB. Contact Mrs B. Baker
Tel: 01548 511272 Fax: 01548 511421

Between Star Point and Prawle Point, South Allington House is a working farm situated in a quiet Hamlet, surrounded by beautiful grounds. This location is perfect for unwinding in the peace and quiet and relaxing in one of the 2 rooms with a four poster bed. Conveniently located near Salcombe and Kingsbridge for you to take advantage of the water sports/leisure amenities they offer.
9 VARIOUS ROOMS WITH EN SUITE OR PRIVATE FACILITIES.
CHILDREN 4+.

Prices from £21.50 to £30

---

62 KINGSBRIDGE

SHIP & PLOUGH The Promenade, Kingsbridge, Devon, TQ7 1JD. Tel: 01548 852485.

In a town centre location, making it handy for the amenities Kingsbridge has to offer. Each room has a colour television and tea/coffee making facilities. Rates vary due to season of booking.
5 DOUBLE. 3 SELF CATERING FLATS (2 BEDROOMED) WITH BATHROOM & KITCHEN.

---

63 LANGPORT

THE OLD MILL Knole, Long Sutton, Langport, Somerset, TA10 9HY. Contact Mrs Paula Barber
Tel: 01458 241599 Fax: 01458 241710.

SOMERTON 3m. The Old Mill has been converted into accommodation in an ideal location for business or leisure, just off the A372. Bath, Bristol, Wells and Taunton all within 1 hour. Close to historic houses and gardens, aircraft and motor museums and sports venues. High quality furnishings and facilities in all rooms. Farmhouse breakfasts made using local produce. Golf course, pubs and restaurant all close.
2 DOUBLE, 1 TWIN, ALL EN SUITE OR PRIVATE FACILITIES.

Prices from £24 to £27

---

64 LANGPORT

GOTHIC HOUSE Muchelney, Langport, Somerset, TA10 0DW. Contact Joy Thorne Tel: 01458 250626.

YEOVIL 12m. Gothic House offers peaceful surroundings and warm hospitality to its guests. This Victorian Farmhouse has spacious, comfortable rooms that are well furbished. Well situated for visiting the many attractions nearby, including historic houses and gardens. The area is renowned for coarse fishing, basket making and cider orchards. 3 DOUBLE EN SUITE.

Prices from £18 to £24

---

65 LAUNCESTON

THE OLD VICARAGE Treneglos, Launceston, Cornwall PL15 8UQ. Contact Mrs Maggie Fancourt
Tel & Fax: 01566 781351.

The Old Vicarage is a Grade 2 listed building in a picturesque rural setting near the north Cornwall coast. Ideally located as a touring base. Excellent food and hospitality are their forte, offering the highest standards throughout and ensuring absolute comfort. Award-winning local pub. Closed November to March.
2 DOUBLE EN SUITE. CHILDREN 5+.

Prices from £23 to £25

66 LAUNCESTON

BERRO BRIDGE HOUSE North Hill, Launceston, Cornwall PL15 7NL. Contact Elizabeth Matthews Tel & Fax: 01566 782714.
Berro Bridge House is set in gardens on the edge of the river Lynher and has its own fishing rights. Near the tors of Bodmin Moor this traditional Cornish House ideally placed for outdoor exploration is also close to horse riding and golf facilities and plenty of good country pubs within easy reach.

Prices from £20 to £22.50

67 LAUNCESTON

MAD HATTER'S TEASHOP 28 Church Street, Launceston, Cornwall, PL15 8AR. Tel: 01566 777188.
Situated in the centre of Launceston, close to attractions such as Launceston Castle, Steam Railway and the Otter Sanctuary. A Lewis Carroll theme prevails with a mad hatter in residence every Saturday and holiday. The teashop has been a finalist in the Top Tea Place of the Year Award '96 and '97 and has received the Heartbeat Award. The Menu is innovative, including Mad Hatter's Platters (ploughmans), Alice's Sandwiches, Mad Hatter's specials, and the Dormouse selection. An extensive range of teas and coffees is available and teapots are available for sale.

68 LISKEARD

LAMPEN MILL St. Neot, Liskeard, Cornwall, PL14 6PB. Contact Mrs Heather Pearce Tel & Fax: 01579 321119.
Lampen Mill rests in the tranquil Glynn Valley with easy access to the A30 and A8, conveniently placed for excursions to Plymouth and the whole of Cornwall. The mill has been converted for accommodation but still retains the original water wheel dating from 1740. Surrounded by 8 acres of woodland attracts many kinds of wildlife including herons and kingfishers. Excellent local pub which provides good food. Golf and sailing nearby. 2 DOUBLE, 1 TWIN, ALL EN SUITE.

Prices from £22 to £25

69 LISKEARD

HIGHER TREVARTHA FARM Pengover, Liskeard, Cornwall, PL14 3NJ. Contact Kathyrn Sobey Tel: 01579 343382.
Within 200 acres of farmland, an acre of walled garden surrounds the 17th century Grade II listed building of Higher Trevartha Farmhouse. The Sobey family have worked the farm for over 100 years. Carp fishing on the two ponds. Situated in the perfect place to explore Devon and Cornwall; Plymouth 16 miles, Looe 7 miles. 1 DOUBLE, 1 TRIPLE, 1 FAMILY EN SUITE.

Prices from £18.50 to £22

70 LOOE

BUCKLAWREN FARM St. Martin-By-Looe, Looe, Cornwall, PL13 1NZ. Contact Mrs J. Henly Tel: 01503 240738 Fax: 01503 240481 E.mail: Bucklawren@compuserve.com.
Bucklawren Farm sits in beautiful countryside and is only 3 miles from the port of Looe and 1 mile from the beach. The furnishings are to a very high standard at this 19th century farmhouse where guests can relax in a modern conservatory. Traditional farmhouse fayre can be enjoyed in a relaxed and friendly atmosphere. Closed November to March. 1 TWIN, 2 DOUBLE, 2 FAMILY, ALL EN SUITE. CHILDREN 5+.

Prices from £20 to £22

71 LOOE

TALEHAY FARM Pelynt, Looe, Cornwall, PL13 2LT.
Contact Mr & Mrs Brumpton Tel & Fax: 01503 220252.
POLPERRO 4m. No longer a working farmstead this 17th century building, offering a high standard of accommodation, is only few miles from Looe and Polperro. The countryside surrounding Talehay Farm is designated as an area of outstanding natural beauty. It is only 3 miles from the coast and attractions throughout Cornwall are within easy reach. 1 TWIN, 1 DOUBLE, 1 FAMILY 3/4, EN SUITE.

Prices from £19 to £22

72 MEVAGISSEY

FOUNTAIN INN Cliff Street, Mevagissey, Cornwall, PL26 6QH.
Contact Mr Moore Tel: 01726 842320.
A 15th century inn with 2 bars open all day. Food served lunchtime and evening, beers served are; Labatts, Scrumpy Jack, Guinness, Murphy's and local real ales Tinners and Hicks. Sky TV shown. Live entertainment on Friday. ACCOMMODATION AVAILABLE.

73 MINEHEAD

THE OLD PRIORY Dunster, Minehead, Somerset, TA24 6RY.
Contact Jane Forshaw Tel: 01643 821540.
The Old Priory, built by Benedictine monks in the 12th century, stands within idyllic walled gardens next to the church in Dunster. The house still keeps some medieval features but is modern enough to provide a high standard of accommodation. One room with 4 poster bed. Farmhouse breakfasts. Closed Christmas Day. 2 TWIN (1 GROUND FLOOR), 1 DOUBLE, EN SUITE OR PRIVATE FACILITIES. CHILDREN 12+.

Prices from £22.50 to £30

74 MINEHEAD

HIGHER RODHUISH FARM Rodhuish, Minehead, Somerset, TA24 6QL. Contact Mrs J. Thomas Tel & Fax: 01984 640253.
Higher Rodhuish Farm offers warm hospitality and home cooking using local and home-grown produce. Situated on the edge of Exmoor National Park it is a working farm with sheep, beef cattle and arable crops. Ideally located for visiting the coast or the moors, walking, fishing and horse riding. Evening meals by arrangement. 2 DOUBLE,1 TWIN, SOME WITH PRIVATE FACILITIES.

Prices from £16 to £19

75 MINEHEAD

THE HORNER TEA GARDENS Horner, Minehead, Somerset, TA24 8HY.
Tel: 01643 862380.
Set in a Grade II listed building on Exmoor, the Tea Gardens are close to Dunkery Beacon and Horner Water. A Cream Tea is available consisting of scones, jam and cream as is a Special Cream Tea which includes cakes as well. All cakes and scones are home baked and a variety of light lunches are also on offer along with a range of teas and coffees.

76 MORETON HAMPSTEAD
WHITE HART The Square, Moretonhampstead, Devon, TQ13 8NF.
Contact Mr Campbell Tel: 01647 440406.
An 18th century inn with a relaxed atmosphere. Open all day with food available lunchtime and evening. Beers served; Strongbow, John Smiths, Websters, Kronenberg and Guinness. Jazz band (Sunday nights) and Folk group (Thursday nights) play monthly. ACCOMMODATION AVAILABLE.

Prices from £30

77 NEWQUAY
OCEAN BREEZE GUEST HOUSE 22 Edgcumbe Avenue, Newquay, Cornwall, TR7 2NH. Contact Pete & Anna Tel: 01637 850187.
A warm welcome extended to all motorcyclists. Club breaks welcomed. Close to Newquay's famous nightlife.

78 NEWQUAY

COLAN BARTON, Colan, Newquay, Cornwall, TR8 4NB. Contact Anna Machin Weaver Tel: 01637 874395 Fax: 01637 881388.
This Grade 2 listed farmhouse, built in 1632, is set in 11 acres. Surrounded by countryside and well off the beaten track, it is in an ideal spot for touring the cliffs of the north Cornish coast and miles of hidden beaches. The grounds are home to dogs, horses and chickens etc. There is a pond and a walk across the fields reveals a beautiful stream. Closed October to February. 2 DOUBLE (1 EN SUITE), 1 TWIN.

Prices from £15 to £22

79 NEWTON ABBOT

BULLEIGH PARK Ipplepen, Newton Abbot, Devon, TQ12 5UA.
Contact Angela Dallyn Tel & Fax: 01803 872254.
The small family farm of Bulleigh Park is in a delightful rural setting with panoramic views of the south Devon countryside. It is centrally located for the coast, Dartmoor, Totnes and Torquay. Home-made preserves and an excellent farmhouse breakfast can be enjoyed at the house, as can the baby grand piano by pianists. Closed Christmas and New Year. 1 DOUBLE, 1 DOUBLE/TWIN/FAMILY, EN SUITE OR PRIVATE FACILITIES.

Prices from £17 to £21

80 NEWTON ABBOT
THE OLD COTTAGE TEA SHOP 20 Fore Street, Bovey Tracey, Newton Abbot, Devon, TQ13 9AD. Tel: 01626 833430.
The Tea Shop was established in the 1950s and has in the past been a winner of Britain in Bloom due to its hanging baskets and window boxes. Cream Teas are a speciality as are fruit pies, pasties and locally made ice cream. Most of the fare is made on the premises with a range of teas on offer.

81 NEWTON ABBOT

PENPARK Bickington, Newton Abbot, Devon, TQ12 6LH. Contact Mrs Madeleine Gregson Tel: 01626 821314 Fax: 01626 821101.
Within beautiful surroundings of Dartmoor National Park sits the country house of Penpark. Magnificent hill-top views, all-weather tennis court and five acres of gardens. Rooms are spacious and well furnished. A terrific blend of elegance and comfort with a homely atmosphere. Closed Christmas. 2 TWIN, 3 DOUBLE, 1 FAMILY, ALL EN SUITE.

Prices from £23 to £25

TOP CLASS PROTECTION AT A PRICE THAT WON'T MAKE YOUR JAW DROP.

Just £169.99

One look at the latest technology in the Tri-composite shell and one button, one-movement easy flip-up system, and you'll realise what great value this helmet is. From just £154.99 we beat any comparable helmet on the market.

● 2.2mm anti-fog and anti-scratch 50% tinted visor. ● Quick release chin strap with security ring. ● Fully detachable, washable and breathable lining. ● Front chin and head ventilation with air ducted polystyrene liner and rear extractor. ● Removable nose guard and wind cuff. ● BS6658 type A with Gold ACU Sticker.

For a colour brochure on the Vemar range, price list and UK dealer list. FREEPHONE 0800 7836178, fax or e-mail.

VEMAR

UK importers & distributors: Nevis Marketing Ltd., Unit 12, Priory Industrial Park, Airspeed Road, Christchurch, Dorset BH23 4HD
Tel: 01425 273344. Fax: 01425 273311. E-mail: info@nevism.co.uk Website: www.nevism.co.uk

82 NEWTON ABBOTT
PRIMROSE COTTAGE Lustleigh, Newton Abbott, Devon, TQ13 9TB.
Tel: 01647 277365.
Set within Dartmoor National Park, opposite Lustleigh Village Church, The cottage dates back to the 15th century. Light lunches are available all day and set menus or a combination of the fare on offer comprise the choices for Afternoon Tea. Homemade cakes are a speciality and ensure a very loyal clientele.

83 NORTH BOVEY
RING OF BELLS North Bovey, Devon, TQ13 8RB. Tel: 01647 440375
E.mail: ringof.bellsin@compuserve.com.
A delightful 13th century thatched village inn providing first class accommodation. Each room has tea/coffee facilities and there is a television available in the lounge bar. 3 DOUBLE/TWIN, ALL EN SUITE.

Prices from £25

84 OKEHAMPTON

HIGHER CADHAM FARM Jacobstowe, Okehampton, Devon, EX20 3RB. Contact Jenny King
Tel: 01837 851647 Fax: 01837 851410.
The 180 mile long 'Tarka trail' on the river Okement is where Higher Cadham Farm is situated and where a family of otters have sometimes been spotted. The farm that is home to beef cattle and sheep has many nature trails that provide an opportunity to spot kingfishers, foxes and badgers etc. The building has recently been renovated with oak beams and stonework, giving a warm feeling to the dining room. Credit Cards Accepted. Closed December and New Year. 1 SINGLE, 2 DOUBLE, 3 TWIN, 3 FAMILY, MOST EN SUITE. CHILDREN 1+.

Prices from £18.50 to £25

85 OKEHAMPTON

FAIRWAY LODGE Thordon Cross, Okehampton, Devon, TQ13 9EL. Contact Mrs Daphne Burgoine Tel: 01837 52827.
Fairway Lodge is a modern house situated on an organic smallholding and is home to a small heard of Shetland ponies. On the edge of Dartmoor it is in an ideal location to explore the area including the 'Tarka Trail' a little way down the road. Riding stables and golf course nearby. Evening meals use home grown produce. Closed January 2nd until Easter. 2 DOUBLE, 1 FAMILY, ALL EN SUITE.

Prices from £20 to £25

86 OKEHAMPTON

HIGHER COOMBEHEAD HOUSE Sticklepath, Okehampton, Devon, EX20 1QL. Contact Mrs V Dixon Tel: 01837 840240.
Higher Coombehead House is just off the A30, within Dartmoor National Park. It is a thatched country home with the accommodation in a self-contained wing that used to be a chapel. Your host with be delighted to show you the model steam railway that runs through the large sloping garden. Ideally situated for North and South Devon, Dartmoor and many inland and coastal attractions. Closed Christmas. 2 DOUBLE, 1 TWIN, EN SUITE OR PRIVATE FACILITIES.

87 PENRYN

PROSPECT HOUSE 1 Church Road, Penryn, Cornwall, TR10 8AD. Contact Mr & Mrs Budd Tel & Fax: 01326 373198.
The late Georgian residence of Prospect House is situated north of Falmouth on the edge of Penryn in a perfect location to explore mid and west Cornwall. The house has been thoughtfully modernised to provide full en suite facilities, keeping the original features preserved. There are also some outstanding restaurants only a few minutes away. 1 TWIN, 2 DOUBLE, ALL EN SUITE. CHILDREN 12+.

⬚ ✄ Ⓢ　　　　　　　　　　　　　　　　**Prices from £25**

88 PENZANCE

ROSEUDIAN Crippas Hill, St. Just, Penzance, Cornwall, TR19 7RE. Contact Mr & Mrs M. Mercer Tel: 01736 788556.
Roseudian is a traditional modernised Cornish cottage with a warm and friendly atmosphere. Lands End, St Ives and St Michaels Mount are all within easy reach. Nice coastal walks. The cottage is south facing with terraced gardens. We only use fresh garden produce in season. Closed November to February. Children welcome 7 plus. 1 TWIN, 2 DOUBLE, ALL EN SUITE. CHILDREN 10+.

✄ Ⓢ　　　　　　　　　　　　　　　　**Prices from £20**

89 PENZANCE

WARWICK HOUSE 17 Regent Terrace, Penzance, Cornwall, TR18 4DW. Contact Mrs Mclennan Tel: 01736 363881.
The relaxed atmosphere and pretty bedrooms within Warwick House mirror the beauty of its location by the seafront. The house, which is within walking distance from the town centre, has a patio area that flourishes with colourful flowers during the summer months. There are tropical gardens nearby or Land's End and St. Michael's Mont a little further afield. Closed November to January. 6 ROOMS, SOME EN SUITE. CHILDREN 5+.

⬚ ✄ Ⓢ　　　　　　　　　　　　**Prices from £19 to £22**

90 PENZANCE

BORAH CHAPEL Lamorna, Penzance, Cornwall, TR19 6BQ. Contact Mrs Lynn Crawford Tel: 01736 810143.
Converted into a family home in 1990 Borah Chapel, which stands above Lamorna Cove, has light spacious accommodation and a friendly atmosphere. The Sunday school, having its own entrance, has been converted into a living area with vaulted ceilings and beams. Coastal walks, bird watching, fishing, golf and scuba diving are some of the activities available near by. There is also the Standing Stones and an open air theatre within a short ride from Borah Chapel. 1 TWIN/FAMILY, 1 DOUBLE, BOTH EN SUITE.

⬚ ✄ Ⓢ　　　　　　　　　　**Prices from £19 to £20.50**

91 PIMPERNE

THE ANVIL Salisbury Road, Pimperne, Dorset, DT1 8UQ. Contact Mrs Palmer Tel: 01258 453431 Fax: 01258 480182.
Picturesque thatched inn dating back to 1535, in Pimperne village 2 miles north east of Blandford on A354. Mouth watering restaurant menu. Tasty bar meals. 11 BEDROOMS, ALL EN SUITE.

⬚ Ⓢ　　▭ ◉ _VISA_ Ⓢ ▭　　**Prices from £50 to £75**

A few more 'Welcome' signs to look out for

**The most reliable bikes
on the planet***

**The UK's fastest growing
biking organisation**

**The award-winning
Motorcycle Appreciation
Course**

* Rider Power Survey – RiDE Magazine, September 1999

...and some 'Welcome' telephone numbers.

Two years free AA
membership on bikes of
125cc and above

Two years unlimited
mileage warranty on bikes of
125cc and above

0345 585 570

For details on the entire Honda range
of motorcycles and scooters

0800 731 8180

For the Honda UK Riders Club
and Motorcycle Appreciation Course

92 PLYMOUTH

IRVINE'S BED & BREAKFAST 50 Grand Parade, West Hoe, Plymouth, Devon, PLI 3DJ. Contact Mrs Irvine
Tel: 01752 227739.
Overlooking Drake's Island and Plymouth Sound, Irvine's Bed And Breakfast offers comfortable accommodation with excellent facilities. It is within walking distance of the city centre, Barbican and other attractions. Situated in the ideal place for passengers using the ferries. Closed January. 1 TWIN, 1 DOUBLE. NO CHILDREN.
⌀ S

Prices from £15

93 PLYMOUTH

WINDWHISTLE FARM Hemerdon, Plympton, Plymouth, Devon, PL7 5BU. Contact Rosemarie & Tony Giblett
Tel & Fax: 01752 340600.
Bordered by woods and the Dartmoor National Park, Windwhistle Farm is a country guest house set in 2 acres of gardens in the idyllic South Hams countryside. Evening meals are cooked using fresh local ingredients. Riding, sailing, fishing and clay pigeon shooting are available nearby. Wide variety of wildlife in the area. Closed Christmas and New Year. 2 SINGLE (1EN SUITE), 1 DOUBLE/TWIN EN SUITE, 1 DOUBLE. CHILDREN 10+.
⌀ ⌀ S

Prices from £21 to £27

94 PLYMOUTH

CROWN YEALM Newton Ferrers, Plymouth, Devon, PL8 1AW. Contact Mrs. Jill Johnson Tel & Fax: 01752 872365.
The south facing Crown Yealm overlooks the estuary of the river Yealm from the waterside village of Newton Ferrers. The rooms are large and overlook gardens to the waters edge, the beds are comfortable and the breakfasts good. There is a Bistro nearby that offers a good choice of meals. Private car park accessible by a flight of stairs. Closed end of September to mid October. 1 FAMILY, 1 DOUBLE, 1 TWIN.
⌀ ⌀ S

Prices from £20 to £21

95 POLPERRO
THE PLANTATION CAFE The Coombes, Polperro, Cornwall, PL13 2RG.
Contact Maurice and Anne Vaughn Tel: 01503 272223.
Set in the picturesque fishing village of Polperro, the Cafe has featured on local radio, television and even in a Japanese magazine. The proprietors are founder members of the Guild of Tea Shops and have created a Victorian ambience in their premises. Cornish cream teas are available, comprising home made scones, jam and local cream. Other specialities include Cornish ice cream, Cornish fruit bread and Cornish pasties. A wide range of teas is on offer including unusual varieties.

96 PORLOCK
CAMELLIA COFFEE HOUSE High Street, Porlock, Somerset, TA24 8PT.
Tel: 01643 862266.
As well as offering food, second hand books, garden art, hampers, chocolates and greetings cards are on sale in this coffee house. It is situated near the centre of Porlock village which itself is near Exmoor. Cream teas are available as are hand made cakes and a variety of unusual sandwiches. There is also a wide range of speciality teas to choose from.

97 PRINCETOWN
PLUME OF FEATHERS INN The Square, Princetown, Devon, PL20 6QQ.
Located in The Square, this is Princetowns oldest inn , dating from 1785. Each room has tea/coffee facilities and a colour television. Also available are hostel facilities with up to 42 beds and camping facilities.
1 DOUBLE, 1 SINGLE, 1 FAMILY (3 PERSONS).

Prices from £15

98 SHEEPWASH
HALF MOON INN The Square, Sheepwash, Devon, EX21 5NE. Tel: 01409 231376.
Each room has tea/coffee facilities, telephone and television. 12 TWIN/DOUBLE ALL EN SUITE. 2 SINGLE WITH PRIVATE BATHROOMS.

Prices from £32 to £55

99 SHEPTON MALTET

PARK FARM HOUSE Forum Lane, Bowlish, Shepton Mallet, Somerset, BA4 5JL. Contact Mrs M Grattan Tel: 01749 343673 Fax: 01749 345279.
WELLS 4m. Previously a working farm, the 17th century Park Farm House is set in a tranquil garden. Bath and Bristol both 18 miles away. Cheddar, Wookey Hole, Ebbor Gorge and Glastonbury are within easy reach. Good local restaurants and pubs. The area has many historic houses and gardens. Not suitable for wheelchairs. 1 TWIN EN SUITE, 1 FAMILY SUITE OF DOUBLE, TWIN AND BATHROOM.
ⓞ Ⓢ

Prices from £17.50

100 SIDMOUTH

CASTLE HILL HOUSE Sidbury, Sidmouth, Devon, EX10 0QD. Contact Mrs L. Webb Tel: 01395 597451.
Only 10 minutes motoring away from the seafront at Sidmouth, Castle Hill House stands high upon a hill offering fantastic views of the Devon countryside or across to the sea from every room. The best of hospitality is offered at the house, set within 4 acres of gardens/grounds. Tennis court available. Closed November to March inclusive. 1 DOUBLE, 1 TWIN/FAMILY, 1 SINGLE.
ⓞ ⌇ Ⓢ

Prices from £20

101 SOUTH MOLTON
THE PARLOUR 112 East Street, South Molton, Devon, EX36 3DB. Tel: 01769 574144.
Set in an attractive Georgian building, the Parlour is decorated in the style of a 1900s front parlour with a selection of small antiques for sale. It is close to Exmoor and the Quince Honey Farm. The menu is constantly updated to include new and different types of cake and there are fifteen different types of tea are on offer.

102 ST AGNES
DRIFTWOOD SPARS HOTEL Trevaunance Cove, St Agnes, Cornwall, TR5 0RT. Tel: 01872 552428.
Set in the attractive town of St Agnes, convenient for all the attractions the region has to offer, Driftwod Spars is an attractive well appointed establishment. 9 DOUBLE, 1 SINGLE, 1 TWIN, 3 FAMILY, 1 SUITE WITH SPACE FOR 4/5.
Ⓢ

Prices from £30 to £33

103 ST JUST
STAR INN Fore Street, St Just, Cornwall, TR19 7LL. Tel: 01736 788747.
In the attractive town of St. Just this cosy establishment offers the ideal location from which to explore Cornwall. 3 DOUBLE ROOMS, 1 EN-SUITE.

Prices from £15 to £20

104 ST. AUSTELL

POLRUDDON FARM Pentewan, St. Austell, Cornwall, PL26 6BJ. Contact Mrs Jackson & Mrs Bainbridge Tel & Fax: 01726 842051.
MEVAGISSEY 2m. Acres of coastal farmland and woodland, with private access to a beach and the National Trust's Coastal Path make up Polrudden Farm. One hour away from anywhere in Cornwall, 5 minute walk away from Pentewan Sands, the farm is close to some excellent restaurants. Closed December and January. 1 DOUBLE EN SUITE, 2 TWIN (1 EN SUITE, 1 PRIVATE). CHILDREN 12+.

Prices from £20 to £25

105 ST. AUSTELL

POLTARROW FARMHOUSE St. Mewan, St. Austell, Cornwall, PL26 7DR. Contact Judith Nancarrow Tel & Fax: 01726 67111.
Poltarrow Farmhouse has a high standard of accommodation set in 45 acres and is close to the south coast of Cornwall, between Penzance and Plymouth. Pony rides, play area and games room at these self-catering cottages will keep the children amused and the 3 acres of woodland and heated pool can be enjoyed by all the family. The excellent restaurants of St. Austel are only a few minutes ride away. Closed Christmas. 3 DOUBLE, 1 TWIN, 1 FAMILY, ALL EN SUITE.

Prices from £22

106 ST. GILES IN THE WOOD
CRANFORD INN St. Giles in the Wood, Devon, EX38 7LA. Tel: 01805 623309.
Cranford Inn is made up of converted stables and other farm buildings, providing comfortable holiday accommodation. SELF-CONTAINED, 2 BEDROOMED.

Prices from £55

107 TAUNTON
STABLE COTTAGE TEA ROOMS Triscombe, Bishops Lydeard, Taunton, Somerset, TA4 3HG. Tel: 01984 618239.
Situated near the Quantock Hills and the West Somerset Railway, the Tea Rooms were once the stable yard to Triscombe House. A cosy atmosphere is provided by log fires and wood panelling. There is a wide range of afternoon teas as well as an extensive selection of speciality teas and coffee

108 TAUNTON

WEST VIEW Minehead Road, Bishops Lydeard, Taunton, Somerset, TA4 3BS. Contact Mrs A. Pattemore Tel & Fax: 01823 432223.
In the Village of Bishop's Lydeard West View stands as an attractive listed Victorian house. Close to West Somerset Steam Railway, 5 miles from Taunton in Somerset. Ideally situated for visits to the north & south coasts, Quantock Hills, Brendon Hills, Exmoor, Glastonbury, Bath and Exeter. Closed Christmas Day. 2 TWIN, 1 DOUBLE EN SUITE.

Prices from £18 to £22

109 TAUNTON

MERLANDS Biscombe, Churchingford, Taunton, Somerset, TA3 7PZ. Contact Mrs Morley Tel & Fax: 01823 601606.
TAUNTON/HONITON 10m. Merlands is an attractive cottage offering comfort and tranquillity in the beautiful Blackdown Hills. There is an extensive garden with sun terrace, a wildflower meadow with stream and woodland. Walks may offer sightings of deer, badgers and buzzards. Breakfast made with home-grown produce, in season. 2 DOUBLE EN SUITE. CHILDREN 8+.

Prices from £20

110 TINTAGEL

9 ATLANTIC WAY, Tintagel, Cornwall, PL34 0DF.
Contact Robert & Jillian Dicker Tel & Fax: 01840 770732.
Situated near Tintagel Church, an area that is rich in history and legend this spacious, modern home offers a warm welcome and wonderful views overlooking cliffs and sea. Over 60 miles of cliff top scenery can be enjoyed from Bude to Padstow and on to the giant stacks of Bedruthian Steps. The beaches of Trebarwith and Bossiney are a short ride away as is Bodmin Moor, Boscastle and Padstow. The pubs, shops and restaurants of Tintagel are only a few minutes walk away. 2 DOUBLE, 1 TWIN, PRIVATE FACILITIES AVAILABLE. COUPLES ONLY.

Prices from £20 to £22

111 TIVERTON

THE OLD MILL Shillingford, Bampton, Tiverton, Devon, EX16 9BW. Contact Mrd D. Burnell Tel & Fax: 01398 331064.
BAMPTON 2m. Formerly water powered, The Old Mill has been recently converted into luxurious accommodation with beautiful riverside gardens. The accommodation is organised into 3 suites all with private bathroom, 2 having private lounge. Shooting and fishing nearby. Excellent choice of evening meals available. Restaurant licence. DOUBLE/TWIN BEDROOMS WITH PRIVATE BATHROOM AVAILABLE. CHILDREN BY ARRANGEMENT.

Prices from £26 to £32

112 TIVERTON
FOUR AND TWENTY BLACKBIRDS 43 Gold Street, Tiverton, Devon, EX166QB.
Tel: 01884 257055.
A traditional atmosphere prevails in these tea rooms set at the bottom of Lowman Green Clock Tower. Local attractions include Tiverton castle and the Great Western Canal. Antiques are available for sale upstairs while the selection of food on offer downstairs includes Cream Tea, Queens Tea, Kings Tea and Blackbirds Tea. A wide selection of speciality teas and home baked cakes is available.

113 TOPSHAM
GEORGIAN TEA ROOM 35 High Street, Topsham, Devon, EX3 0ED.
Contact Heather Knee Tel: 01392 873465.
Set in an attractive town with many buildings of Dutch origin, the Tea Room is near the Quay Antique Centre. The establishment has won the Heartbeat award for the 5th year and appears in two Egon Ronay guides. Home made cakes, scones and jams are on offer along with light lunches, hot and cold food and 'Slimmers Desserts'. A wide range of teas is on offer and all food is made using traditional methods and fresh local produce where possible.

114 TORPOINT

SHEVIOCK BARTON Sheviock, Torpoint, Cornwall, PL11 3EH. Contact Carol & Tony Johnson Tel & Fax: 01503 230793 E.mail: 101723.2442@compuserve.com.

LOOE 9m. Sheviock is a small village is an area of outstanding natural beauty and Sheviock Barton is situated in centre directly opposite a 14th century church. The farmhouse is 300 years old but has been restored and now has full central heating and a 4 oven Aga. There is also a club house for all ages. The beach and golf course are within 1 mile. Twenty minutes to Plymouth, Looe and Polperro. 1 FAMILY EN SUITE, 1 DOUBLE EN SUITE, 1 DOUBLE, PRIVATE BATHROOM.

🗗 ⅍ Ⓢ   **Prices from £18**

---

115 TORQUAY

THE TUDOR ROSE TEA ROOMS AND RESTAURANT 14 Victoria Parade, Torquay, Devon, TQ1 2BB. Tel: 01803 296558.

Set in a historic building overlooking the marina, the Tea Rooms are close to Cockington, the model village, Kents Cavern, Paignton Zoo and Torre Abbey. The period decor is to such a high standard that it was featured in a 1993 article in the Times and creates a pleasant atmosphere in which to sample the fare on offer. Cream Teas are available as are ranges of ice creams and speciality teas.

---

116 TORQUAY

WESTCOTT HOUSE 86 Babbacombe Road, Torquay, Devon, TQ1 3SW. Contact Wendy Evans Tel: 01803 325657.

100 yards from Coastal Path with stunning views across Babbacombe and Lyme Bay. Lots of 'eateries' nearby and local nightlife. Dartmoor 15m, M5 20 minutes. Bikes garaged.

🗗 Ⓢ   **Prices from £16**

---

117 TORQUAY

HUNTERS MOON HOTEL Torquay, Devon. Contact Biking Bros. Tel: 01803 294760.

The biker friendly hotel located in the heart of the English Riviera and Devon Countryside. Superb base for ride-outs and touring. Group bookings welcome for clubs.

🗗 Ⓢ

---

118 TORQUAY

CHELSTON MANOR HOTEL Old Mill Road, Torquay, Devon. Tel: 01803 605142.

Each room of this 17th century building has tea/coffee facilities, television and radio. There is also an extensive breakfast menu. 11 DOUBLE, 2 TWIN, 1 SINGLE ALL EN SUITE.

Prices from £25

---

119 TORQUAY

REDLANDS 317 Babbacombe Road, Torquay, Devon, TQ1 3TB. Contact Don & Rita Tucker Tel: 01803 298702.

Situated at the Babbacombe end of Torquay, Redlands is a comfortable private house near beaches and coastal walks. South Devon is easily accessible from Torquay as is Exeter, South Hams and Dartmoor, all approximately 1 hour away. Ample off road secure parking. Near a bus route into Torquay. Closed October to Easter. 2 DOUBLE EN SUITE, 1 TWIN WITH PRIVATE FACILITIES. NO CHILDREN.

⅍   **Prices from £17 to £20**

Think movement

Touring E N J O Y T O U R I N G *style*

GIVI has many years of experience in the motorcycle sector and carries out continuous research into new technology, with innovative materials, ensuring the best quality, design and reliability.

Today we provide the most complete range of cases, all of which are equipped with the patented Monokey locking device and mounting system.
It offers specific features for most motorcycles...

Technical Helpline 01327 312081

@ givi@globalnet.co.uk

01327 706220

Unit 4, Royal Oak Court,
Royal Oak Way,
Royal Oak Ind. Est,
Daventry, Northants,
NN11 5PQ.

fit the bike

120 TOTNES
GREYS DINING ROOM 96 High Street, Totnes, Devon, TQ9 5SN. Tel: 01803 866369.
Set in Totnes High Street, popular for its interesting shops and street market, Greys Dining Room offers a wide ranging menu. Cream teas, a selection of home baked cakes and thirty seven different teas and infusions are all on offer. Local attractions include the Norman Castle, the 14th century church, the River Dart and the Dartington Cider Press Centre.

---

121 TOTNES
THE BAY HORSE INN 8 Cistern Street, Totnes, Devon, TQ9 5SP.
Contact Kevin & Nicola Tel: 01803 862 088.
Always 3 Real Ales, 3 Lagers, bottled Beers and Guinness. Food served daily from 12 noon to 4pm. ROOM ONLY £10, ROOM WITH B&B £15 OR BRING YOUR OWN SLEEPING BAG AND SLEEP ON THE FLOOR £5.

Prices from £5 to £15

---

122 TRURO
CITY INN Pydar Street, Truro, Cornwall, TR1 3SP. Tel: 01872 272623.
Set in the historic city of Truro and close to all the attractions this offers including the cathedral and local shops. The establishment offers hot drink facilities in all rooms as well as colour television. TWO DOUBLE AND ONE SINGLE ROOM.

Prices from £18.50

---

123 TRURO
AVALON TEA ROOM Coast Road, Porthtowan, Truro, Cornwall, TR4 8AR.
Contact Ann and terry Luckwell Tel: 01209 890751.
Near to Porthtowan beach, this Tea Room is convenient for walkers and surfers. A wide selection of locally baked scones, cakes and biscuits is on offer as are sandwiches and a range of speciality teas and coffees.

---

124 TRURO
THE CHAPTER HOUSE REFECTORY 21 Old Bridge Street, Truro, Cornwall, TR1 2AH.
Tel: 01872 223 214 & 276 782 Fax: 01872 277.
Located in the modern Chapter House, this Refectory provides a range of light meals and refreshments. Meals, snacks and puddings prepared on the premises. MON-FRI 10AM-4PM SATURDAY 10AM-2PM.

---

125 TRURO

MANOR COTTAGE GUEST HOUSE Tresillian, Truro, Cornwall, TR2 4BN. Contact Mrs Moyle Tel: 01872 520212.
Built circa 1820, Manor Cottage is a Georgian house furnished with old pine/oak furniture and patchwork quilts. There is a licensed restaurant open Thursday – Saturday (reservation required) where the dishes are made from local produce. The cottage is located on the A390, 3 miles from Truro many gardens of Cornwall are nearby. Closed Christmas. 1 SINGLE, 1 TWIN, 2 DOUBLE, 1 FAMILY, PRIVATE FACILITIES AVAILABLE.

Prices from £18 to £24

126 TRURO

LANDS VUE Three Burrows, Truro, Cornwall, TR4 8JA. Contact David & Molly Hutchings Tel: 01872 560242 Fax: 01872 560950.
Three miles from the sea, just off the A30, Lands Vue is situated among 2 acres of tranquil gardens which can be used for recreation or just to enjoy the scenery. There is a large dining room with a panoramic view where a plentiful farmhouse breakfast can be enjoyed or relax in front of the TV in the lounge. There are excellent pubs and restaurants nearby. Closed Christmas and New Year.
2 TWIN, 1 DOUBLE, ALL EN SUITE. CHILDREN 12 +.

Prices from £22 to £24

127 UMBERLEIGH

FARRIERS Chittlehamholt, Umberleigh, North Devon, EX37 9NS. Contact Mrs Mil Campion Tel & Fax: 01769 540605.
SOUTH MOLTON 5m. Between the rivers Taw and Mole, the pretty village of Chittlehamholt is where Farriers is situated. There is a guest TV sitting room or peaceful garden in which to relax. Ten golf courses locally, including three championship courses. Local fishing can be arranged. National trust properties and RHS Rosemoor 25-40 minutes away. Closed Christmas and New Year.
1 DOUBLE EN SUITE, 1 TWIN EN SUITE, 1 SINGLE.

Prices from £17 to £25

128 UMBERLEIGH

THE VILLAGE SHOPPE AND TEA ROOMS The Square, Atherington, Umberleigh, DEvon, EX37 9HY. Contact Jo and Chris Hart Tel: 01769 560248.
Dating from 17th century with exposed beams and inglenook fireplace. Central to many Devon attractions. Home-cooked menu including cream teas, all day breakfast and Sunday lunches. Evening meals available.
1 DOUBLE, 1 TWIN, 1 SINGLE.

129 WEDMORE

NUT TREE FARM Stoughton Cross, Wedmore, Somerset, BS28 4QP. Contact Anne Firmager Tel & Fax: 01934 712404 E.mail: Melvyn.firmager@netgates.co.uk.
WELLS 9m. Nut Tree Farm, set in 2 acres of semi-wild garden and orchard is a 16th century farmhouse. Extensive menu, including traditional English or wholefood breakfast. Comfortable lounge with an inglenook fire. A gallery displays the work of Melvyn Firmager, internationally renowned turner, with wood turning courses available. Golf course within walking distance. Wells, Cheddar and Glastonbury within easy reach. 2 DOUBLE, 1 TWIN, EN SUITE OR PRIVATE FACILITIES. NO CHILDREN.

Prices from £19.50 to £21

130 WELLS

INFIELD HOUSE 36 Portway, Wells, Somerset, BA5 2BN. Contact Mr & Mrs R. Betton Foster Tel: 01749 670989 Fax: 01749 679093.
Infield House backs on to woodlands and is a restored Victorian townhouse. Situated on the A371 to Wells it is just a few minutes walk from the High Street, Market Square, the cathedral and other historic buildings. Wonderfully furnished to complement this period house. Well placed for visits to Cheddar, Wookey Hole, Ebbor Gorge and Glastonbury. 2 DOUBLE, 1 TWIN, ALL EN SUITE. CHILDREN 12+.

Prices from £21 to £24.50

131 WESTWARD HO! **FOUR WINDS Cornborough Road, Westward Ho!, Devon, EX39 1AA. Contact Polly & Steve Evers Tel: 01237 421741.**

Four Winds is situated near the long sandy beaches of Westward Ho! and a links golf course. It is a lovely country house in a peaceful location with gardens, croquet lawn, children's play area and lawn tennis. The home is friendly and informal and the rooms are attractive. Home grown produce is provided by the vegetable garden and free range hens. 1 FAMILY, 1 DOUBLE, 1 TWIN, ALL EN SUITE/PRIVATE FACILITIES.

Prices from £18 to £20

---

132 WILLITON
VELLOW TEA GARDENS Vellow, Stogumber, Williton, Somerset, TA4 4LS. Contact Ann Bryant Tel: 01984 656411.

Set in an acre of lush gardens, the Tea Rooms are near a number of local attractions including Vellow Pottery, Bee World and West Somerset Railway. Food is beautifully presented and the selection includes home made cakes, cheeses and scones. The Vellow Tea Garden Special consists of vanilla ice cream, fresh fruit, raspberry sauce, laced with Tequila.Closed end September until 15th April 2000.

---

133 YEOVIL
THE WALNUT TREE West Camel, Nr. Yeovil, Somerset, BA22 7QW. Contact Peter Ball Tel: 01935 851992 & 01935 851292.

This is a tranquil village inn, with an excellent reputation for fine food and very homely accommodation, We offer all the facilities you would expect and much more. our restaurant is Egon Ronay recommended for both food and accommodation for the past 4 years running. We have a wide selection of wines and the owner Peter Ball is the Chef. 7 BEDROOMS ALL EN SUITE AND 1 FOUR POSTER.

Prices from £46 to £76

---

134 YEOVIL

THE SPARKFORD INN Sparkford, Nr. Yeovil, Somerset, BA22 7JN. Tel: 01963 440218 Fax: 01963 440358.

The Sparkford Inn has two bar areas decorated and furnished in a tradition style with many antiques, pictures and photographs. Our restaurant and carvery are decorated similarly. We have a carvery with traditional roasts, fish and vegetarian foods all available. We have cask, Bass and Worthington Beers, and guest beers. We welcome motorcyclists. You can eat with us, stay with us or drink with us, you will enjoy our Country Inn. BEDROOMS SINGLE TWIN AND FAMILY ROOMS ALL EN SUITE.

Prices from £29.50 to £39.50

1 ABBOTSBURY
THE OLD SCHOOLHOUSE 1 Back Street, Abbotsbury, Dorset, DT3 4JP.
Tel: 01305 871808.
Set near the Abbotsbury Swannery, Tithe Barn, St Catherines Chapel and Chesil Beach, The Schoolhouse is decorated in the style of the 1920s and '30s. A gift shop is also available where a variety of locally made gifts can be bought. Set teas along with home made cakes and a range of speciality teas are all available. Children under five are not admitted.

2 ALTON

VINE FARMHOUSE Isington, Bentley, Alton, Hampshire, GU34 4PW. Contact Mrs G. Sinclair Tel & Fax: 01420 23262 E.mail: VINEFARM@aol.com.
Vine Farmhouse, is set in its own farmland half way between Alton and Farnham overlooking the river Wey. Oxford, Winchester, Stonehenge and the New Forest within 45 miles. In an area rich with local attractions, Birdworld, Farnham Castle, Jane Austen's house and steam museum are just some within easy reach. Pubs and restaurants nearby. Closed Christmas. 1 DOUBLE/FAMILY EN SUITE, 1 SINGLE, 1 DOUBLE.

Prices from £17.50 to £22.50

3 ANDOVER

BROADWATER Amport, Andover, Hampshire, SP11 8AY. Contact Mrs Carolyn Mallam Tel & Fax: 01264 772240 E.mail: carolyn@dmac.co.uk.
A listed thatched cottage, Broadwater offers a relaxed, cosy atmosphere in a peaceful village setting. Just 1 mile from the A303, this secluded family accommodation makes an excellent stopover for touring many of the local attractions, including Stonehenge. Credit cards accepted. 2 TWIN EN SUITE, FLAT SLEEPS 2/4.

Prices from £25

4 ARUNDEL
BEAM ENDS COUNTRY TEA ROOM Hedgers Hill, Walberton, Arundel, West Sussex, BN18 0LR. Tel: 01243 551254.
The Tea Rooms are set in a 16th century thatched cottage near a variety of local attractions including Arundel, Climbing Beach and Binsted Woods. Morning coffee, lunches and afternoon teas are all available and home made with fresh ingredients.

5 ARUNDEL

MILL LANE HOUSE Slindon, Arundel, Sussex, BN18 0RP. Contact Mrs Fuente Tel: 01243 814440 Fax: 01243 814436.
Set in a 3 acre garden, Mill Lane House offers superb views to the coast. The local area is almost completely owned by the National Trust and there is excellent bird watching and walks over the South Downs hills. Ideally located for visits to Arundel Castle, Goodwood and Chichester. Portsmouth 25 miles away. Evening meals by arrangement or from the 2 pubs nearby. DOUBLE, TWIN AND FAMILY ROOMS, ALL EN SUITE.

6 ARUNDEL

DELGAR HOUSE The Street, Patching, Arundel, West Sussex, BN13 3XF. Contact Heidi & Andrew Stevens
Tel: 01903 871331 & 0585 921237.
ARUNDEL 5m. Delgar House is in a traditional peaceful village in the Sussex Downs. The 18th century cottage, originally a coach house offers accommodation in the main house or a self contained annexe with its own kitchen and bathroom. Arundel Castle, Parham House and Gardens are nearby. The coast at Littlehampton is 5 miles away. 1 DOUBLE, 2 FAMILY (1EN SUITE).
Prices from £16 to £22

7 BALCOMBE
THE BALCOMBE TEA ROOMS Bramble Hill, Balcombe, West Sussex, RH17 6HR. Tel: 01444 811777.
Situated in an area of outstanding natural beauty the Tea Rooms are well placed to enjoy several local attractions including Borde Hill Gardens, Nymans Gardens, Balcombe Lake, Ardingley Reservoir and High Beech Gardens. Cream teas are a speciality as are home made cakes and fresh strawberries and raspberries. Local preserves and crafts are also available to buy.

8 BARTON-ON-SEA
SEA COTTAGE TEA SHOPPE Marine Drive, Barton-on-Sea, Hampshire, BH25 7DZ. Tel: 01425 614086.
Situated on a cliff top with views of The Needles and the Isle of Wight. The Tea Shoppe specialises in healthy food and has won a Healthy Heartbeat Award for three years in a row. Afternoon tea with home made fare are available. The Tea Shoppe can be booked for parties.

9 BATH
OPEN HOUSE COFFEE SHOP Manvers Street Baptist Church, Manvers Street, Bath, BA1 1JW. Tel: 01225 333 223.
Set in Manvers Street Baptist Church, the Open Coffee House is a warm, welcoming environment in which to enjoy a range of hot and cold beverages and food. Located in the heart of Bath, this is an ideal meeting place for friends. Typical dishes include lentil and chive or coriander soup, roast chicken and broccoli mornay. MONDAY-SATURDAY 10AM-4.30PM SUNDAY CLOSED.

10 BATH

ASHLEY VILLA HOTEL 26 Newbridge Road, Bath BA1 3JZ.
Contact Rod & Alex Kitcher
Tel: 01225 421683 Fax: 01225 313604.
Comfortably furnished licensed hotel with relaxing informal atmosphere, situated close to the city centre. This small friendly hotel has recently been refurbished throughout. It has an outdoor swimming pool with garden patio and car park. You can be sure of a warm welcome from the resident owners. 14 BEDROOMS SINGLES AND DOUBLES, ALL EN SUITE WITH TV, DIRECT DIAL TELEPHONE, TEA/COFFEE FACILITIES.

Prices from £59 to £89

11 BATH

BROMPTON HOUSE St. Johns Road, Bath, North Somerset BA2 6PT. Contact Mr & Mrs Selby Tel: 01225 420972 Fax: 01225 420505.
Elegant Georgian residence (former rectory 1777), family owned and run. Car park and beautiful secluded gardens. Only 6 minutes to main historic sites. Tastefully furnished with fully equipped en suite bedrooms and delicious breakfasts. 18 BEDROOMS SINGLES, TWINS AND DOUBLES, ALL EN SUITE.

Prices from £32 to £80

12 BATH

BURGHOPE MANOR Winsley, Bradford-upon-Avon, Bath, North Somerset BA15 2LA. Contact Mr Denning Tel: 01225 723557 Fax: 01225 723113.
An historic 13th century country home set in beautiful countryside on the edge of the village of Winsley. Steeped in history, first and foremost a living family home, carefully modernised. A wealth of historic features complement present day comforts. 8 BEDROOMS SINGLES AND DOUBLES, ALL EN SUITE.

Prices from £65 to £90

13 BATH

OAKLEIGH HOUSE 19 Upper Oakfield Park, Bath, North Somerset BA2 3JX. Contact Jenny King Tel: 01225 315698 Fax: 01225 448223.
Quietly situated Victorian home only 10 minutes walk from the city centre, with splendid views over Georgian Bath. All luxury rooms en suite. Tempting choice of breakfasts. Closed Jan 5th - Feb. 12th. 4 BEDROOMS SINGLES AND DOUBLES, ALL EN SUITE. ALL CREDIT CARDS ACCEPTED.

Prices from £35 to £65

14 BATH

MEADOWLAND 36 Bloomfield Park, Bath, North Somerset, BA2 2BX. Contact Cathrine Andrew Tel & Fax: 01225 311079.
Meadowland is an award winning accommodation set in its own tranquil grounds a short distance from the beautiful city of Bath. There is a comfortable drawing room and beautiful gardens surrounding this elegant house. An excellent selection of restaurants and pubs within easy reach. Private secure parking. 2 DOUBLE, 1 TWIN ALL EN SUITE.

Prices from £30 to £35

15 BATH

KINLET GUEST HOUSE 99 Wellsway, Bath, North Somerset, BA2 4RX. Contact Mrs Bennett Tel & Fax: 01225 420268.
Kinlet Guest House is a small Victorian house with a friendly and relaxing atmosphere. There is a frequent bus service to the centre of Bath a short walk away. Jenny Bennett will be delighted to advise you on local attractions and visits further afield. The restaurants and pubs of Bath provide an excellent and varied choice of places to dine. 1 DOUBLE, 1 FAMILY, 1 SINGLE.

Prices from £18 to £20

16 BATH

THE OLD RED HOUSE 37 Newbridge Road, Bath, North Somerset, BA1 3HE. Contact Mrs Chrissie Besley Tel: 01225 330464 Fax: 01225 331661.
The Old Red House was a patisserie and baker's shop built 100 years ago. It was Alfred Taylor's famous Gingerbread House and still retains its original charm and stained glass windows. Now a warm, comfortable family home, it is uniquely decorated with pictures and family treasures. Good pubs and restaurants nearby. Varied original breakfast menu. 3 DOUBLE, 1 TWIN/FAMILY, EN SUITE OR PRIVATE FACILITIES.

Prices from £21 to £33

17 BATH

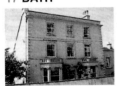

IRONDALE HOUSE 67 High Street, Rode, Bath, North Somerset, BA3 6PB. Contact Jayne & Olwen Holder Tel & Fax: 01373 830730.
Irondale House is an extensively refurbished detached Georgian home with walled gardens and wonderful views. Visits to Stonehenge, Salisbury and Glastonbury or Longleat House and Safari park are easily accessed from this location. There are also many more National Trust properties and places of interest nearby. Credit cards accepted. Closed Christmas and New Year.
1 DOUBLE/TWIN/FAMILY EN SUITE, 1 DOUBLE PRIVATE, 1 FAMILY SUITE.

Prices from £30 to £32.50

18 BEACONSFIELD
THE OLD TEA HOUSE 7 Windsor End, Beaconsfield, Buckinghamshire, HP9 2JJ. Tel: 01494 676273.
The Old Tea House is a Grade 1 listed building set in attractive Beaconsfield. Nearby attractions include Bekonscot Model Village, the Odds Farm Rare Breed Centre, Wycombe Chair Museum and the Chiltern Open Air Museum. A selection of freshly baked cakes are available as are sandwiches, cream teas, speciality teas and coffees and light lunches.

19 BILLINGHURST

HILLAND Stane Street, Billinghurst, Sussex, RH14 9HN. Contact Mrs Wakeling Tel: 01403 782029.
Hilland Farm is in a delightful country setting where a warm and friendly welcome greets you when you arrive. All bedrooms have a view of the South Downs. Good farmhouse breakfasts. Situated just off the A29, it is well located for visits to Arundel Castle, Goodwood, Amberley chalk pits and many other local attractions. Closed Christmas and New Year. 2 DOUBLE/TWIN, 2 FAMILY EN SUITE.

Prices from £20 to £22

20 BLANDFORD FORUM
MANOR HOUSE FARM Ibberton, Blandford Forum, Dorset, DT11 0EN. Contact Mrs Old Tel: 01258 817349.
A small 16th century manor house, which at one time was given to Catherine Howard by Henry VIII, now a farmhouse and working farm in an unspoilt village. 3 BEDROOMS, 2 EN SUITE.

Prices from £14 to £32

AKITO

AFFORDABLE QUALITY

21 BLANDFORD FORUM
THE WILLOWS 5 Blandford Road, Shillingstone, Blandford Forum, Dorset DT11 0SG. Tel: 01258 861167.
Set in an eighteenth century cob and brick cottage at the foot of Hambledon Hill, The Willows are convenient for those exploring the Wessex Ridgeway as well as the Georgian town of Blandford Forum. Home made cakes and scones are on offer as are a variety of teas including Ceylon, Darjeeling and Earl Grey.

22 BOURNEMOUTH
HIGHCLERE 15 Burnaby Road, Alum Chine, Bournemouth, Dorset, BH4 8JF. Contact Mr Baldwin
Tel: 01202 761350 Fax: 01202 767110.
A charming and welcoming family hotel with many original Victorian features. A choice of excellent, plentiful dishes at meal times. Five minutes walk from the beach. Closed November to March inclusive. 9 BEDROOMS, ALL EN SUITE.

Prices from £19 to £46

23 BOURNEMOUTH
QUALITY HOTEL 8 Poole Road, Bournemouth, BH2 5QU.
Tel: 01202 763 006 Fax: 01202 766 168 E.mail: admin@gb641.u-net.com.
Located off A338 towards Bournemouth Int. Centre. Quality accommodation with many facilities including food and drink with wines and beers available and rooms with cable TV. Golf nearby and lots of attractions including Cerne Abbas Giant, Poole Pottery and Brownsea Island. Special package for bikers £26 per person inc. breakfast and dinner. Subject to availability. Must be booked through Central Reservations 0800 44 44 44. 57 BEDROOMS.

24 BRADING (IoW)
PENNY PLAIN TEA ROOM AND GARDEN 44 High Street, Brading, Isle of Wight, PO36 0DN. Tel: 01983 407649.
The Tea Room is not far from the Isle of Wight Wax Museum and the Lilliput Dolls' Museum. A variety of teas and coffees are available as are home made scones and gateaux. A particular speciality are the hot scotch pancakes with maple syrup, double cream and roast almonds.

25 BRIDPORT
FROGMORE FARM Chideock, Bridport, DT6 6HT. Contact Mrs Norman
Tel: 01308 456 159.
A charming 17th century farmhouse where guests can expect a warm and friendly welcome. Rooms are finely decorated and offer many facilities. Located near Lyme Bay the house is also ideally situated to explore the variety of attractions in Dorset. 3 BEDROOMS, 2 EN SUITE.

Prices from £23

26 BRIGHTON
THE COACH HOUSE TEA ROOMS 108A Old London Road, Patcham Village, Brighton, Sussex, BN1 8YA. Contact Mrs Harriet Hawley Tel: 01273 553243.
Set in the village street of old Patcham village the Tea Rooms are close to a range of interesting attractions including the oldest tithe barn in Sussex as well as one of the oldest dovecotes in existence. The property is a former coach house which is decorated with harnesses and brasses. Food on offer is home made and includes quiches, cakes, cream teas and vegetarian options. The speciality teas on offer include herbal and fruit varieties.

27 BRIGHTON
THE LOAVES AND FISHES CAFE Brighthelm Church & Community Centre, North Road, Brighton, BN1 1YD. Tel: 01273 821 512.
Church and community centre cafe serving breakfasts, light lunches and other refreshments. Breakfasts and baked potatoes served between 10am and 2.30pm and home cooked lunches available between 12.30 and 2pm. Delicious food including soup of the day, pork chops and vegetables, pasta bake and lasagne. Average lunch (2 courses) £3.10.

28 CERNE ABBAS

LAMPERTS COTTAGE Sydling St. Nicholas, Cerne Abbas, Dorset, DT2 9NU. Contact Nicky Willis Tel: 01300 341659 Fax: 01300 341699.
Dorchester 8m. Chalk streams and fields encircle the thatched 16th century Lamperts Cottage. Bedrooms are well furnished with dormer windows under the eaves and the dining room has a large inglenook fireplace, old bread oven and original beams. Well placed for touring local attractions, beaches a half-hour ride away. Closed Christmas. Credit Cards Accepted. 1 TWIN, 1DOUBLE, 1 DOUBLE/FAMILY. CHILDREN 8+.

▢ ⅍ Ⓢ   **Prices from £20**

29 CHALE (IoW)

CLARENDON HOTEL Chale, Isle of Wight, PO38 2HA. Contact John and Jean Bradshaw Tel: 01983 730431 Fax: 01983 730431.
Situated in the attractive village of Chale on the Isle of Wight. An ideal location to either enjoy the numerous attractions the island has to offer or to simply unwind. 9 SINGLE, 3 SUITES. ALL ROOMS ARE EN-SUITE.

VISA   **Prices from £25 to £50**

30 CHALE (IoW)
WIGHT MOUTH INN Chale, Isle of Wight, PO38 2HA. Contact Mr Bradshaw Tel: 01983 730 431.
Bikers receive a warm welcome at this establishment, which is open from 11am to midnight. The Wight Mouth Inn specialises in a huge variety of whiskies - over 365, and there is a selection of 6 real ales. Hot food served all day. Live entertainment every night.

31 CHALE (IoW)

CHALE BAY FARM & SEAGULLS RESTAURANT Military Road, Chale, Isle of Wight, PO38 2JF. Contact Mr Bradshaw Tel & Fax: 01983 730431.
Set amongst superb surroundings of a Japanese water garden with fabulous views of the sea, sunset, the Needles and Tennyson Downs. Eight luxurious bedrooms, excellent cuisine and wines, 365 whiskies, 6 real ales and nightly entertainment. 8 BEDROOMS, ALL EN SUITE.

Prices from £28 to £58

32 CHALFONT ST GILES
TEA-TIME 4A High Street, Chalfont St Giles, Buckinghamshire, HP8 4QP. Tel: 01494 871099.
Located in a pretty location on a village green near the John Milton museum. The Tea Room offers either the Traditional Tea comprising scones and tea or the Village Tea consisting of sandwiches and either scones or cake, with a pot of tea. Take away service is available as are breakfast, snack and lunch options.

33 CHARMOUTH
WIND IN THE WILLOWS TEA GARDEN Riverway, Charmouth, Dorset, DT6 6LS. Tel: 01297 560384.
Set on a Jurassic coastline with excellent fossil collecting and walking opportunities. The Tea Garden, as the name suggests, is based on the theme of the Wind in the Willows. Children and dogs are welcome to enjoy the cream teas and home made cakes as well as ginger beer and orange cordial.

34 CHICHESTER
ST MARTIN'S TEA ROOMS 3 St Martins Street, Chichester, West Sussex, PO19 1NP. Contact Keith Nelson Tel: 01243 786715.
Set in a restored medieval building the Tea Rooms have a unique atmosphere. The emphasis is on healthy food and the Tea Rooms have received the Heartbeat Award for Healthiest Food and Preparation. Organic bread, cakes and scones are all home-made and ingredients comprehensively listed. No convenience foods and no microwaves. A wide range of speciality teas available. Open Mon-Sat 9-6pm.

35 CHICHESTER
BISHOP BELL ROOMS REFECTORY The Cloisters, Chichester Cathedral, Chichester, West Sussex, PO19 1PX. Tel: 01243 783 718.
Located in the Cloisters this refectory has large, bright rooms which face a walled garden. Cheerful staff that are always ready to help. Enjoy home made quiches and salads, hot dishes and home made cakes and desserts. MON-SAT, 9.30AM-5PM. CLOSED SUNDAY. CLOSED CHRISTMAS AND EASTER.

36 CHIPPENHAM

ELM FARMHOUSE The Green, Biddestone, Chippenham, Wilts, SN14 7DG. Contact Mrs Elaine Sexton Tel & Fax: 01249 713354.
BATH 10m. Made out of Cotswold stone, Elm Farmhouse was built in the 18th century and is situated opposite the duck pond in the lovely village of Biddestone, 5 miles from the M4. Large, elegant bedrooms overlook the duck pond or the walled garden. Footpaths through picturesque countryside and two pubs/restaurants are an easy stroll away. Well situated for Bath, Castle Coombe, Avebury and other historic attractions. 1 FAMILY, 2 DOUBLE (1 WITH 4-POSTER), ALL EN SUITE WITH PRIVATE FACILITIES.

Prices from £22.50 to £25

37 CHIPPENHAM **FAIRFIELD FARM Upper Wraxall, Chippenham, Wiltshire SN14 7AG. Contact Mrs J. McDonough**
Tel: 01225 891750 Fax: 01225 891050.
BATH 10m. Fairfield Farm is a family run farmhouse built of Cotswold stone with a large garden. Only 6 miles from the M4 it is ideally situated for Bath, Stonehenge, Lacock, Castle Coombe and the Cotswolds. Horse riding, golf, pubs and restaurants nearby. Ample secure parking. 1 TWIN,1 DOUBLE/FAMILY, BOTH WITH PRIVATE FACILITIES.

Prices from £20

38 CHIPPENHAM
THE NEELD ARMS INN The Street, Grittleton, Chippenham, Wiltshire.
Contact Bill and Sara Clemence Tel: 01249 782470.
This is a 17th Century family run Inn, set in the beautiful village of Grittleton, only 1 1/2 miles from the Castle Coombe race course. We serve delicious homemade food. We traditional ales. All rooms have colour TV and tea and coffee making facilities. Secure parking at the rear of the pub.
6 EN SUITE BED AND BREAKFAST ROOMS.

39 CHICHESTER **HATPINS Bosham, Old Bosham, Chichester, Hampshire, PO18 8HG. Contact Mrs Mary Waller Tel & Fax: 01243 572644.**
CHICHESTER 3m. A short walk from the quit waterfront at Old Bosham is the attractive home of Hatpins. The artistic talent and flair of your host is evident in the unique décor of each room. Portsmouth, Chichester, Fishbourne Roman Palace and Goodwood House are nearby. 4 DOUBLE, 1 TWIN, EN SUITE OR PRIVATE FACILITIES.

Prices from £25 to £40

40 CHRISTCHURCH **OLD STABLES 186 Salisbury Road, Burton, Christchurch, Dorset, BH23 7JS. Contact Mrs Ann Dow Tel: 01202 478755.**
BOURNEMOUTH 6m/CHRISTCHURCH 3m. Old Stables has been converted from a stable block to the local Manor House into comfortable accommodation. It is set in a large landscaped garden with stables and paddocks. Patio garden and many animals - a horse, cats and a dog. It is only 3 miles from the coast and 3 miles from the New Forest and Christchurch. Closed Christmas. 1 DOUBLE WITH PRIVATE BATHROOM.

Prices from £20

41 CORSHAM **THURLESTONE LODGE 13 Prospect, Corsham, Wiltshire, SN13 9AD. Contact Mrs V. Ogilvie-Robb Tel & Fax: 01249 713397.**
BATH 8m. Set in beautiful landscaped gardens, Thurlestone Lodge is a spacious Victorian home within easy walking distance of the Corsham centre. Well equipped rooms with colour TV. Ideally located for Bath, the Cotswolds, Stonehenge and other historic attractions. Closed Christmas. 1 DOUBLE, 1 TWIN/FAMILY.

Prices from £17 to £19

42 CRAWLEY

APRIL COTTAGE 10 Langley Lane, Ifield Green, Crawley, Sussex, RH11 0NA. Contact Liz & Brian Pedlow Tel: 01293 546222 Fax: 01293 518712.
April Cottage offers a delightful homely atmosphere, 10 minutes from Gatwick. All rooms are tastefully decorated and there is holiday parking and courtesy travel to Gatwick by arrangement. Shops, pubs, buses and mainline railway to London nearby. Traditional English Breakfast served. 1 SINGLE, 1 TWIN, 1 DOUBLE, 1 FAMILY. CHILDREN 6+.

Prices from £21 to £30

43 DENHAM

LA CAPELLE, RESTAURANT FRANCAIS, Station Parade, Denham, Buckinghamshire, UB9 5ET. Tel: 01895 833048.
For over ten years it has been our pleasure to offer the very best in freshly prepared food and fine wines. We reflect the flavours of the Mediterranean in our restaurant.The Tudor style restaurant and adjoining Tapas Bar offers quality meals at value for money prices. We welcome motorcyclists and we are in one of the most delightful parts of Buckinghamshire. We have a private and secure parking area. We are open Monday to Saturday for dinner and Monday to Friday for lunch.

44 DORCHESTER

3 MANOR FARM COTTAGES Lower Waterston, Dorchester, Dorset, DT2 7SS. Contact Mrs Liz Hardman Tel & Fax: 01305 848160.
3 Manor Farm Cottages is a renovated Victorian farm cottage in the small hamlet of Lower Waterston. Set in a picturesque garden that runs down the river piddle, the area offers a variety of attractions, walking, fishing, historic houses etc. Coast is within easy reach (10miles). Evening meals available. 1 DOUBLE, 1 TWIN, BOTH EN SUITE. CHILDREN 8+.

Prices from £17 to £18

45 DORCHESTER

YALBURY PARK Frome Whitfield Farm, Dorchester, Dorset, DT2 7SE. Mrs Bamlet Tel: 01305 250366 & 01305 260070.
A luxurious new stone farmhouse, Yalbury Park is situated on a 170 acre mixed farm. It is situated in parkland made famous by Thomas Hardy's Valley of the Great Dairies and near the river Frome. Large south facing garden with rare and unusual plants. Near historic towns and beaches - outdoor activities can be arranged. 1 DOUBLE/TWIN, 2 FAMILY, ALL EN SUITE.

Prices from £22 to £25

46 EASTBOURNE

FAR END 139 Royal Parade, Eastbourne, East Sussex, BN22 7LH. Contact Mr Callaghan Tel: 01323 725666.
Sea front hotel with friendly welcome, alongside pretty Princes Park. Wonderful sea views from the first floor lounge; views of park and sea from most bedrooms. Private car park. 10 BEDROOMS, 5 EN SUITE.

Prices from £17 to £180

47 EMSWORTH

MERRY HALL HOTEL 73 Horndean Road, Emsworth, Hampshire, PO10 7PU. Contact Mrs Twine Tel: 01243 431377.
Situated in the coastal town of Emsworth, Merry Hall Hotel is a modern hotel with a cosy atmosphere. The rooms overlook large private gardens and are well equipped. 9 BEDROOMS, 6 EN SUITE.

Prices from £24 to £50

48 FERNDOWN

SMUGGLERS COTTAGE 577 Wimborne Road East, Ferndown, Dorset, BH22 9NW. Contact Robert Marshall Tel: 01202 870738 Fax: 01202 870766.
RINGWOOD 5m. Smugglers Cottage was built in the 16th century and is steeped in the history of smuggling - part of the house is built from timber from a wrecked Spanish galleon. The cottage and tea rooms are situated on the main road giving easy access to all local destinations. 2 DOUBLE, 1 TWIN, 1 SINGLE.

Prices from £20 to £30

49 FINDON

RACEHORSE COTTAGE Nepcote, Findon, Sussex, BN14 0SN. Contact Mr & Mrs Lloyd Tel: 01903 873783.
WORTHING 4m. The picturesque Racehorse Cottage offers a warm friendly welcome. Situated in the peaceful village of Findon with an 11th century church, it is in an excellent location for touring southern England. Home made bread, jams and marmalade at breakfast can be enjoyed. Close to Arundel and Brighton. Closed Christmas. 2 TWIN. CHILDREN 5+.

Prices from £17 to £21

50 GILLINGHAM

STOUR CROSS FARM West Stour, Gillingham, Dorset, SP8 5SE. Contact Mrs C. Trim Tel & Fax: 01747 838183.
SHAFTSBURY 4m. Stour Cross Farm is a Scandinavian house on a working dairy farm that overlooks Blackmore Vale. A warm welcome awaits with comfortable rooms and full English breakfast. Walking, fishing, horse riding and shooting nearby. Ideal location for touring; Shaftsbury 10 mins, coast 45 mins, 8 mile from Stourhead. Closed Christmas Day. 1 DOUBLE, 1 TWIN, BOTH WITH PRIVATE FACILITIES.

Prices from £19 to £20

51 GODSHILL (IoW)

THE OLD WORLD TEA GARDENS High Street, Godshill, Isle of Wight, Hampshire, PO38 3HZ. Contact Lora Dixley and Andrew Parsons Tel: 01983 840637.
The Tea Gardens are close to numerous attractions including a model village, toy museum and Natural History Centre. On offer are cream teas, including a diabetic option, a selection of cakes and teas and coffees.

52 GUILDFORD
GUILDFORD CATHEDRAL REFECTORY Stag Hill, Guildford, Surrey, GU2 5UP. Tel: 01483 560 471.
This Cathedral Refectory offers a warm and friendly atmosphere in which to sit and enjoy a range of tasty meals and snacks. Homemade cakes, sandwiches and salads are just a few of the snacks. Meals include casserole of lamb with apricots and almonds, lentil bake and for dessert sunflower and chocolate cookies. Average lunch £6.10.

53 HANNINGTON
THE OLD RED HOUSE Hannington, Northhamptonshire. Tel: 01604 781 341.
Situated on the A43 between Kettering and Northampton, The Old Roadhouse has a wide variety of good drinks including cask beers, and food. Free camping to Bikers who use the pub. Barbecue available if booked in advance. Space available for Rallies. Honda Owners Club Northants Branch meets here.

55 HENFIELD

YEOMANS HALL Blackstone, Henfield, Sussex, BN5 9TB. Contact Alan & Caroline Kerridge Tel & Fax: 01273 494224.
BRIGHTON 6m. The rooms at Yeomans Hall have comfortable, stylish furnishings and inglenook fireplaces. It is a listed 15th century hall house with an attractive cottage garden situated in the heart of the farming hamlet of Blackstone, close to the A23. Conveniently close to Brighton and National Trust properties. Closed Christmas and New Year. 2 DOUBLE, 1 SINGLE, ALL EN SUITE.

🗔 ⅍ Ⓢ   **Prices from £21 to £26**

56 HENLEY ON THAMES
CRISPIN'S RESTAURANT AND TEA ROOMS 52 Hart Street, Henley on Thames, Oxfordshire, RG9 2AU. Contact Rodney Newbold Tel: 01491 574232.
Being located on the Thames, the Tea Rooms are very convenient for boating enthusiasts. An Edwardian atmosphere is created with potted palms and a mahogany bar. Cream teas are a speciality as are home made cakes and pastries. A selection of teas and coffees are available.

57 HORLEY

STAITH HOUSE 22 Russells Crescent, Horley, Surrey, RH6 7DN. Contact Mrs Mardell Tel & Fax: 01293 785170.
GATWICK. Situated 3 minutes away from Horley, the family run Staith House offers continental breakfasts served in the comfortable lounge/breakfast room. All bedrooms have telephones. Free transport available to and from the airport. 1 DOUBLE, 2 TWIN.

58 HORLEY

ACORNS GUEST HOUSE 125 Balcombe Road, Horley, Surrey, RH6 9BG. Contact Mrs Gibbs Tel & Fax: 01293 820423.
GATWICK. Acorn is a comfortable family home situated in the residential area of Horley, only a few minutes from Gatwick. Built at the turn of the century, this relaxed home is conveniently close to pubs, restaurants and shops. Close to M23. Continental breakfast with early departures catered for. 1 DOUBLE, 1 TWIN/ FAMILY, EN SUITE OR PRIVATE.

Prices from £15 to £20

59 HORSHAM
DOG & DUCK 824 Dorking Road, Kingsford, Horsham, West Sussex, RH12 3SA. Contact Darren Gaul Tel: 01306 627 295.
Enjoy a wide selection of drinks in pleasant surroundings. Food is served weekdays 11am to 3pm and all day Saturday and Sunday. VFR owners Club meet every other week.

60 LEIGH

HERONS HEAD FARM Mynthurst, Leigh, Surrey, RH2 8QD. Contact Mrs Dale Tel: 01293 862475 Fax: 01293 863350 E.mail: heronshead@clara.net.
GATWICK 5m. The typically English Herons Head Farm is a listed 16th century beamed farmhouse and stable block. Situated in 5 acres of gardens and paddocks there is a small lake, tennis courts and heated swimming pool. Near Dorking and Reigate and Leigh with its many inns and restaurants. Gatwick 10 minutes away, secure parking with airport transfer for £10 per week. 1 TWIN, 1 DOUBLE/FAMILY, ALL EN SUITE.

Prices from £18 to £28

61 MARLOW

THE BULL INN The High Street, Bishan, Marlow, Buckinghamshire, SL7 1RR. Tel: 01628 484734.
The Bull Inn dates back to the 12th century. It is the perfect venue for French Continental cuisine. In addition to it's bar, restaurant and private gardens, its upper floors offer superb facilities for conferences, motorcycle and business meetings. It is also very suitable for your private parties etc. Our menu and wine lists are extensive and as comprehensive as anywhere. We are open from Monday to Sunday for dinner and Sunday to Friday for lunch. There ample secure parking and we are only 5 minutes from the M40 and M4 motorways.

62 MARLOW
BURGERS OF MARLOW The Causeway, Marlow, Buckinghamshire, SL7 1NF. Tel: 01628 483389.
Set in a tastefully decorated 17th century listed building the Tea Room is well priced and comfortable. A selection of home made cakes and pastries is available along with a selection of speciality teas. Cooked dishes are also available if a cream tea does not appeal.

63 MELKSHAM

THE SHAW COUNTRY HOTEL Bath Road, Shaw, Melksham, Wiltshire, SN12 8EF. Contact John & Gay Lewis
Tel: 01225 702836 & 01225 790321 Fax: 01225 790275.
This hotel is all that you would wish for . You can be assured of the very best personal service from John and Gay. This typical hotel reputedly built during the 16th Century offers superb first class accommodation. We have a luxury honeymoon suite, with a four poster bed and jacuzzi. The Mulberry restaurant offers superb English and French cuisine.
12 EN SUITE BEDROOMS.

64 MILTON ABBAS
THE TEA CLIPPER 53a The Street, Milton Abbas, Dorset, DT11 0BP.
Tel: 01258 880223.
The Tea Clipper is pleasantly situated in the village of Milton Abbas, close to Milton Abbey, Park Farm Museum and the Rare Breeds Centre. A gift shop selling wooden toys, hand made jewellery and preserves, among other items is incorporated. Cream Teas are available and all bread, cakes and scones are home made on the premises. A wide range of teas is available.

65 NEW FOREST

PRIMROSE COTTAGE Fritham, New Forest, Hampshire, SO43 7HH. Contact Maureen & Barry Penfound Tel: 01703 812272.
A pretty Victorian forest cottage situated on the edge of the hamlet of Fritham, with direct access to ancient woodlands and forest plains where ponies, deer and cattle roam freely. Eight miles from Lyndhurst, 4 miles from M27. Quiet, comfortable accommodation with private bathroom and TV lounge. Reduction for stays of three nights or more. 1 DOUBLE/TWIN/FAMILY WITH PRIVATE BATHROOM.

Prices from £20

66 NEWBURY

CLEREMEDE Foxes Lane, Kingsclere, Newbury, Berkshire, RG20 5SL. Contact Mrs S. Salm
Tel: 01635 297298 Fax: 01635 299934.
BASINGSTOKE 9m. Close to Watership Down, Cleremede is on the edge of the village Kingsclere. It has a large garden and breakfast is served in the conservatory during the summer. The village has good eating places. Newbury 9 miles away. Ample secure parking. Convenient location for Heathrow airport.
2 TWIN EN SUITE, 1 DOUBLE PRIVATE BATHROOM. CHILDREN 10+.

Prices from £20 to £25

67 NEWBURY
THE COOPERS ARMS 39 Bartholomew Street, Newbury, Berkshire, RG14 5LL.
Tel: 01635 47469.
Sample Arkell's of Swindon and a host of other drinks. Sunday lunch only. Newbury MAG meetings every Wednesday at 8.30pm.

68 PETERSFIELD

DUNVEGAN COTTAGE Frogmore Lane, East Meon, Petersfield, Hampshire, GU32 1PW. Contact Jenny D'Amato Tel & Fax: 01730 823213.
PETERSFIELD 5m. The Domesday village of Eastmeon is where Dunvengan Cottage is situted. The rooms have a good view of the rolling South Downs, the South Downs Way runs through the village. Guest rooms are in a separate, purpose built wing. Closed Christmas. 1 DOUBLE EN SUITE, 3 TWIN (2 EN SUITE), 2 FAMILY (1 EN SUITE).

🗑 ✂ S   **Prices from £18 to £22**

69 PETERSFIELD

DRAYTON COTTAGE East Meon, Petersfield, Hampshire, GU32 1PW. Contact Mrs Joan Rockett Tel: 01730 823472.
PETERSFIELD 7m. An attractive 200 year old flint & chalk building, Drayton Cottage has recently been modernised giving guests their own entrance and stairs. The River Meon passes in front of the attractive garden. East Meon with its Norman church is 1 mile away. Portsmouth and Winchester are 1/2 hour away. 1 DOUBLE/TWIN EN SUITE, 1 DOUBLE PRIVATE.

✂ S   **Prices from £20 to £22**

70 POOLE

HIGHWAYS GUEST HOUSE 29 Fernside Road, Poole, Dorset, BH15 2QU. Contact Mr & Mrs Bailey Tel: 01202 677060.
POOLE 1m. Highways guest house is ideally situated for touring Dorset. It is 1 mile from Poole, 2 miles from Sandbanks and 5 miles from Bournemouth. For travellers further afield, there is easy access to the ferry port for travel to and from France. All rooms can be accessed at all times and are well furbished. A good selection of restaurants nearby. 1 TWIN, 2 DOUBLE, ALL EN SUITE.

🗑 ✂ S   **Prices from £22.50**

71 POOLE

THE LORD NELSON The Quays, Poole, Dorset, BH15 1HJ. Contact Ray Forrest Tel: 01202 776226.
Every Tuesday two or three thousand or more bikers come to this area of Poole to meet and discuss biking. They are all welcome in our pub and we sell every thing from beers to coffee and much more. Next door there is a kiosk where a complete range of food is available and they are certainly biker friendly. Come and visit us you will feel part of the ambience and see all the hundreds and hundreds of bikes.

72 POOLE

THE JOLLY SAILOR The Quays, Poole, Dorset, BH15 1HJ. Contact Samantha Fraser Tel: 01202 674138.
The motorcyclists come in their thousands to the Quays in Poole every Tuesday night. We have lots of entertainment and a friendly atmosphere you will enjoy. We have agood range of beers and soft drinks.

IF YOU
WANT TO IMPRESS
YOUR MATES
LET THEM
BORROW IT.

BMW Information: 0800 777 119

Bikes

73 PORTSMOUTH

ASHWOOD GUEST HOUSE 10 St. Davids Road, Southsea, Portsmouth, Hampshire, PO5 1QN. Contact Mrs Rogers Tel: 01705 816228 Fax: 01705 753955.

A large Victorian house on a quiet tree lined road, Ashwood has been converted into a guesthouse with attractive rooms. Ideally placed for visitors wishing to travel by ferry. Portsmouth and Southsea have magnificent shopping centres and are steeped in maritime history. Isle of Wight 10 minutes by hovercraft. Closed Christmas. 2 DOUBLE, 1 TWIN, 2 FAMILY, 2 SINGLE. CHILDREN 1+.

Prices from £16 to £20

74 READING

COMFORT INN 119 Kendrick Road, Reading, Berkshire, RG1 5EB. Tel: 0118 931 1311 Fax: 0118 931 4136.

Located on the M4 Junction 11 then A33. Attractive accommodation in quiet location. Rooms offer high standards of comfort. Enjoy a day out in Legoland (25 miles), Windsor (22 miles) or visit the city centre and the University. Special package for bikers £26 per person inc. breakfast and dinner. Subject to availability. Must be booked through Central Reservations 0800 44 44 44. 35 BEDROOMS.

⑤ ♨

75 READING

648-654 OXFORD ROAD Reading, RG30 1EH. Tel: 0118 950 0541 Fax: 0118 956 7220.

Located on Junction 10 M4-follow A329 or Junction 12 M4 & follow A329. Nearby places of interest include the town centre, Beale Park (6 miles), Wellington Country Park (6 miles) or take a day trip to Windsor (22 miles). Special package for bikers £26 per person inc. breakfast and dinner. Subject to availability. Must be booked through Central Reservations 0800 44 44 44. 95 BEDROOMS.

🍸 ⑤ ♨

76 RINGWOOD

BURBUSH FARM Pound Lane, Burley, Ringwood, Hampshire, BH24 4EF. Contact Mrs Carole Hayles Tel & Fax: 01425 403238.

In the tranquillity of the New Forest, Burbush Farm sits in 12 acres of grounds. Delicious, Aga-cooked farmhouse breakfasts, fresh farm eggs, home-made marmalade. Walking, horse riding, cycle hire, sailing, golf and badger watching available nearby. Closed Christmas and New Year. 3 DOUBLE, ALL EN SUITE. NO CHILDREN.

Prices from £25

77 RINGWOOD

THE STRUAN COUNTRY INN Horton Road, Ashley Heath, Ringwood, Hampshire, BH24 2EG. Tel: 01425 473 553.

A superb country inn open all day, serving food lunchtime and evening. ACCOMMODATION AVAILABLE.

Prices from £45

78 ROMSEY

COBWEB TEA ROOMS 49 The Hundred, Romsey, Hampshire, SO51 8GE. Tel: 01794 516424.

Set in a Georgian property close to Romsey Abbey, the Tea Rooms are traditionally decorated and have a pleasant atmosphere. Nearby attractions include Broadlands, King Johns House, Hilliers Arbretum and Mottisfont Abbey. Cobwebs Cream Tea comprises scones with cream, jam and tea. Freshly baked cakes and pastries are also available with a selection of teas.

IF YOU'VE NOTHING TO PROVE PROVE IT

Bikes

79 ROMSEY

SPURSHOLT HOUSE Salisbury Road, Romsey, Hampshire, SO51 6DJ. Contact Anthea Hughes Tel & Fax: 01794 512229.
This house, originally built for one of Cromwell's generals, was extended in the 1830's. Spursholt House is surrounded by impressive topiary, paved terraces and a view of Romsey Abbey. The furniture in the rooms is in keeping with the character of the house, one bedroom has oak panelling and all contain extra large beds. Closed Christmas and New Year. 1 TWIN, 1 DOUBLE,1 FAMILY, ALL EN SUITE.

Prices from £22 to £27

80 RYDE (IoW)

ASHLAKE FARMHOUSE Ashlake Farm Lane, Wooton Creek, Ryde, Isle of Wight, PO33 4LF. Contact Carol Pearce Tel & Fax: 01983 882124.
The grounds of Ashlake Farmhouse slope down towards Wootton Creek. In this lovely 17th century stone farmhouse breakfasts are served in the beamed dining room or on the terrace overlooking the creek. Evening meals by prior arrangement. The Fishbourne ferry is close by, Ryde is 3 miles. Closed Christmas and New Year. 1 DOUBLE, 1TWIN, 1 FAMILY, ALL EN SUITE/PRIVATE FACILITIES.

Prices from £20 to £25

81 SALISBURY

TOWN FARM BUNGALOW Sixpenny Handley, Salisbury, Wiltshire, SP5 5NT. Contact Mrs Ann Inglis Tel & Fax: 01725 552319.
SHAFTESBURY/SALISBURY 12m. Town Farm Bungalow offers a warm welcome in a quiet location just off the beaten track. The sitting room opens into the garden and excellent breakfasts, tea and coffee are served around a large table in the dining room. Within easy reach of the south coast, Salisbury, Stonehenge and other attractions. The area is popular with walkers because of the magnificent views across three counties. 2 DOUBLE, 1 TWIN, EN SUITE AVAILABLE.

Prices from £17.50 to £20

82 SALISBURY
THE COFFEE SHOP Salisbury Cathedral, Salisbury, Wiltshire, SP1 2EJ.
Tel: 01722 555175 Fax: 01722 555 169.
A spacious coffee shop with a wide range of snacks and quick meals. Enjoy summer coffee in the Cloisters. Stays open for concerts and other events. MON-FRI 9AM-5PM.

83 SALISBURY

LAMB AT HINDON HOTEL High Street, Hindon, Salisbury, Wiltshire, SP3 6DP. Contact Mr Croft Tel: 01747 820573 Fax: 01747 820605 E.mail: the-lamb@demon.co.uk.
Situated in an attractive Wiltshire village, this small 17th century building has open log fires and a wealth of history. 14 BEDROOMS, ALL EN SUITE.

Prices from £40 to £70

84 SALISBURY

MADDINGTON HOUSE Shrewton, Salisbury, Wiltshire, SP3 4JD. Contact Dick & Joan Robathan Tel & Fax: 01980 620406.
The elegant 17th century Maddington House is situated in the centre of a pretty village near two pubs - all serving great food. Stonehenge is only 2.5 miles away and Bath, Salisbury and the New Forest are easily reached. Breakfast consists of home made preserves and eggs laid by their own hens. Closed Christmas and New Year. 1 SINGLE, 2 DOUBLE (1 EN SUITE), 1 TWIN/FAMILY EN SUITE.

Prices from £23 to £25

85 SALISBURY

LITTLE LANGFORD FARM Little Langford, Salisbury, Wiltshire, SP3 4NR. Contact Patricia Helyer Tel: 01722 790205 Fax: 01722 790086.
A working dairy and arable farm, Little Langford sits in the rolling hills of Wiltshire Downs. Situated in large pleasant gardens and delightful countryside, this magnificent farmhouse has spacious, tastefully decorated rooms in keeping with the period of the house. Comfortable lounge, dining and billiard rooms. Near Stonehenge, Salisbury and Bath. Good pubs nearby. Closed Christmas and New Year. DOUBLE/TWIN/FAMILY ROOMS, ALL EN SUITE OR PRIVATE.

Prices from £23 to £25

86 SALISBURY

MANOR FARM Burcombe, Salisbury, Wiltshire, SP2 0EJ. Contact Mrs. S. A. Combes Tel: 01722 742177 Fax: 01722 744600.
Just a short distance from the A30 within easy access of Stonehenge and Salisbury, Manor Farm sits in the pretty village of Burcombe. Bath, Winchester, Dorchester and the New Forest within 1 hour's drive. Wonderful local walks. Closed December to February inclusive. 1 DOUBLE, 1 TWIN, BOTH EN SUITE.

Prices from £21 to £23

87 SALISBURY

BRIDGE FARM Lower Road, Britford, Salisbury, Wiltshire, SP5 4DY. Contact Mrs Hunt Tel & Fax: 01722 332376.
Bridge Farm, to the south of Salisbury, has a beautiful garden backing onto the river. It is a charming 18th century farmhouse on a working farm with views of the cathedral spire. Ideally located for visiting the cathedral, Stonehenge and many other local attractions. 2 DOUBLE, 1 TWIN, ALL EN SUITE.

Prices from £45 to £50

88 SHANKLIN (IoW)
BRAEMAR 1 Grange Road, Shanklin, Isle of Wight, PO37 6NN. Contact Mr Wilson Tel & Fax: 01983 863172.
Located in the island's most attractive area, acclaimed Braemar Hotel is sited in a quiet corner of Shanklin's Olde Village. The beach, chine, shops and countryside only minutes away. Excellent cuisine and choice of menu. Private car park. Open all year round. 11 BEDROOMS, ALL EN SUITE.

[S] VISA

Prices from £22 to £204

89 SHANKLIN (IoW) **MELBOURNE ARDENLEA Queens Road, Shanklin, Isle of Wight, PO37 6AP. Contact Mrs Danson Tel: 01983 862283 Fax: 01983 862865.**

SHANKLIN. Family run hotel in pleasant gardens. Long established, giving personal service. Centrally situated and near to all of Shanklin's facilities, yet in a lovely peaceful area. Closed Nov-Feb. 56 BEDROOMS, ALL EN SUITE.

Prices from £25 to £42

90 SHANKLIN (IoW)
DUNNOSE COTTAGE TEA ROOMS Luccombe Chine, Shanklin,
Isle of Wight PO37 6RH.
Tel: 01983 862585.
Dunnose Cottage is set in three acres of its own award winning gardens filled with herbaceous borders and roses. The building itself is 16th century Grade II listed and newly refurbished. The menu is extensive offering breakfasts, lunches, main courses and afternoon tea. An extensive range of speciality teas, coffees and cold drinks are also available.

DO NOT BELIEVE EVERYTHING YOU READ

MOTOR CYCLE NEWS
The latest Triumph could snatch best sports tourer crown

BIKE
It's not just good, it's brilliant

SUPERBIKE
It doesn't just match the opposition, it beats them...

MOTORCYCLE SPORT
A benchmark bike for the burgeoning sports tourer all-rounder class

TEST RIDE THE SPRINT ST YOURSELF AT A TRIUMPH DEALER NEAR YOU

Triumph's all new Sprint ST sports tourer utilises the powerful 955ccc fuel injected engine as used in the current Daytona 955i. The three cylinder engine has been tuned for optimum mid-range performance. The new model features an all new perimeter frame designed with lightweight and stable handling as priorities, and single sided swingarm. The silencer is moveable to facilitate the close fitment of colour co-ordinated luggage available as an optional Triumph accessory.

All new Triumph motorcycles carry 2 years unlimited mileage warranty, one year's free RAC European Cover, and one year's free membership of The Rider's Association Of Triumph. For a competitive rider insurance quotation phone the TriumphCare Insurance hotline now on: 01708 768613.

91 SHERBORNE

ALMHOUSE FARM Hermitage, Holnest, Sherborne, Dorset, DT9 6AH. Contact Mrs Jenny Mayo Tel & Fax: 01963 210296. Almshouse Farm is a working dairy farm in Dorset overlooking Blackmore Vale. The listed building with charming garden, retains its aged beauty whilst having every modern convenience. Traditional farmhouse breakfast will satisfy the biggest of appetites, ready to explore the beautiful encircling fields and lanes. Closed December and January. 1 TWIN, 2 DOUBLE, ALL EN SUITE. CHILDREN 10+.

ⓞ ⅀ Ⓢ   **Prices from £20 to £24**

92 SOUTHAMPTON

THE VILLAGE TEA ROOMS High Street, Hamble, Southampton, Hampshire, SO31 4HA. Tel: 01703 455583.
Situated in Hamble, the setting for television's Howards Way, the Tea Rooms are close to the Royal Victoria Country Park and Burslem Windmill. The building itself was originally a rope makers and coffin makers workshop and is reputedly haunted. Full English breakfast, light lunches, cream teas and a selection of cakes are available. An adjoining gift shop stocks 'Hamble' china, books and guides detailing local attractions.

93 SOUTHAMPTON

GLEN REST Bourne Road, Woodlands, Southampton, Hampshire, SO40 7GR. Contact Mrs Rosemary Sawyer Tel: 01703 812156.
LYNDHURST 5m. Glen Rest is a detached house offering a warm welcome and friendly atmosphere. It is only 5 minutes from the M27, junction 1 in an ideal location for exploring the New Forest or coastal areas. Southampton city centre is 15 minutes away. Closed December and January. 1TWIN/FAMILY, 1 DOUBLE/FAMILY.

ⓞ ⅀ Ⓢ   **Prices from £17.50 to £19**

94 STURMINSTER NEWTON

LOVELLS COURT Marnhull, Sturminster Newton, Dorset, DT10 1JJ. Contact Mrs M. Newson-Smith Tel: 01258 820652 Fax: 01258 820487.
STURMINSTER NEWTON 4m. With far reaching views across Blackmore Vale, Lovells Court is an old house with character. It has oak panelling and spacious en suite rooms furnished with antique pine. Ideally located for exploring Hardy country, Sturminster Newton and the two cathedral cities of Wells and Salisbury. Good choice of evening meals from the village inn. One hour from the Dorset coast. Large rooms available for seminars/courses. 1 DOUBLE, 1 TWIN, BOTH EN SUITE, 1 DOUBLE WITH PRIVATE BATHROOM. CHILDREN 12+.

ⓞ ⅀ Ⓢ   **Prices from £24**

95 WALLINGFORD

ANNIE'S TEA ROOMS 79 High Street, Wallingford, Oxfordshire, OX10 0BX. Tel: 01491 836308.
Set in a 17th century building near the castle gardens and river, Annies Tea Rooms offer a varied menu in a beautiful setting. Cake Tea, Cottage Tea, Afternoon Tea, High Tea, Cream Tea and Tea Cake Tea are all on the menu. Thirty different varieties of home-baked cakes are available and a wide range of tea is on offer.

96 WAREHAM

WEST COOMBE FARMHOUSE Coombe Keynes, Wareham, Dorset, BH20 5PS. Contact Mr and Mrs Brachi Tel: 01929 462889 Fax: 01929 405863.
LULWORTH COVE 3m. West Coombe Farmhouse, from the Georgian period, sits in a small village near Lulworth cove and is well situated to explore the natural and historic attractions in Dorset. Outdoor activities such as horse riding and golf are nearby. Mountain bikes available for guests. Short breaks with dinner available October to March. Closed Christmas. 1 DOUBLE EN SUITE, 1 DOUBLE/TWIN PRIVATE, 1 SINGLE (ONLY LET WITH OTHER ROOMS). CHILDREN 12+.

☐ ✄ S **Prices from £20 to £25**

97 WARMINSTER

SPRINGFIELD HOUSE Crockerton, Warminster, Wiltshire BA12 8AU. Contact Rachel & Colin Singer Tel: 01985 213696.
Springfield House is situated on the edge of the famous Longleat Estate in the Wylye Valley. It is a charming, welcoming house built in the 17th century with tastefully furnished rooms, a beautiful garden, woodland views and lawn tennis court. Historic attractions such as Stonehenge and the Cities of Salisbury and Bath are easily reached. 2 golf courses nearby. Good pubs a short walk away. 2 DOUBLE, 1 TWIN, ALL EN SUITE. CHILDREN 12+.

☐ ✄ S **Prices from £25 to £28**

98 WELLS

THE CLOISTER RESTAURANT Wells Cathedral, Wells, Somerset, BA5 2PA. Tel: 01749 676 543 Fax: 01749 676 543.
Set in the original stone cloister of the Cathedral, the restaurant offers lunches and teas. Try the wonderful brie and roast vegetable flan or the Somerset pork and roast apple casserole. MON-SAT 10AM-5PM SUNDAY 12.30AM-5PM.

99 WEYMOUTH

FOX BARROW HOUSE The Square, Langton Herring, Weymouth, Dorset, DT3 4HT. Contact Mrs S. A. Andrews Tel: 01305 871463 Fax: 01305 871995 E.mail: Fox.Barrow@wdi.co.uk.
Ideal for walking, bird watching and touring the surrounding attractions, Fox Barrow House is in the centre of a small village on the Heritage Coast. A tastefully restored former Victorian farmhouse offers select accommodation with a warm, homely atmosphere. Chesil Beach and the sub tropical gardens at Abbotsbury are within easy reach. Closed December 15th to January 15th. Ring for details of short break offers. 2 DOUBLE EN SUITE, 1 TWIN PRIVATE BATHROOM, 1 SINGLE. CHILDREN 7+.

☐ ✄ S **Prices from £20 to £22.50**

100 WICKHAM

MONTROSE Solomons Lane, Shirrel Heath, Wickham, Hampshire, SO32 2HU. Contact Mrs Y. Chivers Tel & Fax: 01329 833345.
FAREHAM 5.5m. Montrose is set in a quiet village close to Southampton and Portsmouth. The detached Victorian house has a large garden and floral patio surrounded by wonderful views of the countryside. The self-contained guest accommodation has superb furnishings providing a relaxed atmosphere. Closed Christmas. 1 TWIN, 2 DOUBLE (1 EN SUITE). NO CHILDREN.

☐ ✄ S **Prices from £22 to £25**

101 WIMBORNE

HOPEWELL Little Lonnen, Colehill, Wimborne, Dorset, BH21 7BB. Contact Esther & Tony Perks Tel: 01202 880311 & 0183 264908 E.mail: tonyp@hopewell.cw.net.
WIMBORNE MINSTER 3m. Hopewell is a modern family home, built by your hosts, within easy reach of Poole and Bournemouth. There are free-range chickens and ducks within the 6 acre garden that also includes a wooded area. Ideal for business or leisure breaks. Ample secure parking. 1 DOUBLE/FAMILY EN SUITE, 1 TWIN EN SUITE, 1 SINGLE WITH PRIVATE BATHROOM.

Prices from £20 to £25

102 WINCHESTER
THE CATHEDRAL REFECTORY Inner Close, Winchester, SO23 9LS. Tel: 01962 857258 Fax: 01962 857252.
A modern building set behind a medieval wall and within 50 metres of historic Winchester Cathedral. A wide range of meals and snacks available. Average lunch £5. MON-SAT 9.30AM-5PM SUNDAY 10AM-5PM.

103 WINSLOW
JENNIE WRENS TEA ROOMS 23 Market Square, Winslow, Buckinghamshire MK18 3AB. Contact Brian and Sheila Spatcher Tel: 01296 715499.
Located near a variety of local attractions including Winslow Hall, Keach's Chapel and Claydon House, the Tea Rooms evoke a bygone era with wood panelled rooms furnished with embroidered cushions. The Tea Rooms have won the W.I. Best Ladies Loo in Buckinghamshire award, 1994 as well as the Roy Castle Good Air Award. Afternoon Tea and Farmhouse Tea are available as are all day breakfasts, salads jacket potatoes and home made cakes along with a variety of teas.

104 WISBOROUGH GREEN

LOWER SPARR FARM Skiff Lane, Wisborough Green, Sussex, RH14 0AA. Contact Mrs Sally Sclater Tel: 01403 820465.
PETWORTH 5m. Lower Sparr Farm is a converted farmhouse set in quiet surroundings. Friendly and comfortable atmosphere at this family home where the bedrooms look out over the garden and tennis court to the pastureland beyond. It is off the beaten track but close to several villages and within easy reach of the M25. Gatwick and the south coast are 30 minutes away. Closed Christmas and New Year. 1 DOUBLE, 1 TWIN, 1 SINGLE, ALL WITH PRIVATE FACILITIES.

Prices from £22 to £25

105 ZEALS

CORNERWAYS COTTAGE Longcross, Zeals, Wiltshire BA12 6LL. Contact Irene & John Snook Tel & Fax: 01747 840477.
MERE 2m. An 18th century cottage, Cornerways offers a high standard of accommodation. Excellent breakfasts are served in the old dining room. Situated just off the A303 it is ideally located for travel to Stonehenge, Longleat and Stourhead. Horse riding, walking, fishing and golf available nearby. Evening meals by prior arrangement. Closed Christmas and New Year. 1 TWIN PRIVATE, 2 DOUBLE EN SUITE. CHILDREN 8+.

Prices from £18 to £19

1 ARUNDEL

COMFORT INN Cross Bush, Arundel, West Sussex, BN17 7QQ.
Tel: 01903 840840 Fax: 01903 849 849 E.mail: admin@gb642.u-net.com.
Located on Junction A284/A27 East of Arundel. Enjoy comfortable surroundings and a friendly atmosphere. Rooms are decorated to a high standard and have a hospitality tray. There is a bar and restaurant serving good food and drinks. Mini gym, cable TV and conference facilities. Local places of interest include Arundel Castle and Cathedral. Special package for bikers £26. per person inc. breakfast and dinner. Subject to availability. Must be booked through Central Reservations 0800 44 44 44. 55 BEDROOMS.

2 ASHFORD

LION HOUSE High Halden, Ashford, Kent, TN26 3LS.
Contact Gerald & Caroline Mullins Tel & Fax: 01233 85046.
Lion House is set in a large mature garden by the village green next to pub, shop and historic church. A friendly welcome awaits you at this comfortable, centrally heated en suite accommodation with TV tea/coffee making facilities, private bathroom and patio garden. Near Leeds and Sissinghurst castles and Tenterden. Evening meals by arrangement. Closed Christmas. 1 SINGLE EN SUITE, 1 TWIN/FAMILY EN SUITE.

Prices from £18 to £20

3 ASHFORD

HEGDALE FARM HOUSE Hegdale Lane, Challock, Ashford, Kent, TN25 4BE. Contact Mrs Valerie Baxter Tel: 01233 740224.
CANTERBURY 10m. Set in large garden and 4 acre grounds, the 16th century Hegdale Farm House has beamed ceilings and inglenook fireplaces that add to the welcoming atmosphere. Ideally located for Canterbury, Leeds Castle, Ashford International Terminal (7 miles) and easy access to M2/M20 and ferry ports. Good selection of local pubs. Country walks, horse riding, golf and gliding available nearby. Single guests welcome at no extra charge. 1 DOUBLE EN SUITE, 1 TWIN/FAMILY PRIVATE.

Prices from £20 to £22.50

4 ASHFORD

ELVEY FARM Pluckley, Ashford, Kent, TN27 0SU.
Contact Mrs Harris Tel: 01233 840 442 Fax: 01233 840 726.
Relax in this wonderful, luxury country hotel set on a working farm. Situated in peaceful surroundings this property offers many modern facilities. Licensed bar and dining room. Families welcome. 9 BEDROOMS ALL EN SUITE.

Prices from £39.50 to £65.50

5 ASHFORD

STOWTING HILL HOUSE Stowting, Ashford, Kent, TN25 6BE.
Contact Mrs R. Latham Tel: 01303 862881 Fax: 01303 863433.
CANTERBURY 8m. With glorious views of the North Downs, Stowting Hill House is an 18th century Manor house built onto a 16th century farmhouse. It has a spacious cosy interior and an attractive garden with tennis court. Ten miles from the Channel Tunnel – ideal for visiting France as well as the local attractions Kent has to offer. Evening meals on request or there is an excellent local pub. Closed Christmas and New Year. 3 TWIN (2 EN SUITE). CHILDREN 10+.

Prices from £27.50 to £35

6 ASHFORD

HOGBEN FARM Church Lane, Aldington, Ashford, Kent TN25 7EH. Contact Mrs R. Martin Tel: 01233 720219.
ASHFORD/HYTHE 6m. Hogben Farm is set in 16 acres of grassland with cattle, sheep and horses in the beautiful Kent countryside. This attractive 16th century house has a beamed sitting room withglenook fireplace and a conservatory and beamed dining room where breakfast is served. It is 15 minutes from the Le Shuttle terminal and 25 minutes from Dover. Canterbury and Rye are within 40 minutes. 1 DOUBLE EN SUITE, 2 TWIN (1 EN SUITE).

Prices from £20 to £22.50

7 ASHFORD

THE COACH HOUSE Oakmead Farm, Bethersden, Ashford, Kent, TN26 3DU. Contact Bernard & Else Broad Tel: 01233 820583 Fax: 01233 820583.
One mile from Bethersden village with its many pubs, The Coach House offers a warm welcome and breakfasts of your choice cooked with local produce. Within easy reach of the many historic and picturesque tourist attractions the area has to offer. Secure courtyard parking. Dutch spoken. Closed November to February inclusive. 1 TWIN, 1 FAMILY, BOTH EN SUITE, 1 DOUBLE PRIVATE ROOM.

Prices from £19 to £25

8 ASHFORD

OAK TREE FARM TEAROOMS Lymbridge Green, Stowting, Ashford, Kent TN25 6BL. Tel: 01233 750297.
Set in an attractive building close to Lyminge Forest, the Tea Rooms offer a traditional yet varied menu. Cream Tea, Welsh Tea or Farmhouse Tea are all options as well as a selection of home baked cakes. Salads are available as are roast lunches on Sundays.

Prices from £38 to £44

10 BEXHILL-ON-SEA

HARTFIELD HOUSE 27 Hartfield Road, Cooden, Bexhill on Sea, East Sussex, TN39 3EA. Contact Tony & Maggie Mansi Tel & Fax: 01424 845715.
The attractive, spacious Hartfield House is situated in a quiet residential area. Easy access to the beach and promenade from which the town can be reached in a pleasant 15 minute walk. The house offers wonderful views over the large garden to the English Channel. Lounge, sun lounge and garden are available for guests to use at their leisure. Closed December and January. 1 TWIN, 1 DOUBLE FAMILY, BOTH WITH PRIVATE FACILITIES. CHILDREN 10+.

Prices from £25 to £27.50

11 BEXHILL-ON-SEA PARK LODGE 16 Egerton Road, Bexhill-on-Sea, East Sussex, TN39 3HH. Tel: 01424 216547 Fax: 01424 217460.

Family run, informal hotel with character. Located in a quiet area of Bexhill but near shops, park and seafront. Rooms are very comfortable with en suite, Cable TV, telephone and tea/coffee facilities. 10 BEDROOMS SINGLES AND DOUBLES, 8 EN SUITE.

Prices from £21 to £46

12 BRABOURNE

MEADOWSWEET Manor Pound Lane, Brabourne, Kent TN25 5LG. Contact Mrs Susan Cullen Tel & Fax: 01303 813905 E.mail: meadowsweet@onet.co.uk

ASHFORD 5m. Only 15 minutes away from the channel routes, Meadowsweet makes an excellent stop over to take day trips into France. It is situated at the foot of the North Downs within easy reach of many places of interest. Excellent local pubs for evening meals. 2 DOUBLE, 1 TWIN, EN SUITE OR PRIVATE FACILITIES. CHILDREN 10+.

Prices from £22.50 to £24

13 BRIGHTON
PASKINS TOWN HOUSE 19 Charlotte Street, Brighton, BN2 1AG. Contact Mr Marlowe Tel: 01273 601 203 Fax: 01273 621 973.

Paskin's Town House is a delightful hotel located in a Victorian conservation area. Ideal for visiting Brighton and all its attractions. A good range of food available including organic and natural food and hearty vegetarian breakfasts. 19 BEDROOMS, 16 EN SUITE.

Prices from £22.50 to £85

14 BRIGHTON
ALLENDALE 3 New Steine, Brighton, BN2 1PB. Contact Mrs Heard Tel: 01273 675 436 Fax: 01273 602 603.

A warm, homely atmosphere greets you at this small, privately owned hotel. Allendale has developed a good reputation for its good food and excellent service. Close to Brighton with all its amenities. 13 BEDROOMS, 9 EN SUITE.

Prices from £25 to £36

15 BRIGHTON
QUALITY HOTEL West Street, Brighton, East Sussex, BN1 2RQ.
Tel: 01273 220 033 Fax: 01273 778 000 E.mail: admin@gb057.u-net.com.
Located on A259 towards city centre. Modern accommodation with good facilities and comfortable surroundings. Local places of interest include Brighton's Sealife Centre and Borde Hill Gardens as well as Bowplex Paradise Park. Special package for bikers £26. per person inc. breakfast and dinner. Subject to availability. Must be booked through Central Reservations 0800 44 44 44. 138 BEDROOMS.

16 CANTERBURY
SOUTH WOTTON HOUSE Capel Lane, Petham, Canterbury, CT4 5RG.
Contact Mrs Mount Tel: 01227 700 643 Fax: 01227 700 613.
Set in extensive gardens this lovely farmhouse is surrounded by fields and woodlands. Rooms are co-ordinated and have a private bathroom. Bedrooms are comfortable and there are tea/coffee making facilities in each room. Bikers welcome. 2 BEDROOMS, BOTH EN SUITE.

Prices from £20 to £38

18 CANTERBURY
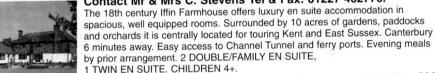

IFFIN FARMHOUSE Iffin Lane, Canterbury, Kent, CT4 7BE.
Contact Mr & Mrs C. Stevens Tel & Fax: 01227 462776.
The 18th century Iffin Farmhouse offers luxury en suite accommodation in spacious, well equipped rooms. Surrounded by 10 acres of gardens, paddocks and orchards it is centrally located for touring Kent and East Sussex. Canterbury 6 minutes away. Easy access to Channel Tunnel and ferry ports. Evening meals by prior arrangement. 2 DOUBLE/FAMILY EN SUITE, 1 TWIN EN SUITE. CHILDREN 4+.

Prices from £22.50 to £30

19 CANTERBURY
HALF MOON & SEVEN STARS The Street, Preston, Canterbury, Kent, CT3 1EB.
Contact D. Sharp & M. Cawston Tel: 01227 722296.
Beers served include Greene King, Triumph, Shepherd Neame Master Brew plus a Guest ale. Three lagers, Guinness, Mild and two Ciders. A wide range of food is available served Mon-Sat 11am-9.30pm including traditional English and South East Asian cuisine. Take away available Friday night. Delicious Sunday roast from 12 noon till late. Music every two weeks on Sundays. Ring for details. Food served up to 6pm only, but sandwiches available. A barbecue is available but please book in advance.

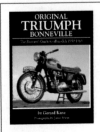

20 COLCHESTER

THE OLD MANSE 15 Roman Road, Colchester, Essex, CO1 1UR. Contact Mrs Wendy Anderson Tel: 01206 545154 E.mail: Website: www.doveuk.com/oldmanse.
Lovely homely B&B serving fabulous breakfasts. The Old Manse is in the centre of Colchester, close to shops, a variety of restaurants, fast food establishments and pubs. Colchester is a motorcycle friendly town and bikers are welcome everywhere.

21 CRAYFORD
THE CRAYFORD ARMS 37 High Street, Crayford, Kent, DA1 4HH. Tel: 01322 521 467.
Drinks served include Master Brew, Spitfire, Bishops Finger and Lager. Bikers meet Tuesdays. Scooter club on Mondays. All made welcome.

22 CROWBOROUGH
PLOUGH & HORSES Walshes Road, Crowborough, East Sussex, TN6 3RE. Contact Brenda Newton Tel: 01892 652614.
Bikers are always welcome at this Free House, which is open from 11am - 2.30pm and 6pm-11pm on weekdays, 12pm-4pm and 6pm-11pm on Sundays. The restaurant serves a wide variety of dishes and there is always a selection of real ales to choose from. ACCOMMODATION AVAILABLE.

Prices from £25 to £45

23 CUXTON
THE ROCHESTER QUEEN FLOATING PUB Port Medway Marina, Station Road, Cuxton, Kent, ME2 1AB. Tel: 01245 400 264.
MCC nights Thursday and Friday. Relax in comfortable surroundings and enjoy a good selection of food and beverages. Food is served all day every day; 11am-11pm during weekdays and 12 noon to 10.30pm Sunday.

24 DOVER
SUNSHINE COTTAGE Mill Lane, Shepherdswell, Dover, Kent, CT15 7LQ. Contact Barry & Lyn Popple Tel: 01304 831359 & 01304 831218.
CANTERBURY 7m. Sunshine Cottage is a 17th century Grade II listed cottage on the village green between Dover & Canterbury, one mile from the A2. Beamed and sympathetically furnished: two lounges and courtyard garden for guests' use. 10 mins from Dover docks and 20 mins from Channel Tunnel.
1 DOUBLE/TWIN SHARED FACILITIES, 1 DOUBLE PRIVATE FACILITIES, 1 FAMILY.

Prices from £22 to £25

25 DOVER

BEULAH HOUSE 94 Crabble Hill, Dover, Kent, CT17 0SA. Contact Mrs Owen Tel: 01304 824615.
This fine house is set in 1 acre of stunning topiaried gardens. The accommodation offers a warm atmosphere, coupled with spacious lay out and elegant furnishings. Port of Dover and Channel Tunnel only a quick drive away. Garages available. 6 BEDROOMS, 4 EN SUITE.

Prices from £25 to £44

26 EASTBOURNE
QUALITY HOTEL Grand Parade, Eastbourne, Sussex, BN21 3YS.
Tel: 01323 727 411 Fax: 01323 720 665 E.mail: admin@gb610.u-net.com.
Located near the sea front, Quality Hotel offers a warm welcome and comfortable surroundings. Guests have cable TV and tea/coffee making facilities. Beachy Head 2 miles, Drusillas Park Zoo 9 miles and Marina 2 miles. Special package for bikers £26. per person inc. breakfast and dinner. Subject to availability. Must be booked through Central Reservations 0800 44 44 44. 115 BEDROOMS.

---

27 FAVERSHAM

THE GRANARY Plumford Lane, Off Brogdale Road, Faversham, Kent, ME13 0DS. Contact Annette Brightman
Tel & Fax: 01795 583416 E.mail: thegranary@compuserve.com.
CANTERBURY 12m. The Granary is situated 15-20 minutes from Canterbury, five minutes from the M2 with easy access from London (1hour). Set in beautiful countryside the delightfully furnished rooms retain a rustic charm and the guests' own lounge has a balcony overlooking the rural landscape. 30 minutes to Folkestone and Dover. Closed Christmas. 1 TWIN, 1 DOUBLE, BOTH EN SUITE, 1 FAMILY FOR 3, PRIVATE.

Prices from £23

---

28 FAVERSHAM
THE DUKE OF KENT Thanet Way, Faversham, ME13 9HU. Contact Dave Ansell
Tel: 01227 751150 Fax: 01227 751672 E.mail: dave@dukeofkent.freeserve.co.uk.
The Duke of Kent is a famous and internationally well-known bikers pub. Bikers come here from all over Europe. On the 1st & 3rd Monday each month we hold the Honda Owners club meetings. On the 1st Wednesday each month we hold the East Kent Advanced motorcycle training session.
Also we hold general bikers meetings. We do bar snacks and have good range of beers and lagers. We have camping facilities and we hold regular rallies during the summer months.
One of the real motorcyclists welcome pubs.

---

29 FOLKESTONE
CHARLOTTE EMILY'S VICTORIAN TEA ROOMS 2-4 Old High Street, Folkestone, Kent, CT20 1RL. Tel: 01303 220732.
Located near Folkestone harbour, the Tea Rooms have a Victorian theme with waitresses dressed in Victorian clothes. The Tea Rooms are family run and provide an extensive menu. Roast dinners, vegetarian options, English breakfasts, a children's menu and fresh sandwiches are all available. There is also a patisserie offering home made cakes and a selection of teas and coffees.

---

30 HERNE BAY

FOXDEN 5 Landon Road, Herne Bay, Kent, CT6 6HP.
Contact Mr M. Williams Tel: 01227 363514.
Set in a peaceful residential location, Foxden is a spacious 1920's house in the Victorian seaside town of Herne Bay. Fresh flowers, books, tea/coffee facilities and colour TV are in every room. Delightful garden with fishponds. Substantial breakfast served. Short walk to the sea, cliff walks and town centre. 7 miles from Canterbury and 40 minutes from Channel Tunnel and ferry ports. Private secure parking. 2 DOUBLE EN SUITE, 2 SINGLE. CHILDREN 10+.

Prices from £20 to £40

31 HYTHE
THE PRINCE OF WALES Dymchurch Road, Hythe, Kent, CT21 6NB. Tel: 01303 266270.
Under new management. Bikers club meet every Wednesday.

---

32 LAMBERHURST

LAMBERHURST The Down, Lamberhurst, Kent, TN3 8ES.
Contact Christine Dickens
Tel: 01892 890891 Fax: 01892 526133.
An attractive 18th century house, originally four cottages, with beams and inglenooks, surrounded by commonland. Close by are Scotney Castle, Bayham Abbey, Bewl Water and Owl House Gardens and opposite is the local vineyard - the visitor is spoilt for choice. Ideal location for touring and walking. The bedrooms are decorated in a cottage style. Closed Christmas to February inclusive. 1 DOUBLE PRIVATE, 1 TWIN EN SUITE. CHILDREN 5+.

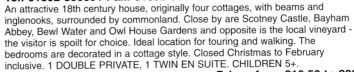 **Prices from £18.50 to £22**

---

33 LAMBERHURST
LAMBERHURST TEA ROOMS The Down, Lamberhurst, Kent, TN3 8ES.
Tel: 01892 890891.
Conveniently located near Scotney Castle, Bayham Abbey ruins, Owl House Gardens and Bewl Water. The Tea Rooms occupy a pretty 18th century property set in picturesque countryside and are run by helpful staff. Fare on offer includes home made bread, cakes, jam and scones as well as a wide range of speciality teas.

---

34 LEWES
CLARA'S 9 High Street, East Hoathly, Lewes, East Sussex, BN8 6DR.
Tel: 01825 840339.
Set in a building dating back to 1760, Clara's is opposite the house of Thomas Turner, diarist 1754-1765. The Tea Rooms offers home made cakes scones and jam as well as a selection of teas are available. Clara's also incorporates a gift shop selling home made preserves, gifts, cards and Rowan yarns.

---

35 MAIDSTONE

HOMESTEAD Greenhill, Otham, Maidstone, Kent, ME15 8RR.
Contact Mrs K. George Tel: 01622 862234 & 0850 516891.
Situated in the peaceful village of Otham, Homestead is a 16th century beamed farmhouse set in large gardens. It is a traditionally furnished family home with the bedrooms overlooking the surrounding countryside. Leeds Castle, the M20 are only 2 miles away and Maidstone is only a few minutes away. The Channel Tunnel is 20 minutes away. Close to country pubs serving evening meals. Closed Christmas and New Year. 1 TWIN, 2 DOUBLE (1EN SUITE).

Prices from £16 to £20

---

36 PENSHURST
FIR TREE HOUSE TEA ROOMS Penshurst, Kent, TN11 8DB. Tel: 01892 870382.
The Tea Rooms are situated in the centre of Penshurst village close to Penshurst Place, an interesting local attraction. Afternoon Tea is a particular speciality and includes scones, sandwiches, cake and tea. All the food is home baked and complemented by a range of teas.

SWiFT

"a concept of excellence"

James Whitham

David Jefferies

Race suits

Race gloves

Helmets

Paddock jackets

Rainwear

For your free catalogue contact:
Lloyd Lifestyle Ltd
Pallet Hill Penrith • Cumbria CA11 0BY
Tel: 017684 83784 • Fax: 017684 83212
Email: info@lloydlifestyle.com

Lloyd LIFESTYLE

37 ROBERTSBRIDGE
KNOLLY'S Bodiam, Robertsbridge, East Sussex, TN32 5UD. Tel: 01580 830323.
Situated in an area of outstanding natural beauty and recommended by Egon Ronay. Cream teas, home made cakes and local strawberries are all specialities. A variety of teas including Assam, Darjeeling, Earl Grey and Lapsang are available and there is a craft and gift shop.

38 RYE

FIDDLERS OAST Watermill Lane, Beckley, Rye, Sussex, TN31 6SH. Contact Nick & Ruth Wynn Tel & Fax: 01797 252394 E.mail: fiddlersoast@compuserve.com.
Fiddlers Oast, formerly an oasthouse is 15 minutes away from the ancient port of Rye. It is situated within 2 acres of grounds in a tranquil location close to the Kent and Sussex border. Battle, Bodiam, Tenterden and Hastings are all within easy reach. Closed Christmas.

Prices from £18.75 to £24.50

39 RYE

SPRINGETTS Goatham Lane, Broad Oak, Rye, East Sussex, TN31 6EY. Contact Mrs A. Morris Tel: 01424 882242.
BATTLE 7m. Springetts can be found off the B2089 on a quiet country lane. Guests have own entrance leading to a lounge for their use. A choice of home-made preserves are available at breakfast. National Trust properties and the historic towns of Rye and Battle are within easy reach of this lovely house. Closed November to February inclusive. 1 TWIN, 1 DOUBLE, BOTH EN SUITE. CHILDREN 12+.

Prices from £17.50

40 SANDWICH
LITTLE COTTAGE TEA ROOMS The Quay, Sandwich, Kent, CT13 9EN. Tel: 01304 614387.
Delightfully set on the backs of the River Stour in the mediaeval town of Sandwich the Tea Rooms specialise in healthy food, having won the Healthy Heart Award and three Clean Food Awards. Cream teas are available as are breakfasts, light lunches and Sunday lunch.

41 SEAFORD

THE OLD PARSONAGE West Dean, Alfriston, Seaford, Sussex, BN25 4AL. Contact Raymond & Angela Woodhams Tel: 01323 870432.
EASTBOURNE 5m. The Old Parsonage is next to a 12th century church and within walking distance of the Cuckmere Estuary. Set in the delightful quiet hamlet of West Dean in the heart of Friston Forest and within easy reach of Beachy Head. Built in 1280, it is supposedly the oldest, continuously inhabited, small medieval house and features spiral staircases. Closed Christmas and New Year. 3 DOUBLE, ALL PRIVATE BATHROOMS. CHILDREN 12+.

Prices from £25.50 to £35

42 SEVENOAKS
THE TEA HOUSE 17 High Street, Borough Green, Sevenoaks, Kent, TN15 7QE.
A traditional atmosphere prevails in this 18th century former butcher's shop. The afternoon special comprises tea with home made scone and jam, a choice of sandwiches and cake.

43 SEVENOAKS

AUSTENS COTTAGE South Park, Sevenoaks, Kent, TN13 1EL.
Contact Mr & Mrs W. Campbell
Tel: 01732 452988 & 01732 451729.
The cosy family home of Austens Cottage is in a quiet residential area, only 2 minutes from the town centre which has good restaurants, pubs and a theatre. Visits to Knole, Chartwell, Hever Castle and Penshurst are within easy reach. Off road secure parking available. 1 TWIN EN SUITE.

[图] [✄] [S]   **Prices from £22.50**

44 TERLING
OLD BAKERY Waltham Road, Terling, Essex, CM3 2QP.
Contact Mrs T Lewis Tel: 01245 233363.
Set in a charming Essex village, the hotel offers an ideal base in which to enjoy the countryside and local pubs. The home cooking is superb and strongly recommended. ALL ROOMS ARE EN SUITE.

Prices from £20

45 TONBRIDGE
QUAINTWAYS TEA ROOMS High Street, Penshurst, Tonbridge, Kent, TN11 8BT.
Tel: 01892 870272.
The Tea Rooms occupy a converted bakehouse in the centre of the village. An antiques showroom and gift shop adjoin Quaintways where a variety of locally made gifts can be purchased. Light lunches and cream teas are on offer as are home made tea breads, local cream and a variety of teas.

47 TUNBRIDGE WELLS

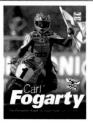

HAMSELL WOOD FARM The Forstal, Eridge, Tunbridge Wells, Kent, TN3 9JY. Contact Bridget Capsey Tel: 01892 864326.
Hamsell Wood Farm is situated in beautiful countryside and offers wonderful panoramic views. Within 1 hour from the south coast and Gatwick. Close to Hever Castle, Penshurst and many beautiful, public gardens. Closed Christmas and New Year. 1 DOUBLE, 1 TWIN/TRIPLE.

[图] [✄] [S]   **Prices from £18 to £20**

48 UCKFIELD

OLD MILL FARM High Hurtswood, Uckfield, Sussex, TN22 4AD. Contact Mrs P. Sharpe Tel & Fax: 01825 732279.
CROWBOROUGH 4m. Old Mill Farm is a converted Sussex barn complex, renovated and restored since the storm of 1987 to make a lovely home whilst still retaining character. Set in a secluded scenic valley on the edge of the Ashdown Forest, surrounded by 55 acres of pasture. Tunbridge Wells 12 miles, Gatwick 20 miles. Full English breakfast is served. FAMILY EN SUITE, 2 GROUND FLOOR TWIN WITH PRIVATE/EN SUITE FACILITIES.

Prices from £20 to £24

49 WHITSTABLE
WINDY RIDGE Wraik Hill, Whitstable, Kent, CT5 3BY. Contact Jean and John Hawkins Tel: 01227 263506 Fax: 01227 771191.
CANTERBURY 5m. Situated high up on the outskirts of Whitstable, Windy Ridge enjoys panoramic views of the Thames Estuary and the Isle of Sheppey. Close to the Thanet Way and M2. Also convenient for Faversham and Canterbury. Ample secure parking, evening meal by arrangement. Ground floor bedroom suitable for disabled. 2 SINGLE, 3 DOUBLE, 3 FAMILY, ALL EN SUITE. 4 POSTER (WEDDING SUITE).

Prices from £25 to £30

1 CHEAPSIDE
THE PLACE BELOW St Mary-Le-Bow Church, Cheapside, London, EC2V 6AU.
Tel: 0171 329 0789.
Situated just down the road from St Pauls, The Place Below is an award winning restaurant that serves vegetarian food. Typical dishes include mushroom and artichoke soup, aromatic sweet potato gratin with salad leaves and hazelnut and honey tart. MON-FRI 7.30AM-2.30PM SATURDAY & SUNDAY CLOSED. CLOSED CHRISTMAS AND BANK HOLIDAYS.

2 EPPING

BROOKLANDS 1 Chapel Road, Epping, Essex, CM16 5DS.
Contact Les & Ray Bayliss Tel: 01992 575424.
A comfortable home with attractive gardens and terraced seating area, Brooklands is located in a quiet, central position near shops, pubs, restaurants and the Central Line underground station. On the edge of Epping Forest it is only 3 mile from the M25 and M11 providing easy access to Stansted, Heathrow and Gatwick airports. £35 single, £45 double. Closed Christmas. 2 FAMILY, 1 DOUBLE, ALL EN SUITE OR PRIVATE.

🖸 ⅓ S   **Prices from £35 to £45**

3 GREENWICH
PETER DE WIT'S CAFE 21 Greenwich Church Street, Greenwich, London, SE10 9BJ.
Tel: 0181 305 0048.
Situated in the Heart of Greenwich and its attractions including the Cutty Sark, the Greenwich Observatory and the Maritime Museum. Although relaxed, the staff are happy to help in any way and add to the cafe's friendly atmosphere. The menu offers cream teas, home made cakes and pastries, and sandwiches. A wide range of teas is available.

4 HEATHROW
COMFORT INN Shepiston Lane, Hayes, Heathrow, Middlesex, UB3 1LP.
Tel: 020 8573 6162 Fax: 020 8848 1057.
Located on the M4 Junction 4, Heathrow Airport then follow signs for "all other routes", Hayes and A312 and the hotel is after the fire station. Good location with easy access to many different routes. Visit Windsor castle (13 miles), Ascot Racing Course (20 miles) and Thorpe park (12 miles). Special package for bikers £26. per person inc. breakfast and dinner. Subject to availability. Must be booked through Central Reservations 0800 44 44 44. 80 BEDROOMS.

🍷 S ⚲

5 LONDON
COMFORT INN 5-7 Frognal, Hampstead, London, NW3 6AL.
Tel: 020 7794 0101 Fax: 020 7794 0100.
Located off Finchley Road (A41). Relaxed and friendly atmosphere in comfortable surroundings. Nearby places of interest include Hampstead Heath, Camden Market and Madame Tussauds. Special package for bikers £26. per person inc. breakfast and dinner. Subject to availability. Must be booked through Central Reservations 0800 44 44 44. 57 BEDROOMS.

🍷 S ⚲

6 LONDON
COMFORT INN 18-19 Craven Hill Gardens, London, W2 3EE. Tel: 020 7262 5644 Fax: 020 7262 0673.
Located on the Westway A50 (M). Attractive building in good location. Theatres, bars and restaurants, Hyde Park, Oxford Road on the doorstep. Special package for bikers £26. per person inc. breakfast and dinner. Subject to availability. Must be booked through Central Reservations 0800 44 44 44. 60 BEDROOMS.

7 LONDON
22-32 WEST CROMWELL ROAD Kensington, London, SW5 9QA.
Tel: 020 7373 3300 Fax: 020 7835 2040 E.mail: admin@gb043.u-net.com.
Good accommodation in excellent location. All the attractions of London within easy reach. Special package for bikers £26. per person inc. breakfast and dinner. Subject to availability. Must be booked through Central Reservations 0800 44 44 44. 125 BEDROOMS.

8 LONDON
QUALITY HOTEL 8-14 Talbot Square, London, W2 1TS. Tel: 020 7262 6699 Fax: 020 7723 3233.
From Marble Arch, follow Bayswater Road to Sussex Gardens, Talbot Square 2nd on left. Rooms are well equipped and very comfortable. Bar and restaurant offering good food and drink in relaxing surroundings. Nearby places of interest include West End Theatres, London Zoo, Museums, Harrods, Madame Tussauds and much, much more. Special package for bikers £26. per person inc. breakfast and dinner. Subject to availability. Must be booked through Central Reservations 0800 44 44 44. 75 BEDROOMS.

9 LONDON
QUALITY HOTEL 82-83 Eccleston Square, London, SW1V 1PS. Tel: 020 7834 8042 Fax: 020 7630 8942.
High standard of accommodation in comfortable surroundings. Lots to do and see including visiting nearby Buckingham Palace, Westminster Abbey, Harrods and Tate Gallery. Special package for bikers £26. per person inc. breakfast and dinner. Subject to availability. Must be booked through Central Reservations 0800 44 44 44. 115 BEDROOMS.

10 LONDON
COMFORT INN 82-86 Belgrave Road, London, SW1V 2BJ. Tel: 020 7828 8661 Fax: 020 7821 0525.
M4 from Heathrow. A high standard of accommodation in a central location. Guests have full use of the bar. City Centre London offers lots of things to see and do. Special package for bikers £26. per person inc. breakfast and dinner. Subject to availability. Must be booked through Central Reservations 0800 44 44 44. 58 BEDROOMS.

11 LONDON
AARON HOTEL 8 Forty Lane, Wembley, London, HA9 9EB.
Tel: 0181 9085711 Fax: 0181 3850472 E.mail: ww.aaronhotel.com.
We are a small family-run bed and breakfast guest house who offer our guests a warm and friendly welcoming stay with us. All our rooms have tea/coffee making facilities and television. Convenient for London city centre, touring and Wembley Stadium. We offer drying facilities, should you require them. 10 BEDROOMS, ALL EN SUITE.

Prices from £45 to £55

12 LONDON
COMFORT INN 11-13 Penywern Road, Earls Court, London, SW5 9TT.
Tel: 020 7373 6514 Fax: 020 8370 3639.
Located Marble Arch-A4, left onto Earls Court Road. Great facilities with all the places of interest in city centre London close at hand. Special package for bikers £26. per person inc. breakfast and dinner. Subject to availability. Must be booked through Central Reservations 0800 44 44 44. 49 BEDROOMS.
🍽 ⑤

13 LONDON
QUALITY HOTEL 122 Church Road, Crystal Palace, London, SE19 2UG.
Tel: 020 8653 6622 Fax: 020 8771 1506.
Located on the A23, follow signs to Crystal Palace. Excellent standards of accommodation, food and drink. Ideal for exploring London and its many attractions. Special package for bikers £26 per person inc. breakfast and dinner. Subject to availability. Must be booked through Central Reservations 0800 44 44 44. 150 BEDROOMS.
🍽 ⑤ ♨

14 LONDON
COMFORT INN 5-7 Princes Square, Bayswater, London, W2 4NP.
Tel: 020 7792 1414 Fax: 020 7792 0099.
Ideal location with all the shops and attractions of central London nearby. Visit Hyde Park, Kensington Palace, Harrods, Earls Court Exhibition, Portobello Market and much more. Special package for bikers £26. per person inc. breakfast and dinner. Subject to availability. Must be booked through Central Reservations 0800 44 44 44. 65 BEDROOMS.
🍽 ⑤

15 LONDON
THE WREN AT ST JAMES' 35 Jermyn Street, London, SW1Y 6DT. Tel: 0171 437 9419.
Simple, split-level restaurant with outside seating available in the courtyard. Art and pictures in the restaurant are for sale. Enjoy hot pot, chilli bean casserole on a jacket potato and potato and spinach tikkies. MON-SAT 8AM-7PM SUNDAY 10AM-5PM. CLOSED CHRISTMAS AND SOME BANK HOLIDAYS.

16 LONDON
CAFE IN THE CRYPT St Martin In The Fields, Trafalgar Square, London, WC2N 4JJ.
Tel: 0171 839 4342 Fax: 0171 839 5163.
A wonderful atmosphere in this cafe located beneath the vaulted ceilings of the Crypt. An imaginative range of food. Sample the heavenly traditional puddings. MON-SAT 10AM-8PM SUNDAY 12NOON-8PM. CLOSED CHRISTMAS AND EASTER.

17 LONDON
FALCON HOTEL 11 Norfolk Square, Hyde Park, Paddington, London, W2 1RU.
Tel: 0171 723 8603

A small family run budget style B&B hotel conveniently situated in tree-lined street in the Paddington/Hyde Park area. Oxford Street, Marble Arch, Madame Tussaud's and other attractions are all within easy reach. Full English Breakfast. Tea and coffee making facilities and TV. 20 BEDROOMS, ALL EN SUITE.

Prices from £40 to £65

18 LONDON
ATHENA HOTEL 112 Sussex Gardens, Hyde Park, Paddington, London, W2 1UA.
Tel: 0171 706 3866.

Family run hotel in a restored Victorian listed building, professionally designed and tastefully decorated with lifts to all floors. Within easy reach of the West End and Knightsbridge and other London attractions making it an ideal base for shopping and sightseeing. Full English Breakfast. Tea and coffee making facilities and satellite TV. 26 BEDROOMS. ALL EN SUITE.

Prices from £45 to £90

19 LONDON
GOWER HOTEL 129 Sussex Gardens, Hyde Park,
London W2 2RX. Tel: 0171 262 2262.

Small family run bed and breakfast hotel, conveniently situated in the Paddington/Hyde Park area. Within easy reach of Paddington Station, restaurants, shops and other London attractions. All rooms have recently been refurbished to a high standard with tea and coffee making facilities and TV. Full English Breakfast. Tea and coffee making facilities and TV. 21 BEDROOMS. ALL EN SUITE.

Prices from £40 to £70

20 LONDON
THE QUEENS HOTEL 33 Anson Road, Tufnell Park, LONDON, N7 0RB.
Tel: 0171 607 4725

A small Victorian family run budget bed and breakfast hotel, with many attractive features. A comfortable and afforable location to explore London, without being in its busy centre. Close to London Zoo, Regents Park, Camden Town and historical Highgate. Full English Breakfast. Tea and coffee making facilities and TV. 38 BEDROOMS. ALL EN SUITE.

Prices from £25 to £50

21 SARRATT
THE CRICKETERS The Green, Sarratt, Hertfordshire.
Contact Simon Tel: 01923 263729.

The Cricketers is a pretty country pub near Rickmansworth, with restaurant service available and an excellent range of quality wines. Saloon and public bars with many facilities. Extensive range of beers, lagers and soft drinks. Well attended bikers' meetings held every Wednesday at 7pm. Featured regularly in Motorcycle News.

22 SHEPPERTON

OLD MANOR HOUSE Squires Bridge Road, Littleton, Shepperton, Middlesex, TW17 0QG. Contact Mrs M. Hoyle Tel: 01932 571293.
An historic house dating back to the reign of Henry VII, Old Manor House is set in 5 acres of grounds with the river Ash running through. The location is ideal for travellers using Heathrow Airport. Hampton Court, Windsor and London are easily accessible. Panelled dining room where breakfast is served while there is a wide selection of pubs/restaurants available for evening meals. Closed Christmas and New Year. 1 DOUBLE EN SUITE, 1 TWIN, 1 SINGLE. CHILDREN 5+.

Prices from £22.50 to £28

23 SIDCUP

THE WOODMAN Black Fen Road, Sidcup, Kent, DA15 8PR. Contact John Harmon Tel: 0181 850 3181.
The Woodman is a very famous motorcyclists pub with a live rock venue bar. Midnight license for 6 nights of the week. Extensive menu including bar snacks. Food is all home cooked and prepared. Good and extensive range of beers, lagers, wines and spirits. Every Tuesday the Tsunami motorcycle club meets here.

24 SOUTHWARK

THE CHAPTER HOUSE Southwark Cathedral, Montague Close, Southwark, London, SE1 9DA. Tel: 0171 378 6446.
Pizza Express run this restaurant in the Chapter House and there is a delicious range of Italian pizzas, soups and salads as well as a range of hot and cold beverages. MON-FRI 10AM-4PM SATURDAY & SUNDAY CLOSED.

25 ST. ALBANS

WREN LODGE 24 Beaconsfield Road, St. Albans, Hertfordshire, AL1 3RB. Contact Mrs Gill Rennick Tel: 01727 855540 & 0836 295196 Fax: 01727 766674.
Wren Lodge is in the heart of the historic St. Albans. Each room of this Edwardian house is decoratively painted in a different style. Well located for travel to many historic locations including the Cathedral, museums, Roman ruins. Well located to explore beautiful Victorian villages and delightful runs throughout the local countryside. During the summer the delicious breakfast is sometimes served on the patio surrounded by attractive gardens. 2 SINGLE, 2 TWIN/DOUBLE EN SUITE.

Prices from £25 to £28

1 ABERGAVENNY

AENON HOUSE 34 Pen-Y-Pound, Abergavenny, Monmouthshire. Contact Clare & Jim Vickers Tel: 01873 858708 & 01873 850656.

Aenon House is a comfortable family home set within a walled garden with comfortable accommodation and relaxed friendly atmosphere. It is only a short walk into Abergavenny and is ideally located for river, canal and hill walks or visiting the castles of Wales. Amidst the Welsh countryside, pockets of industrial archaeology can also be discovered. Closed mid December to mid January. 1 DOUBLE, 1 TWIN, PRIVATE FACILITIES.

⊡ ⅟ S   **Prices from £17 to £20**

2 BETWS-Y-COED

TAN DINAS Coed Cynheleir Road, Betws-y-Coed, Gwynedd, LL24 0BL. Contact Ann Howard Tel: 01690 710635 Fax: 01690 710815.

Set in 3 acres of woodland with scenic views, Tan Dinas is a Victorian house, offering modern facilities while retaining the character of its period. Situated in Betws-y-coed it is an ideal location for walkers and climbers, centrally located for Snowdonia and the castles of North Wales. Evening meals available. 6 DOUBLE/TWIN/FAMILY, SOME EN SUITE.

⊡ ⅟ S   **Prices from £19 to £25**

3 BRECON

PILGRIMS RESTAURANT Priory Close, Priory Hill, Brecon, Powys, LD3 9DP. Tel: 01874 625222.

Situated in the peaceful location of Priory Close, Pilgrims Restaurant in Heritage Centre Brecon Cathedral, serves light refreshments through the day and a la carte lunches in beautiful surroundings. Typical dishes include pork cassoulet, broccoli and stilton quiche and homemade soups. TUESDAYS-SATURDAYS 10.30-4.30PM CLOSED SUNDAY & MONDAY. OPEN BANK HOLIDAY.

4 BRECON

DOLYCOED Talyllyn, Brecon, Powys, LD3 7SY. Contact Mrs Mary Cole Tel: 01874 658666.

Dolycoed is a comfortable, friendly family home built at the turn of the 20th century. It is situated above Llangorse Lake near the Brecon Beacons National Park, an area with many outdoor activities on offer. It is an ideal base for touring central southern Wales. Closed December. 1 TWIN, 1 DOUBLE (EN SUITE SHOWER ONLY).

⅟   **Prices from £18**

5 BRECON

GLYNDERI Talyllyn, Brecon, Powys, LD3 7SY. Contact Mrs Copping Tel: 01874 658263 Fax: 01874 658363.

Set in a secluded position close to Llangorse Lake and within the Brecon Beacons, Glynderi is a country house surrounded by 4 acres of trees and garden. There is a walled herbaceous garden with a large pond surrounded by garden and lawns. The 35 foot long conservatory is where breakfasts and evening meals (by prior arrangement) are served - the meals are made with ingredients from the garden in season. Closed Christmas and New Year. 2 DOUBLE, 1 TWIN, ALL EN SUITE.

⊡ ⅟ S   **Prices from £18 to £20**

6 BRECON

TY TROSNANT Talyllyn, Brecon, Powys, LD3 7SY.
Contact Mrs June Rennison Tel: 01874 658681.
Ty Trosnant means 'house over the stream' and is situated on the outskirts of Talyllyn within a family run farm. A welcoming family atmosphere, comfortable accommodation and afternoon tea on the terrace with home-made cakes and preserves is offered to guests. Pleasant walks and pony trekking available in the area. Closed November to February inclusive. 1 DOUBLE PRIVATE BATHROOM (EXTRA DOUBLE ROOM AVAILABLE). CHILDREN 4+.

📷 ⚰ Ⓢ   **Prices from £17 to £18.50**

7 BUILTH WELLS

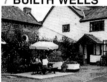

ORCHARD COTTAGE Erwood, Builth Wells, Powys, LD2 3EZ.
Contact Pat & Alan Prior Tel: 01982 560600.
The 200 year old, modernised Orchard Cottage is situated in the centre of a small village, where your hosts will help plan your sightseeing routes. The one acre garden runs down to the river Wye, offering fishing and magnificent views. There are 2 inns 100 metres away providing good value evening meals. It is well located for touring the Wye Valley, Brecon Beacons National Park, Ellan Park and the rest of mid Wales. Closed Christmas. 2 DOUBLE (1 EN SUITE), 1 TWIN. SINGLES.

📷 ⚰ Ⓢ   **Prices from £22 to £26**

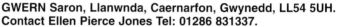

8 CAERNARFON

GWERN Saron, Llanwnda, Caernarfon, Gwynedd, LL54 5UH.
Contact Ellen Pierce Jones Tel: 01286 831337.
Gwern is a modern farmhouse on a working beef and sheep farm situated near Caernarfon with its medieval castle. The Foryd Nature Reserve on the Menai Strait is next to the farm where beautiful views of Anglesey and Snowdonia can be enjoyed from the farmhouses' large bedrooms. A varied breakfast menu using local produce and home made preserves is available. Closed December to Easter. 1 DOUBLE/TWIN EN SUITE, 1 FAMILY EN SUITE.

⚰ Ⓢ   **Prices from £20 to £22**

9 CAERNARFON

CLYDFAN Carmel, Caernarfon, Gwynedd, LL54 7SA.
Contact Mr & Mrs Briggs Tel: 01286 881104 Fax: 01286 880600.
A typical Welsh cottage on the edge of Carmel, Clydfan is situated in the foothill of Snowdonia. The accommodation is comfortable and the private entrance and guests lounge offers a magnificent view of Caernarfon Bay. Suitable location for touring north/mid Wales, seaside resorts, castles and Snowdonia. Closed Christmas and New Year. 1 DOUBLE, 1 TWIN.

⚰ Ⓢ   **Prices from £16**

10 CARDIFF
QUALITY HOTEL Merthyr Road, Cardiff, CF15 7LD.
Tel: 02920 529988 Fax: 02920 529977.
Located on the M4 Junction 32 A4054. Modern accommodation offering many facilities including a leisure centre, cocktail bar and restaurant. Nearby attractions include Cardiff Castle, Cardiff Bay as well as all the shops, bars and nightclubs in Cardiff city centre. Special package for bikers £26. per person inc. breakfast and dinner. Subject to availability. Must be booked through Central Reservations 0800 44 44 44.
95 BEDROOMS.

🍴 Ⓢ ⚲

11 CEREDIGION

Y GELLI Lovesgrove, Aberystwyth, Ceredigion SY23 3HP. Contact Pat Twigg & Tony Wheeler Tel: 01970 617834.
Modern well equipped farmhouse, Y Gelli is set in 22 acres of countryside just outside Aberystwyth. Rooms have colour TV and the family room has a bathroom and is linked to a children's bedroom. One bedroom is on the ground floor with en suite. The farmhouse is well located for touring the west Wales countryside and seaside surrounding Aberystwyth. Evening meals by arrangement. 2 TWIN (1 EN SUITE), 1 DOUBLE, 1 SINGLE, 1 FAMILY EN SUITE.
Prices from £17 to £22

12 CHEPSTOW
ST MARY'S TEAROOMS 5 St Mary's Street, Chepstow, Monmouthshire, NP6 5EU. Tel: 01291 621 711.
Located just off the High Street, St Mary's Tea Rooms have many local attractions including Chepstow Castle, the Wye Valley, Tintern Abbey and the Forest of Dean. In warmer weather guests can sit outside in the cobbled street or in the enclosed courtyard and there are separate Tea Rooms available for smokers and non-smokers. Cream Tea includes two scones with jam and clotted cream and a pot of tea. Home made local dishes including Welsh Rarebit and speciality farm-made ice creams from the Wye Valley. ALL YEAR ROUND, MONDAYS TO SATURDAYS 9AM-5PM. CLOSED ON SUNDAYS. EARLY CLOSING DURING WINTER MONTHS.

13 CHEPSTOW

BRIDGE HOUSE Pwllmeyric, Chepstow, Monmouthshire, NP16 6LF. Contact Mrs B. Gleed Tel: 01291 622567.
Bridge House is a 200 year old family home situated 1 mile from the M48. Set in country surroundings the house has a guest lounge, conservatory and an attractive garden. Exploring the Wye Valley, Chepstow and golf at St. Pierre are some of the activities to be enjoyed in the area. Vanity units in all rooms. Closed Christmas. 1 DOUBLE/SINGLE, 1 FAMILY FOR 3/4. CHILDREN 9+.
Prices from £16 to £18

14 COLWYN BAY
QUALITY HOTEL Penmaenhead, Old Colwyn, Colwyn Bay, N Wales, LL29 9LD. Tel: 01492 516 555 Fax: 01495 515 565.
Located on the A55 Exit Old Colwyn, B5383 to A547. Situated in beautiful surroundings overlooking Colwyn Bay. Rooms are decorated to a high standard and have many facilities. Local attractions include Bodnant Gardens (7.5 miles) and Bodelwyddan Castle. Special package for bikers £26. per person inc. breakfast and dinner. Subject to availability. Must be booked through Central Reservations 0800 44 44 44. 44 BEDROOMS.

15 CORWEN

POWYS HOUSE ESTATE Bonwm, Corwen, Denbighshire, LL21 9EG. Contact Mr & Mrs Carnie Tel: 01490 412367.
Powys House provides a peaceful, comfortable location in the Welsh countryside. Swimming pool, 3 acres of well tended gardens and a lawn tennis court. It is easy to find, situated just off the A5, 9 miles from Llangollen. Evening meals and packed lunches available. Closed Christmas. 1 DOUBLE, 1 TWIN, 1 FAMILY (WITH FOUR POSTER), ALL EN SUITE. CHILDREN 3+.
Prices from £20 to £25

16 GLAN CONWY
PLANTERS Tal Goed Nuseries, Glan Conwy, Conwy. Tel: 01492 573073.
Planters is located after taking the second turning on the left after Water Mill and has superb views of the surrounding countryside. A unique setting in a large sunny greenhouse with good views. Friendly staff serving Afternoon Teas, home made specials, soups and pies. Try the Planters Afternoon Tea which consists of a pot of tea and sandwiches with a choice of fillings including tuna, cheese, egg or cucumber. Teas include Assam, Earl Grey, Darjeeling and a range of fruit teas. OPEN DAILY-9.30 TO 5PM CLOSED FROM 24TH DECEMBER UNTIL THE FIRST WEEKEND AFTER NEW YEAR.

17 GWYNEDD
THE OLD TEA ROOMS Barmouth, Gwynedd, Wales, LL42 1EG. Tel: 01341 280 194.
The Old Tea Rooms are located near the harbour and St Davids Church within walking distance of two miles of clean sandy beaches. The Tea Rooms are light and airy and an inglenook fireplace give them a cosy feel. Friendly staff serving Welsh Afternoon and Cream Teas consisting of Welsh Cakes, Bara Brith, Welsh Tea Bread and Welsh scones. Gourmet sandwiches made on a range of breads and tempting cakes and gateaux. SUMMER SEASON (1ST APRIL TO 30TH SEPTEMBER), OPEN EVERY DAY 10.30AM TO 5PM WINTER SEASON (1ST OCTOBER TO 31ST MARCH), OPEN THURSDAYS TO SUNDAYS 10.30AM TO 5PM.

18 HARLECH
HAFOD WEN GUEST HOUSE Harlech, Gwynedd, LL46 2RA.
Contact Jane and Reg Chapman Tel: 01766 780356
E.mail: Hafodwen@enterprise.net.
Situated on the outskirts of Harlech, the house nestles on an escarpment overlooking the sea. there are beautiful views of the sea which is accessible from the garden. Harlech itself has restaurants, a theatre, swimming pool and the famous Royal David Golf Course. The house is well decorated and offers a warm welcome to all. 3 DOUBLE ROOMS, ALL EN-SUITE, ONE WITH SEPARATE CHILDREN'S BUNK ROOM. ONE SINGLE ROOM (EN-SUITE), LARGE FAMILY ROOM - EN SUITE.

Prices from £20 to £26.50

19 HAVERFORDWEST
WILTON HOUSE HOTEL 6 Quay Street, Haverfordwest, Pembrokeshire, SA61 1BG. Contact Philip & Karine Brown Tel: 01437 760 033 Fax: 01437 760 297.

Acclaimed en suite accommodation in quiet location. Delicious and varied menu in the licensed restaurant. Tearooms for a light snack. Swimming pool available. EN SUITE ROOMS.

20 HOLYHEAD
THE OLD RECTORY Rhoscolyn, Holyhead, Anglesey, LL65 2SQ. Contact Leonie & David Wyatt Tel: 01407 860214.
The Old Rectory offers outstanding views of the sea and surrounding countryside. A fine Georgian country house where footpaths lead from the doorstep to wonderful walks around the headland and to the beach at Rhoscolyn. The resort of Trearddur Bay is a few minutes ride away, also golf and leisure centre nearby. Residents' licence. Closed Christmas and New Year. 4 DOUBLE, 1 TWIN, ALL EN SUITE.

Prices from £26 to £29

21 HOLYHEAD

TEGFRYN Rhydwyn, Church Bay, Holyhead, Anglesey, L65 4EB. Contact Jenny & John Wade Tel: 01407 730702.
This modern bungalow in rural surroundings has views to the sea and Holyhead. There are coastal paths, beaches, bird reserves, fishing and golf nearby. It is conveniently placed for the ferry port at Holyhead for trips to Ireland and Snowdonia is a 45 minute drive away. Breakfasts from 6.30am. Closed Christmas. 2 DOUBLE (1 EN SUITE), 1 TWIN. CHILDREN 3+.

Prices from £16 to £20

22 HOLYWELL

THE HALL Lygan-Y-Wern, Pentre Halkyn, Holywell, Flintshire, CH8 8BD. Contact Mrs James Vernon Tel: 01352 780215 Fax: 01352 780187.
Adjoining a Georgian mansion, The Hall is an 18th century cottage in extensive grounds. It has been converted to offer two comfortable bedrooms and guests' sitting room with wood-burning stove. The coastal resorts of North Wales are accessible as are the many inland attractions Wales has to offer. Chester is a short distance away. Good pubs and restaurants nearby. 1 TWIN, 1 DOUBLE, EN SUITE AVAILABLE. CHILDREN 5+.

Prices from £20 to £25

23 LLANDOVERY

LLWYNCELYN GUEST HOUSE Llandovery, Carmarthenshire, SA20 0EP. Contact Mr & Mrs D. C. Griffiths Tel: 01550 720566.
The 150 year old Llwyncelyn Guest House is situated beside the river Tywi, close to the A40 within easy walking distance of the town. There is a friendly atmosphere, comfortable rooms and a dining room with a residential licence where evening meals are served. Fishing, pony trekking and walking is available in the area, near the Brecon Beacons National Park. Closed Christmas. 1 SINGLE, 1 DOUBLE, 3 DOUBLE/TWIN.

Prices from £18 to £25

24 LLANDRINDOD WELLS

BWLCH FARM Llananno, Llandrindod Wells, Powys, LD1 6TT. Contact Dorothy & Roy Taylor Tel & Fax: 01597 840366.
Bwlch Farmhouse overlooks the Ithon Valley and is set amongst rolling hills, just a short distance from the A483. Built in 1522 the house is made of stone and has a unique carved beam in the dining room, where candlelit dinners can be enjoyed with your hosts. Special diets can be catered for by arrangement. Closed November to March inclusive. 1 TWIN, 2 DOUBLE, EN SUITE OR PRIVATE FACILITIES.

Prices from £19.50

25 LLANDYRNOG

BERLLAN BACH Ffordd Las, Llandyrnog, Denbighshire, LL16 4LR. Contact Mrs Joanna Lindfield. Tel/Fax: 01824 790725.
RUTHIN 4m. Berllan Bach (little orchard) is a charming cottage and barn conversion. French windows are in every guestroom and open out into individual patios overlooking the orchard and garden. There is a cosy sitting room with an inglenook fireplace and an airy conservatory where breakfasts and evening meals are served. Ideally located for touring and walking, Offa's Dyke Path, Snowdonia, Ruthin and Chester are within easy reach. 1 DOUBLE, 1 TWIN, 1 FAMILY, ALL EN SUITE.

Prices from £22 to £24

26 LLANEDWEN

CARREG GOCH Llanedwen, Anglesey, LL61 6EZ.
Contact Mrs Margaret Kirkland Tel: 01248 430315.
Carregs Goch has easy access to the coast and nature reserve (6 miles), and Snowdonia (10 miles). It is set well back off the A4080 in 3 acres of gardens and paddock. The ground floor bedrooms have French windows that open into a private patio and garden that gives a magnificent view of Snowdonia. 1 DOUBLE, 1 TWIN.

Prices from £16

27 LLANWRTYD WELLS

THE DROVERS REST RESTAURANT AND TEA ROOMS The Square, Llanwrtyd Wells, Powys, LD5 4RE. Tel: 01591 610264.
Situated in the old spa town of the River Irfon and in between the Cambrian Mountains and Mynydd Eppynt, The Drovers Rest are charming Tea Rooms and Restaurant. Wonderful food cooked by Peter R. James who is Mid Wales Chef Of The Year and one of the top chefs in Great Britain and Ireland. Vintage Motorcycle Club holds meetings here. Enjoy gourmet meals served Friday, Saturday and Sunday or The Special Welsh Tea which consists of wholemeal bread and butter, Caerphilly cheese, tomato and melon and Bara Birth as well as scones, jam and creams. DAILY FROM 9.30AM TO 5PM FRIDAYS, SATURDAYS AND SUNDAYS FROM 7.30PM FOR DINNER. ACCOMMODATION AVAILABLE : 4 DOUBLE ROOMS, ONE EN SUITE.

28 MACHYNLLETH

THE OLD STATION COFFEE SHOP Dinas Mawddwy, Machynlleth, Powys, SY20 9LS. Tel: 01650 531338.
Situated in superb mountain scenery, the Old Station Coffee Shop is on the right of the entrance to Meirion Mill. Originally the waiting room and booking hall of the Mawddwy Railway Station, the shop sells a book tracing its history for just £1.50. There is an extensive menu and customers can choose from home made soups and flans, jacket potatoes and biscuits and scones. Ploughmans, sandwiches and cakes. Take home available, also jams, sweets, books, honey and ice cream. MARCH TO 30th OCTOBER 9.30AM TO 5PM. OPENING TIMES ARE 10AM TO 4PM.

29 MONMOUTH

HENDRE FARMHHOUSE Hendre, Monmouth, Monmouthshire, NP5 4DJ. Contact Mrs Pam Baker
Tel: 01600 740484 Fax: 01633 85782.
The spacious and well furnished 18th century Hendre Farmhouse is set on a working farm and is situated in a picturesque village with the Offas Dyke path running past the gate. The house has a large attractive garden that overlooks open countryside to the Sugar Loaf and Black Mountain range. Well located for touring Monmouthshire. Excellent home cooking. Evening meals by arrangement. Closed Christmas and New Year. 1 DOUBLE/FAMILY EN SUITE, 2 TWIN (1 EN SUITE).

Prices from £20 to £22

30 MONMOUTH

THE SLOOP INN LLandogo, nr Monmouth, Gwent, NP25 4TW. Tel: 01594 530 291.
Sample Wye Valley traditional guest beers in comfortable surroundings. Enjoy a delicious menu in this friendly inn with superb views. Lunch served between 12 noon and 2pm with evening menu from 6.30pm-9pm. 3 DOUBLE, 1 TWIN.

Prices from £27.50

31 NEATH

THE CASTLE HOTEL The Parade, Neath, West Glamorgan, SA11 1RB. Tel: 01639 641119 Fax: 01639 641624.
The Castle Hotel is a former Coaching Inn and was reputedly visited by Nelson. Welsh Rugby was founded here in 1891 and the hotel is ideal for the whole of South Wales. All rooms have satellite TV, telephone, trouser press, hairdryer etc. There is also a fully licensed restaurant and bar. 28 ROOMS, ALL EN SUITE, 1 FOUR POSTER.

32 NEWBRIDGE ON WYE

LLUESTNEWYDD Llysdinam, Newbridge on Wye, Powys, LD1 6ND. Contact Pauline & Chris Burton Tel: 01597 860435.
LLANDRINDOD WELLS 9m. In its remote location in the heart of the Welsh mountains, Lluestnewydd makes the perfect retreat for a relaxing break. There are many walks offering superb bird watching with is a Red Kite feeding centre nearby. The farmhouse offers luxury accommodation with all the comforts of a hotel but with a friendly, personal touch. Oak beamed lounge and dining room where guests can enjoy a candlelit dinner in the warmth of a real log fire. 1 DOUBLE, 1 FAMILY, BOTH EN SUITE, 1 TWIN PRIVATE.

Prices from £16 to £22

33 NEWPORT
PENHOW CASTLE Penhow, Newport, Wales, NP6 3AD.
Tel: 01633 40080 Fax: 01633 400990.
The lovingly furnished and restored, first home of the Seymour family has a variety of period rooms from battlements to kitchens, which can be explored with a Walkman audio-tour. Holds 8 awards for imaginative interpretation and fine restoration. The castle is located in SE Wales between Newport and Chepstow on the A48.

34 NEWPORT

PENTRE-TAI FARM Rhiwderin, Newport, South Wales, NP10 8RQ. Contact Susan Proctor Tel & Fax: 01633 893284.
A 60 acre sheep farm set in peaceful countryside, Pentre-Tai Farm is situated near junction 28 of the M4, 12 miles form Cardiff. The rooms are spacious and well furnished and there are reduced rates for children. The Wye Valley, Brecon Beacons, South Wales coast and the castles around Gwent are all within easy reach. Facilities for tents. Closed December and January. 1 DOUBLE, 1 TWIN EN SUITE, 1 FAMILY EN SUITE.

Prices from £19 to £20

35 NEWPORT
COMFORT INN Magor, Newport, Gwent, NP6 3YL.
Tel: 01633 881 887 Fax: 01633 881896.
Located on the M4, Junction 23A. Comfortable accommodation with restaurant. Golf nearby. Visit Cardiff (11 miles), Brecon Beacons (20 miles) and Chepstow Historic Town (10 miles). Special package for bikers £26. per person inc. breakfast and dinner. Subject to availability. Must be booked through Central Reservations 0800 44 44 44. 43 BEDROOMS.

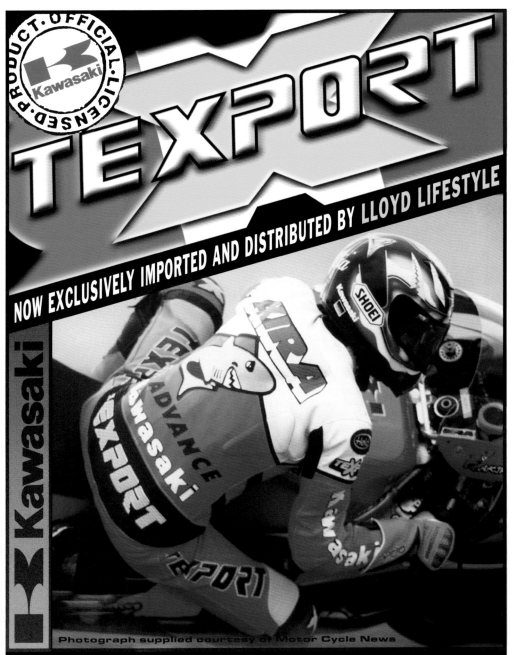

36 NEWPORT

COURT FARM Rogiet, Newport, Monmouthshire, NP6 3UR. Contact Sue Anstey Tel: 01633 880232 & 0403 930922.
Court Farm is set in delightful gardens on a working dairy and arable farm. It is close to junction 23A of the M4 and Severn Bridge and is convenient for touring the Wye Valley, Chepstow and Usk. Many golf courses are within easy access as are Chepstow Racecourse (8 miles) and Cardiff (16 miles). Bristol is also an accessible 17 miles away over the Severn Bridge. 2 TWIN EN SUITE.

⌂ ✂ Ⓢ **Prices from £20 to £25**

37 OSWESTRY

WERNDDU FARM Penybontfawr, Oswestry, Shropshire, SY10 OHW. Contact Mrs Enid Roberts Tel: 01691 860221.
LAKE VYRNWY 5m. Wernddu Farm is a working farm surrounded by tranquil countryside in an ideal location for touring beautiful mid-Wales. Warm welcome, comfortable bedrooms and a farmhouse breakfast is offered to guests. Lakes Vyrnwy and Bala, Pistyll Rhaedar waterfall and an RSPB craft centre are nearby. Walking, cycling and bird watching opportunities available. Closed December. 1 DOUBLE EN SUITE, 1 TWIN WITH PRIVATE BATHROOM. CHILDREN 8+.

⌂ ✂ Ⓢ **Prices from £16 to £18**

38 PENCADER

ARLANDIR Pencader, Carmarthenshire, SA39 9AN. Contact Jacqui Wonfor Tel: 01559 384872 & 01559 384496.
This is a comfortable, family home with a tranquil garden offering extensive views. The excellent home cooking uses organic produce grown by your hosts. It is well located for touring the unspoilt coasts of Cardigan Bay, Pembrokeshire and Carmarthenshire. Colour TV's in all rooms. Pony rides available. Closed Christmas. 1 DOUBLE WITH EN SUITE SHOWER, 1 TWIN/ FAMILY WITH PRIVATE BATHROOM.

✂ **Prices from £16.50 to £18.50**

39 PENRHYNDEUDRAETH

Y WERN Llanfrothen, Penrhyndeudraeth, Gwynedd, LL48 6LX. Contact Mr & Mrs Bayley Tel & Fax: 01766 770556.
PORTHMADOG 6m. 'Y Wern' is a 16th century farmhouse situated off the B4410 within Snowdonia National Park. Set in beautiful countryside, the house has oak beams and inglenook fireplaces with large comfortable bedrooms. Well located for such outdoor pursuits as horse riding, walking, climbing and is central for access to castles, slate mines and the Ffestiniog Railway. Dinner reservations accepted up until 4pm. 5 DOUBLE/TWIN/FAMILY, ALL EN SUITE OR PRIVATE FACILITIES.

⌂ ✂ Ⓢ **Prices from £19 to £22**

40 PONTYPOOL

TY'R YWEN FACH FARM Lasgam Lane, Trevethin, Pontypool, Gwent, NP4 8TT. Contact Mrs Armitage Tel & Fax: 01495 785200.
A remote Welsh long house on the Gwent Ridgeway, Ty'r Ywen Fach Farm is situated in the Brecon Beacons and offers magnificent views across the Usk Valley. The house has plenty of character; inglenook fireplaces, four poster beds, comfortable bedrooms and bathrooms.Pony trekking, canal bohire and walking are enjoyable local activities. Closed Christmas and New Year.

⌂ ✂ Ⓢ **Prices from £20 to £28**

41 PORTHCAWL

THE SEABANK HOTEL The Promenade, Porthcawl, Mid Glamorgan, CF36 3LU. Tel: 01656 782261 Fax: 01656 785363.
In a lovely seaside town the hotel sits in a commanding position overlooking the Bristol Channel. All rooms have satellite TV, telephone, trouser press, hairdryer etc. Equidistant between Swansea and Cardiff. 65 ROOMS, ALL EN SUITE.

42 POWYS
THE COPPER KETTLE 103 The Struet, Brecon, Powys, LD3 7LT. Tel: 01874 611 349.
Award-winning The Copper Kettle is a Grade II listed old worlde tea and coffee shop which displays prints by local and international artists. The Switzerland born owner, Mrs Helga Debroy Summers, speaks English, German and Welsh. Welsh Cream Teas offer a selection of herbal teas, China, Darjeeling and Earl Grey. There are also speciality Welsh cakes and Swiss patisseries. OPEN ALL YEAR; MONDAYS TO SATURDAYS 8AM TO 6.30PM SUNDAYS 9AM TO 5PM.

43 PWLLHELI
THE MILLHOUSE TEA ROOM & RESTAURANT The Mill House, Sarn Meillteyrn, Pwllheli, Gwynedd, LL53 8HF. Tel: 01758 730288.
The Millhouse Tea Room is located in the picturesque Llyen Penninsula, in the market town of Sarn Meillteyrn. Cream Teas with a selection of home made scones, cakes and Welsh Bara Brith. Snacks, lunches and hot meals are served throughout the day and there is also a good evening menu available. Guests are welcome to bring their own wine. Traditional Sunday Lunch available but you must book in advance. Novelty tea pots, mugs and jugs on sale. DAILY 10.45-5PM. CLOSED OCTOBER TO EASTER. EVENING MEALS AVAILABLE WED-SUN 6-8.30PM AND EVERY DAY 6-8.30PM (HIGH SEASON).

44 RHAYADER
CAROLE'S CAKE SHOP AND TEAROOMS Old Swan, West Street, Rhayader, Powys, LD6 5AB. Tel: 01597 811060.
Carole's Cake Shop and Tea-rooms is situated in a small market town east of the Cambrian mountains and within easy reach of the Elan Valley Reservoirs, Gigrin Farm and the Welsh Royal Crystal Factory. It is set in one of the oldest buildings in Rhayader and still retains many of its original features. Welsh Tea consists of a pot of tea, bread and butter, honey and home made jam, two Welsh cakes and Bara Birth. There are lots of other delicious alternatives and there are Welsh hand made chocolates and preserves for sale. SUMMER SEASON; MONDAYS TO SATURDAYS-9AM TO 5PM, SUNDAYS-10.30AM TO 6PM WINTER SEASON; MONDAYS TO SATURDAYS-9AM TO 5PM (EXCEPT THURSDAYS).

45 RHUDDLAN
WHISTLESTOP CAFE 28A HTM Business Park, Rhuddlan, Denbighshire. Tel: 01745 591235.
The hours of this Cafe are Monday - Friday 7am to 4pm except Thursday which is 7am-10/30pm. Saturday and Sunday 9am - 4pm. We serve breakfasts-lunches and all home cooked food.

46 SNOWDONIA
THE OLD FARM HOUSE, Tyddyn Du, Dyffryn Ardudwy, Snowdonia, North Wales. Contact Mick & Jane Tel: 01341 242711.
First class B&B accommodation for bikers with hot spa and heated swimming pool available. ALL ROOMS EN SUITE.

47 ST. CLEARS

COEDLLYS UCHAF Llangynin, St. Clears, Camarthenshire, SA33 4JY. Contact Keith & Val Harber Tel: 01994 231455 Fax: 01994 231441.
CARMARTHEN 12m. Coedllys Uchaf is set in 12 acres of grounds, home to ponies and goats, surrounded by magnificent countryside. It is a tastefully restored 150 year old country house with large, well furnished rooms. Beautiful beaches, golf, castles and many other attractions are within easy reach. Evening meals by arrangement. Closed November and Christmas. 1 DOUBLE, 1DOUBLE/FAMILY, EN SUITE OR PRIVATE FACILITIES.

Prices from £20

48 SWANSEA

THE GROSVENOR HOUSE Mirador Crescent, Uplands, Swansea, SA2 0QX. Tel & Fax: 01792 461522.
Set in the Uplands area of Swansea, the hotel is conveniently close to the city centre. It offers comfortable accommodation with good food and caters for people with special diets. Local attractions include the maritime quarter, the Gower Peninsula and facilities for rock climbing, fishing, golf, tennis, surfing, pony trekking and swimming. ALL EN-SUITE WITH FULL FACILITIES.

49 TENBY
BRAMLEYS TEA ROOMS Plough Penny Nursery, St. Florence, Tenby, Pembrokeshire, SA70 8LP. Tel: 01834 871 778.
Situated on the outskirts of the beautiful village of St. Florence four miles from Tenby, Bramleys tea-room is set in a Scandinavian style log cabin where guests can sit outside in the small garden or veranda. Reasonably priced Cream Tea comprising of home made scones, jam and local clotted cream with a pot of tea. Specialities include Sewin fishcakes, chicken, leek and mushroom pie and Glamorgan sausages. Afterwards sample a delicious blackberry and apple pie. FROM 1ST OF MARCH TO 31ST OCTOBER, OPEN SEVEN DAYS A WEEK-10AM TO 5PM FOR THE REST OF THE YEAR, OPEN THURSDAY TO SUNDAYS-10AM TO 4PM.

50 TENBY

WYCHWOOD HOUSE Penally, Tenby, Pembrokeshire SA70 7PE. Contact Mr C. Ravenscroft Tel: 01834 844387.
Wychwood House has spacious bedrooms, some with a large balcony, four poster bed and a sea view. Four course dinner menu served in the dining room by candlelight. There is a beach nearby where you can walk into the ancient town of Tenby where boat trips are available for visits to the monastic island of Caldey. 1 DOUBLE EN SUITE, 2 FAMILY EN SUITE.

Prices from £21 to £25

51 TYWYN
CEFN COCH Tywyn, Gwynedd, LL36 9SD. Tel: 01654 712193.
Guests can expect a very warm welcome at this former coaching inn which is situated in a Welsh coastal and mountain setting on the outskirts of the Snowdonia National Park. The Tea Room is beautifully decorated in Laura Ashley decor and tea is served on traditional Wedgwood china. In the warmer months, enjoy the superb views outside in the garden. Guests can choose their own afternoon tea from a good selection of sandwiches, light snacks and home made cakes, soups, pates and jams. OPEN DAILY 11AM TO 4.30PM EXCEPT WEDNESDAYS. ACCOMMODATION AVAILABLE-PHONE FOR DETAILS.

52 WELSHPOOL

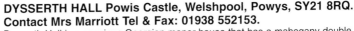

DYSSERTH HALL Powis Castle, Welshpool, Powys, SY21 8RQ. Contact Mrs Marriott Tel & Fax: 01938 552153.
Dysserth Hall is a spacious Georgian manor house that has a mahogany double bed and Victorian brass and painted beds. It is situated close to Powis Castle National Trust with its hanging gardens and deer park. The house has large garden with Victorian kitchen garden. Candlelit dinners and suppers can be enjoyed (by arrangement). Horse riding, golf and swimming nearby. Closed November to February inclusive. 2 TWIN, 1 DOUBLE, 1 SINGLE, 1 FAMILY, EN SUITE/PRIVATE FACILITIES AVAILABLE. CHILDREN 8+.

Prices from £20 to £22.50

1 ATHERSTONE

HAT & BEAVER Long Street, Atherstone, Warwickshire. Tel: 01827 720 300.
Bikers are very welcome at this lively pub. Rock disco every Saturday night. Friendly atmosphere and good ales.

2 BADMINTON

CHESTNUT FARM Tormarton, Badminton, Gloucestershire, GL9 1HS. Contact Mrs Cadet Tel: 01454 218 563.
An attractive stone 18th century farmhouse situated on the outskirts of the Cotswolds just under a mile from the M4. Ideal for visits to Bath and Bristol (12 miles). French, Italian and Spanish spoken. 5 BEDROOMS ALL EN SUITE.

Prices from £25

3 BAMFORD

YE DERWENT Main Road, Bamford, Derbyshire, S33 OAY. Tel: 01433 651 395 Fax: 01433 651 943.
The 100 year old Derwent is situated amidst the rolling hills of the Peak National Park. Guests are assured of comfortable surroundings and good food and ale. 12 BEDROOMS, 6 EN SUITE.

Prices from £25

4 BANBURY

THE OLD RECTORY Warmington, Banbury, Oxon, OX17 1BU. Contact Lady Vivien Cockroft Tel: 01295 690531 Fax: 01295 690526 E.mail: wcockcroft@compuserve.com.
The Old Rectory is a Georgian Grade II listed house standing on the edge of the village green. Warmington is a convenient location for touring the Cotswolds, Oxford, Stratford upon Avon and Bath. Many good restaurants in the area, including The Plough in the village. Closed Christmas and New Year. 1 DOUBLE, 2 TWIN, ALL WITH EN SUITE FACILITIES.

Prices from £25

5 BECKLEY

ROYAL OAK FARM TEA ROOM Beckley, Oxfordshire, OX3 9TY. Tel: 01865 351246.
Situated on the edge of bluebell woods with an adjoining animal garden, the Tea Room has a delightful ambience. On warmer days outdoor seating is available to enjoy food from the extensive menu. Cream Teas, Light lunches, 'Happy Hen' boiled eggs and home made cakes are all on offer.

6 BIRMINGHAM

ALEXANDER 44 Bunbury Road, Northfield, Birmingham, B31 2DW. Contact Mr Jennings Tel & Fax: 0121 475 4341.
Family owned and managed. All rooms en suite with Sky TV and tea/coffee facilities. Off road parking. Please call for a brochure and tariff information. 10 BEDROOMS SINGLES AND DOUBLES, ALL EN SUITE.

Prices from £35 to £60

7 BIRMINGHAM

HIGHFIELD HOUSE Holly Road, Rowley Regis, Birmingham, B65 0BH. Contact Mrs Kilbey Tel: 0121 559 1066.
Small, private, family run commercial hotel which takes great pride in the cleanliness and ambience of the establishment. Home cooked meals.
14 BEDROOMS, 2 EN SUITE.

🔲 Ⓢ MasterCard VISA

Prices from £18

---

8 BIRMINGHAM
QUALITY HOTEL 166 Hagley road, Birmingham, B16 9NZ.
Tel: 0121 4546621 Fax: 0121 456 2935 E.mail: admin@gb605. u-net.com.
Located From M5 to A456. Great facilities at this very comfortable hotel. Restaurant and bar available as well as cable TV, a leisure centre and conference facilities. Places of interest include Edgbaston Cricket Ground and Cadbury World (4 miles). Special package for bikers £26. per person inc. breakfast and dinner. Subject to availability. Must be booked through Central Reservations 0800 44 44 44.
215 BEDROOMS.

🍷 ✶ Ⓢ ♨

---

9 BIRMINGHAM
QUALITY HOTEL & SUITES 267 Hagley Road, Birmingham, B16 9NA.
Tel: 0121 4548071 Fax: 0121 455 6149 E.mail: admin@gb606.u-net.com.
From M5 to A456. Bar and restaurant facilities and mini gym are all available at this comfortable and friendly hotel. Local places of interest include Black Country Museum 12 miles, Warwick Castle 15 miles and Cadbury World 4 miles. Special package for bikers £26. per person inc. breakfast and dinner. Subject to availability. Must be booked through Central Reservations 0800 44 44 44. 166 BEDROOMS.

🍷 Ⓢ

---

10 BIRMINGHAM
QUALITY HOTEL 60/66 Lichfield Road, Sutton Coldfield, Birmingham, B74 2NA.
Tel: 0870 601 160 Fax: 0121 355 0083.
Quality Hotel offers comfortable accommodation and a wide range of facilities. Restaurant and bar, leisure centre and conference facilities. Local attractions include Cadbury World, Drayton Manor, Snow Dome, Alton Towers and the National Indoor Arena. Special package for bikers £26. per person inc. breakfast and dinner. Subject to availability. Must be booked through Central Reservations 0800 44 44 44. 64 BEDROOMS.

🍷 Ⓢ

---

11 BIRMINGHAM
COMFORT INN Station Street, City Centre, Birmingham, B5 4DY.
Tel: 0121 643 1134 Fax: 0121 643 3209.
Relax in comfortable surroundings where there are lots of different things to do and see nearby. All Birmingham City Centre attractions with the NEC (15 minutes), Warwick Castle (20 minutes). Special package for bikers £26. per person inc. breakfast and dinner. Subject to availability. Must be booked through Central Reservations 0800 44 44 44. 40 BEDROOMS.

🍷 ♨

12 BISHOPS CASTLE THE OLD BRICK HOUSE 7 Church Street, Bishops Castle, Shropshire, SY9 5AA. Contact Peter & Phyllis Hutton Tel: 01588 638 471.

Situated in the historic market town of Bishops Castle, The Old Brick GuestHouse is an attractive 18th century house set in a conservation area. A comfortable home to relax in after visiting the scenic hills, valleys and villages of the Shropshite countryside. Wonderful inglenook fireplace in guests lounge. Evening meals available. Closed Christmas. 2 DOUBLE, 1 TWIN, 1 FAMILY, ALL EN SUITE CHILDREN ALL WELCOME.

Prices from £22.50

13 BLADON
PARKHOUSE TEA ROOM AND ANTIQUES 26 Park Street, Bladon, Oxfordshire, OX20 1RW. Contact Hugh and Teresa Thomas Tel: 01993 812817 Fax: 01993 812912.

Situated one mile from Blenheim Place and nearly opposite Bladon Church where Winston Churchill is buried. Park House also provides the opportunity to buy reasonably priced antiques and gifts. Traditional Cream Teas are a speciality but also available are sandwiches, light lunches, and home made cakes. In summer months outside seating is available.

14 BOURTON-ON-THE-WATER

POLLY PERKINS 1 The Chestnuts, High Street, Bourton-on-the-Water, Gloucestershire, GL54 2AN. Tel: 01451 820244 Fax: 01451 820558.

This 300 year old building is ideally situated in the centre of this beautiful village overlooking the river. Family run, offering a warm welcome all year round. Ample secure parking. 8 BEDROOMS, ALL EN SUITE.

Prices from £30 to £45

15 BOURTON-ON-THE-WATER

RIDGE Whiteshoots, Bourton-on-the-Water, Gloucestershire, GL54 2LE. Contact Mrs Minchin Tel: 01451 820660 Fax: 01451 822448.

A large country house set in 2 acres of mature grounds. Spacious bedrooms, two on the ground floor are available with all facilities. Good pubs and restaurants nearby. 5 BEDROOMS, ALL EN SUITE.

Prices from £20 to £40

16 BRIDGNORTH
FALCON St John Street, Lowtown, Bridgnorth, Shropshire WV15 6AS. Contact Mr Pennington Tel: 01746 763134 Fax: 01746 765401.

A 17th century inn with original oak beams located near the bridge at Lowton. Extensively modernised with bedrooms offering all facilities. 14 BEDROOMS SINGLES AND DOUBLES, ALL EN SUITE.

Prices from £35 to £46

SYNCROTEC
The ultimate convertable

SHOEI

SHOEI

Full on technology.

17 BRIDGNORTH
THE QUAYS TEA ROOM & RIVERSIDE GARDEN 45 Cartway, Bridgnorth, Shropshire, WV16 4BG.
Situated on the scenic banks of the River Severn by the old bridge, the Quays Tea Room is a listed building built about 1650 and has a large inglenook fireplace. Scones are baked daily; home made cakes and soup are also on the menu. There is no set Afternoon Tea but regularly changing 'specials' assist guests in their choice. Smoking is not permitted in the tea room, but guests may smoke on the patio when it's open.
TUESDAYS TO FRIDAYS-10AM TO 5PM, SATURDAYS-10AM TO 5.30PM, SUNDAYS 11AM TO 5.30PM.
CLOSED ON MONDAYS.

18 BRIDGNORTH
THE WHEEL Worfield, Bridgnorth, Shropshire, WV15 5NR. Tel: 01744 714 208.
Situated on the A454 Bridgnorth-Wolverhampton road with drinks to suit every taste including Baxters Bitter, mild Lagers and dry ciders. Bikers meetings and barbecue every Wednesday.

19 BRIDGNORTH
NORTHGATE PANTRY Northgate Arcade, High Town, Bridgnorth, Shropshire, WV16 4ER.
Located on the first floor, next to the Northgate Arch, the Pantry is near enough for visitors to take advantage of local places of interest. All food is home cooked and proprietor Lisa Edwards offers a good range of naughty sweets and old fashioned puddings. The main teas available are Assam, Darjeeling and Earl Grey.
MONDAYS TO SATURDAYS - 10AM TO 5PM SUNDAYS - 11AM TO 5PM.

20 BROADWAY
LEASOW HOUSE Laverton Meadows, Broadway, Worcestershire WR12 7NA.
Contact Barbara Meekings Tel: 01386 584 526 Fax: 01386 584 596
E.mail: 100653.3225@compuserve.com.
A beautiful 17th century stone farmhouse, Leasow House is situated in a quiet countryside location. An excellent base from which to explore the Cotswolds, Oxford and Warwick. 7 BEDROOMS, ALL EN SUITE.

Prices from £35 to £65

21 BROADWAY

ASCOT HOUSE Station Road, Broadway, Worcestershire, WR12 7DE. Contact Ms J. Kingdon Tel & Fax: 01386 854 866.
Guests can expect a warm and friendly reception at this attractive property. Situated on the outskirts of Broadway, Ascot House is ideally situated to explore the lovely Cotswolds and the nearby castles and gardens. Closer to home, visit Broadway, reputedly one of the most beautiful villages in Britain. Closed November to February except for 3 or more nights booking. Reductions for stays of 2+ nights. 2 DOUBLE/TWIN/FAMILY EN SUITE CHILDREN 10+.

Prices from £21 to £22.50

22 BUCKINGHAM

FOLLY FARM Padbury, Buckingham, Buckinghamshire, MK18 2HS. Contact Jenny Webb Tel: 01296 712413 Fax: 01296 714923.
Folly Farm is a Victorian Farmhouse situated on the A413 amidst open countryside. It is an arable farm between the market towns of Buckingham and Winslow and is convenient for Silverstone, Waddesdon Manor, Stowe Landscaped Gardens, Althorp Estate and Addington Equestrian Centre. Easily accessible from the M40 and 10 miles from Milton Keynes. Evening meals by arrangement. Closed Christmas. 3 DOUBLE EN SUITE. CHILDREN 12+.

Prices from £18

23 BUXTON

WESTMINSTER 21 Broad Walk, Buxton, Derbyshire SK17 6JR. Contact Mrs Southam Tel: 01298 23929 Fax: 01298 71121 E.mail: cecelia@westminsterhotel.demon.co.uk.
Guests can expect a warm welcome at this spacious family run hotel which overlooks the Pavillion Gardens. Within walking distance is an Opera house and plenty of shops. Colour TV, tea and coffee making facilities. Access to car park via Hartington Road. 12 BEDROOMS, ALL EN SUITE. Colour TV, tea and coffee making facilities. Access to car park via Hartington Road.

Prices from £30 to £56

24 BUXTON
THE DUKE OF YORK 123 St Johns Road, Buxton, Derbyshire, SK17 6UR.
Contact Ken & Angie Waplington
Tel: 01298 24006 Fax: 01298 78182.
The Duke of York is a well know venue for motorcyclists and the are made very welocme in our pub. We are at the Buxton end of the Cat & Fiddle hill which is one on the most popular bikers runs in the area. We serve quality home cooked food, an excellent range of beers and lagers. Special car park for bikes.

25 BUXTON
STADEN GRANGE Staden Lane, Buxton, Derbyshire, SK17 9RZ.
Contact M A Mackenzie Tel & Fax: 01298 72067.
Our lovely bed and breakfast is in the delightful area of the High Peak District of Derbyshire. It is one of the most beautiful areas of England and a very popular area for motorcyclists. We are situated in a very serene and tranquil area close to Buxton. Our rooms are well appointed and you will enjoy your stay with us. We have secure parking and drying facilities available should you need them. NUMEROUS WELL APPOINTED BEDROOMS.

26 BUXTON

SHALLOW GRANGE Chelmorton, Buxton, Derbyshire, SK17 9SG. Contact Christine Holland
Tel: 01298 2378 Fax: 01298 78242.
Prices on application. Spectacular views, wide open spaces and a piece of rural England awaits you at Shallow Grange. Relax in the family atmosphere and sample delicious home cooking and hospitality at its very best. We are a working farm and you are welcome to have a look at our farming activities. We are in the heart of the tourist Derbyshire Dales and we are close to Buxton, Chatsworth House, Bakewell, Castleton, Matlock and Matlock Bath.

🔲 🛏 🍽 Ⓢ

27 BUXTON
CAVENDISH VIEW 108a St Johns Road Buxton, Buxton, Derbyshire, SK17 6UT.
Contact Mr T Conway Tel: 01298 72723.
Situated in lovely scenic countryside with fine views. Special drying facilities and secure parking. All rooms are tastefully furnished with tea and coffee making facilities and TV in every room. Set in a very tranquil and relaxing area, popular with bikers.

28 BUXTON
BULL I' TH' THORN Ashbourne Road, Hurdlow, Buxton, Derbyshire.
Contact Graham Tel: 01298 83348.
This pub, restaurant and bed and breakfast is very popular with motorcyclists. We are on the A515 Buxton - Ashbourne which is a fantastic road for bikers. We hold motorcyling events which are very popular. Caravan and camping site with plenty of available spaces. Caravans £3 per night and camping £1.50 per tent. Restaurant with varied menu and a large range of beers, lagers and wine. EN SUITE ROOMS INCLUDING 1 FOUR POSTER AND DOUBLE BED.

Prices from £66

29 CENTRAL MILTON KEYNES
CORNERSTONE PANTRY Church of Christ the Cornerstone, Central Milton Keynes, Buckinghamshire, MK9 2ES. Tel: 01908 237 777.
Situated within the Ecumenical City Centre Church of Christ the Cornerstone, the Cornerstone Pantry offers good food and drink and a wide variety of events and activities. MON-SAT 10AM-5PM SUNDAY CLOSED. CLOSED CHRISTMAS DAY AND EASTER.

30 CHELTENHAM
IVY DENE HOUSE 145 Hewlett Road, Cheltenham, GL52 6TS.
Contact Mr Hopwood Tel: 01242 521 726.
An attractive home set in pretty grounds. Rooms are comfortable and have many amenities. The city centre and the park are within walking distance. 9 BEDROOMS, 5 EN SUITE.

Prices from £20 to £50

31 CHELTENHAM

FARNCOMBE Clapton-on-the-Hill, Bourton-on-the-Water, Cheltenham, Gloucestershire, GL54 2LG.
Contact Mrs Julia Wright Tel & Fax: 01451 820 120.
A modern yet traditionally built home set in a tranquil location with magnificent views. Ideally situated for day trips to the Cotswolds, Bath, Stratford and Oxford. Enjoy peaceful walks in Clapton a small Hamlet with a charming 12th century church. Nearby bus service to London. Closed Christmas and New Year. 2 DOUBLE ROOMS WITH SHOWER, 1 TWIN EN SUITE CHILDREN 12+.

Prices from £20 to £22

32 CHIPPING CAMPDEN
HOLLY HOUSE Ebrington, Chipping Campden, Gloucestershire, GL55 6NL.
Contact Mrs Hutsby Tel: 01386 593 213.
Situated in a picturesque Cotswold village, two miles from Hidcote Gardens, eleven miles from Stratford upon Avon, there is plenty to see and do. En suite rooms are spacious and offer comfortable surroundings. Unwind and relax in the beautiful garden room. 3 BEDROOMS, ALL EN SUITE.

Prices from £30 to £44

33 CHIPPING NORTON
ANNIE'S COUNTRY PANTRY 22 New Street, Chipping Norton, Oxfordshire. Tel: 01608 641100.
Close to local attractions including The Rollright Stones, Chesterton House and Pool Meadow. Menu includes breakfasts, light lunches and afternoon teas. Cakes, scones and jams are all home made and the local baker is the provider of bread for sandwiches. A variety of teas and coffees are available.

34 CHURCH STRETTON
BELVEDERE Burway Road, Church Stretton, SY6 6DP. Contact Mrs Rogers Tel: 01694 722 232 Fax: 01694 722 232.
An elegant, spacious guest house overlooking its own gardens. Explore the local National Trust hills or nip into town (only 100 yards). 12 BEDROOMS, 6 EN SUITE.

回 S   💳 VISA   **Prices from £24 to £52**

35 CLAPHAM
FOX & HOUNDS 1 Milton Road, Clapham, Bedfordshire, MK41 5AP. Contact John & Anne Chatterley Tel: 01234 352 889.
Wide choice of drinks including McEwans, Eagle, Smooth and Bitter, Murphys, Cider and Red Stripe. Food served from 11am-11pm; Sunday 12 noon-10.30pm. Biker meetings Fridays and Saturdays, rideouts Sunday.

36 COALVILLE
THE VICTORIA, Whitwick Road, Coalville, Leicestershire. Tel: 01530 814 718.
Thoroughbred Biker night on Thursdays. Bar food served Monday to Saturday. Rock bands Friday and Saturday. Disco wednesday, Karaoke Monday. Overnight camping.   S

37 COLEORTON
THE RAILWAY INN Rempstone Road, Gelsmoor, Coalville, Leicester, LE67 8HP. Tel: 01530 222 394.
Bar snacks served Mon-Fri and Sat & Sun from 12 noon onwards. Juke box and pool table. Biker friendly. Four miles from Donnington. Field for camping available. Bikers welcome every evening.

38 CODSALL
FLAPPERS The Square, 1 Church Road, Codsall, Wolverhampton, WV8 1EA. Tel: 01902 845562.
Flappers tea room is combined with a lovely card and gift shop situated in a paved area opposite 'The Crown' only a short distance from the M54 and M6. The menu includes a range of beverages, cold bites, light bites, hot bites and home made desserts, cakes and many flavours of dairy ice cream including Turkish Delight and Butterscotch. MONDAYS TO SATURDAYS 8:30AM-6PM.

39 COVENTRY
QUALITY HOTEL STONEBRIDGE MANOR Birmingham Road, Allesley, Coventry CV5 9BA. Tel: 01203 403 835 Fax: 01203 403 081.
Located on M42 East on A45. Spacious accommodation in good location. Unwind in the relaxed and friendly atmosphere where service with a smile is guaranteed. Places of interest include the NEC 4 miles, Cadbury World and Warwick Castle 5 miles. Special package for bikers £26 per person inc. breakfast and dinner. Subject to availability. Must be booked through Central Reservations 0800 44 44 44. 80 BEDROOMS.

🍴 ♨ ✕ S

40 COVENTRY

SUMMERLANDS GUEST HOUSE 8 Stoney Road, Coventry, Warwickshire, CV1 2NP. Contact Mrs C. Russell Tel: 01203 257 874 Fax: 01203 226 784.
Guests can expect a friendly welcome at this comfortable Victorian town house. Summerlands is within walking distance of the city centre with its cathedral and motor museum and is ideally situated for touring the wonderful countryside. Just a few minutes from the rail station which will take you to the NEC and the Airport. Closed Christmas and New Year. 2 TWIN, 1 DOUBLE, ALL EN SUITE CHILDREN ALL.

Prices from £22 to £24

---

41 DAVENTRY

THREEWAYS HOUSE Everdon, Daventry, Northamptonshire, NN11 6BL. Contact Mrs E. Barwood Tel: 01327 361631 & 0374 428242 Fax: 01327 361359.
A character stone house with delightful garden, Threeways House sits on the green of a conservation village. The guestrooms are separated from the family home, each being extremely comfortable with lovely views and tea/coffee making facilities. Close to many attractions including Silverstone and Althorp. Good value pubs/restaurants nearby. 1 SINGLE, 1 TWIN, 1 DOUBLE/ FAMILY EN SUITE.

Prices from £20 to £27.50

---

42 DERBY
THE LOUDOX ARMS Normanton, Derby, DE23 8ER. Contact Simon & Donna Tel: 01332 342 147.
Friendly staff at this pub where bikers are very welcome. Juke box, pool table and live music and entertainment. Good Ales and food.

---

43 DERBY

RANGEMOOR PARK 67 Macklin Street, Derby, Derbyshire, DE1 1LF. Contact Mrs Richardson Tel: 01332 347252 Fax: 01332 369319.
Acclaimed small hotel with easy access to amenities. Closed Christmas. 20 BEDROOMS, 13 EN SUITE.

Prices from £26 to £53

---

44 DESFORD
THE BLUE BELL Desford, Leicestershire, LE9 9JF. Tel: 01455 822901.
The Blue Bell is a very popular meeting place every Tuesday for lady bikers. If you are a lady and interested in joining the club, then come and visit us here. The Blue Bell has avery warm, cosy and friendly atmosphere and all bikers are welcome here. We serve a nice range of beers, lagers and soft drinks. .

45 DROITWICH

PHEPSON FARM Himbleton, Droitwich, Worcestershire, WR9 7JZ. Contact Mrs Havard Tel & Fax: 01905 391 205.
WORCESTER 6m. Comfort and hospitality abound in this 17th century family house and granary. Enjoy the tranquil surroundings and wander round the grounds of this stock farm. Unwind in lovely rooms with lots of home comforts after touring the beautiful surrounding countryside. Visit the Cotswolds, Birmingham and Worcester. Great selection of restaurants nearby. Closed Christmas and New Year. 1 FAMILY, 2 DOUBLE, 1 TWIN, ALL EN SUITE CHILDREN WELCOME.

✄ Ⓢ   **Prices from £20 to £22**

46 DORRINGTON
HORSE SHOE INN Durrington, Shropshire. Contact Dave Castle.
This pub offers a very warm welcome to Bikers. We hold the meeting of the Salop Motorcycle Club and the Shrewsbury and district Motorcycle Club. Also the Vintage Club. We were recommended to this guide by the Marketing Manager of Morris Motorcycle Oils. We are also close to the A49, which is a very popular bikers run. Come and visit us, enjoy our beers and our friendly Shropshire hospitality.

🍺 🍽 🍺 Ⓢ

47 FARRINGDON
WHITE HORSE INN Woolstone, Faringdon, Oxfordshire, SN7 7GL.
Contact Mr Batty Tel: 01367 820726.
An old English inn, dating from the 16th century, open all day. Home cooked food served between 3pm and 5pm every day. Oak beamed restaurant. Bikers are very welcome. 6 BEDROOMS, ALL EN SUITE.

🅾 Ⓢ   [cards] MasterCard VISA   **Prices from £50**

48 FOUR OAKS
HUNGRY HORSE TEA ROOM Weeford Road, Four Oaks, West Midlands, B75 6NA.
Tel: 0121 323 3658.
Close to Sutton Park and opposite the Moor Hall Hotel, the Hungry Horse Tea Room is an old farmhouse with an outside patio. The majority of the food is home made and guests are at liberty to create their own afternoon tea from the wonderful fare on the blackboard. The portions are generous and there is a full range of hot and cold drinks to complement your food. TUESDAYS TO SUNDAYS - 10AM TO 5PM CLOSED MONDAYS EXCEPT BANK HOLIDAYS.

ORIGINAL SIN

Montana The classic
leather jacket.
Styled for a
streamlined look.

Sting High tech,
high style, one
piece leather suit.

Avalon Waterproof,
windproof,breathable
and armoured.
Outstanding looks

We've been making the most devilish motorcycle gear ever
since god invented two wheels.
Call Belstaff UK for a free brochure on 01782 839879.

49 FRAMPTON ON SEVERN

THE OLD SCHOOL HOUSE Whittles lane, Frampton on Severn, Gloucestershire, GL2 7EB. Contact Mrs C. Alexander Tel: 01452 740 457 Fax: 01452 741 721.
GLOUCESTER 10m. Located in the beautiful village of Frampton on Severn, The Old School House offers relaxed and comfortable surroundings. Situated in a beautiful part of England which is steeped in history, Gloucester, Cheltenham, Bath and Bristol all offer lots to see and do for all ages. Seek out quieter attractions such as Berkeley Castle and the Wetlands Trust. 3 miles from exit 13 on M5. Closed Christmas and New Year. 1 TWIN, 1 DOUBLE/TWIN, BOTH EN SUITE CHILDREN 10+.

Prices from £25

50 GLOUCESTER

VINEY HILL COUNTRY GUEST HOUSE Blakeney, Gloucester, Gloucestershire, GL15 4LT. Contact Mr Humphreys Tel: 01594 516000 Fax: 01594 516018.
A spacious period house just west of Gloucester in an area of outstanding natural beauty. 6 BEDROOMS, ALL EN SUITE.

Prices from £32 to £48

52 GLOUCESTER

GILBERT'S Gilbert's Lane, Brookthorpe, Gloucester, Gloucestershire, GL4 0UH. Contact Mrs Beer Tel & Fax: 01452 812364 E.mail: jenny@gilbersbb.demon.co.uk.
This is a 400 year old listed Tudor building lies beneath the Cotswolds, central to Bath, Oxford and Stratford. A delicious English breakfast is made from the produce of an organic smallholding. 4 BEDROOMS, ALL EN SUITE.

Prices from £24 to £57

53 GLOUCESTER

CARDYNHAM HOUSE The Cross, Painswick, Gloucester, Gloucestershire, GL6 6XA. Contact Carol Keyes Tel: 01452 814 006 Fax: 01452 812 321.
A 15/16th C Grade II listed house which retains much of its original character. Olde Worlde features include open fires, four poster beds and a bread oven. Antiques, murals and garlands of flowers furnish the comfortable rooms. Delicious breakfasts with choice of American pancakes and maple syrup. Evening meals available including Thai cooking. 3 DOUBLE, 2 FAMILY, 1 TWIN CHILDREN 3+.

Prices from £27 to £30

54 GREAT MALVERN ELM BANK 52 Worcester Road, Great Malvern, Worcestershire, WR14 4AB. Contact Richard & Helen Mobbs
Tel: 01684 566 051.

Pamper yourself in peaceful and luxurious surroundings at Elm Bank. A bright, airy lounge with books and local information offers a quiet place in which to sit and read. Take a trip into the nearby town centre or visit the Malvern Hills, Gloucester and Cheltenham; all within easy reach. Packed lunches by prior arrangement. 1 TWIN, 3 DOUBLE, 2 FAMILY, ALL EN SUITE CHILDREN WELCOME.

Prices from £18 to £25

---

55 HARROW
QUALITY HOTEL 12-22 Pinner Road, Harrow, Middlesex, HA1 4HZ.
Tel: 020 8427 3435 Fax: 020 8861 1370.
Located on the A404. Rooms are spacious and comfortable. Local places of interest include Wembley Stadium (4 miles), Windsor Castle (15 miles) and Central London where there is lots to see and do. Special package for bikers £26. per person inc. breakfast and dinner. Subject to availability. Must be booked through Central Reservations 0800 44 44 44. 50 BEDROOMS.

---

56 HATFIELD
QUALITY HOTEL Roehyde Way, Hatfield, Hertfordshire, AL10 9AF.
Tel: 01707 275 701 Fax: 01707 266 033.
Located just off A1 between Junctions 2 and 3. Unusual building set in its own grounds. Rooms are comfortably decorated and are well equipped. Visit the Great Houses of Hatfield, Knebworth, Luton Hoo and the Roman town of Verulanium(St Albans). Special package for bikers £26. per person inc. breakfast and dinner. Subject to availability. Must be booked through Central Reservations 0800 44 44 44. 76 BEDROOMS.

---

57 HATTON
THE WATERMAN Birmingham Road, Hatton, Warwickshire, CV35 7JT.
Tel: 01924 492 427.
Alcoholic beverages including Tetley, Bass, Guest Ales and Cider. Food is served every day of the week with the lunch menu served between 12 noon and 2.30pm and the dinner menu served between 6.30pm-10pm. We serve quality food at reasonable prices and bikers are always welcome. MCC meetings every Wednesday from March to September. Live bands September to March.

---

58 HATTON
THE WATERMAN Birmingham Road, Hatton, Warwickshire, CV35 7JJ.
Tel: 01926 492427.
Truly a bikers family-run pub with a large garden. From March to September every Wednesday is bikers night, where we have literally hundreds of riders. Lots of parking available. Great night out. During the winter (October-February) we have lived bands every Wednesday. See all the latest machines and hear the gossip.

59 HENLEY-ON-THAMES

ALFTRUDIS 8 Norman Avenue, Henley on Thames, Oxfordshire, RG9 1SG. Contact Mrs S. E. Lambert
Tel: 01491 573099 & 0802 408643 Fax: 01491 411747.
Alftrudis is a Grade II listed Victorian home offering friendly and comfortable accommodation. Only 3 minutes walk from the town centre and river, it is situated in a quiet tree lined cul-de-sac with ample parking. Henley, famous for its regatta is conveniently located for Oxford, Windsor and Heathrow Airport. Excellent restaurants and pubs in the area. TWIN AND DOUBLE ROOMS (2 EN SUITE, 1 PRIVATE). CHILDREN 8+.

Prices from £22.50 to £27.50

60 HENLEY-ON-THAMES

LITTLE PARMOOR Parmoor Lane, Frieth, Henley on Thames, Oxfordshire, RG9 6NL. Contact Mr & Mrs W. Wallace
Tel: 01494 881447 Fax: 01494 883012.
Little Parmoor is situated outside the village of Frieth which is close to the M40 and M4 and only 40 minutes from Heathrow Airport. It is a Georgian house set in a beautiful 1 acre garden, is well equipped and has attractive bedrooms. Windsor and Oxford are easily reached as are the many stately homes and gardens in the area. Excellent restaurants and pubs nearby. 2 DOUBLE/TWIN, EN SUITE SHOWER OR BATHROOM, SMALL DOUBLE/SINGLE, PRIVATE BATHROOM.

Prices from £25

61 HEREFORD

UPPER COURT Ullingswick, Hereford, Herefordshire, HR1 3JQ. Contact Susan & Christopher Dalton
Tel: 01432 820 295 Fax: 01432 820 174.
Set in large garden with croquet lawn, orchard and duck pond, Upper Court is a rambling Elizabethan guest house. Comfortably furnished and guests have own panelled sitting room. Located in superb countryside with the Malvern Hills and Black Mountains close by. Enjoy breakfast under the chestnut tree on warm days or around the huge fireplace on chillier days. French speaking. 1 DOUBLE, 1 TWIN/DOUBLE, 1 TWIN, EN SUITE OR PRIVATE AVAILABLE CHILDREN WELCOME.

Prices from £20 to £23.50

62 HEREFORD
THE ANTIQUE TEASHOP 5a St Peters Street, Hereford, Herefordshire, HR1 2LA.
Tel: 01432 342172.
Early Georgian building on the site of St Peters Monastery in a pedestrian area. While enjoying Traditional Cream Tea, guests sit on/at antique furniture that is for sale. Seating outside for those who want to eat al fresco. Traditional Cream and Afternoon Teas are available with a selection of sandwiches and pastries. ALL YEAR ROUND: MONDAYS TO FRIDAYS, SUNDAYS AND BANK HOLIDAYS - 9:45AM TO 5:30PM (JULY AND AUGUST UNTIL 6PM) SATURDAYS: 9:45AM TO 6PM.

63 HEREFORD
CATHEDRAL RESTAURANT 6 College Cloisters, Hereford, HR1 2NG.
Tel: 01432 359 880.
Situated in the Chapter House garden, Cathedral Restaurant offers delicious food and comfortable surroundings. Dishes include ploughmans with local cider, quiche, salad and filled baked potatoes. Average lunch £3.50. MON-SAT 10AM-4.30PM SUNDAY CLOSED.

64 HEREFORD
CAFE @ ALL SAINTS High Street, Hereford, HR4 9AA.
Tel: 01432 370 415 Fax: 01432 370 415.
Set in a stunning Medieval Church and serving fresh food at reasonable prices. Sample a variety of dishes including ploughman's with local cheeses, mushroom and guinness casserole with smoked cheddar mash and thai noodle salad. MON-SAT 8.30AM-5.30PM SUNDAY CLOSED.

65 HIGH WYCOMBE
THE FOX OF IBSTONE COUNTRY HOTEL Ibstone, High Wycombe,
Buckinghamshire, HP14 3GG. Tel: 01491 638289 & 01491 638722 Fax: 01491 638873.
IBSTONE. A privately owned 17th century inn, The Fox of Ibstone is situated in woodlands near chiltern Rideway, opposite Ibstone Common. The inn is popular with business people and weekenders because of the quiet surroundings. There is a friendly atmosphere of a traditional English in with low beams and log fires. Can cater for formal wedding breakfast for up to 55 and can offer buffet facilities for 75. The garden and patio are full of flowers in spring and summer. A small meeting room for 12 persons is available. 1.5 miles from M40 junction 5. 9 ROOMS, ALL EN SUITE.

🖵 ✂ Ⓢ   **Prices from £45 to £98**

66 HUNGERFORD

FISHERS FARM Shefford Woodlands, Hungerford, Berkshire, RG17 7AB. Contact Mrs Mary Wilson Tel: 01488 648466 & 0973 691901 Fax: 01488 648706.
HUNGERFORD 3m. A traditional farmhouse, Fishers Farm is set in a peaceful, secluded location 1 mile from the M4. Well located for visiting the cities of Bath, Oxford, Salisbury, Windsor, Winchester and for touring the downland countryside, villages and attractions like Stonehenge. Heathrow is less than 1 hour away. Indoor heated pool available all year. Excellent home cooking using garden produce. 3 DOUBLE/TWIN/FAMILY, ALL EN SUITE.

✂   **Prices from £25**

67 HUNGERFORD

MARSHGATE COTTAGE HOTEL Marsh Lane, Hungerford, Berkshire, RG17 0QX. Contact Chris & Carole Ticehurst Tel: 01488 682307 Fax: 01488 685475.
A small family run hotel set in beautiful countryside 15 minutes walk along the canal towpath to the centre of Hungerford. The traditionally designed addition to the 1637 thatched cottage houses the guestrooms, most of which having views over the Kennet and Avon Canal. Ideally located for touring southern England and to take canal boat trips. 2 FAMILY, 4 DOUBLE, 2 TWIN, 1 X 4 POSTER, 1 SINGLE, ALL EN SUITE.

🖵 ✂ Ⓢ   **Prices from £24.25 to £27.50**

68 KINGTON

THE WOODLANDS Lyonshall, Kington, Herefordshire, HR5 3LJ. Contact Margaret & John Parker Tel: 01544 340 394.
KINGTON 3m. An unusual half-timbered period house with attractive gardens. Your host and hostess will be more than happy to give you ideas and information and on the local attractions which include the Mortimer Trail and Offa's Dyke. Village pub serving good food within walking distance. Evening meals available. Closed Christmas. 2 TWIN, PRIVATE FACILITIES AVAILABLE CHILDREN WELCOME.

🖵 ✂ Ⓢ   **Prices from £18.50 to £23.50**

69 LONGSTOWE

GLEBE HOUSE Park Lane, Longstowe, Cambridgeshire, CB3 7UJ. Contact Mrs Charlotte Murray Tel: 01954 719509 Fax: 01954 718033.
CAMBRIDGE 9m. Glebe House is a charming 16th century country house situated 15 minutes from Cambridge. It is set in a , acre secluded garden that adjoins the woodlands of Longstowe Hall Estate. Conveniently placed for Newmarket, Ely Cathedral, Wimpole Hall and the Imperial War Museum. Stansted is 35 minutes away. Closed Christmas. 1 DOUBLE EN SUITE, 1 FAMILY PRIVATE.

🖼 ✄ Ⓢ   **Prices from £20**

---

70 LOUGHBOROUGH
QUALITY HOTELS AND SUITES New Ashby Road, Loughborough, LE11 0EX.
Tel: 01509 211 800 Fax: 01509 211 868.
Located on the M1 junction 23 onto A512 towards Loughborough. Quality accommodation with comfortable surroundings. Guests have full use of the leisure centre with swimming pool. Take a day trip to Sherwood Forest (28 miles), Alton Towers (50 miles) and Stanford Hall (5 miles). Special package for bikers £26. per person inc. breakfast and dinner. Subject to availability. Must be booked through Central Reservations 0800 44 44 44. 94 BEDROOMS.

🍷 🕴 Ⓢ

---

71 LUDLOW
THE OLD BAKEHOUSE 6 Tower Street, Ludlow, Shropshire, SY8 1RI.
Tel: 01584 872645.
Originally a 17th century bakery, the tea rooms are situated in a pedestrianised street near to the town centre. The homely Old Bakehouse offers different types of home made scones, cakes and snacks, speciality teas and coffees. There is a larger menu on Saturdays. MONDAYS TO FRIDAYS - 9AM TO 5PM, SATURDAYS - 9AM TO 9PM, SUNDAYS - 10AM TO 6PM CLOSED ON CHRISTMAS DAY.

---

72 LUTON
THE CHEQUERS 112 Park Street, Luton, LU1 3EZ.
Tel: 01234 309 037.
Enjoy a range of drinks in this comfortable pub; John Bull, Tetleys, Boddingtons, Largers and Guinness and more besides. MCC meeting Monday nights. All welcome.

---

73 LUTTERWORTH
ROSEANNES TEA ROOMS 27 Market Street, Lutterworth, Leicestershire, LE17 4QE.
Tel: 01455 552212.
Roseannes Tea Rooms are close to the church made famous by John Wycliffe opposite the Co-op. There is an unusual collection of teapots which add to the character of this cosy tea room. There is no set menu which allows greater freedom of choice for the guest. A range of light lunches available and a selection of cakes and pastries. Speciality teas and coffees available. MONDAYS TO SATURDAYS - 9AM TO 5:30PM OPEN SUNDAYS BY REQUEST.

74 LYDNEY

EDALE HOUSE Folly Road, Parkend, Lydney, Gloucestershire, GL15 4JF. Contact Mr & Mrs Parkes Tel: 01594 562 835 Fax: 01594 564 488 E.mail: edale@lineone.-net.
Attractive Georgian property situated in the Royal Forest of Dean and on the edge of the Nagshead RSPB Nature Reserve. Visitors can enjoy scenic, riverside walks or try out some of the nearby activities which include horse riding, canoeing, fishing and caving. Varied menu serving delicious food. Closed mid December to mid January. 4 DOUBLE, 1 TWIN, MOST EN SUITE NO CHILDREN.

Prices from £20 to £25

75 MACCLESFIELD
THE BUTLEY ASH London Road, Butley, Macclesfield, Cheshire, SK10 4EA. Contact John Chadwick Tel: 01625 829207 Fax: 01625 527323.
We are a very popular Pub Restaurant situated in the heart of rural Cheshire close to Macclesfield, the lovely village of Prestbury and close to Wilmslow, Poynton and Stockport. We have an enviable reputation for quality food and wines in a homely and relaxed pub atmosphere. Motorcyclists are very welcome here and we look forward to entertaining you in this popular venue.

AGON BRISTOL: MOTORCYCLE CITY - 01179 420 500 • BRISTOL: EASY WHEELS 2000 - 01454 320 196 • FLAX BOURTON: BRISTOL SCOOTEI
CENTRE - 01275 463 666 ★ BEDFORDSHIRE LUTON: THE BIKE CONNECTION LTD - 01582 731 855 ★ BERKSHIRE READING: MOTORCYCLE CITY
01189 574 044 • SLOUGH: SUPERBIKING - 01753 811 122 ★ CAMBRIDGESHIRE HUNTINGDON: ST NEOTS - 01480 212 024 • PETERBOROUGH
BERNARDS MOTORCYCLES - 01733 561 062 ★ CHESHIRE STOCKPORT: APRILIA STOCKPORT CENTRE - 0161 442 5805 • WARRINGTON: REVOLUTION
SCOOTERS - 01925 828 787 • WARRINGTON: FOWLERS LTD - 01925 656 528 • WIDNES: SCOOT 'N' COMMUTE - 0151 420 5251 ★ CLEVELAND
REDCAR: PETITE & FRANCE MOTORCYCLES - 01642 475 981 ★ CORNWALL ST IVES: ST ERITH SERVICES - 01736 752 028 ★ CUMBRIA BOWNES!
ON WINDERMERE: ENIGMA - 01539 444 994 ★ DERBYSHIRE CLAYCROSS CLAYCROSS POWERSPORTS - 01246 250 126 • DERBY: TOP MARQUES
01332 703 007 ★ DEVON EXETER: MOTORCYCLES UNLIMITED - 01392 201 750 • NEWTON ABBOT: GRAND PRIX - 01626 335 000 • NEWTON ABBOT
MOTORCYCLE CITY - 01626 331 020 • PLYMOUTH: GT MOTORCYCLES - 01752 559 063 • TORQUAY: PGH MOTORCYCLES - 01803 616 164 ★ DORSE
WEYMOUTH: POWERHOUSE - 01305 266 797 ★ ESSEX BRAINTREE: JOHN PEASE MOTORCYCLES - 01376 321 819 • CHELMSFORD: JOHN PEAS
MOTORCYCLES - 01245 264 350 • COLCHESTER: SUPPLY MOTOR LTD - 01206 210 467 • LEIGH ON SEA: BIKEWISE MOTORCYCLES - 01702 710 12:
• ROMFORD: HYSIDE MOTORCYCLES - 01708 763 360 ★ GLOUCESTERSHIRE CHELTENHAM: AMS - 01242 583 985 ★ GREATER LONDON CHELSEA
RED DEVIL SCOOTERS LTD - 0171 581 2799 • CLAPHAM: MOTORCYCLE CITY - 0171 720 6072 • EALING: BIKESMART - 0181 566 1120 • EAST HAM
EAST LONDON MOTORCYCLES - 0181 472 8301 • GREENFORD: MOTORCYCLE CITY - 0181 578 3218 • HAMMERSMITH: HARRY NASH SCOOTERS
0181 748 2837 • LEE GREEN: HOOTER SCOOTER - 0181 355 8020 • RAYNES PARK: WHEEL POWER - 0181 543 0321 • SEVEN SISTERS: MOTORCYCL
CITY - 0171 561 9500 • SHEPHERDS BUSH: SCOOTER STORE - 0171 610 4331 • SOUTHWARK: BRACKEN - 0171 232 1814 • STRATFORD: STRATFOR
MOTORCYCLES - 0181 555 4346 • WANDSWORTH: AHSAN SCOOTERS - 0181 8744 043 • WEST HAMPSTEAD: SCOOTER POWER - 0171 625 1200
• WILLESDEN GREEN: SUNRISE SCOOTERS - 0181 830 5600 ★ HAMPSHIRE FARNBOROUGH: MOTORCYCLE CITY - 01252 400 000 • GOSPORT: TREVOF
POPE MOTORCYCLES - 01705 521 111 • NEW MILTON: BURSEY ENGINEERING - 01425 612 436 • PORTSMOUTH: MOTORCYCLE CITY - 01705 827
25 • SOUTHAMPTON: PRO-SPORT MOTORCYCLES - 01703 440 595 • SOUTHAMPTON: STRIDES CYCLES - 01703 662 011 ★ HERTFORDSHIR
SHEPRETH: RIGHT TRACK - 01763 262 112 • TRING: MARKET MOTORCYCLES LTD - 01442 822 599 • WATFORD: COLLIN COLLINS - 01923 235 34
★ ISLE OF MAN CASTLETOWN: S & S MOTORS LTD - 01624 823 698 • DOUGLAS: CAR & M/C CENTRE - 01624 614 567 ★ KENT ASHFORD: SIGNPOS
CORNER - 01233 636 699 • PADDOCK WOOD: MOTORCYCLE CITY - 01892 835 353 • ROCHESTER: MARK BOWEN MOTORCYCLES - 01634 721 90(
• HERNE BAY: EXPRESS GARAGE - 01277 364 077 ★ LANCASHIRE BLACKPOOL: STEWART LONGTON CARAVANS - 01253 763 133 • BOLTON: LYTHGO
NISSAN - 01204 388 000 • CHORLEY: STEWART LONGTON CARAVANS - 01257 279 921 • COLNE: JUMBOSTATE LTD - 01282 863 896 • FLEETWOOD
RACEWAYS - 01253 872 037 • LANCASTER: FRANK SHEPARD MOTORCYCLES - 01524 845 167 • ORMSKIRK: BLACKS BIKE SHOP - 01704 897 55
• SOUTHPORT: THE SCOOTER SHACK - 01704 547 177 • WIGAN: KJM SUPERBIKES - 01257 451 656 ★ LEICESTERSHIRE LEICESTER: MARCO
MOTORCYCLES LTD - 01162 623 554 ★

LINCOLNSHIRE BOSTON: RA WILSON - 0120!
356 070 • GRANTHAM: GRANTHAM   CARAVANS - 01476 560 599 • GRIMSBY
JAMBUSTERS - 01472 354 402 • HULL: FIVEWAYS MOTORCYCLE CENTRE - 0148:
455 023 • SPALDING: BROADGATE SCOOTER CENTRE - 01406 364 474 ★ MANCHESTER
ASHTON UNDER LYNE: PHOENIX SCOOTERS   - 0161 343 5355 • ECCLES: CLAYBAN(
MOTOR COMPANY - 0161 788 0471 •   MANCHESTER: MOTO-TECHNIQUE - 0161 83:
3136 • MANCHESTER: MOTORCYCLE CITY -   0161 737 6000 ★ MERSEYSIDE HAYDOCK
UST SCOOTERS - 01744 453 295 •   LIVERPOOL: HOYLAKE CYCLES - 0151 63:
419 • SOUTH WIRRAL: SCOOTERS DIRECT   - 0151 336 3965 • ST.HELENS: MMC - 0174
55 333 ★ MIDDLESEX ENFIELD: SCOOTERS   OF ENFIELD - 0181 292 2003 • HARROV

(W): MACH MOTORCYCLES LTD - 0181 907 6705 • HEATHROW (W): MOTORCYCLE CITY - 0181 890 2913 • SHEPPERTON: JACK LILLEY LTD - 0193:
224 574 ★ NORFOLK KINGS LYNN: EDEN MOTORCYCLES - 01533 679 070 • NORWICH: MOONRAKER MOTORCYCLES - 01603 623 601 • WYMONDHAM
CHRIS CLARKE - 01953 605 120 ★ NORTHAMPTONSHIRE NORTHAMPTON: M & P MOTORCYCLES - 01604 417 000 ★ NORTHUMBERLAND BERWICK
BORDER BIKES - 01289 305 768 • CHOPPINGTON: LIDDELLS OF STAKEFORD - 01670 523343 ★ NOTTINGHAMSHIRE NEWARK ON TRENT: NORTI
NOTTS MOTOR CO - 01636 704 131 • NOTTINGHAM: FOWLERS MOTORCYCLES - 0115 926 7720 • NOTTINGHAM: MARCO★ 0115 950 7912 ★
OXFORDSHIRE BANBURY: MAX MOTORCYCLE CENTRE - 01295 252 506 ★ SHROPSHIRE TELFORD: WYLIE & HOLLAND - 01952 248 868 ★ SOMERSE
BRIDGEWATER: RIDERS - 01278 457 652 • TAUNTON: ATKINS MOTORS SCOOTERS - 01823 254 555 ★ STAFFORDSHIRE BURTON ON TRENT: JACKSON
MOTORCYCLES LTD - 01283 565 154 • CANNOCK: FOWLERS MOTORCYCLES - 01543 428 528 • STOKE ON TRENT: FOWLERS MOTORCYCLES - 0178:
415 768 • TAMWORTH: MOTORCYCLE CITY - 01827 280 905 ★ SUFFOLK BECCLES: L C GREEN & SON - 01502 712 370 • BURY ST EDMUNDS
ASTLANE - 01284 760 916 ★ SURREY CRANLEIGH: FCL - 01483 275 868 • KINGSTON: SCOOTAROUND - 0181 977 7758 • PURLEY: MOTORCYCL
CITY - 0181 763 5700 ★ SUSSEX EAST BRIGHTON: SCOOT-TECH - 01273 626 909 • ST LEONARDS ON SEA: K&S RACING - 01424 439 767 ★ SUSSE
WEST NR CHICHESTER: COLIN STRUDWICK MOTORCYCLES - 01243 544 577 • STEYNING: STEYNING MOTORCYCLES - 01903 814 980 ★ TYNE &
WEAR NEWCASTLE: KAWASAKI NEWCASTLE - 0191 272 3335 • SOUTH SHIELDS: F 1 SPORT - 0191 536 0011 ★ WEST MIDLANDS BIRMINGHAM
PACE - 0121 373 0084 • BIRMINGHAM: SPEEDAWAY - 0121 559 1270 ★ WILTSHIRE SWINDON: FOWLERS MOTORCYCLES - 01793 534 985
WORCESTERSHIRE WORCESTER: PHIL'S MOTORCYCLES - 01905 216 16 ★ YORKSHIRE NORTH RICHMOND: RICHMOND MOTOR COMPANY - 0174:
823 956 • RIPON: SUPASCOOTERS - 01765 690 590 • SETTLE: FH ELLIS - 01729 823 565 • SKIPTON: PETER WATSON (SKIPTON) LTD - 01756 792
711 • YORK: GREENSIDE GARAGE - 01904 798 150 ★ YORKSHIRE SOUTH HALIFAX: RON LEE LTD - 01422 361 108 • SHEFFIELD: HILLSBOROUGI
MOTORCYCLES - 01142 855 580 ★ YORKSHIRE WEST BIRSTALL: KICKSTART UK (EXCEL CARAVANS) - 01924 475 242 • BRADFORD: SCOOTERAMA
01274 678 272 • HUDDERSFIELD: HUDDERSFIELD SUPERBIKES LTD - 01484 421 232 • LEEDS: EDDYS MOTORCYCLE CENTRE - 01132 326 665 ★
SHIPLEY: MOTORCYCLE CITY - 01274 771 122 ★ WALES - CLWYD DENBIGH: A & D MOTORCYCLES - 01745 815 105 ★ GLAMORGAN SOUTH CARDIFF
ROBERT BEVAN & SONS - 01222 227 477 ★ GLAMORGAN WEST PORT TALBOT: KICKSTART - 01639 881 585 ★ SCOTLAND ABERDEEN: SHIRLAWS
01224 584 855 • DUMFRIES: SCOTSPEED - 01387 265 050 • DUNDEE: ALAN DUFFUS MOTORCYCLES - 01382 817 051 EDINBURGH: ALAN DUFFUS
MOTORCYCLES - 0131 622 6220 • FALKIRK: JIM ALLAN MOTORCYCLES - 01324 620 111 • GREENOCK: MOTORCYCLES SALES & SERVICES - 0147!
24 372 • IRVINE: WEST COAST RIDERS - 01294 273 731 • KIRCALDY: ALAN DUFFUS MOTORCYCLES - 01592 264 135 • PAISLEY: TWIST & GO
141 887 5846 ★ NORTHERN IRELAND BALLYMENA: RAYS MOTORCYCLES - 01266 462 05 • BANGOR: SCOTTY MOTORCYCLES - 01247 479 797
BELFAST: EAST END - 01232 731 454 • CARRICKFERGUS: H WILSON & SON - 01960 351 025 • CO. ARMAGH: RS M/C'S • COLERAINE: WRIGHTS
GARAGE - 01265 537 45 • HILLSBOROUGH: GS MOTORCYCLES - 01846 689 777 • LONDONDERRY: RIDE ON - 01504 345 984 • NEWRY: CROSSAN
01693 694 58 • PORTADOWN: HAMILTONS - 01762 334 922 ★ CHANNEL ISLANDS - GUERNSEY ST SAMSONS: RANCHO'S - 01481 432 81

76 MACCLESFIELD
CAT & FIDDLE INN Buxton, Macclesfield, Cheshire, SK11 0AR. Contact Ian & sue Ryder Tel: 01298 23364.

We are situated at the top of the Cat & Fiddle road between Macclesfield and Buxton. This is one of the most popular roads in Derbyshire for bikers and they regularly call in the Cat & Fiddle Inn. The inn is the highest in Cheshire and Derbyshire and is a popular meeting place for bikers. The road is fantastic for biking, but be very careful as it is also dangerous. We have a great variety of beers and lagers and soft drinks and food is available. There are plenty of parking spaces and the views are breathtaking.

77 MALMESBURY

FLISTERIDGE COTTAGE Flisteridge Road, Upper Minety, Malmesbury, Wiltshire, SN16 9PS. Contact Fay Toop-Rose Tel: 01666 860 343.

Secluded country cottage set in beautiful gardens with views of the superb Wiltshire countryside. Bedrooms offer comfortable and attractive surroundings in which to relax. Tour the nearby Cotswolds Water Park and National trust properties or take a day trip to Bath. Delicious breakfast menu. 2 DOUBLE (1 PRIVATE), 1 TWIN CHILDREN 14+.

🖸 ✂ Ⓢ   **Prices from £18 to £23.50**

78 MALVERN
LADY FOLEY'S TEA ROOM Great Malvern Station, Imperial Road, Malvern, Worcestershire, WR14 3AT. Tel: 01684 893 033.

Lady Foley's Tea Rooms are situated on the platform of a charming railway station, where train lovers can watch the trains and enjoy the comfortable surroundings. Tea consists of a sandwich, a home baked scone with jam and cream and a pot of tea. Lovely home baked cakes, scones and lunches. A wide range of sweets including cherry and pineapple cake, date, apple and walnut and lemon meringue pie. Teas include Assam, Darjeeling, Earl Grey and herb teas. MONDAYS TO SATURDAYS-9AM-6PM SUNDAYS-3PM TO 6PM.

79 MAMBLE
MAMBLE TEA ROOM Mamble Craft Centre, Church Lane, Mamble, Worcestershire, DY14 9JY. Tel: 01299 832 834.

Located near Mamble Craft Centre, Mamble Tea Room is in a 17th century barn, right next to a 13th century church. Visit the Craft Centre which has a craft gallery, exhibition room and workshop, and then relax in this spacious Tea Room with views of the Shropshire Clee Hills. Cream Tea with large scone and lots of other tempting alternatives. Baked potatoes with an imaginative range of delicious fillings and a variety of tasty snacks and specials. Hot and cold beverages. TUESDAYS TO SATURDAYS- 10.30AM-5PM SUNDAYS AND BANK HOLIDAYS-11.30AM-5.30PM CLOSED MONDAYS.

80 MATLOCK

ELLEN HOUSE 37 Snitterton Road, Matlock, Derbyshire, DE4 3LZ. Contact Mrs Ruth Lewis Tel: 01629 55584.

A small friendly guest house situated in a quiet location, yet within easy walking or riding distance of Matlock Town centre. We offer bikers a very warm and friendly welcome. We have secure parking and drying facilities. English Tourist Board recommended. Well appointed rooms en suite, centrally heated and double glazed. Hospitality tray and TV in the rooms. We have a nice lounge and lovely garden. Come and visit us.

🎔, 🖸 ♨ ✂ ♟ 🛏 TV Ⓢ ♿

81 MATLOCK

ROBERTSWOOD Farley Hill, Matlock, Derbyshire.
Contact Paul and Daniela Stuart
Tel: 01629 55642 Fax: 01629 55642.
Robertswood is a handsome friendly Victorian family house, set high above Matlock, with spectacular views of the Derwent Valley. Its friendly young owners offer their guests a tranquil and relaxed atmosphere, with traditional values. You can relax in either a double or a twin room. It will be spacious and comfortable, with its own en suite bathroom. Colour TV, radio, hospitality tray and hairdryer. There is lots of entertainment in the area.

82 MEASHAM

THE AUCTIONEER OF MEASHAM High Street Measham, Swadlingcote, Measham, Leicestershire.
Tel: 01530 270 658.
Welcoming family run pub with good Ales including Guest beers. Hot food available at all times, basket meals and take aways also available. Big screen TV and rock disco as well as live bands. Classic music section for the old uns!

83 MILTON KEYNES
QUALITY SUITES & SUITES Monks Way, Two Mile Ash, Milton Keynes, MK8 8LY. Tel: 01908 561 666 Fax: 01908 568 303.
Located on the M1 Junction 14, follow signs A509. Rooms are comfortably furnished and have good facilities. Guests have access to a leisure centre with indoor swimming pool. Enjoy a day out at Silverstone Race Track (15 miles) or Woburn abbey (10 miles). Special package for bikers £26. per person inc. breakfast and dinner. Subject to availability. Must be booked through Central Reservations 0800 44 44 44. 88 BEDROOMS.

84 MORETON-IN-THE-MARSH
ARRETON Station Road, Blockley, Moreton-in-the-Marsh, Gloucestershire GL56 9DT. Contact Mrs G. baylis. Tel & Fax: 01386 701 077 E.mail: bandb@arreton.demon.co.uk.
Situated in an unspoilt village, Arreton is a large, family house with a lovely walled garden. Rooms are decorated to a high standard and beamed lounge creates homely atmosphere. Ideally located to tour the villages of the Cotswalds or visit Warwick, Statford upon Avon and Oxford which are all just a short drive away. Local pub serving good food. 1 DOUBLE, 1 TWIN, 1 FAMILY, ALL EN SUITE CHILDREN WELCOME.
Prices from £20 to £21

85 MORETON-IN-THE-MARSH
OLD COACH HOUSE TEAROOMS Post Office Square, Blockley, Moreton-in-the-Marsh, Gloucestershire, GL56 9BB. Tel: 01386 701545.
The tea rooms are located in an early eighteenth century Coach House and Stables diagonally across the square from the post office. Cream teas comprise of scone, butter, jam and cream with a pot of tea at a very reasonable price. Farmhouse ice cream is a speciality and light lunches, such as home-made soup of the day are offered on the menu. Sunday lunches are also available. SATURDAY AND SUNDAY 10:30AM-5PM.

86 NORTHAMPTON

NOBOTTLE GRANGE Nobottle, Northampton, Northamptonshire, NN7 4HJ. Contact Mrs I. Cocks Tel: 01604 759494 & 07887 850965 Fax: 01604 590799.
Nobottle Grange is only 5 miles from the from the M1, junction 16 and offers spacious rooms and outstanding views over open countryside and woodland. Holdenby and Althorp House are both nearby as are Silverstone, Oxford and Stratford upon Avon. One mile from the Brington villages, both with pubs offering excellent food. 1 DOUBLE/FAMILY, 1 TWIN/FAMILY, BOTH WITH PRIVATE FACILITIES.
Prices from £20 to £25

87 NORTHAMPTON
QUALITY HOTEL Ashley Way, Weston favell, Northampton, NN3 3EA. Tel: 01604 739 955 Fax: 01604 415 023.
Located on the M1, J15 to A45, A43 turn off. Set in own grounds in attractive location. Bar and restaurant facilities serving a wide range of food and drinks. Megabowl Northampton, Wickstead Leisure Park and Towcester Racecourse are nearby places of interest. Special package for bikers £26. per person inc. breakfast and dinner. Subject to availability. Must be booked through Central Reservations 0800 44 44 44. 66 BEDROOMS.

88 NUNEATON
THE HERCULES INN Main Street, Sutton Cheney, Nuneaton, Warwickshire, CV13 0AG. Contact Mark & Belinda Bull Tel: 01455 292 591.
Bikers can expect a warm welcome at this traditional pub. Traditional Ales and food served between 12-2pm and 6.30-9pm.

89 OXFORD

GREEN GABLES 326 Abingdon Road, Oxford, Oxfordshire OX1 4TE. Contact Mr Bhella Tel: 01865 725870 Fax: 01865 723115.
Only 1 mile from the city centre on a regular bus route, Green Gables is an Edwardian house with plenty of character. Comfortable, spacious rooms retain the character of this house, originally built for a local merchant. There is ample secure parking, and a fine walk by the side of the Thames takes you to the centre of Oxford. One room on the ground floor has been adapted for the disabled. Closed Christmas and New Year. 1 SINGLE, 2 TWIN, 4 DOUBLE, 2 FAMILY, MOST EN SUITE.

🖳 ⌇ Ⓢ   **Prices from £22.50 to £28.50**

90 OXFORD
ST. ALDATE'S COFFEE HOUSE 94 St. Aldates, Oxford, OX1 1BP. Tel: 01865 245 952.
Try the excellent selection of pastries, cakes, cooked breakfasts and light lunches. In the summer there is seating available outside where there are superb views of Christchurch college and St. Aldate's Church. Cream teas, strawberries and bottled beers are also on sale. MON-FRI 10AM-5PM SATURDAYS 10AM-6PM.

91 OXFORD
OLD MINT COFFEE HOUSE New Baptist Church, Bonn Square, Oxford, OX1 8LQ. Tel: 01865 250 134.
Located in Charles I Original Mint, this Coffee House serves hearty soups and jacket potatoes. Superb Polish cheesecake for dessert. MON-SAT 10AM-5PM SUNDAY CLOSED.

92 OXFORD
CONVOCATION COFFEE HOUSE St Mary's Church, High Street, Oxford, OX1 4AH. Tel: 01865 794 334.
Located in a 14th century vaulted Old Congregation House of the University Church, offering a wide range of snacks and drinks. Try the speciality cream teas-delicious!. MON-SAT 10AM-6PM SUNDAY 11AM-5PM.

93 OXFORD

HOLLYBUSH GUEST HOUSE 530 Banbury Road, Oxford, Oxfordshire, OX2 8EG. Contact Mrs Field Tel: 01865 554886.
A detached Edwardian house, Hollybush is situated on a main road just north of the Oxford ring road. There is ample secure parking, enabling you to leave your vehicle and take the regular bus service into Oxford, avoiding inevitable parking difficulties. Easy access to the Cotswolds and Witney. Wide variety of breakfasts available. Closed Christmas. 1 TWIN, 1 DOUBLE, 2 SINGLE, EN SUITE AVAILABLE.

🖳 ⌇ Ⓢ   **Prices from £21 to £33**

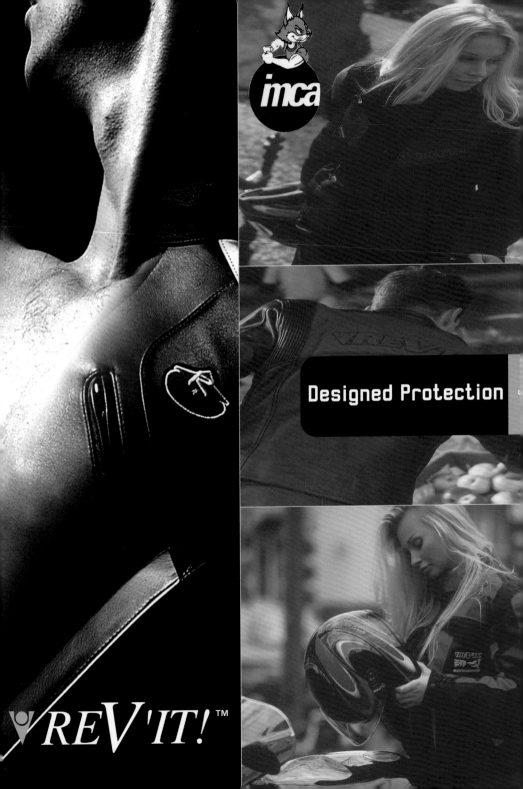

imca

Designed Protection

REV'IT!™

To view the full range of our products please contact our ♥ REV'IT!™ Points.

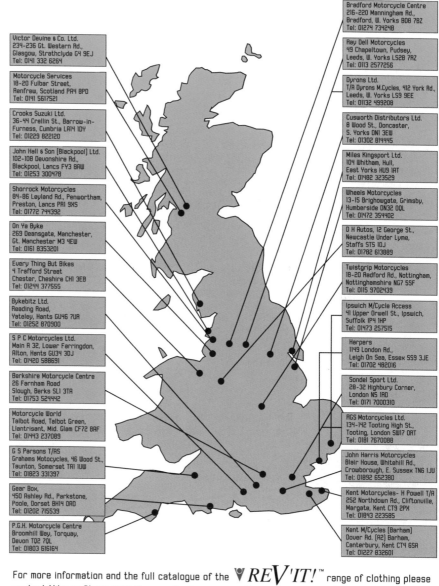

Victor Devine & Co. Ltd.
234-236 Gt. Western Rd.,
Glasgow, Strathclyde G4 9EJ
Tel: 0141 332 6264

Motorcycle Services
18-20 Fulbar Street,
Renfrew, Scotland PA4 8PD
Tel: 0141 5617521

Crooks Suzuki Ltd.
36-44 Crellin St., Barrow-in-Furness, Cumbria LA14 1DY
Tel: 01229 822120

John Hall & Son (Blackpool) Ltd.
102-108 Devonshire Rd.,
Blackpool, Lancs FY3 8AW
Tel: 01253 300478

Shorrock Motorcycles
84-86 Leyland Rd., Penwortham,
Preston, Lancs PR1 9XS
Tel: 01772 744392

On Ya Byke
269 Deansgate, Manchester,
Gt. Manchester M3 4EW
Tel: 0161 8353201

Every Thing But Bikes
4 Trafford Street
Chester, Cheshire CH1 3EB
Tel: 01244 377555

Bykebitz Ltd.
Reading Road,
Yateley, Hants GU46 7UR
Tel: 01252 870900

S P C Motorcycles Ltd.
Main A 32, Lower Farringdon,
Alton, Hants GU34 3DJ
Tel: 01420 588691

Berkshire Motorcycle Centre
26 Farnham Road
Slough, Berks SL1 3TA
Tel: 01753 524442

Motorcycle World
Talbot Road, Talbot Green,
Llantrisant, Mid. Glam CF72 8AF
Tel: 01443 237089

G S Parsons T/AS
Grahams Motocycles, 46 Wood St.,
Taunton, Somerset TA1 1UW
Tel: 01823 331397

Gear Box,
450 Ashley Rd., Parkstone,
Poole, Dorset BH14 0AD
Tel: 01202 715539

P.G.H. Motorcycle Centre
Broomhill Way, Torquay,
Devon TQ2 7QL
Tel: 01803 616164

Bradford Motorcycle Centre
216-220 Manningham Rd.,
Bradford, W. Yorks BD8 7BZ
Tel: 01274 734248

Ray Dell Motorcycles
49 Chapeltown, Pudsey,
Leeds, W. Yorks LS28 7RZ
Tel: 0113 2577256

Dyrons Ltd.
T/A Dyrons M.Cycles, 412 York Rd.,
Leeds, W. Yorks LS9 9EE
Tel: 01132 499208

Cusworth Distributors Ltd.
8 Wood St., Doncaster,
S. Yorks DN1 3EW
Tel: 01302 814445

Miles Kingsport Ltd.
104 Whitham, Hull,
East Yorks HU9 1AT
Tel: 01482 323529

Wheels Motorcycles
13-15 Brighowgate, Grimsby,
Humberside DN32 0DL
Tel: 01472 354402

D H Autos, 12 George St.,
Newcastle Under Lyme,
Staffs ST5 1DJ
Tel: 01782 613889

Twistgrip Motorcycles
18-20 Radford Rd., Nottingham,
Nottinghamshire NG7 5SF
Tel: 0115 9702439

Ipswich M/Cycle Access
41 Upper Orwell St., Ipswich,
Suffolk IP4 1HP
Tel: 01473 257515

Harpers
1149 London Rd.,
Leigh On Sea, Essex SS9 3JE
Tel: 01702 482016

Sondel Sport Ltd.
28-32 Highbury Corner,
London N5 1RD
Tel: 0171 7000310

AGS Motorcycles Ltd.
134-142 Tooting High St.,
Tooting, London SW17 0RT
Tel: 0181 7670088

John Harris Motorcycles
Blair House, Whitehill Rd.,
Crowborough, E. Sussex TN6 1JU
Tel: 01892 652380

Kent Motorcycles- H Powell T/A
252 Northdown Rd., Cliftonville,
Margate, Kent CT9 2PX
Tel: 01843 223585

Kent M/Cycles (Barham)
Dover Rd. (A2) Barham,
Canterbury, Kent CT4 6SA
Tel: 01227 832601

For more information and the full catalogue of the ♥ REV'IT!™ range of clothing please contact Mike or Steve or visit our web site - www.revit.com

Imca ltd
Daventry
Tel 01327 310114

94 PAINSWICK

DAMSELS FARM Painswick, Gloucestershire, GL6 6UD. Contact Mrs Burdett Tel & Fax: 01452 812 148.
A wonderful, rambling 14th century Grade II listed farmhouse situated in quiet countryside. This house has lots of history; Henry VIII used this house as his hunting lodge. Enjoy relaxing, peaceful walks in surrounding countryside or travel further afield and visit Cheltenham and Gloucester which are only a few miles away. Closed November to February inclusive. 3 DOUBLE/TWIN/FAMILY ROOMS CHILDREN WELCOME.

Prices from £20 to £25

95 PAINSWICK

CHANCELLORS TEA ROOMS AND LICENSED RESTAURANT Victoria Street, Painswick, Gloucestershire, CL6 6QA. Tel: 01452 812 451.
Within easy reach of Painswick House and near the village stocks and the church, Chancellors Tea Rooms is a Grade II listed building in Cotswold stone. Cream Tea consists of two scones, jam, cream and a pot of tea. Try Chancellor's Special Afternoon Tea with egg mayonnaise and cress sandwich, home made fruit scone with butter and jam and a pot of tea. Sample the delicious cinnamon butter on home made scones, cakes and teacakes. Assam, Ceylon, China, Earl Grey and Darjeeling all served here. WEEKDAYS AND SATURDAYS 10AM-5PM (CLOSED ON MONDAYS) SUNDAYS 11-5PM.

96 PERSHORE

THE BARN Pensham Hill House, Pensham, Pershore, Worcestershire, WR10 3HA. Contact Mrs Gina Horton Tel: 01386 555 270 Fax: 01386 552 894.
WORCESTER 9m. Set in tranquil surroundings, Pensham Hill House Barn is a converted 19th century barn with delightful original features. Ground floor rooms enjoy wonderful views of the River Avon. Visit Pershore and the splendid Norman Abbey or explore the stunning countryside. Lots of inns and restaurants within walking distance. Guests are welcome to use tennis court, sauna and pool by prior arrangement. 2 DOUBLE, 1 TWIN, ALL EN SUITE.

Prices from £25 to £30

97 READING

DUMBLEDORE Warren Row, Reading, Berkshire, RG10 8QS. Contact Lavina Rashleigh Tel & Fax: 01628 822723.
READING/HENLEY 4m. Dumbledore is a Tudor house with a wealth of beams and character with easy access to the M4, M40 and Windsor. There is a large bountiful garden with glorious views over the surrounding countryside. Maidenhead and Henley are both 4 miles away, Heathrow is within driving distance. Evening meals available, plenty of good pubs/restaurants nearby. Closed Christmas. 1 DOUBLE EN SUITE, 1 TWIN. CHILDREN 10+.

Prices from £28 to £30

98 REDDITCH

QUALITY HOTEL Pool Bank, Southcrest, Redditch, B97 4JS. Tel: 01527 541 511 Fax: 01527 402 600.
Located on M42 Junction 2, A441 Alvechurch Highway. Rooms are attractively decorated and the Hotel is set in its own grounds. Warwick Castle (15 miles), Cadbury World (10 miles) and the Royal Shakespeare Theatre (8 miles) offer lots to see and do. Special package for bikers £26 per person inc. breakfast and dinner. Subject to availability. Must be booked through Central Reservations 0800 44 44 44. 58 BEDROOMS.

99 ROSS ON WYE

RUDHALL FARMHOUSE Ross on Wye, Heresforshire, HR9 7TL. Contact Mrs Heather Gammond Tel: 01989 780 240.
Situated in beautiful, rolling countryside, Rudhall Farmhouse is an attractive Georgian house offering every comfort imaginable. Relax in luxurious rooms that are elegantly furnished and decorated. The nearby Wye Valley and Forest of Dean offers picturesque scenery and peaceful walks. Hearty breakfast cooked on Aga. Closed Christmas and New Year. 2 DOUBLE.

🗔 ✂ Ⓢ

Prices from £22 to £25

100 ROSS ON WYE
THE ANTIQUE TEASHOP 40 High Street, Ross on Wye, Herefordshire, HR9 5HD. Tel: 01989 566 123.
Situated in the market town of Ross on Wye, The Antique Teashop is a traditional teashop where guests sit on antique chairs and tables. Beautiful linen table cloths, bone china and fresh flowers create a refined setting. Traditional Afternoon Tea with finger sandwiches, a home made scone with clotted cream and strawberry jam, home made cakes and pastries and a pot of tea or coffee. MONDAYS TO FRIDAYS 9.45AM TO 5.00PM EXCEPT JULY AND AUGUST WHEN CLOSING TIME IS 5.30PM SATURDAYS 9.45AM TO 5PM SUNDAYS AND BANK HOLIDAYS 9.45AM TO 5.00PM.

101 RUGBY
CRUMB'S TEA ROOMS 3 Southam Road, Dunchurch, Rugby, Warwickshire, CV22 6NL. Tel: 01788 522489.
Crumb's Tea Rooms overlook the hustle and bustle of the ancient village with thatched cottages, stocks on the green and Guy Fawkes house. It is situated just off the A45 at Dunchurch. Tastefully furnished and attractively decorated there is a friendly atmosphere and waitress service. There is a choice of freshly made sandwiches, light lunches or large toasted teacakes available with the Cream Teas. DAILY - 10AM TO 4:30PM CLOSED ON MONDAYS.

102 SAFFRON WALDEN
ROCKELLS FARM Duddenhoe End, Saffron Walden, Essex, CB11 4UY. Contact Mrs Tineke Westerhuis. Tel: 01763 838053 Fax: 01763 837001.
Within the arable Rockells Farm is a Georgian farmhouse surrounded by the Essex countryside. The large garden includes a 3 acre lake for coarse fishing. Close to Audley End House and Duxford Air Museum. London (1 hour), Stansted and Cambridge (30 minutes), Harwich and Felixstowe (60 miles) are easily accessible from this location. Closed Christmas. 1 SINGLE, 1 FAMILY, 1 TWIN, ALL EN SUITE.

Prices from £20

103 SANDY

HIGHFIELD FARM Great North Road, Sandy, Bedfordshire, SG19 2AQ. Contact Margret Codd Tel: 01767 682332 Fax: 01767 692503.
Highfield Farm offers a warm welcome in guest accommodation in converted stables as well as the main farmhouse. The farm is just off the A1, set back by a long private driveway, has ample secure parking. It's centrally located for touring north or south, Cambridge is within easy reach. Guests' sitting room. TWINS, DOUBLES, FAMILIES, MOST EN SUITE.

🗔 ✂ Ⓢ

Prices from £25

104 SANDY
ORCHARD COTTAGE High Street, Wrestlingworth, Sandy, Bedfordshire, SG19 9EW. Contact Mrs Strong. Tel: 01767 631355.
The picturesque part-thatched Orchard Cottage is situated in a pretty village overlooking the countryside. This former bakery is located within easy reach of many attractions including Wimpole Hall, Duxford Air Museum and the city of Cambridge. Convenient for travellers going north and south. Local pub serves evening meals. Closed Christmas. 1 DOUBLE, 1 TWIN, 2 SINGLE.

Prices from £19

105 SIX HILLS
THE WILD OX The Fosseway, Six Hills, Leicestershire LE14 3PD. Tel: 01509 880 240.
Bikers social every friday night. Hot food available as well as bed and breakfast for the travelling biker.

106 SLING
THE MINERS ARMS Sling, Gloucestershire, GL16 8LH. Tel: 01594 834 432.
Wide range of drinks to suit every taste including beers, Ales, Lagers and Guinness. Food served daily. Camping available free. MAG meets every Wednesday. Real ale put – in the Good Beer Guide.

107 SLOUGH
QUALITY HOTEL London Road, Heathrow Airport, Slough, Berkshire, SL3 8QB. Tel: 01753 684 001 Fax: 01753 685 767.
Located on the M4 Junction 5, A4 towards Heathrow. Shuttle service to/from Heathrow Terminals 1/2/3. High standards of comfotable accommodation at this Quality Hotel. Restaurant serves imaginative range of food and drink. Nearby London means that visitors will never be bored! Special package for bikers £26. per person inc. breakfast and dinner. Subject to availability. Must be booked through Central Reservations 0800 44 44 44. 117 BEDROOMS.

108 SOLIHULL
THE MANOR HOTEL Meriden, Solihull, West Midlands, CV7 7NH. Tel: 01676 522735 Fax: 01676 522186.
A picturesque country residence with a warm friendly atmosphere, Manor Hotel is only a few minutes away from the M6, M42, NEC and Birmingham International Airport. Meriden is the 'Centre of England' making it an ideal location for holding conferences or banquets. Award winning Regency Restaurant with two AA Rosettes enjoys a country-wide reputation. Three miles from National Motorcycle Museum. 112 BEDROOMS, 4 CONFERENCE, 2 RESTAURANTS (UP TO 275 PEOPLE), 3 BANQUETING (UP TO 220).

109 SOUTHMOOR

ALPENHAUS Faringdon Road, Southmoor, Oxfordshire, OX13 5AF. Contact Mrs Pat Curtis Tel: 01865 820666 Fax: 01865 821868 E.mail: Bbalpen@aol.com.
A comfortable, modern house in a village 10 miles west of Oxford, Alpenhaus has pleasant rooms that are tastefully decorated. It is conveniently placed for the Cotswolds, Blenheim Palace, Stratford and Warwick. Several pubs and restaurants serving good food nearby. Heathrow is about 1 hour away. Closed Christmas and New Year. 2 TWIN, 1 DOUBLE. CHILDREN 5+.

Prices from £18.50 to £19.50

110 ST ALBANS
COMFORT HOTEL Ryder House, Holywell Hill, St Albans, Hertfordshire, AL1 1HG. Tel: 01727 848 849 Fax: 01727 812 210.
Easy access from M1 (A1) & M25. Attractive accommodation where rooms are well equipped. Local places of interest include Silverstone Race Track, Woburn Abbey, Whipsnade Zoo, Verulanium Museum and Gardens. Special package for bikers £26. per person inc. breakfast and dinner. Subject to availability. Must be booked through Central Reservations 0800 44 44 44. 60 BEDROOMS.

111 ST ALBANS
CHAPTER HOUSE REFECTORY St Albans Cathedral, Holywell Hill, St Albans, Hertfordshire AL1 1BY. Tel: 01727 864 208.
Imaginative range of freshly-cooked and homemade dishes in the dramatic Chapter House setting. Typical dishes include homemade quiche and salad, pork and roast potatoes and a selection of puddings and cakes. MON-SAT 10.30AM-4.30PM SUN 2.30-5PM.

112 ST ALBANS
DUKE OF MARLBOROUGH 110 Holywell Hill, St Albans, Hertfordshire, AL1 1DH. Contact Eamond Murghy Tel: 01727 858 982.
Welcoming pub with good selection of drinks; Tetley, Guest Beer, Carlesberg, Dry Blackthorn and Stella. Food served daily at lunch time only. MAG meetings every Wednesday at 8.30pm. Function room available.

113 STAFFORD
QUALITY HOTEL Pinfold Lane, Penkridge, Stafford, ST19 5QP. Tel: 01785 712 459 Fax: 01785 715 532.
Located between J12 & 13 of M6. Good accommodation in pleasant surroundings. Leisure centre with indoor swimming pool open to guests. Visit Alton Towers, the Black Country Museum and the Bass Museum. Special package for bikers £26. per person inc. breakfast and dinner. Subject to availability. Must be booked through Central Reservations 0800 44 44 44. 47 BEDROOMS.

114 STANDLAKE

HAWTHORN COTTAGE The Downs, Standlake, Oxfordshire, OX 8 7SH. Contact Mrs Susan Peterson Tel & Fax: 01865 300588.
A detached house set amongst mature gardens, Hawthorn Cottage is situated in a pretty Oxfordshire village close to the river Windrush. The self contained guest rooms are beautifully furnished and decorated. Good pub food available within walking distance. Closed December and January. 1 DOUBLE, PRIVATE, 1 TWIN EN SUITE. CHILDREN 3+.

Prices from £20 to £22.50

115 STOW-ON-THE-WOLD

THE OLD GRAIN HOUSE Rectory Barns, Lower Swell, Stow-on-the-Wold, Gloucestershire, GL54 1LH. Contact Mrs Elizabeth Campbell-Winton Tel: 01451 832 348.
The Old Grain House was a former barn that was recently converted to provide unique and lovely accommodation. Situated just 1 mile from Stow on the Wold in the delightful village of Lower Swell. Burford, Bourton on the Water are all close by and there is easy access to Stratford upon Avon, Oxford and Bath (1 hours drive) Closed Christmas and New Year. 1 DOUBLE, 1 SINGLE CHILDREN 5+.

Prices from £23 to £25

116 STRATFORD-UPON-AVON

NEWBOLD NURSERIES Newbold-on-Stour, Stratford-upon-Avon, Warwickshire, CV37 8DP. Contact Roger Everett Tel & Fax: 01789 450 285.
Situated in a rural location, Newbold Nurseri es is a welcoming, modern farmhouse on an arable farm. Spacious bedrooms with every comfort possible. Enjoy the beautiful views. Warwick Castle, Blenheim Palace and the Cotswolds are all within easy reach. Local pubs serving good food. Closed December and January. 1 FAMILY, 1 TWIN, 1 DOUBLE, SOME EN SUITE CHILDREN WELCOME.
🖲 ⅃ S **Prices from £17 to £18.50**

117 STRATFORD-UPON-AVON

MOSS COTTAGE 61 Evesham Road, Stratford-upon-Avon, Warwickshire, CV37 9BA. Contact Pauline & Jim Rush Tel & Fax: 01789 294 770.
An attractive detached cottage with delightful garden. Historic places of interest, theatres and restaurants are all in nearby city centre. Ideal base from which to explore the Cotswolds, the historic Warwick and a variety of National trust Properties. Birmingham airport and NEC are both a 30 minutes drive. Closed Christmas. 2 DOUBLE EN SUITE CHILDREN WELCOME.
🖲 ⅃ S **Prices from £18 to £22**

118 STRATFORD-UPON-AVON

CHURCH FARM Dorsington, Stratford upon Avon, Warwickshire, CV37 8AX. Contact Mrs M. Walters Tel: 01789 720 471 & 0831 504 194 Fax: 01789 720 830.
Situated in a quiet and picturesque village, Church Farm is a working farm which offers comfortable accommodation. Rooms have TV and coffee making facilities. Explore the village and its quaint thatched cottages or travel to Stratford, Warwick, the Vale of Evesham and the Cotswolds. 2 miles to restaurants. 7 DOUBLE/TWIN/FAMILY ROOMS, MOST EN SUITE CHILDREN ALL.
⅃ **Prices from £18 to £20**

119 STROUD

PRETORIA VILLA Wells Road, Eastcombe, Stroud, Gloucestershire, GL6 7EE. Contact Mrs G. Soloman Tel: 01452 770 435.
A well furnished country cottage located in a quiet, picturesque village in the Cotswolds. Enjoy the wonderful gardens and magnificent views. Cheltenham, Bath, Gloucester and Cirencester are all well worth a visit. The Cotswold Way offers scenic walks and abundant wildlife. Closed Christmas. 1 TWIN EN SUITE, 1 DOUBLE AND SINGLE WITH PRIVATE FACILITIES CHILDREN ALL.
🖲 ⅃ S **Prices from £20**

120 STROUD

SOUTHFIELD MILL Southfield Road, Woodchester, Stroud, Gloucestershire, GL5 5PA. Contact Mrs Judy Sutch Tel & Fax: 01453 872 896.
Elegant 18th century converted woollen mill set in peaceful surroundings. Relax in the sitting room or the large garden which has its own lake. Ideally located for touring the Cotswolds. Hire bicycles at the local cycle track. Laundry facilities available at a charge. Local pubs within walking distance. 1 DOUBLE/FAMILY, 1 TWIN, BOTH EN SUITE CHILDREN ALL WELCOME.
⅃ S **Prices from £22 to £25**

121 STUDLEY
HAYE PASTURES FARM Haye Lane, Mappleborough Green, Studley, Warwickshire, B80 7DS. Contact Muriel Richards
Tel & Fax: 01527 852 200.
HENLEY IN ARDEN 4m. Relax in this peaceful location set in an elevated position with superb views of the Warwickshire countryside. Haye Pastures Farm has been recently extended and offers modern yet comfortable accommodation. Easy access to Birmingham, Warwick and Kenilworth. Five minutes from M42 junction 3. 1 SINGLE, 1 DOUBLE EN SUITE, 1 TWIN EN SUITE CHILDREN ALL.

Prices from £25 to £30

122 SWINDON

NORTON HOUSE 46 Draycott Road, Chiseldon, Swindon, Wiltshire, SN4 0LS. Contact Mrs S. Dixon
Tel: 01793 741210 & 0966 282356 Fax: 01793 741020.
Norton house is a large executive family house on the outskirts of the picturesque village of Chiseldon. The bedrooms are spacious, well equipped and overlooking downland countryside. A346 and M4 close by making it easy to tour areas such as the Cotswolds, Oxford, Bath and Stonehenge. Closed Christmas. 1 DOUBLE, 1 TWIN, BOTH EN SUITE, 1 SINGLE, 1 DOUBLE/FAMILY. CHILDREN 5+.

Prices from £20 to £23

123 TELFORD

AVENUE FARM Uppington, Telford, Shropshire, TF6 5HW.
Contact Mrs Mig Jones Tel: 01952 740 253 Fax: 01952 740 401.
Situated in the peaceful Uppington village just 2 miles from M54 (junction 7), Avenue Farm is a charming 18th farmhouse set in a large secluded garden with superb views of the Wrekin. Lots of places of interest close at hand including the Ironbridge museums, Viroconium and the Severn Valley Railway. Easy access to the unspoilt Shropshire countryside. Closed Christmas and New Year. 1 DOUBLE EN SUITE WITH PRIVATE BATHROOM, 1 TWIN, 1 FAMILY CHILDREN WELCOME.

Prices from £20 to £22

124 TELFORD
CLARION HOTEL, MADELEY COURT Telford, Shropshire, TF7 5DW.
Tel: 01952 680 068 Fax: 01952 684 275.
From M54, take J4 onto A464, follow A442 to B4373. A wonderful castle-like building set in its own grounds. Rooms are well equipped and the restaurant serves delicious food and has a good selection of wines. Nearby places of interest include Chatsworth, Alton Towers, Warwick Castle and Cadbury World. Special package for bikers £26. per person inc. breakfast and dinner. Subject to availability. Must be booked through Central Reservations 0800 44 44 44. 47 BEDROOMS.

125 TELFORD

POST OFFICE HOUSE 6 The Square, Ironbridge, Telford, Shropshire, TF8 7AQ. Contact Janet Hunter Tel: 01952 433 201.
An elegant 18th century house overlooking the famous Iron Bridge where guests can expect a relaxed, warm and friendly atmosphere. Ideal for exploring the surrounding Shropshire countryside and its numerous attractions including Weston Park, Bridgnorth, Shrewsbury and the Severn Valley Railway. Visit the nearby Gorge Museum sites which provide an interesting and relaxing day out. 2 DOUBLE (1 EN SUITE), 1 FAMILY CHILDREN ALL.

Prices from £19 to £21

126 TEWKESBURY
TEWKESBURY ABBEY REFECTORY Church Street, Tewkesbury, Gloucestershire, GL20 5RZ. Tel: 01684 273 736.
Delicious homecooked meals and puddings available at this abbey refectory. Typical dishes include steak and kidney pie, lasagne and homemade salads. MON-SAT 10AM-5.30PM SUNDAY 10AM-4.30PM.

127 TEWKESBURY

CORNER COTTAGE Stow Road, Alderton, Tewkesbury, Gloucestershire, GL20 8NH. Contact Caroline & Keith Page Tel: 01242 620 630 & 0370 225 548.
An attractive family home that was originally a pair of farm cottages. Rooms are decorated in a cottage style and offer a comfortable and relaxing atmosphere with views of surrounding area. Cotswolds, Broadway and Tewkesbury are within easy reach. Nearby M5 gives easy access to Gloucester. Excellent eating places nearby. 1 SINGLE, 1 DOUBLE, 1 TWIN EN SUITE CHILDREN ALL.

Prices from £18 to £20

128 WALSALL
QUALITY HOTEL & SUITES 20 Wolverhampton Road West, Bentley, Walsall, Midlands, WS2 0BS. Tel: 01922 724 444 Fax: 01922 723 148.
Located on the M6 Junction 10. Guests can be assured of high quality accommodation. Leisure centre open to guests. Local attractions include the Black Country Museum (12 miles), NEC (19 miles) and Alton Towers (28 miles). Special package for bikers £26. per person inc. breakfast and dinner. Subject to availability. Must be booked through Central Reservations 0800 44 44 44. 155 BEDROOMS.

129 WANTAGE

THE OLD VICARAGE Letcombe Regis, Wantage, Oxfordshire, OX12 9JP. Contact Mrs G.F. Barton Tel & Fax: 01235 765827.
The old vicarage has a charming garden and is set in the pretty village of Letcombe Regis, 1 mile off the Ridgeway long distance walk. The accommodation is elegant and comfortable. It is in an ideal location for visiting The White Horse, Oxford, Blenheim and Bladon. 10 miles from junction 14 of the M4. Evening meals available nearby. Closed Christmas and New Year. 1 DOUBLE/TWIN EN SUITE, 1 SINGLE.

Prices from £22.50

130 WARWICK
44 High Street, Warwick, Warwickshire, CV34 4AX.
Contact Mrs E. Draisley. Tel: 01926 401 512 Fax: 01926 490 809.
Individual Georgian house in Warwick city centre set in peaceful location. Contains 2 guest suites with bedroom, sitting room, bathroom; both suites overlook the garden. The castle, a variety of museums and lots of restaurants are within easy reach. Your hostess can arrange for you to be collected at the station. 2 SUITES, ONE ON THE GROUND FLOOR CHILDREN ALL.

Prices from £25

131 WARWICK
CROFT GUEST HOUSE Haseley Knob, Warwick, Warwickshire, CV35 7NL.
Contact David & Patricia Clapp Tel & Fax: 01926 484 447
E.mail: croftguesthouse@compuserve.com.
Situated in the charming village of Haseley Knob, the Croft Guest House is a friendly family run guest house with wonderful flower gardens. Ideally located for visiting Warwick, Stratford-upon-Avon and Coventry or just relaxing in the comfortable rooms. Home produced eggs and jam as part of breakfast. Closed Christmas. FAMILIES, DOUBLE, TWINS, SINGLES, MOST EN SUITE CHILDREN WELCOME.

⊁ S   **Prices from £23 to £30**

132 WARWICK
QUALITY HOTEL Chesford Bridge, Kenilworth, Warwick, Warwickshire, CV8 2LN.
Tel: 01926 858 331 Fax: 01926 858 153.
From A46 take A452 to Leamington Spa. Traditional style surroundings and well equipped rooms. There are many facilities available including restaurant and bar, entertainment and fishing nearby. Attractions include the NEC, Warwick Castle and Kenilworth Castle. Special package for bikers £26. per person inc. breakfast and dinner. Subject to availability. Must be booked through Central Reservations 0800 44 44 44.
48 BEDROOMS.

𝍮 S ⸙

133 WELWYN
QUALITY HOTEL The Link, Welwyn, Hertfordshire, AL6 9XA.
Tel: 01438 716 911 Fax: 01438 714 065.
Located on Junction 6 A1 (M). Relax in comfortable surroundings where the atmosphere is informal and friendly. Well equipped rooms with TV. Mini gym available for guests. Places to visit include Knebworth House (5 miles), Hatfield House (9 miles) and London (22 miles). Special package for bikers £26. per person inc. breakfast and dinner. Subject to availability. Must be booked through Central Reservations 0800 44 44 44. 96 BEDROOMS.

𝍮 ⌨ 🕱 S ⸙

134 WOLVERHAMPTON
QUALITY HOTEL Penn Road, Wolverhampton, Midlands, WV3 0ER.
Tel: 01902 429 216 Fax: 01902 710 419.
From M6, take J13, A449 turn off. Relax in this attractively decorated hotel. Restaurant and bar offer cosy atmosphere in which to unwind and enjoy a range of food and drink. Leisure centre available. Places of interest include Alton Towers, Cadbury world, Sealife Centre Birmingham and the Severn Valley Railway. Special package for bikers £26. per person inc. breakfast and dinner. Subject to availability. Must be booked through Central Reservations 0800 44 44 44. 92 BEDROOMS.

𝍮 S ⸙

135 WOLVERHAMPTON
THE JUNCTION Holyhead Road, Wolverhampton, Midlands, WV7 3AN.
Tel: 01902 844911.
A large pub with a large selection of drinks to match including Carlsberg, Tetley, Guinness, Strongbow and Scrumpy. Food is also varied with English and Mexican dishes available. Food served weekdays 12 noon till 10pm, Sunday; 12 noon-8pm. MCC night held every Thursday. Beer garden with seating for 100.

S

136 WOLVERHAMPTON
THE HOLLY BUSH A449 Penn Road, Penn, Wolverhampton, WV4 4HU.
Contact Rod & Tash Tel: 01902 342 164.
Bikers are extended a warm welcome at this friendly pub. Drinks include Banks Bitter, original Largers, Irish Hop, Strongbow and Guinness. Delicious home cooked food served daily between 12 noon-3pm. Basket meals on Tuesday evening from 6pm onwards. Outdoor barbecue. Sunday evening is rock disco night. Function room available for up to 300 people. Outside seating area.

137 WOTTON-UNDER-EDGE

BEECH COTTAGE Southend, Wotton-Under-Edge, Gloucestershire, GL12 7PD. Contact Mrs Gloria Gomm Tel: 01453 545 771.
17th century cottage which offers spacious accommodation in 2 acres of grounds. Guests can expect a warm, friendly reception and comfortable rooms with view of the Cotswold escarpment. Lots of places to visit including Berkeley Castle, Dynham Park, Westonbirt and Wetland Trust. Wonderful home cooked breakfast with options for vegetarians. Closed December to February. 1 DOUBLE/FAMILY EN SUITE CHILDREN 7+.

Price £24 (min two nights)

1 BACONSTHORPE
MARGARET'S TEA ROOMS Chestnut Farm House, The Street, Baconsthorpe, Norfolk, NR25 6AB. Tel: 01263 577 614.
Located in the village of Baconsthorpe with easy access to the Norfolk coast, Holt, Sheringham and Cromer. Margaret's Tea Rooms are in a delightful 17th century flint farmhouse. Warm and cosy atmosphere. Home made cakes, pastries, scones, bread and jam. Menu that changes daily and offers a selection of pies, flans, coffee and walnut cake and bread pudding. EASTER TO NOVEMBER-WEDNESDAYS TO SUNDAYS 10.30AM-5PM CLOSED MONDAYS EXCEPT BANK HOLIDAYS. NOV TO EASTER SAT AND SUN ONLY; 11AM-4PM.

2 BURNHAM-ON-CROUCH
YE OLDE WHITE HART The Quay, Burnham On Crouch, Essex, CM0 8AS. Contact John Lewis Tel: 0161 782 106 Fax: 01621 782 106.
Overlooking the River Crouch, Ye Olde White Hart is a 17th century property that still retains some of its original features. Rooms are spacious and finely decorated and there is wonderful exposed brickwork and fireplaces throughout the hotel which give a cosy atmosphere. 18 BEDROOMS, 11 EN SUITE.

🅾 🆂   **Prices from £37 to £65**

3 BURY ST EDMUNDS
TWELVE ANGEL HILL 12 Angel Hill, Bury St Edmunds, Suffolk, IP33 1UZ. Contact John & Bernadette Clarke Tel: 01284 704 088 Fax: 01284 725 549.
Situated in a charming Georgian terrace, Twelve Angel Hill is a wonderfully decorated and furnished award winning hotel. Close by are Abbey Gardens and the Cathedral. Relax in the walled garden and enjoy the fresh air. 6 BEDROOMS, ALL EN SUITE.

🆂   💳 VISA   **Prices from £50.50 to £85**

4 BURY ST. EDMUNDS

CARGATE HOUSE Felsham Road, Bradfield St. George, Bury St. Edmunds, Suffolk, IP30 0AG. Contact Mr & Mrs R.J. Stimson Tel: 01284 386698 & 0802 213344.
Situated next to Bradfield Wood (site of special scientific interest), Cartgate House is a former farmhouse with an attractive garden in the heart of the Suffolk countryside. Close to the attractive towns of Lavenham and Long Melford. Also well located for Stanstead airports and Harwich ferry port. Ample secure parking. 1 DOUBLE, 1 FAMILY, BOTH EN SUITE, 1 SINGLE PRIVATE BATHROOM.

🅾 ✄ 🆂   **Prices from £17 to £20**

5 CAMBRIDGE
ASHTREES 128 Perne Road, Cambridge, CB1 3RR. Contact Mrs Hill. Tel & Fax: 01223 411 233.
Ashtrees is a small family run guest house with a small garden available for guests. Located on a main bus route the hotel is conveniently situated for the city centre and Addensbrooke Hospital. Closed first three weeks in January. 7 BEDROOMS, 3 EN SUITE.

🆂   💳 VISA   **Prices from £20 to £43**

6 CAMBRIDGE
ASSISI GUEST HOUSE 193 Cherry Hinton, Cambridge, CB1 4BX. Contact Julian
Tel: 01223 246 448 & 01223 211 466 Fax: 01223 412 900.
Assisi Guest House is an attractive Victorian family run guest house where bikers are very welcome. Spacious rooms which provide comfortable accommodation and all modern facilities including shower, telephone and a colour TV. Ideal for visiting the nearby city centre of Cambridge with its places of interest, shops, pubs and restaurants. Full English breakfast that will set you up for the day.
17 BEDROOMS, ALL EN SUITE.

Prices from £33 to £75

7 CAMBRIDGE
THE ORCHARD Mill Way, Grantchester, Cambridge CB3 9ND.
Tel: 01223 845 788.
The Orchard Tea Rooms are near to the river, the Meadows and Grantchester village and have been very popular from the 1890's onwards making them a local tourist attraction. Close by there are beautiful riverside walks and a punt hire available. There are a range of light lunches including sandwiches, jacket potatoes and quiche. Afternoon Tea menu includes scones with jam and cream and lovely home baked cakes. DAILY OPENING ALL YEAR- 10AM TO 6PM BUT TIMES MAY VARY ACCORDING TO SEASON.

8 CAMBRIDGE
THE SPREAD EAGLE 67 Lensfield Road, Cambridge CB2 1EN.
Tel: 01223 544 291.
Relax and enjoy good quality food and drink. Drinks include 7 Whitbread Beers plus Guest Beers. Food served all week 12 noon-2.30pm and 5pm-8pm. Bikers meeting every Thursday night.

9 CAMBRIDGE

THE OLD RECTORY High Street, Swaffham Bulbeck,
Cambridge CB5 0LX.
Contact Mrs J. Few-MacKay Tel: 01223 811986
Fax: 01223 812009.
The Old Rectory was formerly the home of Reverend Jenyns, the naturalist and tutor of Charles Darwin. It is a large Georgian house set in 3 acres of grounds with a mill stream. There is a friendly relaxed atmosphere at this traditionally furnished house on the outskirts of Cambridge. Close to Newmarket and Stansted. Harwich 50 miles. Closed Christmas. 2 DOUBLE (1 EN SUITE), 1 TWIN. CHILDREN 12+.

Prices from £22.50 to £30

10 CAMBRIDGE

DYKELANDS GUEST HOUSE 157 Mowbray Road, Cambridge, Cambridgeshire, CB1 4SP. Contact Paul & Alison Tweddell Tel: 01223 244300 Fax: 01223 566746.
In the heart of Cambridge, short distance from the city centre, Dykelands Guest House is situated on the Cambridge ring road. Well equipped bedrooms, two of which on the ground floor, guests' lounge and attractive garden. Credit cards accepted. 9 ROOMS, DOUBLE/TWIN/SINGLE/FAMILY, MOST EN SUITE.

Prices from £18.50 to £22

11 CHELMSFORD

25 WEST AVENUE Maylandsea, Chelmsford, Essex, CM3 6AE. Contact Mrs B. Clark Tel & Fax: 01621 740945.
The modern detached residence at 25 West Avenue has attractive, well equipped bedrooms. Few minutes walk from the river Blackwater, which offers many types of boating activities. Situated in an area with superb views of the countryside. Maldon and South Woodham Ferrers are the nearest towns, 8 miles away and Chelmsford is 16 miles. Closed Christmas. 1 TWIN, 1 DOUBLE. CHILDREN 3+.

Prices from £17 to £19

12 COLCHESTER

HAZEL OAK 28 Seaview Avenue, West Mersea, Colchester, Essex, CO5 8HE. Contact David & Ann Blackmore Tel & Fax: 01206 383030.
Family home situated in tree lined avenue leading to the beach, Hazel Oak offers comfortable ground floor accomm. on the Isle of Mersea, 9 miles from Colchester. The waterfront has two areas, one with fishing and sailing boats, the other a sand and shingle beach used by windsurfers and walkers. Norman castle and museum. Closed Christmas. 1 DOUBLE EN SUITE, 1 TWIN PRIVATE BATHROOM.

Prices from £20 to £22

13 COLCHESTER
THE PLOUGH INN Great Bentley, Colchester, Essex, CO7 8LA. Contact Hazel Woollard Tel: 01206 250563 Fax: 01206 252304.
Wednesday nights are a favourite meeting place for many bikers at this delightful spot in the middle of the lovely Essex countryside. Over 41 acres of unspoiled village green, claimed to be the biggest in England. Home cooking is the speciality. Free house with lovely oakwood bar, relaxing lounge and summertime beer garden.

14 COLCHESTER
THE FLAG, Colchester Road, Wivenhoe, Colchester, Essex CO7 9HS. Contact John Jarrold or Brian Mitchell. Tel: 01206 822830.
Public and saloon bar with home-cooked bar snacks. Pool room and dartboard available, juke box, fruit machine. Wide range of beers, lagers, wines, spirits. Bikers welcome, parking. 4 ROOMS AVAILABLE.

Prices from £25 to £35 + breakfast

15 COLCHESTER
THE WHEATSHEAF, 2 Queen Street, Castle Hedingham, Essex CO9 3EX. Contact Mrs Debbie White. Tel/Fax: 01787 460555. E-Mail: wheatsheaf@castleheddingham.freeserve.co.uk.
Licensed for children. Holds North Essex Harley Davidson Club meetings. Real ales, home-cooked bar snacks and full restaurant service. Extensive wine list. Warm welcome. Ample bike parking space available.

16 COLCHESTER
THE HOLE IN THE WALL, Balkerne Hill, Colchester, Essex CO3 3LA.
Contact Kristian Whitehead. Tel: 01206 760331.
Motorcyclists – come here and have a great night out. Wide range of beers, lagers and a very extensive range of wines, spirits and soft drinks. Ours is an extensive menu and seriously good food is served in the intimate, friendly and warm atmosphere of our restaurant.

17 COLCHESTER
THE FLYING FOX, 216 Harwich Road, Colchester, Essex CO4 3DE.
Contact Mr and Mrs Knights. Tel: 01206 500032.
Karaoke every other Friday, live music on Sundays. Good range of home-cooked bar food. Open all day. Wide range of beers, lagers, spirits and soft drinks.

18 COLCHESTER
THE BUNGALOW CAFE, 45-47 London Road, Marks Tey, Colchester, Essex CO6 1EB. Tel: 01206 210242.
The best bikers cafe in Essex. All day breakfast – the full monty. OPEN 6AM-9PM MONDAY TO THURSDAY, 6AM-5PM FRIDAY AND 7AM-3PM SATURDAY. WE ARE SITUATED NEXT TO RON PARKINSON MOTORCYCLES.

19 COLCHESTER
THE CAMBRIDGE ARMS, 54 Military Road, Colchester, Essex CO1 2AN.
Tel: 01206 500146.
Live bands Fridays and Saturdays. Open to 1am, buskers jam session. Sunday roast 1pm-6pm, wide selection of beers, wines and spirits.

20 CROMER

THE OLD BARN Cromer Road, West Runton, Cromer, Norfolk, NR27 9QT. Contact Mrs Karen Elliot Tel: 01263 838285.
Set in a picturesque village opposite a church, The Old Barn is a charming period house with character and warmth. Converted from the barn, overlooking an attractive secluded garden, the beamed drawing room makes a wonderful room in which to relax after dinner (evening meals by arrangement). Golf, horse riding, sailing and sandy beaches are all nearby. Private secure parking. Closed Christmas. 2 DOUBLE, 1 TWIN, ALL EN SUITE/PRIVATE. CHILDREN 12+.
🗍 ⊁ Ⓢ   **Price £24**

21 DANBURY
TEA ON THE GREEN 3 Eves Corner, Danbury, Essex, CM3 4QF.
Tel: 01245 226 616.
Tea on the Green is adjacent to Danbury village green and has good views of the surrounding National Trust Land. In summer, sit outside and enjoy the fresh air. Traditional Cream Tea comprises two large scones served warm with strawberry or home made preserve and whipped double cream and a pot of speciality tea all for just £3.20. Imaginative menu with delicious home made cakes such as Dutch apple cake, coffee and walnut cake and lemon sponge cake. MONDAYS TO FRIDAYS-8.30AM TO 5PM, SATURDAYS-10AM TO 5PM SUNDAYS-11AM TO 5PM, BANK HOLIDAYS-11AM TO 5PM.

22 DISS
HOLLYBANK High Street, Hopton, Diss, Norfolk, IP22 2QX.
Contact Sue & Tony Tomlinson Tel & Fax: 01953 688147.
Large modern home with tea/coffee facilities and TV in rooms. Lounge for residents and full "Norfolk" breakfast. Ideally situated for touring. Discount for stays of 3 days or longer. DOUBLE AND TWIN ROOMS.
⊙ Ⓢ
Prices from £20 to £30

23 EAST DEREHAM BARTLES LODGE, CHURCH FARM Church Street, Elsing, East Dereham, Norfolk, NR20 3EA. Contact Mrs Bartlett Tel: 01362 637177.
Rooms overlooking idyllic scenery of landscaped meadows and lakes. Perfect for touring or unwinding. Which Bed and Breakfast Guide recommended. Access for disabled. 7 BEDROOMS, ALL EN SUITE.
⊙ Ⓢ 🅿 VISA
Prices from £27 to £56

---

24 ELY
ELY CATHEDRAL REFECTORY The Chapter House, Ely, Cambridgeshire, CB7 4DN. Tel: 01353 660 346.
Situated at the West End of the Cathedral next to the shop, Ely Refectory is a cheerful coffee bar with friendly staff serving a range of food. Typical dishes: homemade soup, quiches and jacket potatoes and cathedral bread pudding. MON-SAT 9.30AM-4.30PM SUNDAY 12NOON-5PM. WINTER CLOSED AT 4PM.

25 ELY
HILL HOUSE FARM 9 Main Street, Coveney, Ely, Cambridgeshire, CB6 2DJ. Contact Mrs Hilary Nix Tel: 01353 778369.
Hill House Farm is set in peaceful surroundings in the small village of Coveney, 3 miles west of Ely. It is a Victorian farmhouse on an arable farm, the bedrooms having their own entrance and guests' lounge overlooking the surrounding countryside. Well located for touring Norfolk, Suffolk and Cambridgeshire. Easy access to Newmarket, Cambridge, Huntingdon and Peterborough. Closed Christmas. 1 TWIN, 2 DOUBLE, ALL EN SUITE. CHILDREN 12+.
⊙ ✗ Ⓢ
Prices from £22 to £24

26 ELY
QUEENSBERRY 196 Carter Street, Fordham, Ely, Cambridgeshire, CB7 5JU. Contact Mrs Jan Roper Tel: 01638 720916 Fax: 01638 720233.
Queensberry is a Georgian house set in large gardens on the edge of the village, just off the A14 on the main Ely to Newmarket A142. Ideal location to tour East Anglia including Newmarket, Cambridge, Ely and Bury St. Edmunds. Restaurants close by. Closed Christmas Day. 1 SINGLE, 1 TWIN, 1 DOUBLE EN SUITE.
⊙ ✗ Ⓢ
Prices from £20 to £25

---

27 FELIXSTOWE
CORNER HOUSE CAFE & TEA ROOM 47 Undercliff Road West, Felixstowe, Suffolk, IP11 8AH. Tel: 01394 283 939.
Corner House is a pleasant Tea Room opposite Leisure Centre and close to ferry, Languard Fort, beach and pier. Guests can choose from a varied menu with a wide selection of home baked cakes, scones and cherry shortbread. Freshly cooked meals inc. breakfast, fish and salads. Teas include Assam and Earl Grey. OPEN ALL YEAR ROUND FROM 9.30AM ONWARDS (CLOSING TIMES VARY ACCORDING TO SEASON) CLOSED MONDAYS EXCEPT BANK HOLIDAYS AND 3 WEEKS OVER CHRISTMAS AND NEW YEAR.

22 FINCHINGFIELD
JEMIMA'S TEA ROOMS The Green, Finchingfield, Essex, CM7 4JX. Tel: 01371 810 605.
Jemima's Tea Rooms overlook the village green and a pond. A 17th century building with traditional atmosphere and original features. The Tea Room caters for coach parties and individuals and the Cream Tea offers home-made scones and cakes and a choice of teas. A menu serving breakfast, snacks and light lunches. Two course carvery lunch on Sundays. SUMMER: MONDAYS TO FRIDAYS 10AM-5.30PM, WEEKENDS 10AM-6PM WINTER; MONDAYS TO FRIDAYS 10AM TO 4PM, WEEKENDS 10AM TO 5PM.

23 GORLESTON ON SEA

WHITE LION INN 13 Cliff Hill, Gorleston on Sea, Norfolk, NR31 6DQ. Contact Mr Lawrie Tel: 01493 662118 Fax: 01493 309980.
An excellent view of the harbour from this inn which is open from 11am- 3pm and 6pm - 11pm on weekdays, 11am-11pm on Saturday, 12 noon-4pm and 7pm-10:30pm on Sunday. Private car park service. B&B. 12 BEDROOMS, ALL EN SUITE.

Prices from £20

24 GREAT DUNMOW
STARR Market Place, Great Dunmow, Essex, CM6 1AX.
Contact Brian Jones Tel: 01371 874321 Fax: 01371 876337.
Established in 1980, Starr Restaurant boasts eight lovely bedrooms overlooking the rear courtyard. Highly reputable for fine food and wine served in beautiful surroundings. Closed 1-7 Jan. 8 BEDROOMS, ALL EN SUITE.

Prices from £60 to £90

25 GREAT YARMOUTH
THE WHITE SWAN Great Yarmouth, Norfolk, NR30 1PU.
Contact Gary Jarvice Tel: 01493 842 027.
Beer menu includes Fosters, Stella, Guinness and John Smiths as well as many others. Good food served Monday-Sunday Noon-2.30pm and 4.30pm-9pm. MCC meetings every Friday.

26 GREAT YARMOUTH

BARNARD HOUSE 2 Barnard Crescent, Great Yarmouth, Norfolk, NR30 4DR. Contact Jill Norris
Tel: 01493 855139 Fax: 01493 843143.
Barnard House is a family home in a residential area near the sea, racecourse, golf links and Norfolk Broads. Guests can relax in the garden or conservatory, or in winter, relax in front of an open fire. Pleasure Wood Hills theme park is a short journey away. Ideal place to stay for business or pleasure. Closed Christmas and New Year. 2 DOUBLE EN SUITE, 1 FAMILY PRIVATE SHOWER ROOM.

Prices from £18 to £20

27 HALSTEAD
TOWNSFORD MILL BED & BREAKFAST Mill House,
The Causeway, Halstead, Essex, CO9 1ET.
Contact Mrs G. Stuckey Tel: 01787 474451.
Mill House is a listed 18th C town house in the market town of Halstead. Adjoining the house is Townsford Mill, originally owned by the Courtauld's family which produced Queen Victoria's mourning gown. The Mill is one of the largest antique centres in the east of England. Pubs and restaurants nearby, and within local travelling distance of Flatford Mill, Hedingham Castle, Colne Valley and is only 30 minutes from Stanstead Airport. 3 DOUBLE EN SUITE (1 CAN BE TWIN). CHILDREN 12+.

Prices from £30 to £48

28 HALSTEAD
KENT HOUSE Church Street, Great Maplestead, Halstead, Essex, CO9 2RQ.
Contact Mrs Eileen Archer. Tel: 01787 460787 & 0498 656822 Fax: 01787 463515.
SUDBURY 7m. The 200 year old Kent House was once a pub in the pretty village in which it is situated, and has been converted into a spacious family home. The Essex countryside, popular with artists, offers pleasant walks and places of interest. Halstead is within 2 miles and Chelmsford, Cambridge and Colchester are all within easy travelling distance. Other local attractions include the Round church at Little Maplestead, the Castle and the Old Colne Railway. Full English Breakfast as well as Continental and Vegetarian versions are available. 2 DOUBLE,1 TWIN, ALL EN SUITE. CHILDREN 12+.

⬛ ⤬ Ⓢ   **Prices from £20 to £25**

29 HATFIELD PEVEREL
THE WICK Terlinghall Road, Hatfield Peverel, Essex, CM3 2EZ.
Contact Mrs Linda Tritton Tel: 01245 380705 & 0976 246082.
CHELMSFORD 5m. The Wick is a Grade II listed 16th century farmhouse in a pleasant rural setting. Large garden, duck ponds and stream. Three attractive, comfortable bedrooms, 1 single, 2 twin with washbasin, sharing large bathroom. Drawing room with log fire. Delicious home-cooked evening meals available on request. Easy access to London, Suffolk and east coast ports. 2 TWIN, 1 SINGLE, PRIVATE FACILITIES AVAILABLE. CHILDREN 10+.

⬛ ⤬   **Prices from £21 to £25**

30 HEACHAM
MILLERS COTTAGE TEA ROOM Caley Mill, Heacham, nr. Kings Lynn,
Norfolk, PE31 7JE. Tel: 01485 570384.
Built as a grain mill in the 19th century and situated on a lavender farm. Lavender theme prevails with lavender tea, lavender scones and lavender lemon sponge available. Adjoining gift shop provides home-made goods to take home.

31 HODDESDON
RYE HOUSE STADIUM Hoddesdon, Hertfordshire, EN11 OE11.
Contact Will Williams Tel: 01992 471 006.
The facilities include cafe, restaurant, video screens and a 500m floodlit track on which we run mini-bikes on a hire and ride basis on Fridays. All motorcyclists welcome.

32 IPSWICH

HIGHFIELD Holbrook, Ipswich, Suffolk, IP9 2RA.
Contact Brian & Sally Morris Tel: 01473 328250.
Highfield has wonderful views of the Stour Valley. Each room has tea/coffee facilities, TV & radio. Walking can be enjoyed in the area around Stour Estuary and Shorley Peninsula has sailing, windsurfing and birdwatching. Hearty English or continental breakfast. 5 miles from Ipswich. Colchester, Felixstowe, Harwich are 14 miles. Evening meals by request. 2 DOUBLE, 1 DOUBLE/TWIN, ALL EN SUITE OR WITH PRIVATE BATHROOM. NO CHILDREN.

⤬   **Prices from £37 to £43**

33 MANNINGTREE

ALDHAMS Bromley Road, Lawford, Manningtree, Essex, CO11 2NE. Contact Mrs C. McEwen
Tel & Fax: 01206 393210 E.mail: coral.mcewen@which.net.
Set in 3 acres of grounds, Aldhams is a converted Queen Anne farmhouse a few minutes from Manningtree and Dedham. Norman castle and leisure centre at Colchester are 10 miles away. Ideally located for travel to the continent, Harwich and ferry port are 20 minutes away. Single guests welcome. Closed Christmas. 1 DOUBLE, 1 TWIN, BOTH EN SUITE, 1 DOUBLE/TWIN.
                                                    Prices from £20 to £22.50

34 NORWICH
BRICKMAKERS PUB 496 Sprowston Road, Norwich, Norfolk, NR3 4OY.
Contact Mandy & Clive Tel: 01603 441 118 Fax: 01603 441 493.
Brickmakers has been awarded "The Motorcycle Friendly Award" and the pub certainly lives up to its reputation. There is a wide selection of drinks and food is served all day. Live music of all kinds here, including rock and blues music.

35 NORWICH
CATHEDRAL RESTAURANT 62 The Close, Norwich, NR1 4EH.
Tel: 01603 471 066 Fax: 01603 766 032.
Located on the first floor of the Monastic Cloisters, Cathedral Restaurant offers a warm, friendly welcome and a wide variety of light lunches and snacks. In summer sit outside on the terrace and enjoy the fresh air. Typical snacks include homemade soups, rolls and sandwiches, jacket potatoes and macaroni and vegetable bake. MON-SAT 10AM-4.30PM SUNDAY CLOSED.

36 NORWICH
MANCROFT OCTAGON Hay Hill, Norwich, . Tel: 01603 610 443.
Part of the beautiful medieval church of St Peter Mancroft and situated in the city centre. Friendly staff serve a range of snacks and refreshments including freshly made rolls and sandwiches, scones and homemade cakes. MON-FRI 10AM-3PM (WINTER CLOSED AT 3PM) SATURDAY & SUNDAY CLOSED.

37 NORWICH
QUALITY HOTEL 2 Barnard Road, Bowthorpe, Norwich, Norfolk, NR5 9JB.
Tel: 01603 741 161 Fax: 01603 741 500.
Located on the A47 to A1074. Hotel with many facilities including leisure centre with indoor swimming pool. Nearby places of interest include Norwich Castle, Norwich Theatre or take a trip out to Great Yarmouth (18 miles). Special package for bikers £26. per person inc. breakfast and dinner. Subject to availability. Must be booked through Central Reservations 0800 44 44 44. 80 BEDROOMS.

38 PETERBOROUGH
PETERBOROUGH CATHEDRAL REFECTORY 24 Minster Precincts, Peterborough, PE1 1XZ. Tel: 01733 555 098 Fax: 01733 552 465.
Friendly coffee shop adjacent to the magnificent cathedral. Choice of light lunches and sandwiches including jacket potatoes, soup of the day with roll and butter and ploughman's lunch. Average lunch £3. MON-SAT 10AM-4PM SUNDAY CLOSED.

SHAD

Explore the four corners

STYLISH, ROBUST CASES FOR
COMMUTING, SPORTS AND TOURING

SH44

The SH44 is a stylish 44 litre capacity topcase that comfortably holds two helmets. It can be complemented with any of the Shad SH90 model versions to make a really spacious three model set. This topcase can be fitted on any of the Shad fittings and comes with an optional brake light unit.

* Other colour options available

SH48

The SH48, the latest product in the Shad range, is a 48 litre capacity topcase that comprises a number of features including a double locking system, two-way safety lock, a double profile rubber seal (for 100% waterproofing), an extra wide reflective strip along with an optional brake light unit.
* Other colour options available

SH30

The SH30 is a topcase with an internal volume of 30 litres. It has been designed as equipment for scooters and small motorcycles in general, even in those models that do not have a carrier, or any element which permits an easy fastening
* Other colour options available

SH25

The SH25, with an internal volume of 25 litres, has been designed for scooters and small motorcycles. Capacity for one integral helmet and other equipment.
Adaptable for the entire range of Shad products.

* Other colour options available

SHAD

39 RETTENDON
THE WHEATSHEAF Main Road, Rettendon, Essex, CM3 8DY. Tel: 01245 400 244.
There is always something going on for Bikers in this lovely pub set in 6 acres of gardens. A Ridleys Pub with 3 Ales always on tap, Rumpus and a one special. Food is served between 11.30am-2.30pm weekdays, 11.30-10pm Saturdays and 12-9.30pm on Sundays.

40 SAXMUNDHAM

DARSHAM OLD HALL Darsham, Saxmundham, Suffolk, IP17 3PR. Contact Mr & Mrs Padfield Tel: 01728 668514.
Darsham Old Hall dates back to 1012 and is supposedly the oldest house in Suffolk. Old beams, timber doors and a galleried hall. Guests rooms are well equipped, overlooking the well kept garden which is part of a 227 acre arable farm. Close to Minsmere Bird Sanctuary, Snape Maltings and Suffolk coast. Pubs and restaurants nearby. 3 DOUBLE, 1 TWIN, ALL EN SUITE OR PRIVATE FACILITIES.

Prices from £40 to £50

41 SOUTH WALSHAM

THE COTTAGES Broad Lane, Pilson Green, South Walsham, Norwich, NR13 6EE. Contact Sandra Jones Tel: 0160 270771 & 01603 270209.
The Cottages are based on a working farm in a quiet country village near the Broads. The rooms have tea and coffee facilities, hand basins and colour television. There is a choice of breakfast menu and the guests' own sitting room with a colour television. There is a secure place for all motorbikes and clothing. 1 DOUBLE, 1 TWIN WITH PRIVATE BATHROOM.

Prices from £16 to £20

42 SUDBURY

COX HILL HOUSE Boxford, Sudbury, Suffolk, CO10 5JG. Contact Mr & Mrs Havard-Davies Tel: 01787 210449.
Cox Hill House overlooks the village and has views over countryside immortalised by Constable's paintings. Finely furnished and decorated. Lavenham, Dedham, Kersey and Sudbury. Harwich, Felixstowe and Stanstead within 1 hour away. 1 TWIN, 1 DOUBLE, 1 GROUND FLOOR TWIN/DOUBLE, ALL EN SUITE OR PRIVATE FACILITIES. CHILDREN 12+.

Prices from £20 to £24

43 THAXTED

PIGGOT'S MILL Watling Lane, Thaxted, Essex, CM6 2QY. Contact Gillian Hingston Tel: 01371 830379 Fax: 01371 831309.
Farmhouse providing excellent accommodation and breakfasts, Piggot's Mill stands in the medieval village of Thaxted. Close to a variety of pubs and restaurants. Within easy reach of the M11 and Stanstead Airport (7 miles). 1 TWIN, 1 DOUBLE, BOTH EN SUITE ON THE GROUND FLOOR.

Prices from £23 to £27

44 THETFORD

WHITE HALL Carbrooke, nr. Watton, Thetford, Norfolk IP25 6SG. Contact Mrs Carr Tel: 01953 885950 Fax: 01953 884420.
White Hall stands in 3 acres of grounds within the Breckland countryside. It is a listed Georgian home with spacious accommodation. Separate drawing and dining rooms for guests. The area offers many places of local interest and is within easy reach of Norwich, Sandringham and the coast. Good local pubs and restaurants. 1 DOUBLE (1 EN SUITE), 1 TWIN.

Prices from £20 to £23

45 THETFORD
COMFORT INN Thetford Road, Northwold, Thetford, Norfolk, IP26 5LQ.
Tel: 01366 728 888 Fax: 01366 727 121.
Located on the M11 Junction 9 to A11 to A134. Comfort Inn is situated in own grounds with car park, gardens and pond. Rooms well equipped with cable TV. Thetford Forest 3 miles, Royal Sandringham 18 miles, Newmarket races 30 miles. Special package for bikers £26. per person inc. breakfast and dinner. Subject to availability. Must be booked through Central Reservations 0800 44 44 44. 34 BEDROOMS.

46 WATERBEACH
GOOSE HALL FARM Ely Road, Waterbeach, Cambridgeshire, CB5 9PG.
Contact Mrs Sylvia Lock Tel & Fax: 01223 860235.
Goose Hall Farm situated off the A10 offers easy access to Cambridge, Ely and Newmarket. It is a lovely, modern farmhouse with ground floor bedrooms overlooking gardens and meadow. A small lake provides the opportunity for bird watching, fishing or a relaxing walk. The M11 is 6 miles away. Closed Christmas and New Year. 4 ROOMS, TWIN/DOUBLE/FAMILY, SOME EN SUITE. CHILDREN 5+. **Prices from £19 to £21**

47 WELLS-NEXT-THE-SEA
THE ANCIENT HOUSE TEA ROOMS Holkham, Wells-next-the-Sea, Norfolk,
NR23 1AB. Tel: 01328 711285.
Easy access to Holkham Hall Estate and Holkham beach. Tea Rooms are located in a building dating back to 1680. Enjoy the choice of quality home-made snacks or more substantial main meals.

48 WELLS-NEXT-THE-SEA
THE STABLES RESTAURANT Holkham, Wells-Next-The-Sea, Norfolk, NR23 1AB.
Tel: 01328 711648.
Set in stable block of Holkham Hall, the restaurant enjoys a beautiful location. Food is home made and a varied menu is available. Speciality teas and coffees. In warm weather food can be consumed on the lawn.

49 WINTERTON-ON-SEA

TOWER COTTAGE Black Street, Winterton-on-Sea, Norfolk, NR9 4AP. Contact Alan & Muriel Webster Tel: 01493 394053.
Opposite a 13th century church in a peaceful village, the charming flint cottage has 3 well equipped bedrooms, 2 on the ground floor overlooking the garden and one is en suite with its own entrance. Home made preserves and seasonal fruits are served at breakfast amongst the grapevines or in the conservatory during the summer. Sandy beach, pub serving good food a few minutes walk away. Norfolk Broads are 2 miles and Norwich 19 miles away. 1 DOUBLE EN SUITE + SITTING ROOM IN CONVERTED BARN, 1 DOUBLE, 1 TWIN. CHILDREN 8+.
Prices from £18 to £20

50 WYMONDHAM

HOME FARM Morley, Wymondham, Norfolk, NR18 9SU.
Contact Mrs M. Morter Tel: 01953 602581.
Home Farm is set in 4 acres of garden and grounds in countryside, 1/2 mile from A11 London to Norwich road. 15 minutes from Snetterton motor racing track, 20 mins from Norwich, 45 mins from Norfolk Broads. Wymondham and Attenborough 3 miles away. Spacious accommodation with inglenook fireplace in the dining room. Closed Christmas. 2 DOUBLE, 1 SINGLE. CHILDREN 5+.
Prices from £17 to £18

2 ASHBOURNE

DOG & PARTRIDGE Swinscoe, Ashbourne, Derbyshire, DE6 2HS. Contact Mrs Stelfox
Tel: 01335 343 183 Fax: 01335 342 742.
Enjoy peaceful and scenic surroundings at this beautifully located country inn. There is a good selection of drinks and food available at the bar with real ales and an imaginative menu. Children and pets welcome. 30 BEDROOMS, 28 EN SUITE, CAMPING ALSO AVAILABLE.

🔟 Ⓢ
Prices from £30 to £70

---

3 ASHBOURNE

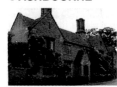

OLDFIELD HOUSE Snelston, Ashbourne, Derbyshire, DE6 2EN. Contact Mrs Jarvis Tel: 01335 324510 Fax: 01335 324113.
ASHBOURNE 3m. Oldfield House is a listed Tudor style house that dates from the 1840's. It is set in the Dove Valley in the small, tranquil village of Snelston 3 miles from the market town of Ashbourne. It is an elegantly furnished house with a relaxing drawing room and rose garden. Easy access to the Peak District National Park and 15 minutes from Alton Towers. Evening meals by arrangement. Closed Christmas and New Year. 1 DOUBLE (+ EXTRA TWIN), PRIVATE BATHROOM.

⚒
Prices from £25

---

4 ASTON-ON-TRENT
THE WHITE HART 21 Derby Road, Aston-on-Trent, Derbyshire, DE73 2AF.
Tel: 01332 792 264.
Drinks served include Pedigree, Marsdens Smooth Brew and many others. BSA Owners Club meets here Wednesdays – all welcome.

---

5 BAKEWELL

HADDON HOUSE FARM Bakewell, Derbyshire, DE45 1BN. Contact Mrs Marilyn Nichols
Tel: 01629 814 024 Fax: 01629 812 759.
Situated in a charming valley, Haddon House is on the ancient Haddon Hall Estate and has an award winning sheep and dairy farm. Rooms are decorated to a high standard and have views over the nearby hills. Attractions include Chatsworth House and fishing on River Wye. Hearty breakfasts prepared on Aga. 1 DOUBLE/TWIN PRIVATE, 1 DOUBLE EN SUITE WITH CONNECTING SINGLE CHILDREN WELCOME.

⚒ Ⓢ
Prices from £30 to £35

not all full stops look the same...

Synonymous with brakes since the
first mechanically propelled vehicles
A pedigree going back as far as 1906

From scooter to superbike, Mini car to
Formula 1 Grand Prix, a brake pad
for all reasons and seasons

What's stopping you?

T01522 888444 **F**01522 888400 **E**lintektl@compuserve.com

6 BASLOW
GOOSE GREEN TEA ROOMS Nether End, Baslow, Derbyshire, DE45 1SR.
Tel: 01246 583000.
Goose Green Tea Rooms overlook Baslow's Goose Green and are next to the village car park. The tea room live up to their name with the predominately green decor, the selection goosey gifts and a large selection of limited edition Derbyshire pictures. Highly recommended by the good cafe guide 1988 and ITV featured the tea-rooms in the series Peak Practice. OPEN DAILY ALL YEAR ROUND: WEEKDAYS - 9:30 TO 5PM WEEKENDS - 9:30AM TO 5:30PM.

7 BELPER

SHOTTLE HALL Shottle, Belper, Derbyshire, DE56 2EB.
Contact Mr Matthews Tel: 01773 550203 Fax: 01773 550276.
Built circa 1850 and set in three acres of grounds in the picturesque Ecclebourne Valley, Shottle Hall is ideally situated for touring the spectacular Derbyshire countryside. Closed Nov. - Christmas. 10 BEDROOMS SINGLES AND DOUBLES, 6 EN SUITE.
🖩 Ⓢ

Prices from £28 to £68

8 BOSTON
COMFORT INN Donington Road, Bicker Bar, Boston, Lincolnshire, PE20 3AN. Tel:
01205 820 118 Fax: 01205 820 228 E.mail: admin@gb607.u-net.com.
Located on Junction of A17/A52. Enjoy high quality accommodation with restaurant and bar facilities offering a good range of food and drink at reasonable prices. Rooms are decorated to a high standard and have good facilities. Leisure centre open to guests. Visit the butterfly/falconry park (16 miles) or Arnhem Museum. Special package for bikers £26. per person inc. breakfast and dinner. Subject to availability. Must be booked through Central Reservations 0800 44 44 44.
🍷 ☆ ♿ Ⓢ

9 BRAILSFORD
THE ROSE & CROWN Main Road, Brailsford, Derbyshire, DE6 3DA.
Contact Steve & Tracy Tel: 01335 340 242.
Enjoy a range of beers including Burtonwood House, Carling, Stella and Dry Blackthorn. Food served every day of the week Noon-2.30pm, Tuesday-Sunday 4pm-9pm. Bikers very welcome.

10 BURTON-UPON-TRENT

WATERSIDE Blacksmiths Lane, Newton Solney, Burton upon Trent, Staffordshire, DE15 0SD. Contact Mrs P. Ratcliffe
Tel & Fax: 01283 702 336.
On the outskirts of Newton Solney, Waterside is an attractive 18th C Georgian farmhouse set in 3/4 acres of mature gardens. Ideal for visiting Alton Towers, Calke Abbey, Kedleston Hall, Melbourne Hall, Sudbury Hall and Donington Park Racing Circuit. M1 and M42 are nearby. Evening meals available by prior arrangement. 1 DOUBLE, 1 TWIN, 1 SINGLE, ALL PRIVATE/EN SUITE FACILITIES CHILDREN WELCOME.
✄

Prices from £22 to £25

11 BUXTON
BUXTONS VICTORIAN GUEST HOUSE 3a Broad Walk, Buxton, Derbyshire, SK17 6JE. Contact Michael & Diane Hames. Tel: 01298 78759.
A unique home built in 1860 for the Duke of Devonshire and situated on a quiet promenade with views of the Pavillion Gardens and Opera house. En suite bedrooms are decorated to a high standard and have TV and tea/coffee facilities. Ideally located for exploring the Peak District and its places of outstanding natural beauty. Visit many nearby stately homes and gardens. Open at Christmas. 3 DOUBLE, 2 TWIN, 2 FAMILY, ALL EN SUITE CHILDREN WELCOME.

⊁ S   **Prices from £21 to £25**

---

12 CHESTER

THE MOUNT Higher Kinnerton, Chester, Cheshire, CH4 9BQ. Contact Mrs J. Major Tel & Fax: 01244 660 275.
Situated within walking distance of Kinnerton village The Mount is an attractive Victorian house set in 3 acres of lovely gardens, open under the National Garden Scheme. Ideally located to explore Cheshire, Shropshire and north Wales. Manchester and Liverpool are also just an hour away. Enjoy an evening meal in one of the pubs at nearby Kinnerton village. 1 KING-SIZE DOUBLE, 1 TWIN, 1 SINGLE, ALL EN SUITE CHILDREN 12+.

⊡ ⊁ S   **Prices from £23 to £30**

---

13 CHESTER

GOLBORNE MANOR Platts Lane, Hatton Heath, Chester, Cheshire, CH3 9AN. Contact Mrs Ann Ikin
Tel: 01829 770 310 & 0374 695 268 Fax: 01829 770 370.
Golborne Manor is a 19th century Manor house situated in a peaceful rural area and set in over 3 acres of garden and grounds. The historic Chester (10 minutes), Manchester and Liverpool (1 hours drive) mean that visitors will never run out of things to do. Unwind in spacious accommodation where there is table tennis and a snooker table available. Good pubs and restaurants close by. 1 TWIN (PRIVATE), 1 FAMILY (EN SUITE SHOWER), 1 DOUBLE EN SUITE CHILDREN WELCOME.

⊡ ⊁ S   **Prices from £30 to £35**

---

14 CHESTER
THE BEEHIVE HOTEL 15 Holle Road, Flockers Brook, Chester, Cheshire, CH2 3NH. Tel: 01244 354 091.
Lots of drinks available including Worthingtons, Stones, Bass Mild, Guinness and Dry Blackthorn. Bar snacks available with food served Monday-Saturday between 11am and 11pm and Sunday; 11am-10.30pm. Entertainment with live bands every Saturday night and pool and snooker tables. Bikers welcome.

---

15 CHESTER
REFECTORY RESTAURANT Chester Cathedral, Chester, Cheshire CH1 2HU. Tel: 01244 313 156.
A 13th century Refectory that used to be the monks' dining hall. The Refectory offers a wide range of food and drink including chicken curry, rice, salad and vegetable lasagne. MONDAY-SATURDAY 9.30-5PM SUNDAY CLOSED.

16 CHESTER

STONE VILLA 3 Stone Place, Hoole Road, Chester, Cheshire, CH2 3NR. Contact David & Brenda Pow Tel: 01244 345 014.
Situated in a quiet cul-de-sac, Stone Villa offers high standards of accommodation and a hospitable welcome. Located in the historic Roman City of Chester with just under a mile to the city centre and a few minutes from the station. Chester offers great shopping facilities and lovely waterside walks. Manchester and Liverpool 1 hours drive. Closed Christmas. 10 ROOMS-TWIN/DOUBLE/SINGLE, ALL EN SUITE CHILDREN ALL.

⌾ ✕ [S]   **Prices from £26 to £31**

17 CHESTER

FIRBANK 64 Tarvin Road, Littleton, Chester, Cheshire, CH3 7DF. Contact Mrs Sue Shambler
Tel: 01244 335 644 Fax: 01244 332 068.
A lovely red brick Victorian house set in attractive gardens with walled courtyard. Period style spacious rooms to unwind and relax in and guests' lounge with open fire, books and piano. Additional self contained coach house also available for bed and breakfast. Nearby Chester offers entertainment and good eating and drinking places. Closed Christmas. 2 KING-SIZE DOUBLE EN SUITE, 1 TWIN EN SUITE CHILDREN NONE.

⌾ ✕ [S]   **Prices from £20 to £25**

18 CHESTER
COTTON FARMHOUSE Cotton Edmunds, Chester, CH3 7PT. Contact Mrs Hill
Tel: 01244 336 699 Fax: 01244 336 699.
Spacious house set in quiet location deep in the Cheshire countryside. Recently renovated, all rooms are comfortably furnished and all have TV, central heating and tea and coffee making facilities. Only a few miles from the historic Roman Chester where there are riverside walks available. Closed Christmas. 3 BEDROOMS, ALL EN SUITE.

⌾ [S]   **Prices from £24 to £48**

19 CHESTER
QUALITY HOTEL Berwick Road, Little Sutton, Chester, L66 4PS. Tel: 0151 339 5121
Fax: 0151 339 3214 E.mail: admin@gb066.u-net.com.
Located on the M53 J5 to A41, A550 turn off. Attractive accommodation in good location. Enjoy a range of facilities including access to the leisure centre. Local places of interest include Chester Zoo, Blue Planet Aquarium and Chester Megabowl. Special package for bikers £26. per person inc. breakfast and dinner. Subject to availability. Must be booked through Central Reservations 0800 44 44 44. 53 BEDROOMS.

🍷 ✳ [S]

20 CHESTER
COMFORT INN Hoole Road, Chester, Cheshire, CH2 3NL.
Tel: 01244 327 542 Fax: 01244 344 889.
Located on the M53 junction 12, A56 towards city centre. High quality accommodation with many home comforts. Rooms have all facilities available including cable TV and tea/coffee facilities. Nearby attractions include Chester Cathedral, Chester Zoo, the River Dee and Wales. Special package for bikers £26. per person inc. breakfast and dinner. Subject to availability. Must be booked through Central Reservations 0800 44 44 44. 31 BEDROOMS.

[S]

21 CHESTERFIELD
THE SOMERSET HOUSE 1 Top Road, Calow, Chesterfield, Derbyshire.
Tel: 01246 278 225.
Bikers can expect a warm welcome at this friendly pub. Food served lunch times and evenings. Drinks include John Smiths, Caffreys and Stones. Juke box plays songs from all decades. Sky TV and pool table.

22 CLEETHORPES
MARPLES TEA ROOMS 6 Seaview Street, Cleethorpes, Lincolnshire, DN35 8EZ.
Tel: 01472 697 188.
Marples Tea Rooms are situated on Seaview Street and are Miss Marple themed. Traditional surroundings and high levels of customer service. Marples Full Afternoon Tea is made up of freshly made sandwiches, scone with whipped cream and preserve, a choice of sweet and a pot of tea. Freshly made scones and cakes, jams, preserves, chutneys and hand made chocolates. Freshly ground coffee and a wide selection of teas including Assam, Ceylon, China, Darjeeling and Earl Grey as well as other speciality teas. MONDAYS TO FRIDAYS-9AM TO 4.30PM; SATURDAYS 9AM TO 5PM SUNDAYS; 9.30AM TO 5PM.

23 DERBY
SERGEANT PEPPERS Burton Road, Derby.
Contact Ronnie & Dave. Tel: 01332 344 732.
Reasonably priced food and drink served at this biker friendly pub. Lunch and evening meal. Rock band Friday and Saturday nights and Jam nights.

24 DERBY
JOUNTY FARMER Kedleston Road, Derby, Derbyshire, DE22 1FZ.
Contact Nigel & Sandra Tel: 01332 292 312.
A whole range of beverages such as Marstons Pedigree, Banks Bitter, Banks No 9, Guinness and Strongbow Cider. Delicious meals and snacks served between 5-9pm Thursday, Friday and Saturday and 4-9pm Wednesday. Lunch 12-2pm. MCC meets every Wednesday at 8pm.

25 DERBY
MELBOURNE HALL TEA ROOMS Blackwell Lane, Melbourne, Derby,
Derbyshire, DE73 1EN. Tel: 01332 864 224.
Melbourne Hall Tea Rooms are located in the grounds of Melbourne Hall, close to the craft centre and the lake. This early 18th century Tea Room used to be the wash/bake house of the Hall. Set tea available for parties at £4.25 a head which consists of assorted sandwiches, scones, jam, a home-made cake and unlimited tea. Smaller tea consisting of two scones with jam, cream and a pot of tea. Teas served include Ceylon and Earl Grey. TUESDAYS TO SUNDAYS-11AM TO 5PM CLOSED ON MONDAYS RESTRICTED OPENING TIMES IN JANUARY AND FEBRUARY.

6 DERBY
ALEXANDRA HOTEL 203 Siddals Road, Derby, Derbyshire, DE1 2QE.
Tel: 01332 293993.
Each room has tea/coffee making facilities and a television. 4 TWIN ROOMS ALL EN SUITE.

Prices from £25 to £35

27 FRODSHAM
THE COTTAGE TEA SHOP 121 Main Street, Frodsham, Cheshire, WA6 7AF.
Tel: 01928 733673.
Charming surroundings with low beamed ceiling, lace tablecloths, bone china and fresh flowers and wonderful home cooked food. Cream Tea comprises of a choice of one or two freshly baked scones, jam, cream and tea or coffee. Afternoon Tea offers a choice of sandwich, a scone and a slice of cake. Teas on offer include Assam, Darjeeling and Earl Grey. Hot and cold meals available including hot pot, quiche and pasta. Children welcome here with colouring books available on request. DAILY - 10AM TO 4:30PM CLOSED SUNDAYS.

28 GEDLING
THE GREY GOOSE Arnold Lane, Gedling, Nottinghamshire. Tel: 0115 987 1335.
The "grandaddy" of all biker pubs where there is a friendly service and a range of drinks and snacks. Function room available for hire.

29 HARTINGTON
CHARLES COTTON HOTEL Hartington, Derbyshire, SK17 0AL. Contact Mrs Stelfox
Tel: 01298 84229.

Prices from £14 to £70

30 HELMSHORE
THE WILLOWS 41 Cherry Tree Way, Helmshore, Rossendale, BB4 4JZ.
Contact Lavinia Tod Tel: 01706 212698.
This cosy establishment promises to be a home from home for the guests staying in it. Evening meals are available on request and rooms have full facilities. TWIN ROOM, DOUBLE ROOM, BOTH EN-SUITE.

Prices from £18

31 HIGH PEAK
COTE BANK FARM Buxworth, Whaley Bridge, High Peak, Derbyshire, SK23 7NP.
Contact Mrs Pamela Broadhurst
Tel & Fax: 01663 750 566 E.mail: cotebank@binternet.com.
BUXTON 7m. A charming Victorian farmhouse with superb views of the Peak District. Relax in the comfortable rooms or the peaceful country garden and curl up by the log fire on chilly evenings. Enjoy excellent home cooked breakfasts. Lyme Park and Chatsworth House are well worth a visit. Good pubs a mile away. Closed December to February inclusive. 2 DOUBLE, 1 TWIN, ALL EN SUITE CHILDREN 6+.

Prices from £20 to £28

32 HOPE VALLEY
EYAM TEA ROOMS The Square, Eyam, Hope Valley, Derbyshire, S32 5RB. Tel: 01433 631274.

The Tea Rooms are set in the village square and exude olde worlde charm and inside the deceptively spacious establishment is a grand piano and a selection of antiques for sale. The Eyam Cream Tea speciality consists of two delicious scones with freshly whipped cream and strawberry jam with a bottomless cup of tea or coffee. TUESDAYS TO SUNDAYS - 10:30AM TO 5:30PM CLOSED ON MONDAYS CLOSED IN DECEMBER AND JANUARY.

33 HORNCASTLE

GREENFIELD FARM Minting, Horncastle, Lincolnshire, LN9 5RX. Contact Mrs Judy Bankes Price, Tel & Fax: 01507 578457.

Greenfield Farm is a comfortable family home, centrally placed and easily accessible one mile from the A158. Set in peaceful countryside, Lincoln Cathedral is 15 minutes and the Wolds are 5 minutes away. At the house there is a guests sitting room with wood burning stove, modern en suite shower rooms, tea/coffee facilities and payphone. Outside an attractive pond, tennis or forest walks can be enjoyed. Traditional pub 1 mile away. Ample secure parking. Closed Christmas and New Year. 1 TWIN, 2 DOUBLE, EN SUITE OR PRIVATE FACILITIES. CHILDREN 10+.

🖾 ⌇ Ⓢ   **Prices from £21**

34 KNUTSFORD
CROSS KEYS INN King Street, Knutsford, Cheshire, WA16 6DT. Tel: 01565 750404.

Set in an attractive village close to Manchester, the Hotel is in an ideal location in which to visit the city or to mere ly enjoy the beautiful scenery in the locality. 9 DOUBLE, 3 SINGLE, ALL EN-SUITE WITH FULL FACILITIES.

Prices from £50 to £75

35 LANGLEY MILL
THE DURHAM OX Cromford Road, Langley Mill, Nottinghamshire. Contact Tony & Maria Tel: 01773 712 806.

Biker night is thursday at this pub with a good selection of drinks and food. Rock bands every Saturday.

36 LEEK
PADDOCK FARM Upper Hulme, Leek, Staffordshire, ST13 8TY. Tel: 01538 300345.

Overlooking Tittesworth Reservoir, Paddock Farm offers comfortable, highly commended accommodation for Bed & Breakfast or Self-Catering. There is a large conservatory and a large private garden that backs onto the Roaches (look out for the Wallaby's!). If cooking breakfast proves too strenuous, the lovely tea rooms (featured in this guide) will provide a hearty meal. The Bed & Breakfast accommodation received 4 diamonds from ETB. Call for a brochure and tariff. 2 EN SUITE, 1 TWIN, 1 FOUR POSTER. 2 SELF-CATERING UNITS (FOR 8 AND 6 PERSONS), £200 TO £500 P/W IN HIGH SEASON. SPECIAL WINTER SELF-CATERING PRICES AVAILABLE (£15 PER NIGHT).

🖾 ⌇ Ⓢ   **Prices from £19 to £22.50**

No, seriously

A brand new Harley-Davidson® for less than £5,000.

Yes, you read that correctly. The Sportster 883, in fact.

With low slung handlebars, solo seat

and sleek shorty dual exhaust.

So go on, pinch yourself. No, it's still there.

And it's still a brand new Harley-Davidson.

And it's still less than £5,000.

37 LEEK
THE ROACHES TEA ROOMS Paddock Farm, Upper Hulme, Leek, Staffordshire, ST13 8TY. Tel: 01538 300 345.
Roaches Tea Rooms are 3 miles from Leek, by the Roaches, overlooking Tittesworth Reservoir. An inglenook fireplace and a wood burner provides cosy atmosphere to this Tea Room which also has superb views. In warmer weather enjoy relaxing in the conservatory or on the patio outside. Home-made cakes, desserts and soups and local produce including honey and free range eggs. Delicious fruit loaf, fruit pie and pavlova with fresh cream. A wide choice of teas including herbal varieties. APRIL-OCTOBER 9AM-5.30PM EVERY DAY. DURING WINTER WEDNESDAY-SUNDAY 9AM-4PM (CLOSED DECEMBER 24, 25, 26), CLOSED JANUARY AND FEBRUARY. OPEN NEW YEARS DAY. ACCOMMODATION AVAILABLE.

38 LINCOLN
LINCOLN CATHEDRAL COFFEE SHOP Lincoln, Lincolnshire, LN2 1PZ. Tel: 01522 544544.
Situated in the Cathedral and close to the town's main shopping centre, the Coffee Shop provides a wide range of refreshments. Home baked cakes and scones are available along with light meals. The selection of drinks includes the Lincoln Cathedral wine.

39 LINCOLN
THE MELROSE TEA ROOMS The Broadway Centre, Woodhall Spa, Lincoln, Lincolnshire, LN10 6ST. Tel: 01526 353842.
Nearby attractions include the Cottage Museum, local woodlands and the Dambuster Memorial. Pleasant decor and waiting service in this fully licensed restaurant which offers traditional Sunday Roast. Full English breakfasts are available.

40 LOUTH
STAGS HEAD FREE HOUSE Main Road, Burwell, Nr. Louth, Lincolnshire, LN11 8PR. Tel: 01507 480 223.
Free House with good selection of Real Ales and food. MCC meets here every Friday and there is a nearby paddock where you may pitch your tent free of charge. Ideal for visiting Cadwell (4 miles). Lunch served between 12 noon and 2pm with evening meals 6.30pm-late. Camping and five caravans.

41 MACCLESFIELD
ANDREW PAJET'S RESTAURANT 72 Chestergate, Macclesfield, Cheshire, SK11 6DY. Tel: 01625 503 733.
Reputedly the biggest breakfast in Macclesfield, for only £5. Fantastic a la carte menu at £20 which uses local and organic farm food. DAILY 12-3PM AND 7PM-MIDNIGHT CLOSED SUNDAYS AND MONDAYS.

42 MATLOCK

FOUNTAIN VILLA 86 North Parade, Matlock Bath, Matlock, Derbyshire, DE4 3NS. Contact Mr Tony Gower Tel: 01629 56195 Fax: 01629 581057.
Fountain Villa is a Georgian town house situated in the Victorian town of Matlock Bath. Wonderful period style furnishings and decorated to a very high standard. Nearby places of interest including Haddon Hall and Chatsworth House. Ideal for exploring the Derbyshire Dales and Peak District. Closed Christmas. 4 DOUBLE, 1 TWIN, ALL EN SUITE OR PRIVATE CHILDREN ALL.
Prices from £20 to £22.50

43 MATLOCK
THE OLD ENGLISH HOTEL 77 Dale road, Matlock, Derbyshire, DE4 3LT.
Tel: 01629 55028.
The Old English is in the centre of Matlock Town and especially makes bikers very welcome. We serve a large range of beers and lagers. We do bar snacks as well as a full restaurant service. We are open all day. 14 ROOMS ALL EN SUITE.

Prices from £19.95

44 MATLOCK
THE FISH POND Matlock Bath, Derbyshire. Contact Keith & Dawn Jacklin.
Tel: 01629 581 000.
Keith & Dawn welcome you to their pub. Food available 7 days, all day at weekends and quality ales and lagers including Tetley, Stella and Carling, Speckled Hen and Bass. Big screen coverage of superbikes and major sports events. Live entertainment 4/5 days a week.

45 MELTON MOWBRAY
HILLSIDE HOUSE 27 Melton Road, Burton Lazars, Melton Mowbray, Leicestershire, LE14 2UR. Contact Sue Goodwin
Tel: 01664 566312 & 0585 068956 Fax: 01664 501819.
A converted 19th century farm building, Hillside House offers magnificent views over rolling countryside and is situated on the edge of Burton Lazars. The accommodation is spacious and very comfortable. Close to Melton Mowbray, famed for Stilton cheese, Hunt cake and pork pies. Well located for Belvoir Castle, Barnsdale, Stamford and Rutland Water. Closed Christmas and New Year. 2 TWIN (1 EN SUITE), 1 DOUBLE EN SUITE. CHILDREN 10+.

Prices from £17 to £27

46 NEWARK

WILMOT HOUSE Church Walk, Dunham-on-Trent, Newark, Nottinghamshire, NG22 0TX. Contact Ruth & David East
Tel: 01777 228226.
A Georgian listed building with oak beams, Wilmot House is situated in the heart of the village close to the church, only a short walk from the river Trent and 6 miles from the A1/A57 towards Lincoln. Comfortable rooms with refreshment trays and colour T.V. Lincoln, Newark, Sherwood Forest and other attractions of Nottinghamshire are within easy reach. Entrance is off the Green. 2 DOUBLE (1 EN SUITE), 1TWIN/TRIPLE, 1 SINGLE. CHILDREN 14+.

Prices from £18 to £27

47 NEWARK
THE MAPLE LEAF Newark, Nottinghamshire, NG24 2AB.
Tel: 01636 687 759.
Drinks include John Smith Smooth, John Smith Cask, Chestnut Mild, Dry Blackthorn, Cider and Boddington Cask. Snacks include tasty cobs and sandwiches. MCC meetings Wednesday. Large Car Park. Function room available. Pool tables.

48 NEWARK
OLLERTON WATERMILL TEASHOP Market Place, Ollerton, Newark, Nottinghamshire, NG22 9AA. Tel: 01623 822 469.
Ollerton Watermill Teashop is a restored 18th century water mill, near Rufford Country Park and Sherwood Forest. There are picturesque views from the glass viewing panel which overlooks the river Mawn where there are often ducks and swans. Pine decor with white walls, china and fresh greenery create a luxurious yet comfortable atmosphere. Cooking is done on the premises and delicious and generous servings of food mean that this Teashop has now won the "Best Afternoon Tea" award twice. MARCH TO NOVEMBER-TUESDAYS TO SUNDAYS 10.30AM TO 5PM OPEN BANK HOLIDAY MONDAYS CLOSED DECEMBER TO FEBRUARY.

49 NEWARK
LORD NELSON INN Besthorpe, Newark, Nottinghamshire, NG23 7HR.
Contact M. Theaker Tel: 01636 892 265.
Friendly pub serving Marstons Beers, Timothy Taylor, Landlord, Abbott Ales, Lagers and Ciders. Excellent freshly prepared a la carte menu, bar menu meals and special Sunday lunch Monday-Saturday 12 noon-2pm, 4.30-9pm and all day Sunday in summer. DOUBLE OR SINGLE.

50 NOTTINGHAM

THE TUDOR LODGE HOTEL 400 Nuthall Road, Nottingham, Nottinghamshire, NG8 5DS. Tel: 0115 9249244 & 9249241 Fax: 0115 9249243.
The Tudor Lodge is owned and run by a small family business offering a personal and friendly service. Each room is central heated with TV, tea/coffee facilities and there is room service for all guests. A full English breakfast is available. Tudor Pub and Steak Bar 150 metres away. 7 BEDROOMS, SOME EN SUITE. £5 WEEKEND DISCOUNT.

Prices from £30 to £60

51 NOTTINGHAM
QUALITY HOTEL George Street, Nottingham, NG1 3BP.
Tel: 0115 947 5641 Fax: 0115 948 3292.
M1 exit 25, A52 onto Lower Parliament Street. Attractive accommodation in ideal situation. Nearby places of interest include Nottingham Castle, Sherwood Forest (9 miles) and American Adventure (10 miles). Special package for bikers £26. per person inc. breakfast and dinner. Subject to availability. Must be booked through Central Reservations 0800 44 44 44. 70 BEDROOMS.

52 NOTTINGHAM
YE OLDE TRIP TO JERUSALEM Brewhouse Yard, Nottingham, Nottinghamshire, NG1 6AD. Tel: 0115 947 3171.
Carved into the rock at the base of Nottingham Castle 1/4 of a mile from the city centre, this is England's oldest inn, dating from 1189. Popular with tourists and locals alike, it has a true medieval feel as you enjoy your traditional Kimberley ale (or whatever takes your fancy) in the multi-levelled caves. There is a terraced beer garden outside and a paved area with tables where you can drink during warm summer nights. MAG meetings on Wednesdays.

53 OLLERTON

MAUN RIVER COTTAGE Main Street, Ollerton, Nottinghamshire, NG22 9AD. Contact Alan & Theresa Morton Tel & Fax: 01623 824746.

Maun River Cottage, situated next to one of 3 pubs in the village of Ollerton retains it's original character with oak beams etc. There is a pretty garden sloping down to the river Maun and a heated swimming pool that guests can use by arrangement from June to September. Sherwood Forest World of Robin Hood, Rutford Lake and Centre Parcs are within 2 miles. 1 DOUBLE, 1 TRIPLE, BOTH EN SUITE.

🗐 ✂ Ⓢ   **Prices from £17.50**

54 OSWESTRY

THE OLD RECTORY Selattyn, Oswestry, Shropshire, SY10 7DH. Contact Mrs Maggie Barnes Tel: 01691 659 708.

Situated on the outskirts of the charming Selattyn village and close to the Welsh border, The Old Rectory offers attractive and spacious accommodation. Ideally located for touring the beautiful surrounding countryside. National Trust properties, Chester and Shrewsbury all offer lots to see and do. After a day's sightseeing unwind in comfortable and relaxing rooms. Closed Christmas. 1 FAMILY EN SUITE, 1 DOUBLE EN SUITE, 1 TWIN CHILDREN WELCOME.

🗐 ✂ Ⓢ   **Prices from £17 to £20**

55 RIDGEWAY VILLAGE

KENT HOUSE COUNTRY KITCHEN Ridgeway Craft Centre, Ridgeway Village, Derbyshire, S12 3XR. Tel: 0114 247 3739.

The Kent House Country Kitchen is just a few minutes away from the Moss Valley where there are various walks available. Traditional surroundings with the original Yorkshire range and oak beams. Enjoy delicious sandwiches and cakes or a selection of hot and cold meals. Teas include China and Earl Grey. OPEN TUESDAYS THROUGH TO SUNDAYS. CLOSED MONDAYS EXCEPT BANK HOLIDAYS.

56 SHAWBURY

UNITY LODGE Moreton Mill, Shawbury, Shropshire, SY4 4ES. Contact Mrs M. Woodcock Tel: 01939 250 831.

Situated on the A53, eight miles north of Shrewsbury, Unity Lodge is a detached house in quiet surroundings. within easy reach are the Ironbridge Gorge Museum, Motor Cross Track, West Midland shooting ground. Enjoy a day trip to the historic Powis Castle or go walking at Long Mynd. Closed Christmas and New Year. 1 SINGLE, 1 TWIN, 1 FAMILY CHILDREN WELCOME.

🗐 ✂ Ⓢ   **Prices from £17 to £18**

57 SHREWSBURY

ADMIRAL RODNEY Criggion, Shrewsbury, Shropshire, SY5 9AU. Contact Bob Jones Tel: 01938 570 313.

A very friendly welcome to all Bikers who visit this delightful pub. Drinks cater for a range of tastes and include Carlesberg, Tetley Keg, Tetley Smooth, Ciders and Guinness. Food available daily. In winter limited opening only.

58 SHREWSBURY

FOXLEIGH HOUSE Foxleigh Drive, Wem, Shrewsbury, Shropshire, SY4 5BP. Contact Barbara Barnes Tel & Fax: 01939 233 528.
Georgian farmhouse with a beautiful Victorian wing, elegant interior with ancestral portraits along the the hall and sitting room overlooking croquet lawn. Attractions include walks along local canals and visits to local gardens, Ironbridge and the famous Follies. Closed Christmas. 1 TWIN, 1 FAMILY SUITE (FOR UP TO 5), PRIVATE FACILITIES AVAILABLE CHILDREN 8+.
Prices from £19.50 to £22

59 SOUTHWELL
MINSTER REFECTORY Church Street, Southwell, Nottingham NG25 0HD. Tel: 01636 815 691.
Visitors can expect a friendly welcome at the Minster Refectory and a wide menu that caters for everybody's tastes. MON-SAT 9.30AM-5.30PM SUNDAY 12NOON-5.30PM.

60 SPALDING

LAVENDER LODGE 81 Pinchbeck Road, Spalding, Lincolnshire, PE11 1QF. Teresa Egleton. Tel: 01775 712800 Fax: 01775 766556.
Lavender Lodge is an Edwardian villa on a tree lined avenue with off street parking, 10 minutes walk from Spalding town centre, the heart of the British bulb, flower and seed industry. The Lincolnshire Fens are within easy reach offering pleasant walks, cycling and bird watching. Ely, Cambridge and Lincoln within easy reach. Closed Christmas. 1 DOUBLE, 1 FAMILY, BOTH EN SUITE.
Prices from £22

61 SPALDING

BARRINGTON HOUSE Barrington Gate, Holbeach, Spalding, Lincolnshire, PE12 7LB. Denny Symonds Tel & Fax: 01406 425178.
Barrington House is situated on the edge of the old market town of Holbeach, 3 minutes walk from several pubs/restaurants and overlooking countryside. It is a spacious Georgian House offering comfortable accomm., the drawing room has a log fire. Payphone and fax facilities available. Ample secure parking. 2 DOUBLE, 1 TWIN, 1 SINGLE, EN SUITE OR PRIVATE FACILITIES. ALSO SELF-CATERING OPTIONS FROM £165 PER WEEK.
Prices from £23 to £40

62 STAMFORD
FRANGIPANI'S TEA ROOMS 3 Red Lion Square, Stamford, Lincolnshire, PE9 2AH. Tel: 01780 762422.
The Tea Rooms are 50 metres away from the building used as a doctors surgery in TV's Middlemarch. Also nearby is Burghley House, the site of filming for The Buccaneers. Cheery atmosphere, helpful staff and displays of local art. Food made to order and staff are willing to prepare items not on the menu.

63 STOKE-ON-TRENT
THE LIMES Cheadle Road, Blythe Bridge, Stoke-on-Trent, Staffordshire, ST11 9PW. Mrs R. Williams Tel: 01782 393 278.
An attractive Victorian property with lots of character set in landscaped gardens. Intricate decor adds charm to this beautifully decorated house where guests can expect a warm and friendly atmosphere. Famous ceramic museums nearby (Wedgwood, Royal Doulton, Spode), stately homes and Peak District. Enjoy an exciting day out at Alton Towers only 8 miles away. Closed Christmas. 1 SINGLE, 1 DOUBLE (WITH SHOWERS), 1 FAMILY CHILDREN 5+ CHILDREN ALL.

64 WELLINGTON
ODDFELLOWS ARMS 65 High Street, Wellington, Shropshire, TF1 1JT.
Contact Mr David Redman Tel: 01952 249 153.
A good selection of drinks including Tetleys Bitter, Worthington, Carling Lager and Cider. Food served between 11am-3pm, 5pm-11pm and 12 noon-10.30pm Sunday. All Bikers welcome. Function room available for up to 80 people.

65 WILMSLOW
HEATHERLEA GUEST HOUSE 106 Lacey Green, Wilmslow, Cheshire, SK9 4BN.
Contact Keith & Marjorie Rogers. Tel: 01625 522 872 Fax: 01625 527 524.
Situated in a quiet residential area, Heatherlea Guest House is a wonderfully refurbished property. Manchester Airport (10 minutes away) and M56 offering easy access to northwest motorway system. Nearby train station where there are frequent trains to Manchester, Liverpool, Chester and the Peak District. Guests can be met at the station. Lots of pubs and restaurants nearby. 2 SINGLE, 1 TWIN, 1 DOUBLE, 1 FAMILY, ALL EN SUITE CHILDREN WELCOME.

Prices from £20 to £30

66 WORFIELD

THE WHEEL Worfield, Shropshire.
This pub is very popular with bikers who meet regularly here, so popular in fact that in summer, the car park is packed full! Enjoy a warm, friendly atmosphere, good food and drink.

[S]

67 WYMONDHAM

THE OLD RECTORY Wymondham, Leicestershire, LE14 2AZ.
Contact Isabel Smeaton Tel: 01572 787583 Fax: 01572 787347.
OAKHAM / MELTON 7m. The Old Rectory is set within secluded grounds 5 miles west of the A1. This Georgian building offers guests comfortable, self-contained accommodation with its own entrance. The cities of Nottingham, Peterborough and Leicester or the activities available at Rutland Water are within easy reach. Turn by wooden bus shelter on Wymondham village green onto Sycamore Lane and bear left. Closed Christmas and New Year. 2 DOUBLE, 1 TWIN, ALL EN SUITE OR PRIVATE FACILITIES.

[🅾] [✄] [S]

Prices from £22.50 to £27.50

68 YORK
BETTY'S CAFE TEA ROOMS 6-8 St Helen's Square, York, North Yorkshire, YO1 2QP.
Tel: 01904 659142.
Betty's Cafe Tea Rooms was opened in 1937 and many of the original features still remain. The tea rooms are very close to York Minster and other local attractions. Cream Tea offers 2 sultana scones with butter, whipped cream and preserve and a pot of tea-room blend tea. St Helena coffee is exclusive to Betty's from the island of St Helena and teas include Assam, Ceylon, China, Darjeeling and Earl Grey. SEVEN DAYS A WEEK - 9AM TO 9PM.

1 ACCRINGTON
MAPLE LODGE HOTEL 70 Blackburn Road, Clayton Le Moors, Accrington, BB5 5JH. Contact Len Haysom Tel: 01254 301 284 Fax: 01254 388 152.
Guests are assured of a warm and friendly welcome at this hotel. En suite rooms with all facilities. Good location with walks nearby.

Prices from £35.50 to £46

2 ALNMOUTH

FAMOUS SCHOONER Northumberland Street, Alnmouth, Northumberland, NE66 2RS. Contact Mr Ord Tel: 01665 830216.
A 17th century inn, renowned for superb food and real ales, only 100 yards from the beach, river and golf course. Many rooms overlook the hotel gardens, estuary and sea. 31 BEDROOMS, ALL EN SUITE.

Prices from £30 to £69

3 ALNWICK

HOTSPUR Bondgate Without, Alnwick, Northumberland NE66 1PR. Tel: 01665 510 101 Fax: 01665 605 033.
Situated near Alnwick Castle and in the town centre, The Hotspur offers a warm and friendly atmosphere. All rooms are decorated to a high standard with many home comforts. Enjoy the excellent standard of food and drink here and choose from a wide range of wines and fine ales. 25 BEDROOMS, ALL EN SUITE.

Prices from £30 to £40

4 ALSTON

HARBUT LAW Brampton Road, Alston, Cumbria, CA9 3BD. Contact Mrs S Younger Tel: 01434 381 950.
A spacious Victorian family home, Harbut Law is set high in the north Pennines with panoramic views of surrounding countryside. Situated in an area of outstanding natural beauty, it is ideal for touring the Lake District, Northumberland and the Scottish Borders. Visit nearby Alston with its quaint cobbled streets and shops and places to eat. England's highest gauge railway 1 mile away. Closed December to March inclusive. 1 DOUBLE EN SUITE, 1 FAMILY WITH PRIVATE BATHROOM, 1 DOUBLE + EN SUITE.

Prices from £15 to £18

5 ALTRINCHAM
QUALITY HOTEL Langham Road, Bowdon, Altrincham, Cheshire, WA14 2HT. Tel: 0161 9287 121 Fax: 0161 927 7560 E.mail: admin@gb064.u-net.com.
From M56, take J7 onto A56. Quality Hotel offers a high standard of accommodation and service. Altrincham and Manchester offer lots to see and do. Places of interest include Tatton Park, Styal Country Park and Granada Studios. Relax in comfortable surroundings where there are restaurant and bar facilities and cable TV. Leisure centre available to guests. Special package for bikers £26. per person inc. breakfast and dinner. Subject to availability. Must be booked through Central Reservations 0800 44 44 44. 89 BEDROOMS.

6 ALTRINCHAM
THE BRICKLAYERS ARMS 68 George Street, Altrincham, Cheshire, WA14 1RS.
Tel: 0161 928 1547.
A good selection of drinks such as Newcastle Brown, Theakstones and Fosters. Food available lunch time only till 2pm. Thick as a Brick MCC meets every Wednesday at 8pm.

---

7 ALTRINCHAM
OLD PACKET HOUSE Navigation Road, Altrincham, Cheshire, WA14 1LW.
Tel: 0161 929 1331.
A charming inn open all day, serving real ale and food (lunchtimes and evenings). ACCOMMODATION AVAILABLE.

---

8 ALTRINCHAM

OLD PACKET HOUSE Navigation Road, Broadheath, Altrincham, Cheshire, WA14 1LW.
Tel: 0161 929 1331 Fax: 0161 929 1331.
Bikers are very welcome in this charming olde worlde inn with a lively yet comfortable atmosphere. A wide range of drinks and food served daily. Accommodation comprises four very luxurious en suite bedrooms.
4 BEDROOMS ALL EN SUITE.
ⓞ Ⓢ   **Prices from £47.50 to £57.50**

---

9 AMBLESIDE

BETTY FOLD Hawkshead Hill, Ambleside, Cumbria, LA22 0PS.
Contact Anthony Marsden Tel: 015394 36611.
HAWKSHEAD 1m. Set in beautiful grounds in the heart of the Lake District and just a few miles from Ambleside and Coniston, Betty Fold is a comfortably furnished home with a welcoming atmosphere. Rooms have lovely views. An ideal location from which to explore the surrounding area, Tarn Hows and the quaint Hawkshead village. Evening meals available by arrangement. 2 DOUBLE, 1 TWIN, ALL EN SUITE.
⚹   **Prices from £22 to £28**

---

10 AMBLESIDE
FISHERBECK Old Lake Road, Ambleside, Cumbria LA22 0DH.
Tel: 015394 33215 Fax: 015394 33600.
Fisherbeck offers high standards of accommodation and a warm and friendly atmosphere. Unwind in spacious rooms that are furnished to provide comfortable surroundings. Good food and drink available. 18 BEDROOMS ALL EN SUITE.
ⓞ Ⓢ   **Prices from £25 to £86**

---

11 AMBLESIDE

ELDER GROVE Lake Road, Ambleside, Cumbria LA22 0DB.
Contact Mr McDougall Tel: 015394 32504.
A charming family run Victorian house offering comfortable accommodation. All rooms are decorated to a high standard. There is a licensed bar, heating and a car park. Open all year.
ⓞ Ⓢ ⚹   **Prices from £23 to £32**

12 AMBLESIDE

LYNDHURST Wansfell Road, Ambleside, Cumbria LA22 0EG. Contact Mrs Green Tel: 01539 432 421 Fax: 01539 432 421. Situated in a quiet area and surrounded by countryside, Lyndhurst offers warm and friendly accommodation with plenty of facilities. Bedrooms with lovely four poster beds available. Enjoy a hearty breakfast in the morning and relax at the cosy bar in the evenings. Special breaks available. 8 BEDROOMS ALL EN SUITE.

Prices from £20 to £26.50

13 AMBLESIDE
SAWREY INN Far Sawrey, Ambleside, Cumbria, LA22 0LQ.
Contact Mr Brayshaw Tel: 01539 443425.
Dating from the 18th century, the inn has been converted from stables into a superb bar full of atmosphere. Open all day with home cooked food served all day. Bikers welcome. BED & BREAKFAST.

Prices from £29

14 AMBLESIDE
SCANDALE BRIDGE COTTAGE Lake District, Ambleside, Cumbria, LA22 9RR.
Contact Derek Sweeney Tel: 017687 72393.
Situated in the heart of the Lake District this Lakeland stone built cottage dates back from the early 18th century. Outside there is a patio and gardens with Scandale Beck nearby. Ideal for visiting the nearby town of Ambleside where there are restaurants, pubs and cinemas or touring the Lake District. Relax in the sitting room with views over Scandale Beck.

15 AMBLESIDE
THE KIRKSTONE PASS INN, Ambleside, Cumbria, LA22 9LQ.
Contact Wally Alexander Tel: 01539 433624.
The management and staff of this pub are all bikers. This Inn is the highest inn in The Lake District and is over 1500ft above sea level. It is located at the very top of Kirkstone Pass, with all it's magnificent views and fantastic countryside. The roads are suitable for biking, with long straights and gentle bends. The pub is over 500 years old with lots of history. We serve bar snacks and have a very good range of beers. The house speciality being hot mulled Austrian wine, at £1:50 per glass. Club meetings welcome.

16 APPERKNOWLE
YELLOW LION High Street, Apperknowle, Derbyshire, S18 4BD. Tel: 01246 413181.
1 DOUBLE, 1 SINGLE, SHARED BATHROOM.

Prices from £12

17 APPLEBY-IN-WESTMORLAND

COURTFIELD Bongate, Appleby-in-Westmorland, Cumbria, CA16 6UP. Contact Mrs Robinson Tel: 017683 51394.
A friendly family run hotel set in three acres of lawned gardens. Ideally located to explore the wonderful Eden Valley. A wide variety of local outdoor activities. 11 BEDROOMS 4 EN SUITE.
🆔 Ⓢ

Prices from £25

STRENGTH
THROUGH STYLE!

WEISE WESTWARD JACKET
The Value Jacket that does it All

Recommended by Ride magazine and described by MCN as "the value jacket that does it all" - the Westward's combination of rugged construction and stylish design offers an ideal all-purpose motorcycle jacket.

- 100% waterproof Cordura shell with breathable Hydratech membrane
- Fixed quilt liner plus removable polyester quilted lining
- Integral pockets on shoulders and elbows for removable protective armour
- Scotchlite 3M reflective piping
- 10 pockets including 2 handwarmer pockets
- Fleece collar with Velcro and buckle fastenings
- Matching trousers available

Retail price £139.99

WEISE WATERFORD II LIMITED JACKET

- Made from 100% Cordura with a breathable membrane
- Detachable lining
- Protector pockets in shoulders, elbows and back accept Weise recommended T Pro CE approved protective armour
- Adjustable belt and velcro wrists
- Fleece collar
- Matching trousers available

Retail price £89.99

Prices correct at time of going to press but may vary.

AVAILABLE FROM WEISE STOCKISTS OR CALL FOWLERS - 0117 977 0466
FOR DETAILS ON THE WEISE RANGE OF CLOTHING

18 ASKRIGG

KING'S ARMS Askrigg, North Yorkshire, DL8 3HQ. Contact Mr Turner Tel: 01969 650 258 Fax: 01969 650 635. Wonderful stone country inn with unique history and character. Rooms are elegantly furnished and comfortable. Try the delicious range of food, wines and beers. 11 BEDROOMS, ALL EN SUITE.

⃞ ⃞ *VISA*

Prices from £50

19 BACUP

OAKENCLOUGH FARM Oakenclough Road, Bacup, Lancashire, OL13 9ET. Contact Chris & Paul Worswick Tel: 01706 879 319 & 0973 314 489. A warm welcome all year round is extended to guests in this very comfortable farmhouse situated on the edge of open moors, yet only half a mile from the centre of the market town. A good location to explore the varied places in the North West, including wonderful countryside, historic houses, city centre museums, the coast & attractive towns and villages. 2 DOUBLE AND 1 TWIN EN SUITE, 1 BUNK BEDROOM. SELF CATERING AVAILABLE.

⃞ ⃞

Prices from £17.50

20 BAINBRIDGE

RIVERDALE HOUSE Bainbridge, North Yorkshire, DL8 3EW. Tel: 01969 650 311. Situated in picturesque Wensleydale, Riverdale House offers comfortable surroundings in which to unwind. Delicious cooking that makes use of fresh ingredients. Closed November to January. 12 BEDROOMS, 11 EN SUITE.

⃞

Prices from £52

21 BAMBURGH

BROOME 22 Ingram Road, Bamburgh, Northumberland NE69 7BT. Contact Mary Dixon Tel: 01668 214 287 & 07971 248 230. Located in the historic village of Bamburgh, Broome has wonderful views of open fields and Bamburgh Castle. Just a 2 minute walk from the village centre and a few minutes walk from the beach, ideally situated for exploring the North Northumberland coast, Northumberland and the Scottish Borders. The sandstone castle overlooks both the village and the beautiful sandy beach with views of the nearby Farne Islands. Golf course 2 miles away. Closed Christmas and New Year. 1 DOUBLE, 1 TWIN, PRIVATE FACILITIES AVAILABLE NO CHILDREN.

Prices from £25 to £30

22 BAMFORD
YE DERWENT Main Road, Bamford, Derbyshire, S33 0AY. Tel: 01433 651395.
Bamford is in the middle of the fabulous scenic views and rolling countryside of Derbyshire. A quaint village with an exclusive charm in fantastic motorcycling country. Noted for the fine food and traditional atmosphere and friendliness. BED & BREAKFAST.

23 BARNARD CASTLE
THE MARKET PLACE TEASHOP 29 Market Place, Barnard Castle, County Durham, DL12 8NE. Tel: 01833 690 110.
The Market Place Teashop is situated near to the Castle ruins, the River Tees and the Bowes Museum. In the past the tea room has been used as a temperance hotel and a gentleman's outfitters. It has a reputation for good food and service and has won an award from the AA. Imaginative menu that caters for a range of tastes. Visitors select their own cakes, scones and speciality teas. A good range of Italian ice creams containing natural fruits and flavours. MONDAYS TO SATURDAYS 10AM TO 5.30PM SUNDAYS 2.30 TO 5.30PM (MARCH TO OCTOBER).

24 BARNARD CASTLE

MARWOOD HOUSE 98 Galgate, Barnard Castle, County Durham, DL12 8BJ. Contact Mr & Mrs J. Kilgarriff Tel & Fax: 01833 637 493.
An attractive Grade II listed Victorian town house, located off the main road with parking. Period fireplace and wonderful embroideries in the lounge make Marwood House a luxurious yet comfortable place to stay. Guests are welcome to use the fitness and sauna room. The city centre is within walking distance and there are many nearby attractions including Bowes Museum and the Dales. Durham and Beamish are also within easy reach. Wonderful meals. Dinner by arrangement. 3 DOUBLE EN SUITE, 2 SINGLE EN SUITE/PRIVATE CHILDREN 10+.

Prices from £18 to £20

25 BISHOP AUCKLAND

LOW CORNRIGGS FARM HOUSE Cowshill in Weardale, Bishop Auckland, County Durham, DL13 1AQ. Contact Mrs Janet Ellis Tel & Fax: 01388 537 600.
Low Cornriggs is situated right in the heart of the North Pennines with views of the Pennines and the unspoilt surrounding area. This modernised 200 year old farmhouse has a conservatory and wonderful home cooked food. Ideal for touring, visiting Alston and Stanthorpe (both 10 miles) and Hexham (19 Miles). Walks and skiing in the area and onsite riding school provides lessons and daily rides. 2 DOUBLE, 1 TWIN/FAMILY, ALL EN SUITE CHILDREN 5+.

Prices from £20 to £23

26 BLACKPOOL

206 NORTH PROMENADE Blackpool, Lancashire, FY1 1RU. Contact Mrs Dixon Tel: 01253 625688 Fax: 01253 624075.
The Stretton is highly commended and is situated opposite the North Pier. Close to all amenities, it offers excellent cuisine and friendly, courteous service. 50 BEDROOMS, 49 EN SUITE.

Prices from £43 to £59

27 BLACKPOOL

WINDSOR PARK 96 Queens Promenade, Blackpool, Lancashire, FY2 9NS. Contact Mr Ramsden Tel: 01253 357025.
The Windsor Park Hotel is situated in one of the most sought after areas of the Fylde coast. Queens Promenade overlooks the north shore cliffs and looks out over the Irish Sea. 11 BEDROOMS, ALL EN SUITE.

Prices from £17 to £40

Whatever your area of interest,
Haynes have got it covered...

From **Car Service and Repair Manuals** covering 95% of cars on the roads today, to **TechBooks** and **Restoration Manuals**…

…Service and Repair Manuals for **motorcycles** ranging from **Superbikes** to **Scooters** and **Motorcycle TechBooks**…

…books for cyclists featuring the best-selling **Bike Book**…

…books for the home covering **Washing Machine** and appliance repairs and **home decorating**…

…books for travelling, including **The Motorcaravan Manual** and the highly regarded **Alan Rogers' Good Camps Guide** series and, last but not least, books for reading and enjoying…

…**Superbikes, Rider Biographies, Ogri, Classic Cars,** and much, much more…

28 BLENCOW
THE CROWN Blencow, Cumbria. Contact Martin & Janette
Tel: 01768 483369 & 0836 515542.

A very friendly pub, well known in the area for our hospitality, with a pool table and darts board. We serve pub food, which is all home made in our own kitchens. We have a wide selection of beers and lagers and a good range of Scottish Malt Whiskies. Come and sample our hospitality. We are only a few hundred yards away from the A66 bikers run. 4 ROOMS A MIXTURE OF TWINS AND SINGLES.

Prices from £20

29 BLENCOW
THE CROWN INN Blencow, Cumbria. Contact Martin and Janette
Tel: 01768 483369 & 0836 515542.

A very popular Inn/Pub with bikers. Warm homely accommodation with the best breakfast either South of the Border or North of it. You will need nothing else for the rest of the day!! Dinner served in the evening. We are located just of the A66 junction 40 on the M6. This is real bikers country and is the gateway to the lakes and the most wonderful scenery. VARIOUS TWIN AND SINGLE ROOMS.

Prices from £20

30 BOLTON
COMFORT INN Horwich, Bolton, Lancashire, BL6 5UZ. Tel: 01204 468 641.

On M61 between junctions 6 and 8. Rooms are decorated to a high standard and facilities include restaurant and bar area and cable TV. Nearby local places of interest such as Granada Studios 5 miles, Wigan Pier 8 miles, Camelot 15 miles the GMEX centre and Blackpool (10 miles). Special package for bikers £26. per person inc. breakfast and dinner. Subject to availability. Must be booked through Central Reservations 0800 44 44 44.

31 BOROUGHBRIDGE ORCHARD COTTAGE Langthorpe, Boroughbridge, Yorkshire, YO51 9BZ. Contact Mrs Marcia Arrowsmith Tel: 01423 323 712 & 0402 949505.

YORK 13m. Orchard Cottage is a spacious family home on the edge of the old town of Boroughbridge. A wood burning stove in the inglenook is great for chilly evenings or enjoy the conservatory overlooking landscaped gardens in summer. The nearby A1 gives easy access to the Yorkshire Dales and Moors. The River Ure offers a lovely walk into the town. Closed Christmas. 1 DOUBLE, 1 TWIN, 1 SINGLE (BUNK BEDS) CHILDREN WELCOME.

Prices from £18

32 BRADFORD
QUALITY HOTEL Bridge Street, Bradford, W. Yorkshire, BD1 1JX. Tel: 01274 728 706
Fax: 01274 736 358 E.mail: admin@gb654.u-net.com.

Located on M62/M606 to city centre. High standard accommodation with eating and drinking facilities. Guests have many modern facilities and full use of the mini gym. Local places of interest include the National Photographic Museum, the largest cinema screen in the UK and easy access to the Yorkshire countryside. Special package for bikers £26. per person inc. breakfast and dinner. Subject to availability. Must be booked through Central Reservations 0800 44 44 44. 60 BEDROOMS.

33 BRADFORD

PARK DRIVE 12 Park Drive, Bradford, Yorkshire, BD9 4DR. Contact Mr Hilton Tel: 01274 480194 Fax: 01274 484869.
This elegant Victorian residence in its delightful woodland setting offers delicious home cooking, friendly personal service and safe parking inside the grounds. 11 BEDROOMS SINGLES AND DOUBLES, ALL EN SUITE.

Prices from £30 to £57

34 BRAITHWAITE

COTTAGE IN THE WOOD Whinlatter Pass, Braithwaite, Cumbria, CA12 5TW. Contact Mr Littlefair Tel: 01768 778409.
A small comfortable private hotel personally run by the Littlefairs who pride themselves in offering excellent food and good wine at reasonable prices. 7 BEDROOMS, ALL EN SUITE.

Prices from £27 to £33

35 BRAMPTON

ABBEY BRIDGE INN Lanercost, Brampton, Cumbria, CA8 2HG. Contact Mr Sayers Tel & Fax: 016977 2224.
Family run in a peaceful riverside setting. This 17th century inn and restaurant offers excellent food and real ales. A good touring centre for Hadrians Wall and the Lakes. 7 BEDROOMS SINGLES AND DOUBLES, 4 EN SUITE.

Prices from £22 to £60

36 BRIDLINGTON
THE OLD SHIP INN St Johns Street, Bridlington, North Yorkshire. Contact Allan & Pat Jimmison.
Traditional old English pub, big on cask ales. Excellent range of real ales, bottled beers and lagers. There is always a good menu of food available, during lunch and evening, and we have an extensive range of all qualities of wines. This Pub is under new management and welcome bikers to come and visit us. Secure parking available.

37 BRIDLINGTON
PARK VIEW 9-11 Tennyson Avenue, Bridlington, North Yorkshire YO15 2EU.
Contact Mr Gaze Tel: 01262 672 140 Fax: 01262 672 140.
A lovely hotel located approx. 200 yards from the beach. There is a car park nearby and a leisure centre. Relax on the beach or enjoy the wide range of things to do and see. 16 BEDROOMS, 4 EN SUITE.

38 BROUGHTON IN FURNESS
OLD KINGS HEAD HOTEL Church Street, Broughton in Furness, Cumbria LA20 6HJ. Tel: 01229 716293.
This is a charming, traditional inn which is open all day with a warm, friendly and traditional atmosphere. Open all day. Home cooked food available all day at reasonable prices. BED & BREAKFAST.

Prices from £18

39 BURNLEY
COMFORT INN Keirby Walk, Burnley, Lancashire, BB11 2DH.
Tel: 01282 427 611 Fax: 01282 436 370 E.mail: admin@gb608.u-net.com.
Located on M65, J9 to Burnley. Good quality accommodation with traditional feel. Rooms decorated to a high standard and many facilities inc. cable TV. Enjoy a good range of meals at the restaurant including traditional dishes and international dishes. Places of interest include Manchester Utd ground, Yorkshire Dales and Camelot Adventure Theme Park. Special package for bikers £26. per person inc. breakfast and dinner. Subject to availability. Must be booked through Central Reservations 0800 44 44 44. 50 BEDROOMS.

🍷 ✗ ⑤

40 BURNLEY
ROSEHILL HOUSE HOTEL Burnley, Lancashire, BB11 2PW.
Contact Mrs Doherty Tel: 01282 453 931 Fax: 01282 453 931.
Located in a quiet area of Burnley, Rosehill House Hotel is a large stone built house set in its own grounds. Unique decor and original features. Rooms are superbly decorated and are centrally heated and have 10 channel satellite. Restaurant and bistro serve delicious food with a choice of English and International dishes. Snooker room available. 23 EN SUITE ROOMS.

⑩ ⑤

41 CARLISLE

ELLENSIDE Ireby, Carlisle, Cumbria, CA5 1EH.
Contact Robin & Anne Binny Tel: 016973 71256.
KESWICK 15m. Ellenside is an attractive house with spectacular views. This early 19thC regency house has much charm. French windows open onto a veranda and garden with tennis court. Enjoy panoramic views of the Lake District, fells and mountains. 2 TWIN, 1 DOUBLE, ALL EN SUITE CHILDREN 3+.

⑩ ✄ ⑤

Prices from £20

42 CARLISLE
AVONDALE 3 St Aidans Road, Carlisle, Cumbria CA1 1LT.
Contact Mrs Hayes Tel: 01228 523 012 Fax: 01228 523 012.
Avondale is an elegant Edwardian house in a peaceful location. Finely decorated with spacious rooms. Close to the city centre and with easy access to the M6, J43. Closed Christmas. 3 BEDROOMS, 1 EN SUITE.

⑩ ⑤

Prices from £20 to £40

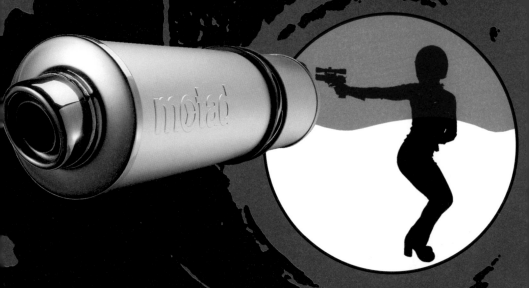

43 CARLISLE
PRIOR'S KITCHEN RESTAURANT The Abbey, Carlisle, Cumbria, CA3 8TZ.
Tel: 01228 543 251 Fax: 01228 547049.
Situated in the vaulted undercroft of the medieval Fratry, Prior's Kitchen Restaurant serves local Cumbrian dishes, soups, salads, sandwiches and freshly baked scones and jam. MONDAY- SATURDAY 9.45AM-4.00PM CLOSED CHRISTMAS DAY, BOXING DAY AND GOOD FRIDAY.

44 CARNFORTH

THE BOWER Yealand Conyers, Carnforth, Lancashire, LA5 9SF.
Contact Sally-Ann Rothwell Tel: 01524 734 585.
A delightful Georgian house situated south of the Lake District and set in an area of outstanding natural beauty. Guests are assured of a friendly reception and a comfortable and relaxing atmosphere. Centrally located for touring the Lakes and Dales and for stopovers en route to Scotland. The owners enjoy bridge and classical music and own a harpsichord. Wonderful meals by arrangement.
1 TWIN/DOUBLE EN SUITE, 1 DOUBLE WITH PRIVATE BATHROOM
CHILDREN 12+.

⬜ ✂ Ⓢ   **Prices from £27 to £32**

45 CHORLEY
TRADER JACKS 38 Hollingshead Street, Chorley, Lancashire PR7 1EP.
Tel: 01257 266 401.
Drinks include Bass and Mathels Brown. MCC meets every Monday-come along!.

46 CLITHEROE
ROSE COTTAGE Longsight Road, Clayton Le Dale, Nr. Clitheroe, Lancashire
BB1 9EV. Contact Marj Adderley Tel: 01254 813 223 Fax: 01254 813 831.
Situated on the A59, 5 miles from the M6 and M65,Rose Cottage offers a warm welcome to motorcyclists. An excellent base from which to explore the beautiful surrounding countryside of the Ribble Valley. En suite with all facilities. Traditional English breakfast included.

⬜ Ⓢ   **Prices from £19**

47 CLITHEROE

BAY GATE FARM Holden, Bolton-by-Bowland, Clitheroe,
Lancashire, BB7 4PQ. Contact Mrs E Townson
Tel: 01200 447643.
Bay Gate Farm is a traditional farmhouse on a working farm, with lovely views of the surrounding countryside. It is ideally located for visiting the Fells and Forest of Bowland and the nearby villages of Skipton and Clitheroe and is only 1 hour from Blackpool. There is a good selection of inns and pubs in the area that offer good country cooking. Dogs welcome. Closed November to February. 3 TWIN, CHILDREN 5+.

Ⓢ   **Prices from £16**

48 CLITHEROE
PENDLE HOTEL Chatburn, Clitheroe, Lancashire, BB7 4JY. Tel: 01200 441 234.
Well known meeting place for bikers with sports biker meetings and lots more. Food served 7.30-10pm. Sunday lunch available. Free trade beer.

49 CLITHEROE
CLARION HOTEL & SUITES Whalley Road, Billington, Clitheroe, Lancashire BB7 9HY. Tel: 01254 822 556.
Located M6, A677, A59 or M65, A6119 and A666. Visit Blackpool Pleasure Beach and Pendle Heritage Centre. After a busy day's sightseeing relax in comfortable surroundings. Hospitality tray in all rooms. Leisure centre available for visitors. Special package for bikers £26. per person inc. breakfast and dinner. Subject to availability. 44 BEDROOMS. Must be booked through Central Reservations 0800 44 44 44.

50 CLITHEROE
HILLCREST TEA ROOMS Mitton Road, Great Mitton, Clitheroe, Lancashire BB7 9PQ. Tel: 01254 826 573.
Located in a small hamlet next to a medieval church with local attractions such as Whalley Abbey and the famous Stoneyhurst college. Customers can expect a warm, relaxing atmosphere and friendly staff. Home made scones and cakes and home grown fruit which is made into pies and jams. A wonderful range of house specialities such as parkin and sticky toffee pudding. Wide selection of teas; Assam, China, Darjeeling and Earl Grey. Hot meals served from 12 noon until 4.30pm. MONDAYS TO WEDNESDAYS- 10AM TO 4.45PM SATURDAYS AND SUNDAYS- 10AM TO 4.45PM.

51 COCKERMOUTH LAKESIDE Bassenthwaite Lake, Cockermouth, Cumbria CA13 9YD. Contact Mr Semple Fax: 017687 76358.

Comfortable accommodation set in beautiful surroundings. Lounge and two bedrooms overlooking the Lake. Large rear garden and a self-contained catering lodge with all facilities. All rooms have colour TV, radio alarms and tea/coffee making facilities. Visit the Georgian town of Cockermouth or the lake town of Keswick. Bird reserve, nature trails and forest walks nearby.
8 BEDROOMS, ALL EN SUITE.
Prices from £25 to £50

52 COCKERMOUTH SOUTHWAITE FARM Cockermouth, Cumbria, CA13 0RF. Contact Mrs Clark Tel & Fax: 01900 822 370.

Children are very welcome on this relaxed and friendly working farm. Southwaite Farm is situated in a secluded part of the Lake District and set in a peaceful location by the River Cocker. The northern lakes of Bassenthwaite, Derwentwater, Crummock Water and Buttermere are all just a short drive away. Excellent and reasonably priced home cooked evening meals available. Closed Christmas. 3 FAMILY ROOMS. CHILDREN WELCOME.
Prices from £16 to £17.50

53 COCKERMOUTH SUNDAWN Carlisle Road, Bridekirk, Cockermouth, Cumbria, CA13 0PA. Contact Mrs Pauline Hodge Tel: 01900 822 384 E.mail: robert.hodge1@virgin.net

A Large Victorian family home which offers comfortable accommodation and a relaxing atmosphere. Set back from the Cockermouth/Carlisle road and very accessible. Enjoy panoramic views of the Lakeland Fells and the historic town of Cockermouth from the sun lounge. Scenic drive to the nearby Lake District. Closed mid December to mid January. 1 TWIN, 1 DOUBLE EN SUITE, 1 FAMILY EN SUITE CHILDREN ALL.
Prices from £17.50 to £19.75

54 COCKERMOUTH

RIGGS COTTAGE Routenbeck, Bassenthwaite Lake, Cockermouth, Cumbria, CA13 9YN. Contact Mrs Wilkinson Tel & Fax: 017687 76580.
An off the beaten track, charming 16th century lakeland cottage set above Lake Bassenthwaite. Retains many of its original features including inglenook fireplace and oak beams. Well furnished bedrooms. Guests met at the station. 1 DOUBLE, 1 TWIN, 1 FAMILY, 1 SMALL SINGLE, SOME WITH PRIVATE FACILITIES CHILDREN 5+.

Prices from £20 to £25

55 COLNE

HIGHER WANLESS FARM Red Lane, Colne, Lancashire BB8 7JP. Contact Mrs Carolle Mitson Tel: 01282 865301.
Higher Wanless Farm is a 250 year old farmhouse set in the rural area of Pendle. There is fishing available in the nearby Liverpool/Leeds canal and there are various scenic walks that run through Pendle Witch and the breathtaking Bronte country. Manchester Airport is 1 hour away. The Farm's Shire horses have proved popular with guests. Closed December to mid January. 1 TWIN/FAMILY EN SUITE, 1 TWIN CHILDREN 3+.

Prices from £20 to £24

56 COLNE
MIDDLE BEARDSHAW HEAD FARM Burnley Road, Trawden, Colne, Lancashire BB8 8PP. Contact Bob & Ursula Mann Tel & Fax: 01282 865257.
A restored farmhouse set in 15 acres of pastures, woods, streams and pools. Some rooms are oak panelled and beamed, with mullion windows. There are log fires and the furnishings complement the period. All rooms have TV and tea/coffee facilities. Theme holidays can be arranged - art tuition, historical or walking. Small campsite with limited facilities that has recently yielded some prehistoric finds. Packed lunches/evening meals provided by request. Guests from abroad welcome, your hosts speak French, Italian, Spanish and some Japanese. 3 SINGLE, 2 DOUBLE, EN SUITE AND SEPARATE SHOWER. YHA CAMPING BARN AVAILABLE (SLEEPS 20) 2 CARAVANS FOR HIRE.

57 CONGLETON
SWETTENHAM ARMS Swettenham Village, Congleton, Cheshire, CW12 2LF. Tel: 01477 571 284.
An attractive country inn serving food lunchtimes and evenings. Quiz night on Tuesdays, music night on Wednesdays.

58 CONISTON
SUN HOTEL AND COACHING INN Coniston, Cumbria LA21 8HQ. Contact Mr Elson Tel: 015394 41248. Fax: 015394 41219.
Welcoming family run Hotel with own gardens and patio area. This magnificent Hotel stands at the foot of the Coniston Old Man. Restaurant serving good home made food and also at adjacent 16thC Inn. En suite facilities and excellent views. This location is ideal for walkers, with direct access to fells. 11 BEDROOMS, ALL EN SUITE.

Prices from £30 to £80

59 CONISTON

CONISTON LODGE Sunny Brow, Coniston, Cumbria, LA21 8HH. Contact Mr Robinson Tel: 015394 41201 Fax: 015394 41201.
This highly acclaimed Lodge won 'RAC Small Hotel of the Year'. Picturesque scenery, peaceful surroundings, excellent home cooking and a very warm welcome. 6 BEDROOMS, ALL EN SUITE.

Prices from £19 to £75

60 CONISTON

ARROWFIELD COUNTRY GUEST HOUSE Little Arrow/Torver, Coniston, Cumbria, LA21 8AU. Contact Mrs Walton Tel: 015394 41741.
Set in peaceful scenery, is this elegant Victorian house with beautiful gardens and views. Breakfasts include home made bread, preserves, home-produced eggs and honey. Immediate access to fells, making this location ideal for walkers. Closed Dec-Feb. 5 BEDROOMS, ALL EN SUITE.

Prices from £21 to £47

61 DARLINGTON
QUALITY HOTEL Scotch Corner, Darlington, North Yorkshire, DL10 6NR. Tel: 01748 850 900 Fax: 01748 825 417 E.mail: admin@gb609.u-net.com.
Attractive hotel on the A66 exit towards Penrith. Friendly staff and comfortable surroundings. Guests have full use of the leisure centre. Restaurant and bar provide a wide selection of foods and drinks. Local places of interest include Catterick Army Camp 6 miles and the Yorkshire Dales 4 miles. Special package for bikers £26. per person inc. breakfast and dinner. Subject to availability. Must be booked through Central Reservations 0800 44 44 44. 90 BEDROOMS.

62 DARLINGTON

CLOW BECK HOUSE Monkend Farm, Croft on Tees, Darlington, County Durham, DL2 2SW. Contact Heather & David Armstrong Tel: 01325 7211075 Fax: 01325 720419.
Clow Beck House is comfortable and welcoming and situated on the edge of the Yorkshire Dales. Rooms are wonderfully decorated and have many facilities. Fishing for fresh trout is available. Enjoy breakfast and dinner in the conservatory overlooking a superb garden. Ideal for exploring magnificent countryside and the east coast. 6 DOUBLE EN SUITE, 2 TWIN EN SUITE, 1 DOUBLE PRIVATE CHILDREN WELCOME.

Prices from £30

63 DARWEN
MARJORY'S TEA ROOM 65 Blackburn Road, Darwen, Lancashire, BB3 1EJ. Contact Marjory Harrison Tel: 01254 776587.
A cosy atmosphere and friendly serviceoffering home baked cakes and scones. Freshly cut sandwiches are available. CLOSED SATURDAY, SUNDAY AND MONDAY. Situated over antique/second hand shop.

64 DARWEN
ST ALBANS GUEST HOUSE 282 Blackburn Road, Darwen, Lancashire. Tel: 01254 702437 & 01254 771202.
A friendly atmosphere prevails in this easily accessible hotel. All local amenities are conveniently close and some rooms have cable television. A full English Breakfast is available as are evening meals on request. WIDE RANGE OF ROOMS INCLUDING EN-SUITE AND FAMILY ROOMS.

65 DEWSBURY
DEWSBURY MINSTER REFECTORY Dewsbury Minster, Dewsbury, West Yorkshire, WF12 8DD. Tel: 01924 457 057.
Located within the Minster and adjacent to the Heritage Centre and Pilgrimmage Trail. This is a friendly tea room serving a range of home cooked foods including sandwiches, cakes and puddings and casseroles. Average lunch is £3.

66 DONCASTER
PREMIER BIKERS CAFE Selby Road, Askern, Doncaster, South Yorkshire, DN6 0EP. Tel: 01302 703100.
We are open Monday to Saturday from 9am to 6pm, Wednesday from 9am to 11pm. Sunday from 10am to 6pm. Food is served throughout the day, varied menu. We hold a bikers meeting every Wednesday and you are very welcome to come and join the meeting. We also have mini Motor racing.

67 DONCASTER
29 KING STREET Thorne, Doncaster, South Yorkshire, DN8 5AU. Tel: 01405 813634.
The Gates Tea Rooms were built in 1700 as the original gate house for carts entering Thorne. The building has since been used as a beer house, stonemasons and cobbler's workshop. The tea room is situated on the main road opposite Wilsons Carpet Warehouse and just one mile fromjunction 6 of the M18. Dark wood tables and chairs complement the wooden beams inside to give the impression of a bygone age. Cream teas are served in a friendly olde worlde style. MONDAYS TO FRIDAYS - 9AM TO 4PM SATURDAY AND SUNDAY - OPEN FROM 7 AM.

68 DRIFFIELD

THE WOLD COTTAGE Wold Newton, Driffield, East Yorkshire, YO25 3HL. Contact Mrs Katrina Gray Tel & Fax: 01262 470696.
FILEY 7m. Spacious Georgian farmhouse in its own grounds, The Wold Cottage offers peace and tranquillity and lovely views of the nearby woodlands. Large rooms are decorated to a high standard and are great to unwind and relax in. Relaxing walks around the fields, exploring the east coast's wildlife and history with Scarborough and Bridlington only a 12 miles drive. Evening meals by prior arrangement. 2 DOUBLE (1X4 POSTER), 1 TWIN, ALL EN SUITE. CHILDREN WELCOME.

Prices from £20 to £26

69 FLEETWOOD
LANTERN TEA ROOMS 30 Kent Road, Fleetwood, Lancashire. Tel: 01253 874418.
Situated near Fleetwood market, a delightful promenade and the Isle of Man ferry, Lantern Tea Rooms offers a warm, cosy atmosphere. Sit outside on the patio in warm weather or enjoy the comfortable surroundings inside on colder days. Good selection of home baked cakes and scones and a wide range of teas including Assam, Ceylon, China, Darljeeling and Earl Grey. WINTER - CLOSED ON WEDNESDAYS.

70 GRANGE-OVER-SANDS

ELTON Windermere Road, Grange-over-Sands, Cumbria, LA11 6EQ. Contact Mrs Crane Tel: 01539 532838.
A small, family run, licensed hotel set in peaceful surroundings. Good food and hospitality. Ground floor accommodation. 7 BEDROOMS, 5 EN SUITE.
🔲 ⑤
Prices from £20 to £48

71 GRASMERE

GRASMERE Broadgate, Grasmere, Cumbria, LA22 9TA. Contact Mr Riley Tel & Fax: 01539 435277.
Situated in an acre of informal gardens running down to the River Rothey, this Victorian house hotel is close to the centre of Grasmere. It also has an award winning restaurant. Closed January. 12 BEDROOMS, ALL EN SUITE.
🔲 ⑤ 💳 VISA
Prices from £35 to £80

72 GRASMERE

MOSS GROVE Grasmere, Cumbria, LA22 9SW. Contact Martin Wood Tel: 01539 435251 Fax: 01539 435685 E.mail: martinw@globalnet.co.uk.
Established since 1894 Moss Grove has been modernised without losing its olde worlde charm. For an excellent start to the day there is a buffet with a selection of cereals, fruit and yoghurts followed by a full English breakfast. All bedrooms have satellite TV, tea/coffee facilities and direct dial phones.The dinner menu offers good home cooked food. Grasmere is an ideal centre for exploring the whole Lake District. Closed December - January. 14 BEDROOMS, 13 EN SUITE.
🔲 ⑤ 💳 VISA
Prices from £26

73 GRASMERE

THE TRAVELLERS REST Grasmere, Cumbria, LA22 9RR. Tel: 015394 35604 & 0500 600725.
Set in a 16th century former coaching inn, The Travellers Rest is full of character and very welcoming. Real ales, fine wines and home cooking are all available. If you should want to venture out, the hotel is situated in the heart of the Lake District and therefore an excellent base for exploring. Local attractions include the Wordsworth Museum, art galleries and craft centres and Grasmere. Special occasions and private receptions are catered for. 4 DOUBLE, 2 TWIN, 1 SINGLE.
Prices from £20 to £31

74 GREENHEAD-IN-NORTHUMBERLAND

HOLMHEAD GUEST HOUSE Thirlwall Castle Farm, Hadrians Wall, Greenhead-in-Northumberland, Carlisle, CA6 7HY. Contact Pauline & Brian Staff. Tel & Fax: 016977 47402.
A former farmhouse retaining original features, Holmhead Guest House is set in a picturesque location. Ask your host for ideas and information about the local area. Bedrooms are comfortable with compact shower and toilet room. Award winning breakfast menu. Evening meals available with guests dining together at one candlelit table, dinner party style. Lounge with bar and TV for guests. Credit cards accepted. 3 TWIN/DOUBLE, 1 FAMILY, ALL EN SUITE. CHILDREN WELCOME.
✄ ⑤
Prices from £27 to £29

75 HALIFAX

WOODLANDS 2 The Grove, Shelf, Halifax, West Yorkshire HX3 7PD. Contact Mrs S. Wood Tel: 01274 677533.
BRADFORD/HALIFAX: 4m. Ten minutes drive from the M606 and M62, Woodlands is situated in a quiet, private lane with off road parking. Easy to get to nearby Pennines and Yorkshire Dales. The garden is particularly stunning and has it's own waterfall. The interior has been decorated in a country style and is furnished with paintings and items collected during the host's travels in Africa. Breakfasts are varied. Restaurant and pubs nearby. Closed Christmas and New Year. 1 SINGLE EN SUITE, 1 DOUBLE PRIVATE BATHROOM CHILDREN 12+.
Prices from £20

76 HALIFAX
GATSBY'S TEA ROOMS 1a Old Market, Halifax, West Yorkshire, HX1 1TN. Tel: 01422 323 905.
Located in Halifax: town centre, Gatsby's Tea Rooms are spacious and have good views. Traditional Cream Tea, sandwiches, scones with preserve and cream and home made cake and pastry. Special items include a weight watchers daily special where points are already worked out and children's menu for the under 12's. MONDAYS TO FRIDAYS-9.30AM TO 4.30PM SATURDAYS-9AM-4.30PM. CLOSED SUNDAYS.

77 HARROGATE

APRIL HOUSE 3 Studley Road, Harrogate, Yorkshire, HG1 5JU. Contact Ruth & David Hayes Tel: 01423 561 879 Fax: 01423 548 149 E.mail: David@April94.Freeserve.co.uk.
An attractive Victorian house with lots of character situated in quiet residential area. Rooms are decorated to a high standard with charming wood panelled doors, mouldings and original fireplaces. Ideally located to explore the magnificent Yorkshire Dales. Fountains Abbey and Harewood House within easy reach. Closed Christmas. 1 SINGLE, 1 DOUBLE, 1 TWIN, 2 FAMILY, EN SUITE/ PRIVATE FACILITIES. CHILDREN WELCOME.
Prices from £20 to £27

78 HARROGATE

BAY HORSE Burnt Yates, Harrogate, North Yorkshire, HG3 3EJ. Contact Mr Robinson Tel: 01423 770230.
Olde Worlde 18th century inn, open all day during the summer, serving food at lunchtime and evenings. Beers served; Theakstons Best, Tetleys, John Smiths Smooth, Fosters and Carlsberg Export. ACCOMMODATION AVAILABLE.
Prices from £28

79 HARROGATE
QUALITY HOTEL 11-19 Kings Road, Harrogate, North Yorkshire, HG1 5JY. Tel: 01423 505 613 Fax: 01423 530 276.
Located on the A59 Kings Road. Attractive hotel set in ideal location. Friendly service and good accommodation with many facilities. Local attractions include the Turkish Baths and the Royal Pump Room Museum. Special package for bikers £26. per person inc. breakfast and dinner. Subject to availability. Must be booked through Central Reservations 0800 44 44 44. 48 BEDROOMS.

80 HARROGATE

ABBEY LODGE 31 Ripon Road, Harrogate, North Yorkshire, HG1 2JL. Contact Mr Naylor Tel: 01423 569712 Fax: 01423 530570.
Well appointed accommodation where you can enjoy a relaxing break with fine cuisine in the the award winning, proprietor run restaurant. Ideally situated for York, the Dales and Moors. 19 BEDROOMS, 14 EN SUITE.

Prices from £29.50 to £62

---

81 HATHERSAGE
SCOTSMAN'S PACK School Lane, Hathersage, Derbyshire. Tel: 01433 650253.
A comfortable pub offering superb accommodation in the Derbyshire village of Hathersage. Each room has central heating, radio, TV and tea/coffee facilities. 3 DOUBLE, 1 TWIN, 1 SINGLE, ALL EN SUITE.

Prices from £29

---

82 HAWKSHEAD

BUCKLE YEAT Buckle Yeat, Hawkshead, Cumbria, LA22 0LF. Contact Mrs Kirby Tel & Fax: 015394 36446 E.mail: buckleyeat@sawrey.demon.co.uk.
Centrally heated and with log fires, this tastefully furnished guest house offers all guests en suite accommodation. Ideally situated for touring and walking. Open all year. 7 BEDROOMS, ALL EN SUITE.

Prices from £22.50 to £50

---

83 HAYFIELD
SPORTSMAN Kinder Road, Hayfield, Derbyshire, SK22 2LE. Tel: 01663 741565.
6 DOUBLE, ALL EN SUITE.

Prices from £45

---

84 HAYFIELD
ROYAL HOTEL Market Place, Hayfield, Derbyshire, SK22 2EP. Tel: 01663 742721.
3 DOUBLE ALL EN SUITE, 1 FOUR POSTER WITH JACUZZI.

Prices from £50

---

85 HEBDEN BRIDGE

REDACRE MILL Mytholmroyd, Hebden Bridge, West Yorkshire, HX7 5DQ. Contact Captain and Mrs A. R Peters Tel: 01422 885563/01422 881569.
A restored Victorian mill, Redacre Mill is set in lovely gardens and waterside lawns. Right on the banks of the Rochdale canal, guests can relax in peace and tranquillity or visit the nearby cities of Manchester and Leeds. It is ideally situated for touring the magnificent Bronte country and the South Pennines. An imaginative dinner menu provides a wide range of delicious meals. 2 TWIN EN SUITE, 2 DOUBLE EN SUITE CHILDREN WELCOME.

Prices from £29

86 HELMSLEY

CROWN INN Market Place, Helmsley, North Yorkshire YO62 5BJ. Contact Mr Hutchinson Tel: 01439 770297 Fax: 01439 771595.
Dating back to the 16th century in a picturesque part of North Yorkshire in an area with super bikers roads. The Crown Inn offers a friendly atmosphere in which to enjoy one of the many well kept beers. Open from 11am - 3pm and 5:30pm to 11pm. Traditionally home cooked food served. 12 BEDROOMS, ALL EN SUITE.

Prices from £30

87 HELMSLEY

LASKILL FARM Hawnby, Helmsley, North Yorkshire, YO6 5NB. Contact Mrs Smith Tel & Fax: 01439 798268.
An attractive, stone built farmhouse situated in the North York Moors National Park near Rivaulx Abbey. It is ideally situated for touring the surrounding places of interest and scenic beauty. York is 45 minutes away. 6 BEDROOMS, ALL EN SUITE.

Prices from £26 to £52

88 HEXHAM

PLANETREES Keenley, Allendale, Hexham, Northumberland, NE47 9NT. Contact Mrs I Lee Tel: 01434 345 236.
ALLENDALE 3m/HEXHAM 12m. Planetrees is located high in the Pennines and has panoramic views of the surrounding area, Hadrian's Wall and the Cheviot Hills. This charming stone cottage is comfortably furnished and is a great place to relax after exploring the stunning countryside. Visit nearby Beamish and Metro City or the Lake District (1 hour's drive). Good local inns at nearby villages. Turn off A686 at the Elks Head pub at Whitfield to get to Keenley. Closed Christmas. 2 DOUBLE (1 EN SUITE), 1 SINGLE CHILDREN 8+.

Prices from £19 to £21

89 HEXHAM

AYDON 1 Osborne Avenue, Hexham, Northumberland NE46 3JP. Contact Mrs Shelagh Potts Tel: 01434 602 915.
A charming Edwardian terraced house set in a peaceful location in the market town of Hexham. Aydon is a large, spacious house retaining many of its period features. Bedrooms are attractively furnished and very comfortable. Separate guest's lounge/dining room with TV and a useful variety of maps and guide books. Hadrian's Wall, museums and other interesting sites only a few miles away. Dinner available if arranged in advance. Closed Christmas. 1 DOUBLE, 1 FAMILY/TWIN/DOUBLE CHILDREN 2+.

Prices from £17.50 to £18

90 HOLMFIRTH
30 UPPERBRIDGE Holmfirth, West Yorkshire, HD7 1JS. Tel: 01484 681408.
This is The Wrinkled Stocking Tea Room seen in the TV series The Last of the Summer Wine and is frequented by the cast of the programme. Local attractions include the summer wine exhibition and the scenery of West Yorkshire. The tea room offers warm and friendly waitress service with food and sandwiches freshly made to order. Cakes are home baked, and the range of teas include Yorkshire, Breakfast Blend, Fine Ceylon, Darjeeling and Earl Grey. OPEN ALL YEAR ROUND SEVEN DAYS A WEEK - 10AM TO 5PM CLOSED ONLY ON CHRISTMAS DAY.

91 HUDDERSFIELD
'MOONRAKER' FLOATING TEAROOM Commercial Mills, Slaithwaite, Huddersfield, Yorkshire, HD7 5HB. Tel: 01484 846370.
Moonraker Floating Tea Room has a distinctive location, on board a narrow boat on the canal between locks 23 and 24. The boat is fitted out in pine creating a warm clean atmosphere. The parking is located near the canal, adjacent to Church Lane in the centre of Slaithwaite. Cakes and biscuits are baked in the galley daily, and there is no set menu for afternoon tea, so there are plenty of options. In warmer weather the ice-cream floats are delicious. Ceylon, Orange Pekoe Darjeeling and Earl Grey are among the teas available.
SUMMER: TUESDAYS TO SATURDAYS - 9AM TO 6PM, SUNDAYS - 10AM TO 6PM, MONDAYS - CLOSED WINTER: MONDAYS AND TUESDAYS - CLOSED, WEDNESDAYS TO SATURDAYS - 9AM TO 4PM, SUNDAYS - 10AM TO 4PM.

92 HULL
COMFORT INN Analby Road, Kingston-upon-Hull HU1 2PJ.
Tel: 01482 323 299 Fax: 01482 214 730.
Located on M62 onto A63 onto A1079 Ferensway. All rooms are furnished and decorated to a high standard. Facilities include cable TV and gym. Visit Humber Bridge, Sea World and York Minster (37 miles). Special package for bikers £26. per person inc. breakfast and dinner. Subject to availability. Must be booked through Central Reservations 0800 44 44 44. 59 BEDROOMS.

93 HULL
QUALITY HOTEL 170 Ferensway, Kingston-upon-Hull, Hull, HU1 3UF.
Tel: 01482 325 087.
HULL. Located on the M62 onto A63 onto A1079 Ferensway. Guests can be assured of a warm and friendly welcome and a high standard of accommodation. Facilities include tea/coffee making facilities and cable TV. Humber Bridge (2 miles) and Sea World (18 miles) are some of the many places to visit in this area. Special package for bikers £26. per person inc. breakfast and dinner. Subject to availability. Must be booked through Central Reservations 0800 44 44 44. 155 BEDROOMS.

94 INGLETON

SPRINGFIELD Main Street, Via Carnforth, Ingleton, North Yorkshire, LA6 3HJ. Contact Mr Thornton
Tel & Fax: 015242 41280.
A detached, family run6 Victorian villa with fountain in the front. Set in its own grounds with great views and backing on the the River Greta. Closed Christmas.
5 BEDROOMS, ALL EN SUITE.

Prices from £22 to £46

95 KEIGHLEY

MOORFIELD GUEST HOUSE 80 West Lane, Haworth, Keighley, West Yorkshire, BD22 8EN. Contact Barry and Pat Hargreaves
Tel & Fax: 01535 643689.
Moorfield Guest House is a detached Victorian guest house with stunning views of the Bronte country. Between Haworth village and the moors, the Bronte Parsonage Museum and the famous Main Street are within easy walking distance. Relax in the friendly and comfortable dining room and look out over the gardens and cricket ground. Closed Christmas and New Year. 1 SINGLE, 2 TWIN, 3 DOUBLE, 1 FAMILY, MOST EN SUITE. CHILDREN WELCOME.

96 KENDAL
THE KENT TAVERN Kent Street, Kendal, Cumbria, LA9 4AT.
Contact Christien & Cameron Bolton Tel: 01539 722 410.
Bikers can expect a warm and friendly welcome at this pub. Drinks include Boddingtons Trophy, Stella, Strongbow and Guinness.

97 KENDAL

SUMMERLANDS TOWER Endmoor, Kendal, Cumbria, LA8 OED.
Contact Hazel & Michael Green
Tel & Fax: 015395 61081
Previously a Victorian Gentleman's residence, Summerlands Tower has been renovated to a beautiful country house retaining many of its original features. Summerlands is set in a peaceful area overlooking 3 acres of mature gardens and borders the Lake District and the Yorkshire Dales. Visit the nearby Sizergh Castle and Levens Hall. 3 miles from M6, junction 36. Closed November to February. 1 DOUBLE EN SUITE, 1 TWIN PRIVATE, 1 TWIN CHILDREN 12+.

Prices from £22.50 to £28

98 KENDAL

CROOK HALL Crook, Kendal, Cumbria, LA8 8LF.
Contact Mrs P Metcalfe Tel: 01539 821 352.
W'MERE/KENDAL 5m. Crook Hall is a 17th century historic working farm with original features and spacious accommodation. Situated in a quiet private farm lane between Windermere and Kendal with views to the Lakeland Hills. Explore the footpaths that stretch over the farmland. Wonderful oak panelling in the TV lounge. Closed December to March inclusive. 2 DOUBLE, 1 DOUBLE/FAMILY EN SUITE CHILDREN WELCOME.

Prices from £18 to £22.50

99 KESWICK

WHITE STONES Underskiddaw, Keswick, Cumbria, CA12 4QD.
Contact Mrs M Houldershaw Tel: 017687 72762.
An unusual Victorian residence set in peaceful and attractive grounds and gardens, with panoramic views of the surrounding valleys and fells. Between Bassenthwaite Lake and Derwentwater and near Keswick, a small market town. Walks, climbing and fishing are all available. Closed Christmas and New Year. 3 DOUBLE, 1 FAMILY CHILDREN WELCOME.

Prices from £17 to £20

100 KIRKBY STEPHEN
KINGS HEAD VILLAGE PUB Raven Stonedale, Kirkby Stephen, Cumbria.
Contact Gordon Stewart Tel: 01539 623 284.
Drinks include 3 Real Ales and smooth Cask Ales. Food is served all day and there is a choice of snacks and meals. Warm, friendly atmosphere where bikers are very welcome. Accommodation also available.

Prices from £30

101 KNUTSFORD
DOG INN Well Bank Lane, Over Peover, Knutsford, Cheshire, WA16 8UP.
Tel: 01625 861421.
Situated 10 minutes outside Knutsford in Over Peover, the Dog is a superb country inn serving food lunchtime and evening. ACCOMMODATION AVAILABLE.

102 LANCASTER
THE FARMERS ARMS Penny Street, Lancaster, Lancashire, LA1 1AT.
Contact Tony Williams Tel: 01524 36368.
A Biker friendly place that welcomes you to try a wide selection of food and drink. Beverages include Thwaites Traditional and Smooth, Carling, Carlsberg, Guinness and Guinness Gold. Food available all day. MAG meetings every other Monday.

103 LANCASTER
THE THREE MARINERS St. Georges Kuay, Lancaster, Lancashire, LA1 1EE.
Contact Les & Rhiannon Layton Tel: 01524 388 957.
Second oldest pub in the country established 1213 with Beers; Flowers, Tetleys, Tetleys Smooth and Guinness. Food available 12-2.30pm with evening meals on request. Lancaster and Morecombe MCC meet every Wednesday night.

104 LANCASTER
LANCASTER PRIORY REFECTORY Lancaster Priory Church, Lancaster
Lancashire LA1 1YZ. Tel: 01524 65338.
Spacious, quiet, welcoming converted choir vestry with a wide variety of food and drink. Snacks include soup and sandwiches, cakes and baked potatoes. MON-SAT 10AM-4PM SUNDAY CLOSED.

105 LEEDS

WIKE RIDGE FARM Wike, Shadwell, Leeds, West Yorkshire LS17 9JF. Contact Mrs Jill McCandish Tel: 0113 266 1190.
Wike Ridge Farm is a stone farmhouse that retains its old character with oak beams and log fires. With views of the lovely gardens and farmland, the house also overlooks golf courses to the North Yorkshire Moors. Situated to the edge of a quiet village yet with easy access to the M1, A1, M62, York and 2 miles from Harewood House. 1 DOUBLE, 1 TWIN/FAMILY, 1 SINGLE. CHILDREN WELCOME.
🅓 ⌇ Ⓢ **Prices from £18**

106 LEVENS

BIRSLACK GRANGE Hutton Lane, Levens, Windermere, South Cumbria, LA8 8PA.
Contact Jean & John Carrington-Birch. Tel: 015395 60989.
KENDAL 5m. A converted barn, Birslack Grange is situated on the outskirts of the peaceful rural village of Levens, winner of Cumbria's Best Kept Village Award. Spacious lounge with wonderful views of the famous Lyth valley and Lakeland Fells. Sizergh Castle, Levens Hall Southern Lakes and Beatrix Potter attractions are all close at hand. 1 DOUBLE, 2 TWIN, 1 TWIN/FAMILY, ALL EN SUITE CHILDREN 7+.
⌇ **Prices from £20**

107 LEYBURN
GOLDEN LION Market Square, Leyburn, North Yorkshire, DL8 5AS.
Contact Mrs Wood Tel: 01969 622161.
Open all day, food served at lunchtime and evening. Beers served are; John Smiths Smooth, Theakstons Best, Fosters, Strongbow, Guinness and Oliver John Bitter (local independent brew). Live entertainment on Sunday. ACCOMMODATION AVAILABLE.

108 LIVERPOOL
LIVERPOOL CATHEDRAL REFECTORY Liverpool Cathedral, Liverpool, L1 7AZ.
Tel: 0151 709 6271 Fax: 0151 709 1112.
A large 80 seater restaurant situated in the Liverpool Cathedral Refectory. There is a good range of food here to suit all tastes with all meals freshly made on the premises. MON-SAT 10AM-4PM SUNDAY 12NOON-5PM.

109 MANCHESTER
QUALITY HOTEL Waters Reach, Trafford Park, Manchester, M17 1WS.
Tel: 0161 873 8899 Fax: 0161 872 6556.
MANCHESTER. Located on the M6, junction 7, A56 to Manchester. A welcoming smile and comfortable surroundings are offered in this hotel with high class accommodation. Rooms are comfortably furnished with tea/coffee making facilities and cable TV. Local places of interest include Manchester United Football Club, Granada Studios, the G-Mex Exhibition Centre and the Lowry Centre. Special package for bikers £26. per person inc. breakfast and dinner. Subject to availability. Must be booked through Central Reservations 0800 44 44 44. 111 BEDROOMS.
🍸 Ⓢ

110 MANCHESTER
COMFORT INN Hyde Road, West Gorton, Manchester, M12 5NT.
Tel: 0161 220 8700 Fax: 0161 220 8848.
MANCHESTER. Located on the junction of the A57/A6010. Enjoy a good standard of accommodation with many facilities. Local places of interest include Granada Studios, Manchester United Stadium and Manchester City Stadium. Special package for bikers £26. per person inc. breakfast and dinner. Subject to availability. Must be booked through Central Reservations 0800 44 44 44. 90 BEDROOMS.
🍸 🎄 Ⓢ ⚐

111 MANCHESTER
THE CROWN TAVERN Booth Street, Manchester.
Contact Peter Tel: 0161 237 0801.
Every Sunday is bikers night (you are welcome any night) We have a rock disco with the Satan Slaves, selected drinks at £1 each. Full range of beers, wines and spirits and full menu is available.

112 MIRFIELD

FIVE ARCHES Calder Farm, Sand Lane, Mirfield, West Yorkshire, WF14 8HJ. Contact Jean and Keith Crabtree Tel: 01924 498699.
MIRFIELD 1m. Five Arches is situated in a tranquil location with views over the moorland to nearby towns. There is easy access to Huddersfield (4 miles), the M62 (3 miles) and Leeds (10 miles). An ideal spot for business people and tourists. On the doorstep of Dewsbury District Golf Club where visitors are welcome. 2 TWIN (1 EN SUITE, 1 PRIVATE), 1 FAMILY (EN SUITE) CHILDREN 10+.

113 NELSON IN PENDLE
LOVETT GUEST HOUSE, 6 Howard Street, off Carr Road (B6249), Nelson In Pendle, Lancashire. Contact Lesley Chisnell Helm Tel: 01282 697 352 Fax: 01282 700 186.
Situated in a beautiful and historical area, Lovett Guest House offers comfortable accommodation where bikers are particularly welcome. Warm hospitality and reasonable prices. Excellent base for touring.

🔲 🆂   **Prices from £19.50 to £37**

114 NETHER WASDALE
SCREES HOTEL Nether Wasdale, Cumbria, CA8 1LE. Tel: 01946 726262.
This homely hotel offers good quality accommodation in an attractive environment. Convenient for local attractions including the Lake District. 2 EN-SUITE ROOMS, 1 TWIN, 1 DOUBLE.

                                       Prices from £23 to £40

115 NEWCASTLE UNDER LYME
COMFORT INN Liverpool Road, Newcastle Under Lyme, Staffordshire, ST5 9DX. Tel: 01782 717 000 Fax: 01782 713 669.
Located on Junction 16 M6 then A500 to A34. Furnished and decorated to a high standard, Comfort Inn has lots to offer including a mini gym for guests use and bar and restaurant. There are many attractions nearby including Waterworld (2 miles), Alton Towers (18 miles) and Festival Park (3 miles). Special package for bikers £26. per person inc. breakfast and dinner. Subject to availability. Must be booked through Central Reservations 0800 44 44 44. 75 BEDROOMS.

🍷 🍴 🆂 ⚓

116 NEWCASTLE UPON TYNE
COMFORT INN CARLTON 82-86 Osborne Road, Jesmond, Newcastle Upon Tyne, NE2 2AP. Tel: 0191 281 3361 Fax: 0191 281 7722.
Located on the A1 to A167 to A1058 then left. Quality accommodation in good location. Nearby attractions include Gosforth Racetrack (3 miles), Eldon Shopping Mall (3 miles) and Quayside (1 mile). Special package for bikers £26. per person inc. breakfast and dinner. Subject to availability. Must be booked through Central Reservations 0800 44 44 44. 35 BEDROOMS.

🍷 🔲 🍴 🆂 ⚓

117 NORTHALLERTON

NURSERY COTTAGE Leeming Bar, Northallerton, North Yorkshire, DL7 9BG. Contact David & Edna Braithwaite Tel: 01677 422 861 Fax: 01677 426 847.
BEDALE 2m. Nursery Cottage is an attractive, modernised cottage and guests are assured of a warm and friendly welcome with complimentary home-made scones and tea on arrival. Just off the A1, it is ideally located for touring the Dales and Moors and visiting historic abbeys. Closed November to February inclusive. 1 DOUBLE, 1 TWIN/TRIPLE, PRIVATE FACILITIES AVAILABLE CHILDREN 12+.

118
NORTHALLERTON

WELLFIELD HOUSE North Otterington, Northallerton, North Yorkshire, DL7 9JF. Contact Mrs Hill Tel: 01609 772 766.
Situated on a working sheep and arable farm, Wellfield House is an attractive building in a peaceful setting. Has large garden with patio and fishpond and coarse fishing available (no charge). Nearby Yorkshire Moors and Dales for walks and other activities. Convenient for those travelling to/from Scotland and using the A1. Local village inns provide good food. Closed Christmas. 1 FAMILY, 1 TWIN, 1 DOUBLE PRIVATE BATHROOM CHILDREN WELCOME.

Prices from £18 to £22

---

119 NORTHWICH
QUALITY HOTEL London Road, Northwich, Cheshire, CW9 5HD. Tel: 01606 44443 Fax: 01606 42596.
Located on the M6 exit 19 A556 to Northwich then A533. Unique accommodation in own grounds. Hotel offers many facilities including mini gym. Places of interest include Englands only floating hotel, Beeston Castle (6 miles), Chester Zoo (20 miles) and the Boat Museum (16 miles). Special package for bikers £26. per person inc. breakfast and dinner. Subject to availability. Must be booked through Central Reservations 0800 44 44 44. 60 BEDROOMS.

---

120 PENRITH
TOPOS ITALIAN RESTAURANT Penrith, Cumbria. Contact John Tel: 01768 866987.
We are a very popular Italian restaurant in the heart of Penrith, the gateway to the English Lakes. Ask anybody they will tell you where we are. We serve the finest quality italian traditional foods. We have a full and quality range of wines. All our food is cooked and prepared by John the owner and chef. We welcome motorcyclists. Some of our best customers are motorcyclists, including the editor. This is one of his favourite eating places.

---

121 PENRITH
THE VILLAGE BAKERY Melmerby, Penrith, Cumbria, CA10 1PT. Tel: 01768 881 515.
A 200 year old converted stone barn with views of the distant Pennine hills. Restaurant shop selling a range of fresh bread, cakes, biscuits, puddings, jams and a range of baking equipment. Imaginative menu which includes bacon & avocado on sunflower bread and smoked trout on Borodinsky bread. Afternoon Tea includes delights such as organic simnel cake, organic cheese scone with butter or Grasmere gingerbread. Teas served include loose leaf teas and there are a range of other drinks including home made lemonade. MONDAYS TO SATURDAYS-8.30AM TO 5PM SUNDAYS-9.30AM TO 5PM.

---

122 PICKERING
ABBEY TEA ROOM, Rosedale Abbey, Pickering, Yorkshire, YO18 8SA. Tel: 01751 417 475.
Opposite the church with views of the village green, Abbey Tea Room is warm and cosy with pretty decor. Yorkshire Cream Tea offers a scone with strawberry jam, whipped cream, home made cake and a pot of tea. Freshly prepared sandwiches and home baked cakes and scones. Try the delicious ginger scone with ginger jam and cream, or apricot and cheese gateau. Teas include Ceylon, Darjeeling and Earl Grey. EASTER TO END OF OCTOBER- 10.30AM TO 5.30PM (CLOSED WEDNESDAYS).

123 PRESTON

JENKINSONS FARMHOUSE Alston Lane, Longridge, Preston, Lancashire, PR3 8BD. Contact Mrs E. J. Ibison Tel: 01772 782624.
PRESTON 8m. Jenkinsons Farmhouse is an olde worlde farmhouse with oak beams, inglenook fireplace and four poster beds. Situated 15 minutes from the M6, junction 31 off the B6243. Near the Ribble Valley it is surrounded by herbaceous gardens in idyllic countryside. Complementary afternoon teas on arrival. Ideally located to stop off for journeys between London and Scotland. Closed Christmas. 3 TWIN, 2 DOUBLE, 1 SINGLE. CHILDREN 12+.

🔲 ⌇ 𝕊   **Prices from £20 to £25**

124 PRESTON

MIDDLE HOLLY COTTAGE Middle Holly Lane, Forton, Preston, Lancashire, PR3 1AH. Contact Jack & Kate Worsnop Tel: 01524 792 399.
LANCASTER 7m. Middle Holly Cottage is a tastefully refurbished former coaching inn offering high quality accommodation. En suite Bedrooms have colour TV, telephones and other extras. Convenient for Preston, Blackpool and Lancaster and ideal for stopover to/from the north and Scotland. Nearby pubs and restaurants. 1 SINGLE, 1 FAMILY, 1 TWIN, 3 DOUBLE, ALL EN SUITE CHILDREN ALL.

🔲 ⌇ 𝕊   **Prices from £19.75 to £26.50**

125 PRESTON
DOG & PARTRIDGE 44 Friargate, Preston, Lancashire PR1 2AT.
Contact Ronnie Fitzpatrick Tel: 01772 252 217.
DOG & PARTRIDGE, PRESTON. Special welcome to bikers at this pub with secure motorcycle park. Real Ales include Bass and Whitbread. Bar lunches are from 12-2.00pm, served 6 days a week. Pub games available. Rock disco every Thursday and Sunday.

𝕊

126 RIBCHESTER
THE NEWDROP INN Ribchester, Lancashire, . Tel: 01254 878 338 Fax: 01254 878 542.
THE NEWDROP INN, RIBCHESTER. Family run Country Inn situated in the Ribble Valley specialising in home cooked foods. Delicious food available with an a la carte menu, table d'hote, lunches (Sundays) and bar meals. Wedding parties & dinner dances are catered for.

127 RICHMOND
THE WHITE HOUSE Anvil Square, Reeth, Richmond, North Yorkshire, DL11 6TE. Tel: 01748 884763.
Close to the countryside and many local crafts, The White House, located opposite Barclays Bank in Reeth, offers good views and pleasant decor enhanced by the fine bone china on the table. There is no set menu, but the variety of cakes, scones and jams are home-made and sandwiches are served with a huge salad. Assam Darjeeling and Earl Grey are the traditional teas on offer. There is also a selection of herbal teas. OPEN DAILY FROM 10:30AM TO 4:30PM (SUNDAY LUNCH ONLY) CLOSED WEDNESDAYS AND THURSDAYS CLOSED DURING FEBRUARY.

128 RIPON

YEW TREE FARM Kirkby Malzeard, Ripon, North Yorkshire, HG4 3SE. Contact Mrs Barbara Atkinson Tel & Fax: 01765 658 474.
Situated in the Dales village of Kirkby Malzeard, Yew Tree Farm offers accommodation in converted farm buildings. The Dales, the ancient town of Ripon, and the floral town of Harrogate are just a handful of the attractions that are right on the doorstep. Visit the world famous Old Peculiar at nearby Masham. 3 TWIN, 2 DOUBLE, 1 FAMILY, ALL EN SUITE, 4 ON GROUND FLOOR CHILDREN WELCOME.

✄ S **Prices from £22.50**

---

129 RIPON
BLACK A MOOR Boroughbridge Road, Ripon, North Yorkshire, HG4 5AA. Contact Margaret Alice Perez Tel: 01765 603 511.
We are a main road side inn and an award winning "motorcycle friendly" public house that specialises in Spanish Tapas food. Relax in this modern restaurant and let us serve you with home-made snacks or dinner in the evening. A good range of beers, wines and spirits. Function room available.

---

130 ROCHDALE
THE DOG AND PARTRIDGE 370 Oldham Road, Rochdale, Lancashire, OL11 2AL. Tel: 01706 645858.
Motorcyclists are very welcome at this pub. Every Tuesday night is bikers night. The Rochdale Road Runners Bikers Club meet here every Tuesday. They plan the next weeks activities, runs, socials and charity events etc. We provide FREE OF CHARGE FOOD on bikers night. The pub is part of the Bramwells Food Group. We do a comprehensive range of bar snacks.

---

131 ROCHDALE
THE MUCKY DUCK 81 Drake Street, Rochdale, Lancashire OL14 1SD. Contact Phil & Ivy Tel: 01704 351 624.
Bikers welcome at this friendly pub. Alcoholic beverages include Scottish & Newcastle Beers, Fosters, Websters, Ciders and Guinness. Live music Thursday and Sunday and every other Tuesday.

---

132 ROSSENDALE
THE ROYAL HOTEL 729 Baccup Road, Waterfoot, Rossendale, Lancashire BB4 7EU. Contact Mr Horsfall Tel: 01706 214 493 Fax: 01706 215 371.
ROSSENDALE. Biker friendly hotel where all rooms have en suite facilities. Free entrance to Club Royal for residents. Hearty breakfast served from 7am with food available all day. Large function room available. Group discounts on request.

⌾ S **Prices from £22.50**

---

133 SCARBOROUGH
THE DONNINGTON HOTEL 13 Givendale Road, Scarborough, Yorkshire, YO12 6LE. Tel: 01723 374394. E-mail: www.epoch.co.uk/donnington
Accommodation run by bikers, for bikers. Very secure parking in alarmed garage with CCTV. Close to Olivers Mount race track and some of the best biking roads in Yorkshire.

⌾ S

134 SCARBOROUGH HOLLY CROFT 28 Station Road, Scalby, Scarborough, North Yorkshire, YO13 OQA. Contact John and Christine Goodhall Tel: 01723 375 376 Fax: 01723 360 563.

A lovely Victorian detached house with a large garden situated in the village of Scalby on the outskirts of Scarborough. Enjoy a game of Billiards or unwind in the peaceful conservatory. Ideal for countryside walks and touring the North Yorkshire Moors. Easy access to Castle Howard, Burton Agnes and Bempton Cliffs RSPB nature reserve. The nearby Alan Ayckbourne theatre, pubs and restaurants guarantee good food and entertainment .Closed Christmas and New Year. 1 DOUBLE PRIVATE BATHROOM, 1 TWIN EN SUITE SHOWER CHILDREN 5+.

🔲 ✂ ⓢ   **Prices from £22.50**

---

135 SETTLE

THE OAST GUEST HOUSE 5 Pen-y-Ghent View, Church Street, Settle, North Yorkshire, BD24 9JJ. Contact Margaret King Tel: 01729 822989.

The Oast Guest House is within walking distance of Settle and Pen-y-Ghent, one of the three peaks of the Ribble valley. Settle, an unspoilt market town, is situated in the Yorkshire Dales. Enjoy a scenic trip on the Settle - Carlisle railway line. Evening meals and packed lunches provided. Vegetarians catered for. 1 SINGLE, 2 TWIN, 2 DOUBLE, 1 FAMILY MOST EN SUITE OR PRIVATE FACILITIES CHILDREN 5+.

🔲 ✂ ⓢ   **Prices from £17 to £23**

---

136 SETTLE
GOLDEN LION HOTEL Duke Street, Settle, North Yorkshire, BD24 9DU.
Contact Mr Phillip Longrigg Tel: 01729 822203.

A traditional, busy Thwaites' inn open all day with food served lunchtime and evening. Beers served are: Thwaites, Carling and Carlsberg. ACCOMMODATION AVAILABLE.

Prices from £23.50

---

137 SKIPSEA

THE GRAINARY Skipsea Grange, Hornsea Road, Skipsea, Yorkshire, YO25 8SY. Contact Frances Davies Tel: 01262 468 745 & 01262 468 440.

HORNSEA 5m. The Grainary is a converted granary and is part of a farm that is over 5 generations old. Located on the east coast, it is a few minutes stroll to the sea. The Grainary has a homely atmosphere and being well equipped with games it would be ideal for families with young children. Guests have free membership of the nearby leisure complex and caravan site with swimming pool, bars and night club. 1 SINGLE, 2 DOUBLE/FAMILY, ALL EN SUITE CHILDREN WELCOME.

🔲 ✂ ⓢ   **Prices from £18 to £20**

---

138 SKIPTON

ALTON HOUSE 5 Salisbury Street, Skipton, North Yorkshire, BD23 1NQ. Contact Mrs Phillis Sapsford Tel & Fax: 01756 794780.

A delightful Victorian town house, Alton House offers a warm and friendly welcome and comfortable beds. Set in a quiet area off Gargrave road, the nearby town centre with its many attractions is only a few minutes walk away. Ideally located for touring the Yorkshire Dales. Special rates for out of season breaks. Closed December and the New Year. 1 TWIN, 2 TRIPLE CHILDREN 10+.

✂   **Prices from £17.50 to £20**

139 SKIPTON
**THE PRIEST'S HOUSE Bardon Tower, Skipton, North Yorkshire, BD23 6AS.
Tel: 01756 720 616.**
Situated in a 15th century priests house, close to Stirred Woods and right in the heart of the magnificent Yorkshire Dales. Tea terrace at the tower offers light snacks for bikers and hikers with dainty or doorstep sandwiches. Menu includes biscuits, crumpets, pancakes and a selection of cakes and puddings. Range of speciality teas to suit every taste including fruit and herbal teas. SUMMER (MARCH TO OCTOBER) OPEN SATURDAYS AND WEDNESDAYS 10.30 TO 5PM CLOSED NOVEMBER TO MID MARCH.

140 SKIPTON

DALE HOUSE Cove road, Malham, Skipton, North Yorkshire, BD23 4DH. Contact Gill and Andy Jessup Tel: 01729 830664.
A large 18th century house with its own walled grounds, Dale House is situated in Malham, a bustling village in the Yorkshire Dales. Malham has many attractions including Malham Cove and Gordale Scar, which were painted by Turner and Malham Tarn, the inspiration for Kingsley's The Waterbabies. The National Park Centre, pubs and craft shops also offer relaxing walks and a range of activities. 2 DOUBLE (1 EN SUITE), 1 TWIN CHILDREN ALL.
🖻 ⅍ Ⓢ **Prices from £20 to £25**

141 SOUTHPORT
**NOSTALGIA TEA ROOM 215-217 Lord Street, Southport, Merseyside, PR8 1NZ.
Tel: 01704 501 294.**
Listed building in half-timbered black and white style with window tables looking out onto the Victorian arcade of Lord Street. A light and airy interior with personally designed bamboo furniture. Sample the range of home made meals and soups or enjoy a Cream Tea, Afternoon Tea or Special Afternoon Tea. TUESDAYS TO SATURDAYS-9.30AM TO 5PM, SUNDAYS- 10AM TO 5PM. CLOSED ON MONDAYS. OPEN BANK HOLIDAYS 10AM TO 5PM.

142 SPENNYMOOR

IDSLEY HOUSE 4 Green Lane, Spennymoor, County Durham, DL16 6HD. Contact Mrs Joan Dartnell Tel: 01388 814 237.
DURHAM 6m. Idsley House, a detached Victorian house, is located just 6 miles south of Durham Castle and Cathedral. Ideally situated for those wishing to tour the north east, North Yorkshire, Northumbria and the nearby borders of Scotland. Beamish Open Air Museum, Bowes museum at Barnard Castle and the North Yorkshire National Parks are all within easy driving distance. Breakfast is served in the conservatory. On junction A167/A688. Credit cards accepted. Closed Christmas and New Year. Evening meals by arrangement. 1 DOUBLE, 2 TWIN, 1 FAMILY, 1 SINGLE, MOST EN SUITE CHILDREN 5+.
🖻 ⅍ Ⓢ **Prices from £24 to £35**

143 SUNDERLAND
**QUALITY HOTEL Witney Way, Boldon, Sunderland, Tyne & Wear, NE35 9PE.
Tel: 0191 519 1999 Fax: 0191 519 0655.**
Located on Junction of A19/A184. High standard of accommodation and facilities at this hotel. Enjoy the use of leisure centre with indoor swimming pool. Places to visit include Metro Shopping Centre (9 miles), Wildfowl Reservation (2 miles) and Durham Cathedral (18 miles). Special package for bikers £26. per person inc. breakfast and dinner. Subject to availability. Must be booked through Central Reservations 0800 44 44 44. 82 BEDROOMS.
🍷 Ⓢ ⚲

144 THE BORDERS
GRAHAM ARMS HOTEL Longtown, The Borders, Cumbria, CA6 5SE.
Tel: 01228 791213 Fax: 01228 792830 E.mail: hotel@cumbria.com.
The Graham Arms Hotel is a former Coaching Inn, less than 7 miles from the M6 and Scottish Border. The ideal overnight stop or perfect touring base for the Scottish Borders, English Lake District, Hadrians Wall, Keilder Forest and the Solway Coast. The fine biking roads and spectacular scenery abound. the rooms are comfortable and there is excellent food and drink. Special short-break rates are available. Secure courtyard parking. Established venue for touring clubs and individuals. Visit our website www.cumbria.com/hotel.

🅐 🆂

145 THIRLMERE

THE KINGS HEAD HOTEL Thirlmere, Cumbria, CA12 4TN.
Tel: 0500 600 725.
Near Keswick. Enjoy comfortable surroundings in this 17th century former coaching Inn located in beautiful countryside. Bedrooms are individually furnished and have colour TV, tea and coffee making facilities and superb views of the Fells. Ideal for exploring the breathtaking countryside. Free membership to Low Wood Health, Fitness and Leisure Club with gymnasium, swimming pool and sauna. Delicious food served in restaurant. 18 BEDROOMS, 9 DOUBLES, 4 TWINS, 2 FAMILY, 4 SINGLE.

146 THIRSK
ANGEL INN Long Street, Topcliffe, Thirsk, Yorkshire, YO7 3RW.
Contact Mr Adron Tel: 01845 577237.
A charming 17th century inn with a friendly atmosphere. Open all day with food available all day.
ACCOMMODATION AVAILABLE.

147 THORNTON
TIFFINS TEA SHOP Marsh Mill Village, Thornton, Lancashire. Tel: 01253 857 100.
A purpose-built Tea Room situated on the edge of the village square. Well known locally for its range of high quality home baked cakes. Food is freshly prepared and beautifully presented. A full menu includes light lunches, hot meals, toasts, salads and a children's menu. Try the speciality; Lancashire Bagging afternoon tea which offers two thick slices of Borrowdale Tea Loaf with creamy Lancashire cheese and butter with tea for one. MONDAYS TO SATURDAYS-10AM TO 5PM SUNDAYS-11AM TO 5PM WITH LAST ORDERS FOR FOOD AT 4.30PM.

148 TODMORDEN
SPORTSMAN ARMS Kebs Road, Kebcote, Todmorden, Lancashire, OU4 8SB.
Visit this biker-friendly, highest pub in Lancashire. Restaurant and bar snacks available Wednesday to Sunday. Open all day Saturday and Sunday. Drinks include cask guest Ales, Caffreys, Carling Premier and Guinness.

149 ULVERSTON

COBBLESTONES Causeway End, Ulverston, Cumbria
LA12 8JW. Contact Hazel & David Brown. Tel/fax: 015395 31391.
NEWBY BRIDGE 3m. Cobblestones is a charming 16th century former farmhouse with delightful original features. Set in a peaceful and picturesque location with views of the surrounding meadow, forest and moorland. Centrally situated between Lake Windermere and Coniston Water and ideal for touring the Lake District. A short drive brings you to Grizedale Forest and Hawkshead. Wonderful home cooked food. Bicycle hire available. 20 minutes from M6 and easy access from A590. 2 DOUBLE, 1 TWIN/DOUBLE, ALL EN SUITE CHILDREN ALL.

Prices from £22 to £26

FOWLERS

Discover a two-wheeled society you only dreamed of...

No more wondering who you can ask to come for a spin, no more staring blankly at a map for inspiration - just join Fowlers Riders Club...!

Life will never be the same again - yours that is!

It's Fun!

- **Evening Ride Outs**
- **Sunday Breakfast Runs**
- **Ride Outs to Britain's top race meetings**
  Including the British Superbikes Championships and the British Grand Prix
- **Factory Visits** - *Visit the Triumph factory*
- **Weekend Ride Away Trips**

It's Fantastic!

- **Track Days** - *Special prices for FRC members at Castle Combe and Mallory Park*
- **Advanced Rider Training**
  10% reduction available for FRC members
- **Theme Park Weekends**
  Big thrills at Alton Towers at reduced prices
- **Genuine Motorcycle Parts** - *10% reduction on production of a FRC card at Fowlers branches*
- **Big Rock Intercontinental Bike Tours**
  10% discount available to FRC members

& It's Free!

- **No Membership Fees** • **Introductory Goody Bag**
- **Free Quarterly magazine, 'The Flying F'**
- **FRC Information Hotline**
- **Promotion Evenings & Barbecues**

To join Fowlers Riders Club, call Barry Maunders at Fowlers on 0117 977 0466

Or
ww

150 WAKEFIELD
ST CATHERINES CHURCH CENTRE Doncaster Road, Belle Vue, Wakefield, West Yorkshire WF1 5HL. Tel: 01924 211 130 Fax: 01924 211 010.
A recently renovated church and community centre which is warm and welcoming and has a large menu selection. MON-FRI 9AM-4PM SATURDAYS & SUNDAYS.

151 WARRINGTON
THE IMPERIAL Bewsey Road, Warrington, Cheshire, WA5 5LG. Tel: 01925 437 255.
Wide range of Beers and Lagers. MAG meets every Thursday at 8.30.

152 WHITBY

NETHERBY HOUSE 90 Coach Road, Sleights, Whitby, North Yorkshire, YO22 5EQ. Contact Peter O' Brien Tel & Fax: 01947 810 211.
A lovely Victorian stone house set in 2.5 acres of garden and bordering the North Yorkshire Moors National Park. Stunning walks in this scenic Heartbeat country. The coast and the fishing port of Whitby are just 3.5 miles away. The evening meals are varied and eating times are flexible. There is a games room available to guests. Four poster bed. Private parking. Closed January. 1 SINGLE, 3 DOUBLE, 2 TWIN, 1 FAMILY, ALL EN SUITE CHILDREN ALL.

⌾ Ⓢ **Prices from £17.50 to £25**

153 WHITBY
FLASK INN Robin Hoods Bay, Fylingdales, Whitby, North Yorkshire, YO22 4QH. Tel: 01947 880305.
Originally a 17thC monks hostelry with food served lunchtime and evening. ACCOMMODATION AVAILABLE.

154 WIGAN
QUALITY HOTEL Riverway, Wigan, WN1 3SS. Tel: 01942 826 888 Fax: 01942 825 800.
WIGAN. From M6, take J25/26, A49 turnover. Good accommodation in pleasant surroundings. Rooms are decorated to a high standard. There are shopping facilities close at hand and places of interest include Granada Studios, Blackpool, Camelot Theatre, Chester and the Lake District. Special package for bikers £26. per person inc. breakfast and dinner. Subject to availability. Must be booked through Central Reservations 0800 44 44 44. 88 BEDROOMS.

🍷 Ⓢ ♿

155 WIGAN
QUALITY HOTEL Prescott Road, Up Holland, Nr. Skelmersdale, Wigan, WN8 9PU. Tel: 01695 720 401 Fax: 01695 50953.
Located on the M58 Junction 5-1 mile. Traditional looking accommodation offering a relaxed, comfortable atmosphere. Restaurant and cocktail bar facilities. Nearby places of interest include Wigan Pier, Granada Studios and The Albert Dock. Special package for bikers £26. per person inc. breakfast and dinner. Subject to availability. Must be booked through Central Reservations 0800 44 44 44. 55 BEDROOMS.

🍷 Ⓢ ♿

156 WIGAN
THE CHATTERIES TEA ROOMS 7 Jaxons Court, Wigan, Lancashire, WN5 1LR.
Tel: 01942 820 988.
The Chatteries Tea Rooms can be found in an olde world complex to the side of Wigan station, not far from the Wigan Pier. Varied menu for breakfast, lunch and afternoon tea. Cream Tea offers a scone with cream and preserve and a pot of English Breakfast Tea. Good menu including hot pot with red cabbage or beetroot a pot of tea or coffee and a scone or Eccles cake. Teas served include Assume, Ceylon, Darjeeling and Earl Grey. MONDAYS TO SATURDAYS-9AM TO 4.30PM SUNDAYS-CLOSED.

157 WINDERMERE
LOWTHER COTTAGE Lake District, Windermere, Cumbria.
Contact Derek Sweeney Tel: 0500 600 725.
A highly commended 16th century listed cottage with many original features including oak beams and flagstone stairways. Rooms are decorated to a high standard and offer a cosy atmosphere. Wonderful sitting room with traditional atmosphere and colour TV. Shops, pub and restaurant within walking distance. Pets taken if well behaved and arranged in advance. 2 BEDROOMS, 1 DOUBLE, 1 TWIN.

158 WINDERMERE

HAISTHORPE HOUSE Holly Road, Windermere, Cumbria LA23 2AF. Contact Mick & Angela Brown. Tel: 015394 43445 Fax: 015394 48875. E.mail: haisthorpe@clara.net.
Haisthorpe House is a charming traditional lakeland stone house situated in a quiet area of Windermere. Guests are assured of high quality accommodation and service in this friendly family run guest house. Ideally located for exploring the Lake District. Local restaurants, shops and train/coach station with free collection by arrangement. Guests have free membership of leisure complex. Credit cards accepted. 3 DOUBLE, 1 TWIN, 1 FAMILY 1 SINGLE, ALL EN SUITE OR PRIVATE FACILITIES.

Prices from £17 to £22

159 WINDERMERE

BEAUMONT Thornbarrow Road, Windermere, Cumbria LA23 2DG. Contact Bob & Maureen Theobald Tel: 015394 45521 Fax: 015394 46267.
Beaumont is an elegant Victorian house midway between Windermere and Bowness, set in one acre of beautifully landscaped gardens with wonderful views of the Fells. Guests have free membership of the Parklands Country Club Leisure Complex. Visit the many attractions in Windermere where there are some fabulous eating places. 3 DOUBLE, 2 FAMILY, ALL EN SUITE CHILDREN ALL.

Prices from £23 to £37

160 WORKSOP
FROG AND NIGHTGOWN 30 Carlton Road, Worksop, Nottingham, S80 1PH.
Contact Roy Borrowdale.
Reasonably priced food and drink at this biker friendly pub. Barn available for F.O.C overnight stay. A welcome barbecue can also be arranged.

161 YORK

SOUTHLANDS Hutington Road, York, North Yorkshire, YO3 9PX. Contact Mrs Klavenes. Tel: 01904 766 796 Fax: 01904 764 536. Southlands is a large, detached house on the outskirts of York, set in tranquil grounds with private parking. The city centre is 2 miles away and there is a regular 5 minute bus journey that will take you there. Rooms are of a high standard and there is a separate lounge available for guests. Ideal for visiting the stunning Yorkshire countryside and for sampling its many attractions. From Huntingdon/Strensall roundabout on A1237 head for York/Huntingdon. Southlands house is 1.3 miles on left. Closed mid December to mid January. 2 DOUBLE, 2 TWIN/FAMILY, ALL EN SUITE CHILDREN 9+.

Prices from £19 to £28

---

162 YORK

CLARK'S TEA ROOMS Market Place, Easingwold, York, North Yorkshire YO61 3AG. Tel: 01347 823 143.
Situated close to the North Yorkshire Moors, Clark's Tea Rooms are located in the market square of a charming Georgian town overlooking the green. Afternoon Tea consists of a range of sandwiches, savouries such as pasties, sausage rolls, cakes and scones. Owners have their own bakery which produces the bread, cakes and pastries found here. Specialities include Yorkshire curd tarts, fruit cake and local Wensleydale cheese. Visit their bakery at 195 Long Street where breakfast is available. MONDAYS TO THURSDAYS-10AM TO 5PM FRIDAYS AND SATURDAYS-9.30AM TO 5PM.

---

165 YORK

WAKENDALE HOUSE Oldstead Grange, Coxwold, York, North Yorkshire, YO61 4BJ. Contact Mrs M.J Banks Tel: 01347 868351. THIRSK 8m. Wakendale House offers accommodation with a traditional farming family. Superb views of wooded valleys and hills in a peaceful setting and located half a mile from Oldstead village. Guests are welcome to look around the extensive farmlands. Closed November to February inclusive. 1 DOUBLE, 1 TWIN, 1 FAMILY FOR 4 CHILDREN ALL.

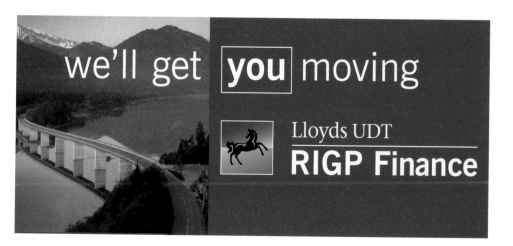

166 YORK
QUALITY HOTEL LADY ANNE MIDDLETON Skeldergate, York, North YorkshireYO1 6DS. Tel: 01904 611 570 Fax: 01904 613 043.
Located on the A64 from Leeds to York, then A1036. Elegant property in leafy surroundings. Rooms are individually decorated and furnished. Leisure centre, fishing and golf nearby. Places of interest include York Minster, Cliffords Tower and the Jorvik Centre. Special package for bikers £26. per person inc. breakfast and dinner. Subject to availability. 52 BEDROOMS. Booked through Central Reservations 0800 44 44 44.

167 YORK

WHITE DOVES GUEST HOUSE 20 Claremont Terrace, Gillygate, York, North Yorkshire, YO3 7EJ. Contact Mr & Mrs Pearce Tel: 01904 625 957.
Located in a quiet cul-de-sac, this Victorian guest house is 5 mins walk from York Minster and the City Centre. Restaurants just around the corner. Rooms are comfortable and provide excellent rest after a busy day's sightseeing in the City or in the surrounding Moors and Dales. Closed during Christmas. 3 DOUBLE EN SUITE, 1 FAMILY PRIVATE CHILDREN 5+.

Prices from £20 to £24

168 YORK

ARNOT HOUSE 17 Grovesnor Terrace, York, North Yorkshire YO3 7AG. Contact Mrs & Miss Sluter-Robbins Tel & Fax: 01904 641 966.
CITY CENTRE. The house offers modern amenities whilst also retaining its period features with Victorian style bedrooms. Overlooking the Park and Minster, it is only a 5 minute walk from York Minster with city centre shops and restaurants just a few minutes away. The nearby Moors and Dales are just an hours drive away. Breakfast menu that caters for vegetarians. Private parking. Closed Christmas. 3 DOUBLE, 1 TWIN, ALL EN SUITE CHILDREN 12+.

Prices from £24 to £27.50

169 YORK

MANOR FARMHOUSE Main Street, Sutton upon Derwent, York, North Yorkshire, YO41 4BN. Contact Mrs Diana Arnold Tel: 01904 608 009.
A former farmhouse, Manor Farmhouse is set in an attractive village just 7 miles drive from York. Rooms are well decorated and spacious. Separate lounge for guests. Parking space. Easy access to York's many attractions including the Yorkshire Air Museum (1.5 miles away). A traditional pub serving excellent food is a few minutes stroll. 2 DOUBLE, 1 TWIN, 1 SINGLE, ALL EN SUITE.

Prices from £20 to £22.50

170 YORK

ALDER CARR HOUSE York Road, Barmby Moor, York, North Yorkshire, YO4 5HU. Contact Mrs C. Steel Tel: 01759 380 566 & 0585 277 740.
YORK 8m. Alder Carr House is a Georgian style house set in extensive grounds. Guests can be assured of a warm and friendly welcome and a quiet, relaxing atmosphere. Spacious rooms with views of the surrounding countryside. Pocklington, a nearby market town, boasts a range of traditional and alternative eating places. Sample the traditional delights of Yorkshire. Your historian hostess will be happy to share her extensive knowledge of the local attractions. Closed Christmas and New Year. TWIN/DOUBLE/FAMILY ROOMS, ALL EN SUITE WITH PRIVATE FACILITIES CHILDREN ALL.

Prices from £17

1 ABERDEEN

ABERDEEN SPRINGBANK GUEST HOUSE 6 Springbank Terrace, Aberdeen, Aberdeenshire, AB11 6LS. Tel: 01224 592048.

Family run Guest House 5 minutes from the city centre, rail, bus and ferry terminals, theatre and restaurants. Near Duthie Park. En route to Royal Deeside and castle trail. All rooms have tea/coffee facilities and TV. ALL ROOMS EN SUITE.

Prices from £16 to £25

2 ABERDEEN

KILDONAN 410 Great Western Road, Aberdeen, Aberdeenshire, AB10 6NR. Contact Ann Dey Tel: 01224 316115.

Kildonan is a warm and friendly guest house with modern facilities and a TV in every room. The mornings are a treat with a traditional Scottish breakfast to set you up for an enjoyable day at Deeside or Donside which are only a short distance away. Closed from Christmas - New Year. 6 BEDROOMS, 5 EN SUITE.

Prices from £20 to £30

3 ABERDEEN

BIMINI GUEST HOUSE 69 Constitution Street, Aberdeen, Aberdeenshire, AB2 1ET. Contact Colin Morrison Tel: 01224 646912 Fax: 01224 646755.

Bimini is a short stroll from the seafront, local golf courses and a variety of city centre attractions. This guesthouse offers comfortable accomodation with a relaxing atmosphere. 8 BEDROOMS, 6 EN SUITE.

Prices from £20 to £50

4 ABERDEEN

FOURWAYS 435 Great Western Road, Aberdeen, Aberdeenshire, AB1 6NJ. Contact Mr Milne Tel & Fax: 01224 310218.

Fourways is situated in a quiet residential area of Aberdeen. Ideal for exploring Royal Deeside. Rooms are attractively decorated and offer comfortable surroundings and a television. 6 BEDROOMS, ALL EN SUITE.

Prices from £25 to £40

5 ABERLADY

KILSPINDIE HOUSE Main Street, Aberlady, East Lothian, EH32 0RE. Tel: 01875 870 682.

Open all day serving a good range of beers, real ales, spirits and wine. Bar food and restaurant available. ACCOMMODATION AVAILABLE.

6 ACHARACLE

STRONTIAN HOTEL Strontian, Acharacle, Argyllshire, PH36 4HZ. Contact Mr & Mrs Cunningham Tel: 01967 402029 Fax: 01967 402314.

We are a small and very friendly hotel and we welcome motorcyclists to come and stay with us. We are located by the shores of Loch Sunart. We have a fully licensed restaurant where we serve tasteful food. The bedrooms are elegantly furnished and well appointed. This is a very lovely part of Scotland with lochs and fishing, walking, shooting and a super place to relax and enjoy your self. It is centrally located to tour the area from.

7 AIRDRIE
THE FOURWAYS Black Street, Airdrie, ML6 6LX. Tel: 01234 743 498.
Bikers can expect a hospitable welcome at this pub which serves a variety of beverages including Tennents, lager, Blackthorn and Guinness. Bar lunches daily from 12 noon-3pm. Evening meals and bar snacks available Thursday, Friday, Saturday and Sunday. Bikers meet on Sundays.

8 ARGYLL
ARDSHEAL HOUSE Kentallen of Appin, Argyll, PA38 4BX.
Contact Mr & Mrs N. Sutherland Tel: 01631 740 227 Fax: 01631 740 342.
A historic 16th century mansion situated on the shores of Loch Linnhe and set in 800 acres of gardens, fields and woodlands. A truly amazing property decorated to a very high standard with billiard table. Ideally located to explore nearby Fort William and the surrounding countryside. Varied course set dinner menu.

Prices from £39 to £42

9 ARGYLL OF BUTE
KIRKTON HOUSE Darleith Road, Cardcross, Argyll of Bute, Argyll, G82 5EZ.
Contact Mr & Mrs Macdonald Tel: 01389 841 951 Fax: 01389 841 868
E.mail: Kirktonhouse@compuserve.com.
Enjoy a peaceful setting with wonderful views of the Clyde in this award winning 18thC converted farmstead. Modern amenities, a friendly service, an open fire in the guest lounge and home cooking guarantee a relaxing and comfortable stay. Walks and weekday golf. Discounts for longer stays. Closed December and January 4 DOUBLE/TWIN/FAMILY EN SUITE, 2 TWIN EN SUITE. CHILDREN ALL.

Prices from £29.50 to £35

10 AULTBEA
ALTBEA HOTEL Aultbea, Ross-shire, 1V22 2HX. Tel: 01445 731 201.
Wonderful 18th century hotel on the shores of Loch Ewe. Open all day serving bar food. ACCOMMODATION AVAILABLE.

11 AULTBEA
DRUMCHORK LODGE Aultbea, West Ross, IV22 2HU.
Groups and rallys welcome at this pub offering a traditonal Scottish atmosphere. Scottish ales, 200 malt whiskies in "water of life" bar. Restaurant serving delicious meals. ACCOMMODATION AVAILABLE. FREE CAMPING ALSO.

Prices from £25

12 AYR
QUALITY HOTEL Burns Statue Square, Ayr, KA7 3AT.
Tel: 01292 263 268 Fax: 01292 262 293.
Located on the A70 from South, A77 from North. Attractive building with a high standard of accommodation and service. There is a full fitness centre available including sauna and jacuzzi. Restaurant and bar offer comfortable surroundings in which to relax and unwind. Places of interest include the nearby beach, Seaworld (7 miles) and Culzean Castle and Country Park (2 miles). Special package for bikers £26. per person inc. breakfast and dinner. Subject to availability. Must be booked through Central Reservations 0800 44 44 44. 75 BEDROOMS.

13 AYRSHIRE
THE BALGRAY INN Ayrshire, KA15 1HP. Tel: 01505 504 122.
Tennent's House and a wealth of other beverages served here. Strathgryffe MCC meet every Monday at 8.30pm.

14 BALLACHULISH
LYN-LEVEN GUEST HOUSE Ballachulish, Highland, PA39 4JW.
Contact Mr & Mrs J.A. MacLeod Tel: 01855 811392 Fax: 01855 811600.
Award winning licenced accommodation overlooking Loch Leven in the Highlands of Scotland. Ideal location for touring, fishing, walking and climbing.

🔲 Ⓢ   **Prices from £22**

15 BALLATER
BANK HOUSE Station Square, Ballater, Aberdeenshire, AB35 5QB.
Contact Mr & Mrs Chalmers Tel: 013397 55996.
Located in the picturesque village of Ballater, Bank House has wonderful views of Lochnagar and the nearby mountains. Ideally located to explore Royal Deeside, historical castles and whisky distilleries. Activities include gliding, and winter skiing. Plenty of superb restaurants in Royal Deeside.
1 DOUBLE, 1 TWIN, 2 FAMILY, ALL EN SUITE. CHILDREN ALL.

🍴   **Prices from £20 to £23**

16 BALLATER
OAKLANDS HOUSE 30 Braemar Road, Ballater, Aberdeenshire, AB35 5RL.
Contact Evechen & Peter Duff Tel: 013397 55013.
Set in the scenic village of Ballater, Oaklands is a delightful Victorian property with beautiful surroundings. The nearby Cairngorm and Grampian mountains offer a rich landscape with glorious panoramas. Balmoral Castle, whisky distilleries, walks and fishing are just some of the many attractions. Aberdeen just 1 hour. Closed October to April inclusive. 2 DOUBLE, 1 TWIN, ALL EN SUITE. CHILDREN ALL.

🍴 Ⓢ   **Prices from £20 to £24**

17 BALLINDALLOCH BRIDGE OF BROWN TEA ROOMS & CRAFT SHOP Tomintoul, Ballindalloch, Banffshire, AB37 9HR. Contact Graham & Susan Larrington. Tel & Fax: 01807 580335.

Bikers are always welcome at our tea room. We are motorcyclists ourselves and can offer advice and information on local runs and places to visit. Bikers can dry their clothing and in winter we have a log fire burning. We open at 8am and offer a full menu all day. We specialise in home baking and have a craft shop. We have mountain bikes for rent, or we have outdoor clothing if you fancy a highland walk. We are in the middle of the Grampians, close to Aviemore, for skiing in the Winter or for you to relax and enjoy some of the most breathtaking scenery in Scotland. We are on the famous 'whisky trail'. In our craft shop you can buy motorcycle products, maps etc and you can also receive model aircraft construction and flight tuition if you fancy something different.

🔲 ☆ £ Ⓢ

18 BANCHORY
BURNETT ARMS 25 High Street, Banchory, Aberdeenshire, AB31 5TD. Tel: 01330 824 944.
18th century Inn situated in the town centre. Tempting bar snacks and meals available. ACCOMMODATION AVAILABLE.

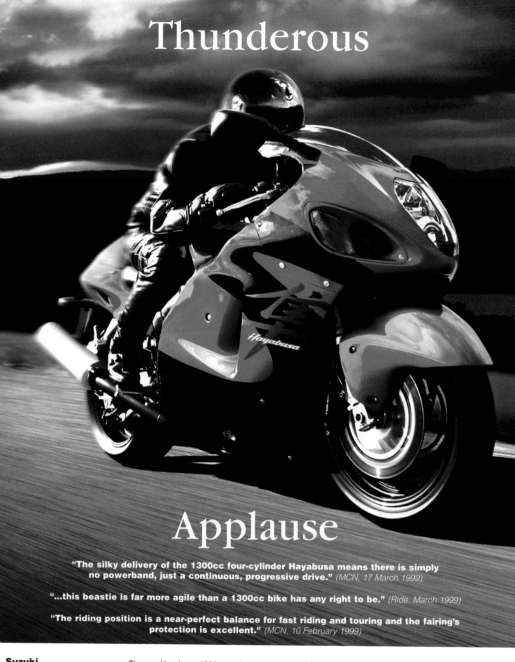

Thunderous

Applause

"The silky delivery of the 1300cc four-cylinder Hayabusa means there is simply no powerband, just a continuous, progressive drive." *(MCN, 17 March 1999)*

"...this beastie is far more agile than a 1300cc bike has any right to be." *(Ride, March 1999)*

"The riding position is a near-perfect balance for fast riding and touring and the fairing's protection is excellent." *(MCN, 10 February 1999)*

**Suzuki
GSX1300R Hayabusa**

The new Hayabusa. 1300cc engine, awesome 175PS, revolutionary aerodynamics and exceptional handling. Hardly surprising that the reception by the press to the new GSX1300R has been deafening in its praise. Spend a few quiet moments, think what your reaction will be, then call us for your copy of the MCN road test. If you expect a lot from your motorcycle, we'll expect your call. **01892 707001**.

**Suzuki Information Department, PO Box 56, Tunbridge Wells, Kent TN1 2XY
or visit our website at www.suzuki.co.uk**
Details correct at time of going to press.

SUZUKI
Ride the winds of change

19 BANFF
THE ORCHARD Duff House, Banff, Aberdeenshire, AB45 3TA.
Contact Mrs Mackie Tel & Fax: 01261 812146 E.mail: jma691429@aol.com.
A warm and friendly welcome is assured at this traditional house, set in three-quarters of an acre of grounds, enjoying complete privacy. Within walking distance of Banff and Duff House Royal Golf Club.
1 DOUBLE, 1 SINGLE, 2 TWIN, ALL EN SUITE.

🗑 Ⓢ   **Prices from £20**

---

20 BANFF
BANKHEAD CROFT Gamrie, Banff, Aberdeenshire, AB45 3HN.
Contact Lucy R. Smith Tel & Fax: 01261 851 584.
Comfortable country cottage set in peaceful surroundings. All Bedrooms have en suite facilities. Within easy reach of whisky trails, castles and bird sanctuaries. Ideal for exploring the charming fishing villages of the North East. Delicious breakfasts and evening meals that use home grown ingredients. Aberdeen and Inverness both 1 hour. 1 FAMILY, 1 DOUBLE, 1 TWIN, ALL EN SUITE. CHILDREN ALL.

🗑 ✂ Ⓢ   **Prices from £17 to £18**

---

22 BY BANCHORY
ROWANBANK By Banchory, Aberdeenshire, AB31 6NL.
Contact Mrs Pat Mallen. Tel & Fax: 01330 824 257.
Rowanbank is a modern stone house located on Royal Deeside. Spectacular views with Ballater and Braemar just a short drive. Nearby places of interest include Crathes, Drum and Dunotter Castles. Ideal base for exploring the rich variety of Deeside. Closed Christmas and New Year. 1 TWIN, 2 DOUBLE, 2 PRIVATE BATHROOMS CHILDREN 5+.

🗑 ✂ Ⓢ   **Prices from £18**

---

23 BY BEAULY
ARDGOWAN LODGE Wester Phoineas, By Beauly, Inverness-shire, IV4 7BA.
Contact Liz Brown & Peter Redsell Tel & Fax: 01463 741 745.
Set in 2 acres of secluded gardens, Ardgowan Lodge is part of a former Victorian coach house. Furnished and decorated to a high standard and very comfortable. Easy access to the Highlands and Inverness. Further afield the Isle of Skye, John O' Groats and the whisky country of Speyside. A wide range of attractions including wonderful scenery, historic castles and museums. Tasty home cooked dinners.
2 DOUBLE EN SUITE, 1 TWIN PRIVATE CHILDREN 12+.

🗑 ✂ Ⓢ   **Prices from £18 to £20**

SV650S and SV650
Engineered to deliver a brilliant response

Suzuki
SV650S/SV650

Here it is... 'astonishingly high standards of handling for a middleweight...' *MCN, Dec 1998*; '...the SV's 90 degree, liquid-cooled vee twin engine kicks out as much horsepower as the 100cc bigger Monster...' *Which Motorcycle, Feb 1999*; 'Alloy frames are rare on budget bikes and this one's beautifully made...' *Ride, Feb 1999*; 'The SV is stuffed full of character...' *Bike, Feb 1999*; 'Big fun' *MCN, Dec 1998*. If you expect a lot from your motorcycle, we'll expect your call. **01892 707001.**

Suzuki Information Department, PO Box 56, Tunbridge Wells, Kent TN1 2XY or visit our website at www.suzuki.co.uk
Models shown are the sports faired SV650S and the sports naked SV650. Details correct at time of going to press.

SUZUKI
Ride the winds of change

24 BY CUPAR
TODHALL HOUSE Dairsie, By Cupar, Fife, KY15 4RQ.
Contact Joan & Gill Donald Tel & Fax: 01334 656 344.
ST. ANDREWS 7m. Country house with extensive views over the Eden Valley. Cupar and St. Andrews nearby, Todhall is ideally located for exploring the historic Kingdom of Fife and its many attractions. Visit Edinburgh (1 hour) or relax in the wonderful grounds that boast lovely rosebeds. Closed November to February. 1 DOUBLE, 1 TWIN, BOTH EN SUITE BATH/SHOWER, 1 DOUBLE EN SUITE SHOWER.

🗗 ⅍ Ⓢ   VISA ⬤   **Prices from £25 to £32**

25 CAIRNDOW
THISTLE HOUSE St. Catherines, Cairndow, Argyll, PA25 8AZ.
Contact Donald & Sandra Cameron Tel: 01499 302 209 Fax: 01499 302 531.
INVERARAY 15m. Built in Victorian times, Thistle House is a spacious country home on the Loch Fyne shores with views of Inveraray and the castle. Argyll Forest Park is nearby and there is lots to do here including walking, climbing, fishing, golf and pony trekking. Enjoy cruises on Loch Lomond, Loch Awe and the Clyde. Closed November to March inclusive. 2 DOUBLE, 1 TWIN, 1 FAMILY, ALL EN SUITE CHILDREN ALL.

⅍   **Prices from £19 to £25**

26 CAITHNESS
BILBSTER HOUSE Wick, Caithness, Highlands, KW1 5TB.
Contact The Stewart family Tel & Fax: 01955 621 212.
WICK 5m. An elegant 18th century listed country house set in 5 acres of woodlands and gardens. Comfortable, traditionally furnished bedrooms with electric blankets provided. Visit Caithness and its many attractions including the famous John O'Groats and Orkney Islands. Closed Christmas and the New Year. 2 DOUBLE (1 EN SUITE), 1 TWIN EN SUITE CHILDREN ALL.

⅍   **Prices from £16 to £17**

27 CALLANDER
ANNFIELD North Church Street, Callander, Perthshire, FK17 8EG.
Contact Mrs Greenfield Tel: 018773 30204.
CALLANDER. Family run stone built guesthouse located in a quiet setting off the main street in Callander. The Scottish Highlands and the Trossachs are within easy reach and nearby Callander has lots of shops and restaurants. Climb the Callander Crag (1000 feet) or enjoy activities such as walking, golf, tennis and bowling. Closed Christmas and New Year. 6 TWIN/DOUBLE, 1 FAMILY, SOME EN SUITE CHILDREN 2+.

🗗 ⅍ Ⓢ   **Prices from £20 to £22**

28 CANISBAY
BENCORRAGH HOUSE Upper Gills, Canisbay, Caithness, KW1 4YB.
Tel & Fax: 01955 611449.
Stay at Bencorragh House and enjoy panoramic views across pentland Firth to the Orkney Isles. Rooms are decorated to a high standard and guests are assured of comfortable and relaxing surroundings. Delicious evening meals available. 4 BEDROOMS, ALL EN-SUITE CLOSED JANUARY.

🗗 Ⓢ ♨   ⬤ VISA   **Price: £25 to £40**

29 CARLISLE
BESSIESTOWN FARM COUNTRY GUEST HOUSE Catlowdy, Longtown, Carlisle, Cumbria, CA6 5QP. Contact Margaret & Jack Sisson Tel & Fax: 01228 577 019.
Overlooking the Scottish Borders, Bessiestown is a wonderful farm guesthouse. Ideal stopover for journeys to/from Scotland with easy access to J44 of M6. Excellent for travel to the Lakes, Scotland and Hadrian's Wall. Mouthwatering breakfasts, dinners and sweets. Indoor heated swimming pool open mid May to mid September. 2 DOUBLE, 1 TWIN, 1 FAMILY, ALL EN SUITE CHILDREN 5+.

Prices from £23.50 to £25

30 CARLISLE
STREETHEAD FARM Ivegill, Carlisle, Cumbria, CA4 0NG.
Contact Mrs J Wilson Tel: 01697 473 327.
PENRITH/CARLISLE 9.5M. Streethead Farm is an elegant farmhouse just ten minutes drive from the M6 (junction 41 or 42). Large bedrooms overlook the orchard and ponds which are home to rare breeds of ducks. Scotland and the Lake District 1/2 hours drive away. Speciality sausages as well as other delicious choices for breakfast. Complimentary evening tea for guests. Closed Christmas and New Year.
1 DOUBLE/TWIN/FAMILY, 1 DOUBLE, BOTH EN SUITE CHILDREN 7+.

Prices from £20 to £22

31 CARLISLE
THE GILL FARM Blackford, Carlisle, Cumbria, CA6 4EL.
Contact Mrs D. Nicholson Tel: 01228 675326.
CARLISLE 4m. A large 18th century Georgian farmhouse on a beef/sheep farm set in tranquil countryside. Rooms are decorated to a high standard and there is a spacious lounge with colour TV. Conveniently located for travellers en route to Scotland just three miles from M6 (junction 44) and off A7. Visit the historic Carlisle, Hadrian's Wall, the Lake District and the Scottish Borders. 1 DOUBLE, 1 TWIN, 1 FAMILY CHILDREN ALL.

Prices from £17 to £20

32 CARNWATH
WALSTON MANSIONS FARMHOUSE Walston, Carnwath, Lanark, ML11 8NF.
Contact Mrs Margaret Kirby Tel & Fax: 01899 810 338.
BIGGAR 5m. A lovely farmhouse where children are especially welcome. Biggar market town is just a few miles away and Edinburgh and Glasgow are also easy to get to. Home grown vegetables and meat make delicious evening meals. Dogs by prior arrangement. 1 TWIN, 2 FAMILY CHILDREN ALL.

Prices from £15 to £17

33 CASTLE DOUGLAS
CULGRUFF FARM Crossmichael, Castle Douglas, Dumfries and Galloway, DG7 3BB.
Contact Mrs H. Sledge Tel: 01556 670 285.
DUMFRIES 20m. Magnificent Galloway countryside surrounds Culgruff Farm which is situated between Gretna Green and Stranraer. En suite bedrooms offer a comfortable and relaxing atmosphere. There is birdwatching, golf, fishing and sailing available and wonderful gardens to visit. Closed Christmas and New Year. 2 DOUBLE, 1 SINGLE, ALL EN SUITE CHILDREN NONE.

Prices from £25

34 CATACOL
CATACOL BAY HOTEL Catacol, Isle of Arran, KA27 8HN.
Tel: 01770 830231 Fax: 01770 830350.
Comfortable friendly accommodation where good cooking is a speciality. Extensive bar menu and meals are served from noon untill 10pm. Special breaks, brochure available on request. Open all year.

35 CONNEL
KILCHURN Connel, Argyll, PA37 1PG. Contact Jean Clark Tel: 01631 710 581.
OBAN 5m. Situated in the charming village of Connel, Kilchurn is a detached granite villa with views of Ben Lora. Ideal for visiting the Isle of Mull and Iona and good hill walks nearby. Oban just a few miles away and Fort William 1 hours drive. Closed November to April. 1 TWIN, 2 DOUBLE, ALL EN SUITE CHILDREN 12+.

Prices from £18 to £25

36 CRAINLARICH
CRAIGBANK GUEST HOUSE Crainlarich, Perthshire, FK20 8QS.
Contact Mrs Flockhart Tel: 01838 300 279.
Lovely stone house located in the central Highlands with superb surrounding countryside. Rooms decorated to a high standard and lounge boasts delightful open fire. The Trossachs, Loch Lomond and Glencoe are all just an hours drive away. Walking and fishing provide enjoyable and relaxing activities. Full Scottish breakfast to see you through the day. Closed Christmas. 2 FAMILY, 1 DOUBLE, 3 TWIN (1 EN SUITE).

Prices from £16 to £18

38 CUPAR
NINEWELLS FARM Woodriffe Road, Newburgh, Cupar, Fife, KY14 6EY.
Contact Mrs B. Baird Tel & Fax: 01337 840 307 E.mail: nwfarm@premier.co.uk.
PERTH 10m. Traditional farmhouse with spectacular views of the Tay Valley and Perth mountains. A homely atmosphere in this comfortable home on a working farm. Off A913 and a few minutes from junction 9 of the M90. Explore magnificent countryside and nearby Edinburgh, Perth and St. Andrews. Closed November to March. 1 DOUBLE EN SUITE, 1 TWIN, 1 TRIPLE, BOTH WITH PRIVATE FACILITIES. CHILDREN 9+.

Prices from £18 to £25

39 DALKEITH
BELMONT 47 Eskbank Road, Dalkeith, Midothian, EH22 3BH.
Contact Mrs Margaret Jarvis Tel & Fax: 0131 663 8676.
EDINBURGH 6m. A spacious Victorian house with many original fittings including a period bathroom. Regular and frequent bus service to Edinburgh city centre. Home produced honey with breakfast. Pets welcome. Closed Christmas and New Year. 2 DOUBLE (1 EN SUITE), 1 TWIN/TRIPLE CHILDREN WELCOME.

40 DINGWALL
STATION TEA ROOM & CRAFT SHOP Station Square, Dingwall, Ross-shire, IV15 9JD. Tel: 01349 865894.
Part of Dingwall Railway Station, The Tea Room and Craft Shop is a wonderful welcome to the small market town. Listed building, built in 1886. Cakes, scones and jams are home made and the local baker bakes the bread. Also serves homemade soups and light lunches are also available. SUMMER- MONDAYS TO SATURDAYS 10AM TO 5PM WINTER - MONDAYS TO SATURDAYS 10AM TO 4PM.

41 DRUMNADROCHIT
WESTWOOD Lower Balmacaan, Drumnadrochit, Inverness-shire, IV63 6WU. Contact Sandra Sike Tel & Fax: 01456 450 826.
Situated near Loch Ness, Westwood is a comfortable bungalow with superb views. Glens Affric, Cannich and Strathfarrar are all just 10 miles away and offer scenic walks amongst a variety of wildlife. Ideally located for touring the Highlands and daytrips to Skye and Ullapool. Dinners by prior arrangement. 1 DOUBLE EN SUITE, 1 TWIN EN SUITE, STANDARD SINGLE CHILDREN 8+.

Prices from £17 to £21

42 DUMFRIES
KIRKLAND COUNTRY HOUSE Ruthwell, Dumfries, Dumfriesshire, DG1 4NP. Contact Mr Coatsworth Tel: 01387 254 893 Fax: 01387 262 553.
Friendly family run country house set in own grounds in peaceful countryside location. Nearby activities include birdwatching, golfing and fishing. Table license and delicious meals available. 6 BEDROOMS, ALL EN SUITE.

Prices from £30 to £50

43 DUMFRIES
BUCCLEUCH AND QUEENSBERRY HOTEL Thornhill, Dumfries, DG3 5LU. Tel: 01848 330215.
A good atmosphere at this comfortable pub with food and drink to suit all tastes. Cask ales, bar snacks and evening menu available. ACCOMMODATION AVAILABLE.

44 DUNBAR
OVERCLIFFE 11 Bayswell Park, Dunbar, East Lothian, EH42 1AE. Contact Brenda Bower Tel: 01368 864 004.
Motor Cycle friendly B&B in central situation. Easy access to Edinburgh and only 2 hours from the Newcastle ferry. Licensed premises 5 BEDROOMS, 3 EN SUITE.

Prices from £20

45 DUNFERMLINE
HALFWAY HOUSE Main Street, Kingseat, Dunfermline, Fifeshire, KY12 0TJ. Contact Mr Flemming Tel: 01383 731 661 Fax: 01383 621 274.
Centrally located accommodation just 30 minutes from Princes Street and with easy access to Perth, Stirling and Glasgow. Bar and restaurant offering a wide range of food and drink. 12 BEDROOMS, ALL EN SUITE.

Prices from £37 to £49

46 DUNFERMLINE
HALFWAY HOUSE Main Street, Kingseat, Dunfermline, Fifeshire, KY12 OTJ.
Tel: 01383 731 661.
A relaxing atmosphere in this pub serving bar snacks and meals. Separate restaurant facilities with imaginative and tasty menu. ACCOMMODATION AVAILABLE.

47 ECCLEFECHAN
CRESSFIELD COUNTRY HOUSE HOTEL Ecclefechan, Dumfrieshire, DG11 3DR.
Contact Mr & Mrs Arthur Tel: 01576 300281 Fax: 01576 204218.
This lovely hotel was built in the 1800s and is set in attractive gardens. Meals are freshly prepared every day. Bar meals available all day. We have a good selection of real ales, malt whiskies and bottled beers. We welcome motorcyclists and we are open all the year round. Each of our rooms have tea making facilities, telephones and colour television. 10 ROOMS EN SUITE.

Prices from £26 to £41

48 EDINBURGH
EILDON 109 Newbigging, Musselburgh, Edinburgh EH21 7AS.
Contact Mrs Eve Campbell Roache Tel: 0131 665 3981.
Set in a beautifully restored 19th century town house only 20 minutes drive from Edinburgh city centre. Nearby are Musselburgh sports centre and swimming pool as well as perfect locations for riverside walks. ONE EN SUITE, SLEEPS THREE. ONE DOUBLE, ONE TWIN (SHARED BATHROOM). DISCOUNTS AVAILABLE FOR LONGER STAYS.

Prices from £16 to £24

49 EDINBURGH
DUNSTANE HOUSE HOTEL 4 West Coates, Haymarket, Edinburgh, EH12 5JQ.
Contact Mr & Mrs Derek Mowat Tel & Fax: 0131 337 6169.
Beautiful detached mansion set in delightful gardens. Handy for town centre, good bus service, railway station, golf courses, 15 minutes from the airport, five minutes to Princess Street. Private, family run hotel open all year. Licenced residents bar. ALL ROOMS EN SUITE.

Prices from £27.50 to £44

50 EDINBURGH
VILLA NINA GUEST HOUSE 39 Leamington Terrace, Edinburgh, EH10 4JS.
Tel & Fax: 0131 229 2644.
Very comfortable Victorian terraced house situated in a quiet residential part of the city yet only 10 minutes walk to Princess Street, the castle, theatres, shops and major attractions. TV in all rooms, some rooms with private showers, full cooked breakfast provided.

Prices from £18

51 EDINBURGH
THE IVY GUEST HOUSE 7 Mayfield Gardens, Edinburgh, EH9 2AX.
Tel: 0131 667 3411 Fax: 0131 620 1422 E.mail: ivy.guesthouse@cableinet.co.uk.
A Victorian villa close to the city centre, open all year with private car park. All rooms have central heating, H&C, colour TV, tea/coffee facilities. Public phone available. EN SUITE OR STANDARD ROOMS.

Prices from £18

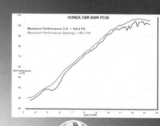

52 EDINBURGH
SOUTHDOWN GUEST HOUSE 20 Craigmillar Park, Edinburgh, EH16 5PS.
Tel: 0131 667 2410 Fax: 0131 667 6056 E.mail: haml20@aol.com.
A wram welcome and personal service is assured at the Southdown Guest House. Conveniently situated on a main bus route in a prime residential area, just 10 minutes from Princess Street. Rooms have Cable/Sky TV, tea/coffee facilities. There is also a lounge with TV. Full Scottish Breakfast provided. Reduced rates for families and groups. ROOMS WITH PRIVATE SHOWER OR FULL EN SUITE.

Prices from £17.50

53 EDINBURGH
LORNE VILLA 9 East Mayfield, Edinburgh, EH9 1SD.
Contact Many & Calum McCulloch Tel & Fax: 0131 667 7159.
Festival city centre guest house offering superb Scottish hospitality and cuisine at affordable prices. Private car park, dinner available, reduced rates for children. SINGLE & FAMILY ROOMS, EN SUITE OR STANDARD.

54 EDINBURGH
7 BLINKBONNY GARDENS Edinburgh, Lothian, EH4 3HG.
Contact Mrs Gena Speirs Tel: 0131 332 3301 Fax: 0131 332 0974.
Situated in a quiet area , detached bungalow, situated off A90 Queensferry Road, in a quiet area near te centre of Edinburgh. Buses, shops, restaurants nearby. Off street, free parking. Travel and tourist advice available. En suite rooms with TV, hairdryer, hospitality tray and well-equipped bathroom. Regular buses provide a short drive to nearby shops and restaurants. Murrayfield rugby stadium just a few minutes walk away. Friendly hosts who will be more than happy to give you information on local places of interest. 1 TWIN/DOUBLE/FAMILY, 1 DOUBLE, 1 TWIN ALL EN SUITE.

Prices from £20 to £25

55 EDINBURGH
CORNERSTONE CAFE St John's Church, West End, Princess Street, Edinburgh,
EH2 4BJ. Tel: 0131 229 0212.
Cornerstone Cafe is in the historic crypt of St John's Church. Range of vegetarian options including roasted vegetables, bean patties and courgette and leek lasagne. Views of the Castle from terrace and graveyard.

56 EDINBURGH
AVERON 44 Gilmore Place, Edinburgh, EH3 9NQ.
Contact Mrs Cran Tel: 0131 229 9932.
Lovely townhouse offering comfortable accommodation. Whilst recently converted, the taste of the history is still present. The townhouse dates back to 1770. We are just 10 minutes walk from Princess Street and the Castle and all the sights of this wonderful city, steeped in Scottish history. 10 BEDROOMS.

Prices from £18 to £32

57 EDINBURGH
ARD-NA-SAID 5 Priestfield Road, Newington, Edinburgh EH16 5HH.
Contact Mrs Olive Lyons Tel: 0131 667 8754 Fax: 0131 271 0960.
Ard-na-said is located in a quiet residential area close to the city centre. Holyrood Park, swimming and a wide variety of pubs and restaurants are all within easy reach. Airport just a few miles away. Guests are assured of a comfortable stay in tastefully decorated rooms. Breakfast menu that caters for vegetarians. 1 FAMILY, 2 TWIN, 2 DOUBLE, 1 SINGLE, ALL EN SUITE CHILDREN ALL.

Prices from £22 to £28

58 EDINBURGH
ALLISON HOUSE 15-17 Mayfield Gardens, Edinburgh, EH9 2AX.
Contact Simon Stone Tel: 0131 667 8049 Fax: 0131 667 5001
E.mail: dh007ljh@msn.com.
Situated 1 mile from city centre, Allison House is a family run hotel with restaurant, bar, conference room and private parking. Theatre, golf and other amenities close at hand. 23 BEDROOMS, 22 EN SUITE.

🔟 Ⓢ ▄◣ VISA
Prices from £25 to £88

59 EDINBURGH
KEW 1 Kew Terrace, Murrayfield, Edinburgh, EH12 5JE.
Contact Alan Gray Tel: 0131 313 0700 Fax: 0131 313 0747.
Refurbished Victorian terraced house close to the city centre. Visit Edinburgh Castle and Murrayfield rugby stadium. Restaurant and bar with snacks available. 6 BEDROOMS, ALL EN SUITE.

🔟 Ⓢ ▄◣ VISA
Prices from £40 to £82

60 EDINBURGH
53 ESKSIDE WEST Musselburgh, Edinburgh, Lothian, EH21 6RB.
Contact Annie Deacon Tel: 0131 665 2875.
Lovely stone built terraced cottage with charming bedrooms. In pleasant location right on the bank of the River Esk. Regular trains and buses bring you to Edinburgh city centre. Enjoy wonderful meals prepared by an expert chef. Please book 24 hours in advance. 1 TWIN, 1 DOUBLE EN SUITE CHILDREN 5+.

�
Prices from £16 to £18

61 EDINBURGH
QUALITY HOTEL Marine Drive, Cramond Foreshore, Edinburgh, EH4 5EP.
Tel: 0131 336 1700 Fax: 0131 336 4934.
Located on the A90 to seafront. Rooms decorated to a high standard. Full fitness centre with sauna and jacuzzi. The restaurant serves a range of tempting dishes and sweets. Places of interest include Edinburgh Castle (4 miles) and Edinburgh Zoo (2 miles). Special package for bikers £26. per person inc. breakfast and dinner. Subject to availability. Book through Central Reservations 0800 44 44 44. 86 BEDROOMS.

🍽 Ⓢ ♨

62 EDINBURGH
QUALITY HOTEL Ingliston, Edinburgh, EH28 8AU.
Tel: 0131 333 4331 Fax: 0131 333 4124.
Located on the A8. Many facilities inc. cable TV, restaurant and bar. Edinburgh Castle (16 miles), Edinburgh Crystal (30 miles), Gyle Shopping Centre (4 miles). Special package for bikers £26 per person inc. breakfast and dinner. Subject to availability. Book through Central Reservations 0800 44 44 44. 95 BEDROOMS.

🍽 Ⓢ ♨

63 EDINBURGH
DORSTAN 7 Priestfield Road, Edinburgh, EH16 5HJ.
Contact Mrs M. Campbell. Tel: 0131 667 5138 Fax: 0131 668 4644
E.mail: reservations@dorstan-hotel.demon.co.uk.
Elegant and tastefully furnished Victorian house close to Edinburgh city centre and all its attractions. Warm and welcoming atmosphere where guests have many home comforts. 14 BEDROOMS, 9 EN SUITE.

Ⓢ ♨

65 EDINBURGH
ASHCROFT FARMHOUSE East Calder, Edinburgh EH52 0ET.
Contact Elizabeth & Derek Scott Tel: 01506 881 810 Fax: 01506 884 327
E.mail: Ashcroftfa@aol.com.
Set in landscaped gardens this modern farmhouse has attractive pine furnished bedrooms. Airport and M8/M9 just five miles away. Walks and sightseeing in wonderful countryside. Delicious breakfast including kippers, salmon and homemade sausage. 2 FAMILY, 3 TWIN, 1 FOUR POSTER DOUBLE, ALL EN SUITE CHILDREN 3+.

Prices from £25 to £28

66 EDINBURGH
A HAVEN TOWN HOUSE 180 Ferry Road, Edinburgh, EH6 4NS.
Tel: 0131 554 6559 Fax: 0131 554 5252.
Elegant Victorian town house located close to the city centre. Beautifully decorated with a welcoming atmosphere. Secure private parking. 12 BEDROOMS, ALL EN SUITE.

Prices from £40 to £90

67 EYEMOUTH
FAIRLAW Reston, Eyemouth, Berwickshire, TD14 5LN.
Contact Katie Henderson Tel: 01890 761 724.
An 18th century farmhouse with original features set in secluded gardens and woodlands. Fairlaw has a wonderful drawing room with log fires that are great for chilly evenings. Ideal for outdoor pusuits including Golf and other historic and cultural activities. Only a few miles from the coast with Edinburgh just an hours drive or less. French and Norwegian spoken. Closed November to March inclusive. 1 DOUBLE, 2 TWIN (1 PRIVATE FACILITIES) CHILDREN ALL.

Prices from £21 to £24

68 FALKIRK
COMFORT INN Manor Street, Falkirk, FK1 1NT.
Tel: 01324 624 066 Fax: 01324 611 785.
Located on the M876 then A883. Traditionally furnished rooms offering comfortable accommodation. Facilities include mini gym and golf nearby. Restaurant and cocktail bar also available. Places of interest include Stirling Castle (6 miles), the Trossachs (10 miles) and the Whisky Centre (16 miles). Special package for bikers £26. per person inc. breakfast and dinner. Subject to availability. Must be booked through Central Reservations 0800 44 44 44. 33 BEDROOMS.

WHEN IT STAYS IN POSITION, SO WILL YOUR BIKE

That's because once switched on, any movement of the small ball bearing inside each Spyball alarm is detected by ultra-sonic transducers which trigger Spyball's ear-piercing siren.

The PATRIOT AM/8510GB is the very latest development from SPYBALL. It exceeds the stringent specifications for security levels recommended by the UK's leading insurance companies and is SOLD SECURE APPROVED. It is a combined immobiliser and alarm system and includes automatic immobiliser arming as well as a **unique 'Emergency disarming' facility which enables the user to disarm the system in the event of loss or failure of the remote control key**.

Other key features of the alarm include:-

● Ignition lock tamper protection.
● LED alarm status indicator.
● Battery back-up siren.
● Anti-grab/anti-scan 'Ghost' coding.
● Low battery consumption – only 3.6mA on/off.

For safety reasons and to satisfy the warranty conditions as well as insurance company requirements, the sale and installation of the alarm is restricted to authorised SPYBALL motorcycle alarm dealers only.

The new alarm which includes 2 remote controls, is guaranteed for 2 years and has a recommended retail price (incl. VAT and installation) of £335.00

For a colour brochure and UK dealer list FREEPHONE 0800 7836178, fax or e-mail.

SPYBALL®

UK importers & distributors: Nevis Marketing Ltd., Unit 12, Priory Industrial Park, Airspeed Road, Christchurch, Dorset, BH23 4HD
Tel: 01425 273344. Fax: 01425 273311. E-mail:info@nevism.co.uk Website:www.nevism.co.uk

69 FALKIRK
OAKLANDS 32 Polmont Road, Laurieston, Falkirk, Central Scotland, FK2 9QT.
Contact Mrs Penny Fattori Tel & Fax: 01324 610 671
E.mail: b-and-b@oaklands.ndirect.co.uk.
An attractive Edwardian family house on the elevated Roman Antonine Mound. Rooms furnished to a high standard ensuring comfort and luxury. Enjoy a variety of outdoor pursuits including walking and golf. Convenient for Edinburgh, Glasgow and Stirling. 5 minutes from the M9 junction 5. Closed mid December to mid January. 1 DOUBLE/FAMILY EN SUITE, 2 EN SUITE CHILDREN ALL.

🖨 ✂ [S]   VISA

Prices from £25

70 FALKLAND
KIND KYTTOCK'S KITCHEN Cross Wynd, Falkland, Fife, KY15 7BE.
Tel: 01337 857477.
Situated beside the village green in the heart of a conservation village, Kind Kyttock's Kitchen was opened in 1970. It is well renowned for its quality food, recommended by Egon Ronay. Cream tea, Afternoon Tea, Scot's pancakes and homemade scones available on the beautifully presented menu. 10:30AM TO 5:30PM CLOSED MONDAYS CLOSED CHRISTMAS EVE UNTIL 5TH JANUARY.

71 FORT WILLIAM
ASHBURN HOUSE Achintore Road, Fort William, Inverness-shire, PH33 6PG.
Contact Sandra Henderson Fax: 01397 706000.
Hospitable welcome at this handsome property. Guests can expect very high standards of comfort and service. Town with restaurants and bars nearby. 7 BEDROOMS, ALL EN SUITE.

🖨 ✂ [S]   MasterCard VISA

Prices from £30 to £70

72 FORT WILLIAM
TRAVEE Corpach, Fort William, Inverness-shire, PH33 7LR.
Contact Mrs M. Cumming Tel & Fax: 01397 772 380.
Travee is a detached house with superb views of the nearby Ben Nevis and Fort William. Ideally situated for touring the Scottish Highlands and its places of outstanding natural beauty. Guests can expect a friendly Scottish welcome. Closed December and January. 2 TWIN (1 EN SUITE), 2 DOUBLE (1 EN SUITE) CHILDREN ALL.

🖨 ✂ [S]

Prices from £16 to £18

73 FORT WILLIAM
FORDON Badabrie, Banavie, Fort William, Inverness-shire, PH33 7LX.
Contact Mrs. Gillies Tel: 01397 772 737.
Set in tranquil surroundings 2 miles from Fort William. Fordon is set on an elevated position and has superb panoramic views to Ben Nevis and Aonach Mhor. Warm, comfortable accommodation with large TV lounge. Outdoor pursuits also available. Closed Christmas. 1 DOUBLE EN SUITE, 1 TWIN, 1 FAMILY. CHILDREN ALL.

🖨 ✂ [S]

74 FORT WILLIAM
ISLANDERS 10 Achnalea, Onich, Fort William, Inverness-shire, PH33 6SA.
Contact Mrs Jennifer Morrison Tel: 01855 821 403.
Situated in one of the most attractive areas of the Highlands, Islanders is a modern detached house with well equipped bedrooms. Ideal for touring the Scottish Hills and visiting the Isles of Mull and Loch Ness. Nearby pool and leisure complex and a range of outdoor pursuits. Restaurants nearby. 1 TWIN EN SUITE (WITH SITTING ROOM), 1 DOUBLE EN SUITE SHOWER CHILDREN ALL.

Prices from £18 to £24

75 FORT WILLIAM
DISTILLERY HOUSE Nevis Bridge, North Road, Fort William, Inverness-shire, PH33 6LR. Contact Mr McPherson Tel: 01397 700 103 Fax: 01397 702 980.
Just 5 minutes from the town centre, Distillery House offers comfortable accommodation in beautiful surroundings. Situated at the end of Glen Nevis, there are some lovely scenic walks close at hand. 6 BEDROOMS, ALL EN SUITE. Self catering apartments available.

Prices from £20 to £35

76 FORT WILLIAM
GLEN SHIEL GUEST HOUSE Achintore Road, Fort William, Highland, PH33 6RW.
Contact Mrs A. Grant Tel: 01397 702271.
Modern purpose house situated near Loch Linnhe with panoramic views of the surrounding mountains. All rooms have colour television and tea/coffee facilties. Car park & garden. On the A82 1.5 miles south of Fort William. 3 DOUBLE EN SUITE, 1 TWIN, 1 FAMILY (3 PERSONS).

Prices from £16

77 FORT WILLIAM
THE WALLACE 6 Kinross Place, Upper Achintore, Fort William, Highland, PH33 6UN.
Tel & Fax: 01397 703635.
Quality B&B in quiet cul-de-sac close to the town centre. All rooms have central heating with colour TV, radio and hospitality tray. Your hosts strive to ensure an enjoyable stay and always look forward to welcoming you on return visits. ALL ROOMS SHOWER/EN SUITE.

78 FORTINGALL
FORTINGALL Aberfeldy, Perthshire, PH15 2NQ. Contact Alan Schofield
Tel & Fax: 01887 830 367.
Situated in Glen Lyon 3 miles from Aberfeldy, Fortingall offers a high standard of accommodation and service. Bar and fully licensed restaurant serving a range of dishes to suit every taste. Yew tree in church 3000 years old. Reputed to be birth place of Pontius Pilate. 10 BEDROOMS, 9 EN SUITE.

Prices from £32 to £60

79 GALASHIELS
ABBOTSFORD ARMS 63 Stirling Street, Galashiels, Selkirkshire, TD1 1BY.
Contact Mandy Tel: 01896 752 517 Fax: 01896 750 744.
A warm, welcoming atmosphere at this tastefully decorated property. Cosy traditional pub serving bar food all day. 14 BEDROOMS, 10 EN SUITE.

Prices from £38 to £58

80 GATEHOUSE OF FLEET

BANK O'FLEET 47 High Street, Gatehouse of Fleet, Kirkcudbrightshire, DG7 2HR.
Contact James Watson Tel & Fax: 01557 814 302.
Attractive building decorated to a high standard and offering a warm, friendly atmosphere in which to relax. Traditional pub serving a range of hot and cold beverages. Beer garden. Open to non residents. 6 BEDROOMS, 5 EN SUITE.

Prices from £30 to £47

81 GIRVAN

GLENDRISSAIG HOUSE Newton Stewart Road, Girvan, Ayrshire, KA26 0HJ.
Contact Mrs McIntosh Tel: 01465 714 631.
A detached farmhouse set in landscaped gardens with views to Arran and Mull of Kintyre, Glendrissaig offers peace, comfort and tranquility. Golf courses, castles and beautiful parks and gardens are just some of the attractions in this lovely, unspoilt part of Scotland. Delicious menu which caters for vegetarians. Closed November to March inclusive. 1 FAMILY, 1 TWIN, 1 DOUBLE, ALL EN SUITE CHILDREN ALL.

Prices from £20 to £25

82 GLASGOW

LOANINGHEAD FARM Balfron Station, Glasgow, Strathclyde, G63 0SE.
Contact Mrs M. Paterson Tel & Fax: 01360 440 432 E.mail: Loaninghead@Virgin.Net.
An early 18th century hunting lodge, Loaninghead has superb views of the Campsie Hills. Ideally situated with the Highland Way and The Trossachs right on the doorstep and Loch Lomond just a ten minute drive away. Off the A811 with easy access to Glasgow and Drymen and with Stirling (20 miles) Edinburgh Airport (50 miles) and Glasgow Airport (20 miles). OPEN ALL YEAR. 1 DOUBLE, 1 TWIN, 1 FAMILY CHILDREN 7+.

Prices from £19 to £25

83 GLASGOW

ACRE VALLEY HOUSE Torrance, Glasgow, G64 4DJ.
Contact Glen & Margie Collins Tel: 01360 620 223.
A Victorian house situated in 2 acres of wonderful gardens. Acre Valley House is centrally situated with Glasgow city centre, Loch Lomond and Stirling just a 1/2 hour drive and Edinburgh 1 hour. The nearby Trossachs and Campsie Hills offer beautiful drives and walks. Comfortable guest's sitting room with log fire provides relaxing atmosphere in which to unwind. Closed Christmas and New Year. 1 TWIN EN SUITE, 1 TWIN PRIVATE, EXTRA ROOM FOR CHILDREN CHILDREN ALL.

Prices from £22 to £30

84 GLASGOW

CHARING CROSS 310 Renfrew Street, Charing Cross, Glasgow, G3 6UW.
Contact Mr Mahmood Tel: 0141 332 2503 Fax: 0141 353 3047.
Situated in Glasgow city centre, Charing Cross is a spacious guest house in pleasant surroundings. All the attractions and amenities of Glasgow right on the doorstep. 24 BEDROOMS, 7 EN SUITE.

Prices from £17.50 to £37

85 GLASGOW
MYFARRCLAN 146 Corsebar Road, Paisley, Glasgow, PA2 9NA. Contact Brenda Farr
Tel: 0141 884 8285 Fax: 0141 581 1566 E.mail: myfarrclan_qwest@compuserve.com.
A warm and friendly welcome at this superb guest house located in a leafy suburb of Paisley. Luxurious accommodation and home cooking. Breakfasts and dinners are a treat. 3 BEDROOMS, ALL EN SUITE.

Prices from £35 to £70

86 GLASGOW
QUALITY HOTEL 99 Gordon Street, Glasgow, G1 3SF.
Tel: 0141 221 9680 Fax: 0141 226 3948.
Located on the M8 exit 19, left into Argyle Street. Ideally placed accommodation with many facilities. Leisure centre available with indoor swimming pool. Transport Museum 1 mile, Art galleries 1 mile and Botanic Gardens 2 miles. Special package for bikers £26. per person inc. breakfast and dinner. Subject to availability. Book through Central Reservations 0800 44 44 44. 222 BEDROOMS.

87 GLENCOE
HOLLY TREE Kentallen, Glencoe, PA38 4BY. Contact Annette
Tel: 01631 740 292 Fax: 01631 740 345.
Located beside Loch Linnhe, Holly Tree guest house has spectacular views. Bar and small restaurant serving a seafood speciality and a range of mouthwatering dishes. Closed November to January. 10 BEDROOMS, ALL EN SUITE.

Prices from £40 to £117

88 GOLSPIE
SUTHERLAND ARMS Main Street, Golspie, Sutherland, KW10 6SA.
Contact Mrs Ross Tel & Fax: 01408 633 234.
Pleasant accommodation in lovely surroundings. High standards of service in this guest house with many facilities. Licensed restaurant and lounge bar for guests. TV available. 15 BEDROOMS, ALL EN SUITE.

Prices from £28

89 GRANTOWN ON SPEY
ROSEGROVE GUEST HOUSE Skye of Curr, Dulnain Bridge, Grantown on Spey, Highland, PH26 3PA. Tel & Fax: 01479 851335.
Ideal for birdwatching, walking, fishing and exploring the mountains and glens of the Scottish Highlands. The food is something special, venison, salmon and Scotch beef. After dinner relax by the log fire enjoying the view over the valley to the Cairngorms. Rosegrove is a holiday for the whole family, children and pets welcome and there is ample parking. DOUBLE, TWIN, SINGLE AND FAMILY ROOMS, SOME EN SUITE.

Prices from £15

90 GRANTOWN ON SPEY
ROSSMOR GUEST HOUSE Woodlands Terrace, Grantown on Spey, Moray PH26 3JU. Contact Sue & Dennis Day Tel & Fax: 01479 872 201.
Situated on the west of Grantown on Spey, Rossmor is an elegant Victorian house with many original features. Attractive rooms and guests' lounge with stunning views. Centre and River Spey are within easy walking distance. Cromdale Hills and nearby pine woods offer scenic walks and superb views. 3 DOUBLE, 3 TWIN, ALL EN SUITE CHILDREN NONE.

Prices from £20 to £22

91 HADDINGTON
EAGLESCAIRNIE MAINS Gifford, Haddington, East Lothian, EH41 4HN.
Contact Barbara & Michael Williams Tel: 01620 810 491
E.mail: williams.eagles@btinternet.com.
Georgian farmhouse in the middle of an award winning mixed farm. Rooms are spacious and comfortable. Borders, Hills and coast nearby. Sample the Lowland Whisky Distillery or visit Edinburgh (17 miles). Closed Christmas and the New Year. 2 DOUBLE EN SUITE, 1 TWIN, 1 SINGLE CHILDREN WELCOME.

Prices from £18 to £25

92 HALKIRK
ULBSTER ARMS Halkirk, Caithness, KW12 6XY. Tel & Fax: 01847 831 206.
Situated in a charming village by a small river, Ulbster Arms is a welcoming hotel with a good standard of accommodation. Award winning restaurant with imaginative menu and tempting desserts.
26 BEDROOMS, ALL EN SUITE.

Prices from £37 to £61

93 HAWICK
DUNIRA HOUSE Buccleuch Road, Hawick, Scottish Borders TD9 0EL.
Contact Mrs J Needham Tel: 01450 378 493.
Set in 1 acre of wooded gardens is Dunira; an attractive Victorian house on the edge of Hawick, overlooking the River Teviot and the nearby award winning Lodge Park. Hawick is a short stroll away. Summer house, separate lounge and 5 hole putting green available to guests. Evening meals by prior arrangement. Closed Christmas and New Year. 2 DOUBLE EN SUITE/PRIVATE, 1 TWIN EN SUITE CHILDREN 12+.

Prices from £20

94 HAWICK
ELM HOUSE 17 North Bridge Street, Hawick, Scottish Borders TD9 9BD.
Contact Mr Neish Tel: 01450 372 866 Fax: 01450 374 175.
Elegant late Victorian house situated within easy reach of the city centre. En suite rooms are tastefully furnished. Licensed premises. 15 BEDROOMS, ALL EN SUITE.

Prices from £25 to £42

95 HAWICK
WINDRUSH Highend, Bonchester Bridge, Hawick, Scottish Borders, TD9 9SA.
Contact Mrs A McFayden Tel: 01450 860 331.
Children are welcome at this friendly family home. Windrush is in a quiet country lane and has lovely views of the rolling Scottish Borders. Activities and attractions include walking, fishing, golf, abbeys and castles. Newcastle, Edinburgh and Carlisle are all just an hour away. Evening meals available by prior arrangement. Local pub 2 miles away. Dogs welcome. Closed christmas. 1 DOUBLE/FAMILY, 1 TWIN CHILDREN ALL.

Prices from £14

96 INNELLAN
OSBORNE Shore Road, Innellan, Argyll, PA23 7TJ.
Contact Mr Carson Tel & Fax: 01369 830 445.
Wonderfully situated accommodation with views of the sea. Games room and lounge bar. High standards of accommodation and a welcoming atmosphere. 4 BEDROOMS, ALL EN SUITE.

Prices from £23.50 to £40

97 INVERNESS
GLENASHDALE Daviot East, Inverness, Inverness-shire, IV1 2EP.
Contact Barbara Kinnear Tel: 01463 772 221 Fax: 01463 772 131.
Glenashdale is a modern house situated in tranquil countryside. Inverness (7 miles) with lots to see and do whilst the surrounding countryside offers relaxing and scenic walks. Just a short drive from the A9, it is ideally located for touring the Highlands. 1 DOUBLE, 1 TWIN, 1 FAMILY, ALL EN SUITE CHILDREN ALL.

Prices from £20 to £22

98 INVERNESS
FAIRFIELD LODGE 39 Fairfield Road, Inverness, IV1 5QD.
Contact Marie MacPherson Tel: 01463 & 237 559.
Fairfield Lodge is a Victorian stonebuilt house set in a peaceful residential area. Inverness city centre (10 minutes) with lots to do including shopping, entertainment and places of historical interest. Excellent base for touring spectacular Highlands. Delicious Scottish breakfast. Inverness Airport 20 minutes drive.
2 DOUBLE EN SUITE, 2 DOUBLE/FAMILY EN SUITE, 1 TWIN PRIVATE, CHILDREN WELCOME.

Prices from £16 to £20

99 INVERNESS
SUNNYHOLM 12 Mayfield Road, Inverness, IV2 4AE.
Contact Agnes Gordon Tel: 01463 231 336.
Spacious bungalow in mature gardens. High quality accommodation with a relaxed atmosphere. Just a few minutes from the town centre. 4 BEDROOMS, ALL EN SUITE.

Prices from £25 to £40

100 INVERNESS
3A RESAURIE Smithton, Inverness, IV2 7NH.
Contact Mrs M.B. Mansfield Tel: 01463 791714.
3 miles east of Inverness with rooms having views across open farmland to the Moray Firth and Ross-shire hills. Ample off road parking. Home baking, high tea or dinner served between 5 and 8 pm (24 hours notice required). Residents lounge. Public transport nearby. 1 DOUBLE EN SUITE, 1 DOUBLE AND 1 TWIN SHARING BATHROOM.

Prices from £15

101 INVERNESS
CULDUTHEL LODGE 14 Culduthel Road, Inverness, IV2 4AG.
Contact David Bonsor Tel & Fax: 01463 240 089.
Attractive Georgian residence set in attractive gardens. Rooms are furnished to a high standard. Nearby town offers shopping and eating facilities and other amenities. 12 BEDROOMS, ALL EN SUITE.

Prices from £45 to £95

102 INVERURIE
FRIDAYHILL Kinmuck, Inverurie, Aberdeenshire, AB51 0LY.
Contact Shena Mcghie Tel & Fax: 01651 882 252.
A unique modern Norwegian/Canadian style home set in peaceful rural location. Beautiful grounds with rockeries and fish ponds. Bedroom with 4-poster bed and a cosy wood panelled sitting room. Castle and whisky trails right on the doorstep. Activities include hill walking,fishing and Archeolink. Newburgh beach (13 miles) where there are seals and seabirds. 1 DOUBLE EN SUITE, 1 DOUBLE PRIVATE CHILDREN ALL.

Prices from £20 to £25

103 ISLE OF ARRAN
LAGG Kilmory, Isle of Arran, KA27 8PQ.
Contact Mr Hull Tel: 01770 870 255 Fax: 01770 870 250.
18th century coaching inn with charming traditional architecture. Set in beautiful lawned gardens with river frontage. Guests here can expect comfort and quality and high standards of service. Licensed premises. TV available. 15 BEDROOMS, ALL EN SUITE.

Prices from £35 to £84

104 ISLE OF LEWIS
GALSON FARM South Galson, Isle of Lewis, HS2 0SH.
Contact Dorothy Russell Tel & Fax: 01851 850 492.
18thC farmhouse with magnificent views of the sea and the surrounding countryside. Visit the Butt of Lewis (10 miles) and return to comfortable accommodation and home cooked meals. 3 BEDS, ALL EN SUITE.

Prices from £29 to £58

105 ISLE OF MULL
RED BAY COTTAGE Deargphort, Fionnphort, Isle of Mull, Argyll, PA66 6BP.
Contact John & Eleanor Wagstaff Tel: 01681 700 396.
Situated on the south west coast of Mull with wonderful views across the Iona Sound and its white beaches. Ideal base for exploring Mull and Iona and the Treshnish Isles. John and Eleanor have adjoining restaurant where they prepare and serve excellent food. Silversmithing course available from your qualified silversmith hostess; enquire for details. 1 DOUBLE, 2 TWIN CHILDREN ALL.

Prices from £16

106 ISLE OF SKYE
ROSKHILL Roskhill, By Dunvegan, Isle of Skye, Inverness-shire, IV55 8ZD. Contact Mrs Griffith Tel: 01470 521317 Fax: 01470 521761 E.mail: stay@roskhill.demon.co.uk.
Centrally located accommodation perfect for exploring the wonderful Isle of Skye. Rooms are comfortable and there is a traditional feel to the dining room with its stone wall and log fire. Mouthwatering home cooked meals available. 5 BEDROOMS, 4 EN SUITE.

Prices from £54 to £70

107 ISLE OF SKYE
HOTEL EILEAN IARMAIN Sleat, Isle of Skye, Inverness-shire, IV43 8QR.
Contact Mrs McKenzie Tel: 01471 833 332 Fax: 01471 833 275.
Excellent Hotel situated on the south side of Skye. Rooms are en-suite with complimentary extras. Romantic atmosphere is enhanced by the wonderfull views of Isle Ornsay harbour. The award winning restaurant serves a variety of sumptuous dishes accompanied by a fine selection of wines and spirits. 12 BEDROOMS, ALL EN SUITE.

Prices from £63 to £125

108 ISLE OF SKYE
25 URQUHART PLACE Portree, Isle of Skye, IV51 9HJ. Contact Mrs Elizabeth Macdonald Tel: 01478 612 374.
Family run guest house situated in quiet cul-de-sac. Next door to Skye Woollen Mill and a mile from city centre. Hosts will be happy to drive guests into town. Portree has good restaurants with seafood specialities.

Prices from £17 to £20

109 ISLE OF SKYE
THE BUNGALOW Herebost, By Dunvegan, Isle of Skye, IV55 8GZ. Contact Samela Macdonald Tel: 01470 521 255.
South facing bungalow with fantastic views over sea and mountains. Well equipped rooms with ironing and drying facilities available. Historic Dunvegan Castle 2 miles. Ideally located for exploring the island with its lovely beaches and sealife. Closed December and January. 1 DOUBLE EN SUITE, 1 DOUBLE PRIVATE CHILDREN ALL.

Prices from £16 to £18

110 JEDBURGH
FROYLEHURST Friers, Jedburgh, Scottish Borders, TD8 6BN. Contact Mrs Irvine Tel & Fax: 01835 862477.
Handsome detached Victorian house located in a peaceful residential area with spacious garden. Just two minutes from the city centre. High standards of comfort and service. 5 BEDROOMS. CHILDREN OVER 5 WELCOME. CLOSED DEC - JAN.

Prices from £32 to £34

111 JEDBURGH
FERNIEHURST MILL LODGE Jedburgh, Scottish Borders, TD8 6PQ. Contact Alan Swanston Tel & Fax: 01835 863279.
Modern purpose built property set in 25 acres overlooking the River Jed. Beautiful surroundings with walks nearby. Other activities include fishing and pony trekking. 9 BEDROOMS, ALL EN SUITE.

Prices from £23 to £46

112 KILMARNOCK
LAIGH LANGMUIR Kilmarnock, Strathclyde, KA3 2NU. Contact Mrs Steel Tel: 01563 538 8270.
A modernised 18th century farmhouse in a tranquil rural setting. Laigh Langmuir is relaxed and friendly and guests are welcome to explore the farm and sit around the cosy log fire. Easy access from Glasgow and the South. Day trips to Arran, Culzean Castle and Loch Lomond. Closed Christmas.
1 FAMILY EN SUITE, 1 TWIN, 1 DOUBLE EN SUITE, 1 SINGLE CHILDREN ALL.

Prices from £15 to £18

113 KILMARNOCK
MUIRHOUSE FARM Gatehead, Kilmarnock, Ayrshire, KA2 0BT. Contact Mrs Love Tel: 01563 523975.
A very comfortable and traditional farmhouse positioned in urban surroundings. We are close to the town of Kilmarnock, the beautiful Ayrshire coast, many golf courses, wonderful country walks. We welcome motorcyclists. 3 BEDROOMS, 2 EN SUITE AND ONE WITH A PRIVATE BATHROOM.

Prices from £17 to £36

114 KINGUSSIE
ROYAL 29 High Street, Kingussie, Scottish Highlands, PH21 1HX. Tel: 01540 661 898.
Hotel with cosy bar. Bar food served and restaurant available. ACCOMMODATION AVAILABLE.

Prices from £20

115 KINROSS
CRAIGTON HOUSE Cleish, Kinross, Tayside, KY13 0LQ.
Contact Mrs Helen Nelson Tel: 01577 850 206.
KINROSS 4m. Set in beautiful gardens, this large family home enjoys views of the Lomond and Ochil Hills. With the motorway just minutes away, Craigton House is ideally located to explore the Scottish Hills and countryside. Visit Edinburgh Castle or St. Andrews many golf courses. Closed mid December to end of January. 1 DOUBLE/TWIN EN SUITE, 1 TWIN, 1 FAMILY CHILDREN ALL.

Prices from £18 to £22

116 KIRKCALDY
COXSTOOL West Wemyss, Kirkcaldy, Fifeshire, KY1 4SL.
Contact Gordon MacIntosh Tel & Fax: 01592 655279.
All our bedrooms have fabulous and panoramic views accross the Firth of Forth. We have an excellent restaurant and use Scottish grown foods. We welcome motorcyclists to our bed and breakfast and we promise you will have a memorable visit to one of the gateways into Scotland. There are many golf courses and some of the most famous in the World, including St Andrews. 21 BEDROOMS ALL EN SUITE.

Prices from £45 to £75

117 KIRKCUDBRIGHT
BENUTIUM 2 Rossway Road, Kirkcudbright, Kirkcudbrightshire, DG6 4BS.
Contact Eileen Garroch-Mackay Tel: 01557 330 788. E-mail: www.benutium.co.uk.
Located in a quiet residential area, this lovely house offers peaceful surroundings and superb views. Enjoy Galloway's rocky coastline, sandy bays, lochs, forests and castles. Visit the charming medieval harbour town of Kirkcudbright with its many attractions. Walkers and cyclists welcome. Evening meals by prior arrangement. Closed New Year. 1 DOUBLE, 1 TWIN, CHILDREN 15+.

Prices from £17.50 to £18

118 KIRKMICHAEL
LOG CABIN Kirkmichael, Perthshire, PH10 7NB. Contact Wend Rattray
Tel: 01250 881288 Fax: 01250 881206.
Perthshire is in an idealistic area for touring. It is very convenient for your entrance into the northerly and the highlands of Scotland. Our Log Hotel is unique and very welcoming. This is a tranquil area and if you wish to come and wind down, this is the place to do it. Motorcyclists are very welcome. 13 BEDROOMS ALL EN SUITE.

Prices from £27 to £52

119 KYLESCU
NEWTON LODGE Kylescu, Sutherland, IV27 4HW.
Contact Myra Brauer Tel: 01971 502070 Fax: 01971 502070.
We are situated in one of the most tranquil areas of Scotland. If you want to relax and wind down this is where to do it. We are approximately 30 miles North of Ullapool. We specialis in seafood in our restaurant and prices are from £15 per person for dinner. We overlook a small sea colony of seals, so bring your binoculars. 7 BEDROOMS ALL EN SUITE.

Prices from £28

FM

ProtectionBeyondconvention

HELMETS

the only way

lintek

T01522 888444 **F**01522 888400 **E**lintektl@compuserve.com

120 LARGS
SOUTH WHITTLIEBURN FARM Brisbane Glen, Largs, Ayrshire, KA30 8SN.
Contact Mary Watson Tel: 01475 675881 Fax: 01475 675080.
Farmhouse accommodation at it's very best. We have lovely peaceful views and are 5 minutes drive from the from the tourist centre of Largs, where the ferries operate to the islands. We offer you a warm welcome, friendly hospitality, and you will always recall our delicious breakfasts. 3 BEDROOMS ALL EN SUITE.

⌗ ☆ Ⓢ **Prices from £20**

121 LASSWADE
CARLETHAN HOUSE Wadingburn Lane, Lasswade, Mid Lothian, EH18 1HG.
Contact Mrs M Dunlop Tel: 0131 663 7047 Fax: 0131 654 2657.
EDINBURGH 5m. Listed Georgian house with pleasant gardens set in a peaceful rural location. With Edinburgh city centre only a 20 minute drive and Edinburgh Bypass 1 mile away there is plenty to see and do. Dinner by prior arrangement. Closed November and Christmas.

⌗ ⤸ Ⓢ **Prices from £30 to £40**

122 LAUDER
THE GRANGE, 6 Edinburgh Road, Lauder, Berwickshire, TD2 6TW.
Contact Tricia and Peter Gilardi Tel: 01578 722649 Fax: 01578 722649.
Very comfortable and large house in our own private grounds. We overlook the Lammermuir Hills and are located on the A68 road and our position is particularly suitable for visiting Edinburgh or touring the Scottish Border Country. We welcome bikers aand offer you both drying facilities and secure parking. 3 BEDROOMS.

⌗ ⛻ Ⓢ **Prices from £16 to £20**

123 LERWICK
GLEN ORCHY HOUSE 20 Knab Road, Lerwick, Shetland Isles, ZE1 0AX.
Contact Mrs Howarth. Tel: 01595 692031 Fax: 01595 692031.
Family owned and run guest house, with excellent facilities, air conditioning, under floor heating. Table de hote menu with food freshly prepared every day. Come and visit the beautiful Shetland Islands. Relax and enjoy this wonderful and tranquil part of Scotland. Bird watching, shooting, fishing and sailing. If you are interested in archeology this is the place to explore. We are centrally located for boats to visit the islands in the area. Next door is a free 9 hole golf course to test your skills. A very popular region for touring motorcyclists. A number of motorcycling rallies take place on the Islands. 14 BEDROOMS ALL EN SUITE.

⌗ ⊜ ☆ ⛻ Ⓢ ▭ 𝘝𝘐𝘚𝘈 **Prices from £34 to £58**

124 LESMAHAGOW
DYKECROFT FARM Kirkmuirhill, Lesmahagow, Lanarkshire, ML11 0JQ.
Contact Mrs McInally Tel: 01555 892 226.
Dykecroft Farm is a modern farmhouse bungalow on lovely working farm. Ideal stop for journeys between north and south with easy access to the M74 and on the A726 (B7086). Glasgow Airport is nearby and Glasgow city centre only 30 minutes by car. Ideal for touring the surrounding countryside. Watersports available at the Strathclyde Country Park and near popular village of New Lanark. Home baking adds to homely atmosphere. 2 DOUBLE AND 1 TWIN CHILDREN ALL.

⤸ Ⓢ **Prices from £19 to £21**

125 LEVEN
MONTURPIE GUEST HOUSE Monturpie, Upper Large, Leven, Fife, KY8 5QS. Contact Mrs Linda Law Tel: 01333 360 254 Fax: 01333 360 850.
ST. ANDREWS 9m. A traditional stone built farmhouse with spectacular views of the Firth of Forth, Edinburgh and the Lothians. Nearby Fife offers a wonderful variety of activities and places to visit. Enjoy walks around National Trust houses and grounds. Closed mid December to mid January. DOUBLE/TWIN/FAMILY ROOMS, ALL EN SUITE CHILDREN 5+.

Prices from £17.50 to £19.50

126 LOANHEAD
CRAIG COTTAGE 5 New Pentland, Loanhead, Midlothian, EH20 9NT. Contact Mrs P. Ciupik Tel: 0131 440 0405.
Craig Cottage offers traditional accommodation with a warm and friendly atmosphere. Excellent bus service to Edinburgh and easy access to city bypass for visits to surrounding Borders. Your hosts will be pleased to indicate places of interest and provide information on local routes. Well behaved pets welcome. Closed November to January. 1 DOUBLE, 1 TWIN. CHILDREN 6+.

Prices from £15

127 LOCH LOMOND
ARDOCH COTTAGE Main Street, Gartocharn, Loch Lomond, Dunbartonshire G83 8NE. Contact Mrs Mabel Lindsay Tel & Fax: 01389 830 452.
Award winning 18th century cottage with views of surrounding farmland. Guests can enjoy private lounge with beautiful log fire. The Trossachs and the Highlands are both within easy reach and it is ideal for touring and visiting Loch Lomond, Stirling and Edinburgh. Glasgow Airport 20 minutes drive. 2 DOUBLE, 1 TWIN, ALL EN SUITE. CHILDREN ALL.

Prices from £25

128 LOCHEARNHEAD
CLACHAN COTTAGE HOTEL, Lochearnhead, Perthshire, FK19 8PU. Tel: 01567 830247 Fax: 01567 830300.
Ours is a very popular venue with motorcyclists – we especially welcome you. This privately run hotel enjoys a spectacular setting on the shores of Loch Earn. Our Loch View Restaurant serves the finest Scottish Cuisine or an extensive choice of bar meals. We are centrally placed for touring including the West Coast, Trossachs, Stirling Castle, Edinburgh and Pitlochry to name a few. For the energetic we have hill-walking, fishing and water skiing. 21 BEDROOMS ALL EN SUITE.

Prices from £28 to £48

129 LOCKERBIE
SOMERTON HOUSE Carlisle Road, Lockerbie, Dumfrieshire, DG11 2DR. Contact Mrs Arthur Tel: 01576 202583 Fax: 01576 204218.
All our bedrooms are elegantly furnished, and we have single, twin, double and family rooms available. All the rooms have telephone, colour TV and tea/coffee making facilities. Rooms have lovely views of the gardens and local coutryside. We have a well stocked bar with real ales and malt whiskies. We specialise in bar meals and an a la carte service is available. We have a new conservatory where your freshly prepared food can be enjoyed. ALL BEDROOMS ARE EN SUITE.

130 MAUCHLINE
AUCHENLONGFORD Sorn, Mauchline, East Ayrshire, KA5 6JF.
Contact Mrs J. Clark Tel: 01290 550761.
The farm is situated in the hills above the picturesque village of Sorn near the River Ayr and a 17th century church. The accommodation is in three attractively furnished bedrooms and a large well appointed residents lounge. 3 BEDROOMS.

Prices from £17 to £27

131 MELROSE
KINGS ARMS High Street, Melrose, Roxburghshire, TD6 9PB. Contact Mr Delgetty
Tel: 01896 822143 Fax: 01896 823812.
This old coaching inn is situated in the heart of the historic part of Melrose. The inn itself is very old and is modernised and offers a very warm welcome to motorcyclists passing through, or wishing to stay a few days in our very pleasant surroundings. We have a superb menu and our eating facilities are very comfortable. 7 BEDROOMS ALL EN SUITE.

Prices from £35 to £65

132 MELROSE
WHITEHOUSE St Boswells, Melrose, Roxburghshire, TD6 0ED. Contact Mrs Tyrer
Tel: 01573 460343 Fax: 01573 460361.
Scottish Tourist Board 4 star accommodation in a former dowager house. There are panoramic views, and we have open log fires with TV. Home cooked dinners and breakfasts served. Very conveniently located for golf, fishing, shooting and walking. 3 BEDROOMS ALL EN SUITE.

Prices from £25 to £30

133 MOFFAT
THE BALMORAL High Street, Moffat, Dumfriesshire, DG10 9DL. Contact Mr Doonan
Tel: 01683 220288 Fax: 01683 220451.
This family run hotel situated in the central part of Moffat is very conveniently located for the West Coast within easy reach of some of the prettiest parts of this area. All our cooking is freshly prepared in our kitchens with that home cooking taste. We serve food all day and have an extensive menu. 16 BEDROOMS ALL WITH EN SUITE INCLUDES 2 FAMILY ROOMS

Prices from £21 to £54

134 MOFFAT
GILBERT HOUSE Old Edinburgh Road, Beechgrove, Moffat, Dumfriesshire
DG10 9RS. Contact Mr Poynton Tel & Fax: 01683 220050.
This delightful detatched Victorian house is located in a quiet residential district and very close to the town centre. It offers a very comfortable and hospitable stay. Moffat is situated very conveniently to enable the visitor to plan touring and sightseeing or just to relax in a very pleasant part of Scotland. 6 BEDROOMS - 5 EN SUITE.

Prices from £20 to £45

135 MOFFAT
BUCHAN GUEST HOUSE Beechgrove, Moffat, Dumfries, DG10 9RS.
Contact Mrs McNeill Tel: 01683 220378.
Large Victorian house with fine views. Comfortable accommodation with rooms having colour TV. Guest lounge with tea/coffee available at all times. Private parking. Moffat is an ideal stopover as it is only 1 mile from the M74. Evening meal optional. DOUBLE, TWIN AND FAMILY ROOMS, MOST EN SUITE.

[S]

Prices from £16

136 MOFFAT
WATERSIDE Moffat, Dumfries and Galloway, DG10 9LF.
Contact Mrs E. Edwards. Tel: 01683 220 092.
Built in 1840, Waterside is a spacious country house with 12 acres of gardens and woodlands and its own streach of river. Relax in the tastefully decorated rooms or the gardens and enjoy the tranquility of the surrounding countryside. Visit the lovely town of Moffat. Traditional Scottish breakfast. Self catering available. Closed end of October to Easter 1 FAMILY, 2 DOUBLE, 1 TWIN, PRIVATE FACILITIES AVAILABLE CHILDREN ALL.

[symbols]

Prices from £19 to £21

137 NAIRN
ALTON BURN Alton Burn Road, Nairn, Nairnshire, IV12 5ND.
Contact Mrs McDonald Tel: 01667 452051 Fax: 01667 456697.
Alton Burn is situated in a very prominent position and overlooks the Moray Firth and Nairn Golf Course. We offer motorcyclists a very warm and relaxed atmosphere in this delightful part of Northern Scotland. Nairn is ideally located to begin your tour of the Highlands and there are wonderful places to visit and see all within easy reach of Alton Burn. If you are a group then we offer discounted prices. Come and stay with us and experience our Highland hospitality. Dinner is from £15:00 25 BEDROOMS ALL EN SUITE.

[symbols]

Prices from £30 to £60

138 NEW ABBEY
ABBEY COTTAGE 26 Main Street, New Abbey, Dumfries, DG2 8BY.
Tel: 01387 850377.
In the picturesque conservation village of New Abbey next to the historic ruin of Sweetheart Abbey lies Abbey Cottage. Healthy delicious food is served in a non-smoking environment and free range eggs and local produce are used in the cooking. Meals are freshly prepared and made toorder. Assam, Lemon, Darjeeling and Earl Grey teas are served together with a selection of speciality coffee's and herbal infusions. 1ST APRIL TO 31ST OCTOBER - 7 DAYS A WEEK 10AM TO 5:30PM NOVEMBER & DECEMBER - WEEKENDS ONLY 11AM TO 5PM CLOSED FROM CHRISTMAS UNTIL THE END OF MARCH.

139 NEW GALLOWAY
KENMURE ARMS High Street, New Galloway, Kirkcudbrightshire, DG7 3RL.
Tel: 01671 420240 Fax: 01671 420240.
We are a very homely Scottish Pub with Bed and Breakfast facilities. We are located on the A762/A713 in New Galloway which is on the shores of Loch Ken. There are many other lochs in the area and both touring and sighseeing are highly recommended. There are lots of watersports inthe region. We offer warm and welcoming hospitality to motorcyclists and we sell fine beers and home cooked bar foods. 12 BEDROOMS - 8 EN SUITE.

[symbols]

Prices from £19

140 NEWTON STEWART
THE CROWN 101 Queen Street, Newton Stewart, Wigtownshire, DG8 6JW.
Contact Mrs Hazel Tel: 01671 402727 Fax: 01671 402727.
Ours is a family run hotel and offer attractively priced accommodation. All our bedrooms are en suite and well appointed. We offer an extensive bar, a la carte and table d' hote menus. If yours is a touring group of motorcyclists we do specialise in groups and offer you a very welcome stay with us. 11 BEDROOMS ALL EN SUITE.

🆔 🛏 🍴 🎒 S   💳 VISA   **Prices from £25 to £60**

141 NEWTONMORE
EAGLE VIEW Perth Road, Newtonmore, Inverness-shire, PH20 1AP.
Contact Nicky Drucquer Tel & Fax: 01540 673 675.
A traditional stone built house with easy access to beautiful Scottish countryside. Guests are assured of a warm and friendly reception at this family run guesthouse where children are especially welcome. Waltzing Waters and the Highland Wildlife park are just a couple of the nearby attractions. Ideally located to explore the Highlands and its beauty spots. A wide variety of summer and winter sporting activities to choose from. Evening meals available. 2 DOUBLE, 1 TWIN, 1 FAMILY, 1 SINGLE, MOST PRIVATE/EN SUITE FACILITIES CHILDREN ALL.

🆔 🍴 S   **Prices from £17 to £22**

142 NORTH BALLACHULISH
CEOL-NA-MARA North Ballachulish, Inverness-shire, PH33 6RZ.
Contact Mrs Annette Laing Tel: 01855 821 338.
GLENCOE 4m. Detached house in stunning location. Enjoy scenic walks in this beautiful area. Guests have free access to the swimming and leisure facilities in local hotel. With Aonach Mor/White Corries 16 miles, skiers and walkers are very welcome. Superb evening meals by arrangement. Closed December to mid January. 2 DOUBLE, 1 TWIN, PRIVATE OR EN SUITE FACILITIES CHILDREN 12+.

🆔 🍴 S   **Prices from £18 to £20**

143 OBAN
KINGS KNOLL Dunollie Road, Oban, Argyll, PA34 5JH.
Tel: 01631 562536 Fax: 01631 566101 E.mail: kingsknoll@aol.com.
A small family run hotel, in a lovely town and located on the A85 from the North and the A816 from the South. Oban is a very convenient touring centre for travel to Mull and other islands by the local ferries. This hotel overlooks the Sound of Kerrara and Oban Bay. Dinner is served from £12:00. We are closed Dec 25-Jan 31. 15 BEDROOMS WITH 13 EN SUITE.

🆔 🛏 S   💳 VISA   **Prices from £18 to £65**

144 OBAN
GLENARA GUEST HOUSE Rockfield Road, Oban, Argyll, PA34 5DQ.
Contact Dorothy Bingham Tel: 01631 563 172 Fax: 01631 571 125.
Just minutes away from the city centre, Glenara enjoys seaviews out over the bay. Rooms are uniquely decorated to a high standard and the double rooms boast lovely king size beds. Oban has lots to see and do. Walking, cycling, sea trips and loch cruises in nearby areas. Menu that caters for vegetarians. Minimum stay 2 nights. Closed January 3 DOUBLE EN SUITE, 1 TRIPLE WITH PRIVATE BATHROOM, 1 SINGLE WITH PRIVATE BATHROOM, CHILDREN 12+.

🍴

145 PAISLEY
ASHBURN Miliken Oark Road, Kilbarchan, Paisley, Renfrewshire, PA10 2DB.
Tel: 01505 705477 Fax: 01505 705477.
For additional prices and information, please contact us. We are within easy reach of Glasgow in a very nice country location. Motorcyclists are very welcome 6 BEDROOMS 2 EN SUITE.

Prices from £26 to £48

146 PENRITH
GREENFIELDS Ellonby, Penrith, Cumbria, CA11 9SJ.
Contact Mrs Green. Tel: 017684 84671.
Greenfields is located in tranquil, rural countryside and provides an excellent base from which to tour the Lake District and visit the scenic Eden valley. Rooms are tastefully decorated and overlook gardens. Your host and hostess will provide advice and assistance as well as a warm and friendly welcome. Good meals available. Closed November to February inclusive. 2 DOUBLE, 1 SINGLE CHILDREN 8+.

Prices from £16 to £18

147 PERTH
CLUNIE 12 Picullen Crescent, Perth, Perthshire, PH2 7HT.
Tel: 01738 623625 Fax: 01738 623625.
We are situated within easy reach of the City Centre for all the sight seeing and entrance to the Highlands if you wish to tour. We offer welcoming and homely accommodation and we are able to provide evening meals by prior arrangement 7 BEDROOMS, ALL EN SUITE.

Prices from £18 to £25

148 PERTH
QUALITY HOTEL Leonard Street, Perth, PH2 8HE.
Tel: 01738 624 141 Fax: 01738 639 912.
Located on the M90/A90 to Kings Place, Marshall Place to Leonard Street. Elegant castle-like building with high standards of comfort and service. Enjoy the use of a full fitness centre with sauna and jacuzzi. Golf nearby. Places of interest include St Andrews (50 miles), Gleneagles (30 miles) and closer to home, Scone Palace (3 miles). Special package for bikers £26. per person inc. breakfast and dinner. Subject to availability. Must be booked through Central Reservations 0800 44 44 44 52 BEDROOMS.

149 PERTH
TOPHEAD FARM Tullybelton, Stanley, Perth, Perthshire, PH1 4PT.
Contact Mrs Dow Tel & Fax: 01738 828 259.
A working farm with magnificent views situated in a peaceful location. Sun lounge overlooking garden and spacious bedrooms with king size beds. Perth and wonderful countryside nearby. Take A9 north out of Perth from Inveralmond roundabout.Take slip road left towards Tullybelton (0.5 mile). Varied breakfast menu 1 DOUBLE, 2 TWIN (1 EN SUITE), PRIVATE FACILITIES AVAILABLE CHILDREN ALL.

Prices from £18 to £22

150 PITLOCHRY
TIGH DORNIE ALDCLUNE Killiecrankie, Pitlochry, Perthshire, PH16 5LR.
Contact Mrs E. Sanderson Tel & Fax: 01796 473 276.
Beautiful Perthshire countryside surrounds this detached house with large garden. Tigh Dornie is just a few miles from Pitlochry with its many attractions. Also an ideal base from which to explore the Highlands, Inverness and Perth. Closed November. 2 DOUBLE, 1TWIN, ALL EN SUITE CHILDREN 12+.

Prices from £21 to £23

151 PITLOCHRY
BALROBIN Higher Oakfield, Pitlochry, Perthshire, PH16 5HT.
Contact Mrs Hohman Tel: 01796 472901 Fax: 01796 474200.
This is a delightful and traditional Scottish house in it's own grounds. It commands impressive and panoramic views. We welcome motorcyclists. 16 BEDROOMS 15 EN SUITE.

Prices from £25 to £64

152 PRESTWICK
GOLF VIEW 17 Links Road, Prestwick, Ayrshire, KA9 1QG.
Contact Mr heslop Tel: 01292 671234 Fax: 01292 671244.
As our name suggests we have lovely views across the Prestwick Golf Course and we are close to the International Airport. A very elegantly furnished house with moderately priced accommodation. Full Scottish breakfast that will send you on your way with fond memories. 6 BEDROOMS ALL EN SUITE.

Prices from £27 to £60

153 ROGART
BEN VIEW Lower Morness, Rogart, Sutherland, IV28 3XG.
Contact Mrs Corbett Tel: 01408 641222.
We offer, peace, quiet comfort and very good food served in a friendly way.We give personal attention and our traditional country farmhouse is located as an ideal base for golfing, hill walking, fishing and is convemient for all coasts. We have a TV lounge and dining room and we welcome motorcyclists.
3 BEDROOMS.

Prices from £14

154 ROSYTH
GLADYER INN 10 Heath Road, Rosyth, Fife, KY11 2BT. Tel: 01383 419 977.
Friendly pub serving bar meals. Guest beers occassionally. ACCOMMODATION AVAILABLE.

155 SLEAT
HOMELEIGH 3 Calgary, Ardvasar, Sleat, Isle of Skye, IV45 8RU.
Contact Rosemary Houlton Tel & Fax: 01471 844 361.
A comfortable modern home with superb views across the Sound of Sleat. Breathtaking views and stunning scenery. Enjoy relaxing walks and abundant wildlife. Skye ferry just a few minutes drive. Closed January
1 SINGLE, 2 TWIN EN SUITE, 1 DOUBLE EN SUITE CHILDREN NONE.

Prices from £15 to £19

RIDING THE STORM

SIDI

STEP INTO THE FUTURE

156 SPEAN BRIDGE
LETTERFINLAY LODGE Lochlochy, Lochlochy, Spean Bridge, Inverness-shire, PH34 4DZ. Tel: 01397 712622.
This is a beautifully situated home by the lochside, the views are wonderful and there is so much to do in the area. Superb motorcycle riding countryside. We serve bar meals and all our food is home cooked and prepared by us. We are closed from November to February. 12 BEDROOMS 9 OF WHICH ARE EN SUITE.

🗓 ☆ 🛏 🍽 Ⓢ   💳 💳 💳 💳   **Prices from £30 to £35**

157 SPEANBRIDGE
LETTERFINLAY LODGE Loch Lochy, Speanbridge, PH34 4D2. Tel: 01397 712 622.
Serves bar meals lunch and evening meals. Sandwiches served all day. Beautiful location by Loch side. ACCOMMODATION AVAILABLE.

158 ST ANDREWS
THE LARCHES 7 River Terrace, Guardbridge, St Andrews, Fifeshire, KY16 0XA. Contact Mrs Mayner Tel: 01334 838008 Fax: 01334 838008 E.mail: thelarches@aol.com.
This is a beautiful old memorial hall with plenty of traditional character. We are ideally positioned for swimming, touring and of course golf. The accommodation offers, full central heating, residents lounge with satellite TV, video player and plenty of films to relax with. We serve wonderful food and offer motorcyclists a very warm welcome. 3 BEDROMMS ALL EN SUITE OR WITH BATHROOM.

🖩 🗓 🛏 ☆ 🛏 🍽 Ⓢ   **Prices from £18 to £44**

159 ST ANDREWS
ARDGOWAN 2 Playfair Terrace, St Andrews, Fifeshire, KY16 9HX. Contact Mr Soutar Tel: 01334 472970 Fax: 01334 478380.
Two star hotel, consisting of 12 en suite bedrooms. We are very centrally situated in St Andrews. You can enjoy our fully licensed bistro bar and a la carte restaurant. Our speciality is fresh fish. 12 EN SUITE BEDROOMS.

🛏 🍽 Ⓢ   **Prices from £29 to £47**

160 ST. ABBS
CASTLE ROCK GUEST HOUSE Murrayfield, St. Abbs, Berwickshire, TD14 5PP. Contact Barbara Wood Tel: 01890 71715 Fax: 01890 71520 E.mail: boowood@compuserve.com.
A lovely Victorian house set on the edge of the cliffs and overlooking the fishing village of St. Abbs. Located in Scotland's beautiful Border country, with a wonderful sandy beach and birdwatching available at St. Abbs Head Nature Reserve. Good sporting facilities nearby with tennis, squash and swimming. All rooms have spectacular seaviews. Honeymoon suite available with bar and whirlpool bath. Delicious evening meals available that caters for vegetarians. Closed December and January.
1 SINGLE, 1 DOUBLE, 1 TWIN, 1 FAMILY, ALL EN SUITE CHILDREN 12+.

✂   **Prices from £23**

161 ST. ANDREWS

ROMAR GUEST HOUSE 45 Main Street, Strathkinness, St. Andrews, Fife, KY6 9RZ. Contact Margaret & Bob Patterson Tel & Fax: 01334 850 308.
Situated in peaceful surroundings, Romar Guest House is a modern bungalow with wonderful views. Visit the famed Old Course or enjoy the charming fishing village of Fife. Glamis Castle and Scone Palace also nearby. Hearty breakfast that will set you up for the day. Closed mid December to mid January. TWIN, SINGLE, FAMILY ROOMS, MOST EN SUITE CHILDREN ALL.

Prices from £18 to £22

162 STIRLING

CAIRNSAIGH Doig Street, Thornhill, Stirling, Perthshire, FK8 3PZ. Contact Fiona & John Boswell Tel & Fax: 01786 850 413 E.mail: cairnsaigh@compuserve.com.
Cairnsaigh is a spacious bungalow in a peaceful setting with excellent views across the Carse of Stirling. Ideal for touring central Scotland. Edinburgh, Glasgow and Perth all within 45 mins. Packed lunch and evening meals. Reductions for off season and longer stays. 2 DOUBLE, 1 TWIN, ALL EN SUITE CHILDREN ALL.

Prices from £24 to £30

163 TILLICOULTRY

WESTBOURNE 10 Dollar Road, Tillicoultry, Clackmannanshire, FK13 6PA. Contact Jane O' Dell Tel: 01259 750 314 Fax: 01259 750 642.
At the foot of Ochil Hills and surrounded by wooded grounds, Westbourne, a former Victorian mill owners' mansion, has log fires and a croquet lawn. Warm and friendly, it is perfect for exploring the nearby Highlands and the rest of central Scotland. On the Mill Trail and close to golf courses. Easy access to Stirling and the M9. Closed Christmas and New Year. 1 TWIN, 1 FAMILY, 1 DOUBLE EN SUITE CHILDREN ALL.

Prices from £21 to £23

164 TONGUE

BEN LOYAL Tongue, Sutherland, IV27 4XE. Tel: 01847 611216 Fax: 01847 611212.
Located in the very North of Scotland in an area with wonderful views and fantastic scenery. Tongue is on the A838 and A836 which runs along the extreme north road from Cape Wrath to John 'o' Groats. Ben Loyal is popular with motorcyclists as they are made very welcome. We offer hospitality comfort and a relaxed atmosphere. We are highly commended for our food. Closed from November to February. 12 BEDROOMS WITH 9 EN SUITE.

Prices from £30 to £40

165 WHITEBRIDGE

WHITEBRIDGE HOTEL Whitebridge, Inverness-shire, IV1 2UN. Tel: 0800 026 6277 Fax: 01456 486413 E.mail: whitebridgehotel@southlochness.demon.co.uk.
We are located on the southern end of Loch Ness. Our hotel is very poular with motorcyclists. We have covered and secure parking, and we have facilities to dry your clothes if necessary. There are some superb bikers roads, in this region with friendly bends alongside Loch Ness and going South. We offer cosy and comfortable accommodation and have bar foods available. 12 BEDROOMS AND 10 EN SUITE.

Prices from £25 to £44

166 WICK

MACKAYS Union Street, Wick, KW1 5ED. Tel: 01955 602 323.
Motorcyclists welcome at this beautifully situated pub. Restaurant with a la carte menu, bar food also available. ACCOMMODATION AVAILABLE.

1 ACHILL ISLAND
ACHILL CLIFF HOUSE Keel, Achill Island, Co. Mayo.
Contact Mrs McNamara Tel: 0984 3400.
Beside the beach this new guest house with panoramic views has a private sauna, residents lounge, TV, hairdryers and trouser press. Excellent restaurant specialising in seafood. 11 BEDROOMS, ALL EN SUITE.

Prices from £44 to £60

2 ADARE
ADARE LODGE Kildimo Road, Adare, Co. Limerick. Tel: 061 396629 Fax: 061 395060.
6 BEDROOMS, ALL EN SUITE.

Prices from £20 to £45

3 ANTRIM
THE RAILWAY BAR 24 Railway Street, Antrim, BT41 4AE. Tel: 01849 428 405.
Formerly famed for its cabaret acts, The Railway Bar is spacious and bright with a cosy atmosphere. Originally built in 1859 but recently renovated, the pub retains many of its original features. Drop in and sample the imaginative and delicious menu that caters for vegetarians.

4 ARDMORE
NEWTOWN VIEW FARMHOUSE Grange, Ardmore, Co. Waterford.
Contact Mrs O'Connor Tel & Fax: 024 94143.
With views of the Atlantic Ocean, this working dairy farm offers en suite rooms with TV and tea/coffee facilities. Award winning seafood dishes, hard tennis court, pony trekking, games room and cliff walks available. Closed November. 6 BEDROOMS, ALL EN SUITE.

Prices from £18 to £46

5 BALLINTOY
THE FULLERTON ARMS 22 Main Street, Ballintoy, Co. Antrim, BT54 6LX.
Tel: (028) 207 69613.
Unique traditional Irish theme bar situated on the Antrim coast, The Fullerton Arms is a wonderful place to stop when exploring the stunning surrounding countryside. Giant's Causeway (6 miles) and Carrick-A-Rede Rope Bridge and White Park Bay all within easy reach offering scenic walks and breathtaking views. Delicious and varied menu. 11 BEDROOMS ALL EN SUITE.

Prices from £25

6 BALLYCASTLE
ANTRIM ARMS 75 Castle Street, Ballycastle. Tel: (028) 207 62284.
Situated in the centre of Ballycastle, Antrim Arms is one of Ireland's oldest hotels. Guests can expect to receive a warm and friendly welcome in this delightful hotel which still retains much of its original character. An ideal base from which to explore the Antrim coast, Giant's Causeway and Bushmills Whisky Distillery. Enjoy fabulous a la carte menu and Irish style High Tea. Children welcome. 5 ROOMS.

7 BALLYMACARBRY
CLONANAV FARM GUEST HOUSE Hire Valley, Ballymacarbry, Co. Waterford.
Tel & Fax: 052 36141 E.mail: clonanav@iol.ie.
Closed 1 November-1 February. 10 BEDROOMS, ALL EN SUITE.

Prices from £27 to £54

8 BALTIMORE
CASEY'S OF BALTIMORE HOTEL Baltimore, Co. Cork. Tel: 028 20197 Fax: 028 20509 E.mail: baltimorecaseys@tinet.ie.
Closed 19-25 Feb, 1-14 Nov, 22-27 Dec. 14 BEDROOMS, ALL EN SUITE.

Prices from £47 to £93

9 BLESSINGTON
DOWNSHIRE HOUSE Blessington, Co. Wicklow. Tel: 045 865199 Fax: 045 865335.
Closed 22 December - 6 January. 25 BEDROOMS ALL EN SUITE.

Prices from £50 to £88

10 BRUFF
BRIDGE HOUSE FARM Grange, Bruff, Co. Limerick. Contact Mrs Barry Tel: 061 390195.
On the R512, this is a 200 year old house situated on a cattle farm 15 minutes south of Limerick city. Archaelogy, fishing and golf nearby. Closed November to February. 4 BEDROOMS, 2 EN SUITE.

Prices from £18 to £36

11 CAPPAGH
CASTLE FARM Millstreet, Cappagh, Co. Waterford. Contact Mr & Mrs Nugent Tel: 058 68049 Fax: 058 68099.
Award winning restored wing of 15th century castle on a large dairy farm. Excellent breakfast menu and elegant decor. Closed mid November - February. 5 BEDROOMS, ALL EN SUITE.

Prices from £27 to £42

12 CARAGH LAKE
CARAGH LODGE Caragh Lake, Co. Kerry. Contact Mrs Gaunt Tel: 066 976 9115 Fax: 066 976 9316.
Set in 7 acres on the shore of Caragh Lake, this is a mid Victorian fishing lodge offering award winning hospitality, comfort and service. Closed October to April. 15 ROOMS, ALL EN SUITE.

Prices from £75 to £200

13 CARLOW TOWN
BARROWVILLE TOWN HOUSE Kilkenny Road, Carlow Town, Co. Carlow. Contact Marie Dempsey Tel: 0503 43324 Fax: 0503 41953.
This regency house is set in its own grounds and has antique furnishings. It is 4 minutes walk from the twon centre, pub and restaurants and is in an ideal location for golf, touring the south east, midlands and Glendalough. 7 ROOMS, ALL EN SUITE.

Prices from £23.50 to £45

14 CARRICKFERGUS
DOBBINS INN Carrickfergus, Co. Antrim, BT38 7AF. Tel: 01960 351905.
Motorcyclists are welcome at this historical 16thC inn. There are regular evening entertainments and drink promotions. Fine ales and food served are of the best traditional quality. ACCOMMODATION AVAILABLE.

Prices from £42

15 CARRICKFERGUS
QUALITY HOTEL 75 Belfast Road, Carrickfergus, Co. Antrim, BT38 8PH.
Tel: 01960 364 556 Fax: 01960 351 620.
Located on the M5 from Belfast to Carrickfergus. Modern, stylish building with good quality accommodation. Facilities include restaurant, cocktail bar with golf and fishing nearby. Places of interest include Carrickfergus Castle (1 mile), Glens of Antrim (30 miles) and Belfast city centre (11 miles). Special package for bikers £26. per person inc. breakfast and dinner. Subject to availability. Must be booked through Central Reservations 0800 44 44 44. 68 BEDROOMS.

16 CARRIGANS
MOUNT ROYD COUNTRY HOME Carrigans, Co. Donegal.
Contact Mrs Martin Tel: 074 40163 Fax: 074 40400.
Offering traditional Irish hospitality this house is perfectly situated for visiting historic treasures, the Giants Causeway and Londonderry is 5 miles away on the R236. A40 off N13/N14. 4 ROOMS, ALL EN SUITE.

Prices from £19 to £32

17 CASTLETOWNBERE
FORD RI Castletownbere, Co. Cork. Contact Marian O'Dricoll and Edward Boyce
Tel: 027 70379 Fax: 027 70506 E.mail: fordrihotel@tinet.ie.
Looking out over Bantry Bay and the fishing port of Castletown Bere, this accommodation offers an excellent menu with seafood a speciality. 19 ROOMS, ALL EN SUITE.

Prices from £30 to £60

18 CASTLEWELLAN
SLIEVE CROOB INN 119 Clanvaraghan Road, Castlewellan, Co Down, BT31 9LA.
Tel: (028) 447 71412.
Slieve Croob Inn offers excellent accommodation with traditional entertainment and a wonderful restaurant. The Slieve Croob Inn has many modern day comforts but still manages to retain its old Irish charm with open fires and slate floors. Situated in magnificent countryside, there are superb views of the Mountains of Mourne, Lough Neagh and Belfast. NEARBY SELF-CATERING ACCOMMODATION.

19 CELBRIDGE
GREEN ACRES Dublin Road, Celbridge, Co. Kildare.
Contact Rose McCabe Tel: 01 627 1163 Fax: 01 627 1694.
Set in its own grounds with car park, this bungalow is 20 minutes away from Dublin, 30 minutes from the airport and ferries. Castletown house is 2km, golf and fishing nearby. Closed Christmas and New Year. 6 ROOMS, ALL EN SUITE.

Prices from £17.50 to £36

20 CLIFDEN
O' GRADY'S SUNNYBANK Church Hill, Clifden, Co. Galway.
Contact Mrs O'Grady Tel: 095 21437 Fax: 095 21976.
A period house with character, situated in its own grounds surrounded by gardens with many interesting features. Outdoor swimming pool. The house overlooks the picturesque town of Clifden. A warm Irish welcome is offered to guests. Closed 3rd November to 14th March. 11 ROOMS. ALL EN SUITE.

Prices from £50 to £60

21 CLIFDEN
MAL DUA Galway Road, Clifden, Co. Galway.
Contact Mrs Duane Tel: 095 21171 Fax: 095 21739 E.mail: maldua@iol.ie.
A mile from Clifden in the heart of Connemara, this family run guest house has spacious bedrooms, all individually designed with TV, radio, telephone and tea/coffee facilities. Closed December. 14 ROOMS, ALL EN SUITE.

Prices from £30 to £60

22 CLIFDEN
HEATHER LODGE Westport Road, Clifden, Co. Galway.
Contact Mr Delapp Tel: 095 21331 Fax: 095 22041 E.mail: 231@tinet.ie.
With splendid views of the lake and mountains, this delightful family home with a warm atmosphere offers a wonderful breakfast menu and home baking. Area of unspoilt beaches, angling and golf. Closed Christmas. 6 ROOMS, 5 EN SUITE.

Prices from £20 to £23.50

23 CLIFDEN
BUTTERMILK LODGE Westport Road, Clifden, Co. Galway.
Contact Pat O'Toole Tel: 095 21951 Fax: 095 21953 E.mail:
buttermilk@connemara.net.
Only 400 metres from the town centre this house with spacious rooms offers every comfort including satellite TV, real turf fires , home baking and wholesome breakfast options. 11 BEDROOMS, ALL EN SUITE.

Prices from £25 to £45

24 CLONAKILTY
CLONAKILTY LODGE Clonakilty, Co. Cork.
Contact Mr McGuire Tel: 023 34466 Fax: 023 33644.
A mixture of ensuite rooms and dormitories within close proximity of golden beaches and town centre. Located 50 metres off the N71. 42 ROOMS, ALL EN SUITE.

Prices from £16.50 to £35

25 CLONAKILTY
DUVANE FARM Ballyduvane, Clonakilty, Co. Cork.
Elegant Georgian house located on a beef farm just 2km from Clonakilty. High standard of accommodation and service in this beautifully situated house. Rooms have brass and canopy beds, TV and tea/coffee making facilities. Meals from local and home produce. All leisure activities nearby.

Prices from £18 to £22

26 CLONMEL
AMBERVILLE Glenconnor Road, Clonmel, Co. Tipperary. Tel: 052 21470.
Lovely spacious bungalow set in own grounds. There is a TV lounge for guests and tea/coffee available. Shops and other facilities nearby. 5 BEDROOMS, 3 EN SUITE.

Prices from £15 to £17

27 CORK
ANTOINE Western Road, Cork. Contact Mr Cross
Tel: 021 427 3494 Fax: 021 427 3092.
A large, attractive house situated just 5 minutes from the city centre. Ideal for exploring Bord Failte. All rooms fully ensuite. 10 BEDROOMS, ALL EN SUITE.

⬚ S

Prices from £25 to £50

28 CORK
ST KILDA GUEST HOUSE Western Road, Cork.
Contact Mr Collins Tel: 353 21 273 095 Fax: 353 21 275 015.
Attractive accommodation just 10 minutes stroll from the city centre with all its attractions. 20 minutes drive to airport and Blarney Castle, 30 minutes to ferryport and Kinsdale which has fabulous restaurants.

⬚ S

29 CORK
QUALITY HOTEL & SUITES MORRISONS ISLAND Morrisons Quay, Cork.
Tel: 00353 212 75858 Fax: 00353 212 75833.
From Airport: Parnell Place into Oliver Street. Well located, facilities inc. restaurant, cocktail bar, cable TV, shopping and golf nearby. Places of interest include Cork city centre, Blarney Castle (10 miles) and Kinsale Town and Midleton Jameson Distillery (12.5 miles). Special package for bikers £26. per person inc. breakfast and dinner. Subject to availability. Book through Central Reservations 0800 44 44 44. 54 BEDROOMS.

S 🍵

30 CRUSHEEN
LAHARDAN HOUSE Crusheen, Co. Clare. Contact Mrs Griffins.
A large, elegant family residence set in own grounds. Rooms are ensuite and have direct dial telephones, hairdryers and central heating. Local activities include fishing, golf and pitch and putt. 8 BEDROOMS, ALL EN SUITE.

⬚ S 🖃 VISA

31 DINGLE
MILLTOWN HOUSE Dingle, Co. Kerry. Tel: 066 915 1372 Fax: 066 915 1095
E.mail: milltown@indigo.ie.
Comfortable accommodation in good location. There are tea/coffee making facilities and food available. Rooms have TV. 10 BEDROOMS, ALL EN SUITE.

Prices from £27.50 to £37.50

32 DINGLE
BOLANDS Goat Street, Dingle, Co. Kerry. Contact Mrs Boland Tel: 066 915 1426.
Accommodation with views of Dingle Bay and offering sky TV. Rooms have many facilities and even orthopaedic beds. Shops and other amenities are within walking distance. 6 BEDROOMS, ALL EN SUITE.

⬚ 🍴 S 🍵

Prices from £15 to £18

33 DUBLIN
CHARLEVILLE LODGE 268-272 North Circular Road, Phisborough, Dublin 7.
Contact Mr Stenson Tel: 01 838 6633 Fax: 01 838 5854.
Beautifully refurbished accommodation combining a traditional feel with modern facilities. 15 minutes walk from O' Connell Street. Bus stops at front door. 30 BEDROOMS, 28 EN SUITE.

⬚ S

34 DUBLIN
COMFORT INN, TALBOT STREET 95-98 Talbot Street, Dublin.
Tel: 00353 1874 9202 Fax: 00353 1874 9672.
Located 10 mins from O'Connell Street. Attractive decor in comfortable surroundings. Facilities include cable TV. All the attractions of Dublin right on the doorstep. Special package for bikers £26. per person inc. breakfast and dinner. Subject to availability. Must be booked through Central Reservations 0800 44 44 44.

35 DUBLIN
EGAN'S HOUSE 7/9 Iona Park, Glasnevin, Dublin.
Contact Robert Devine Tel: 01 830 3611 Fax: 01 830 3312.
Charming property set in peaceful location with easy access to the city centre. Airport, ferry and botanic gardens nearby. 23 ROOMS ALL EN SUITE.

Prices from £26 to £32

36 DUBLIN
GLENVEAGH 31 Northumberland Road, Ballsbridge, Dublin.
Contact Mrs Cunningham Tel: 01 668 4612 Fax: 01 668 4559.
Victorian residence right in the heart of Dublin. City centre less than 2km where there are lots of places of interest. High standard of comfort and service. En suite rooms with cable TV and direct dial telephone.

37 DUBLIN
RAGLAN LODGE 10 Raglan Road, Ballsbridge, Dublin.
Contact Helen Moran Tel: 01 660 6697 Fax: 01 660 6781.
Elegant Victorian residence built in 1861. Decor and furnishings combine to create a lovely traditional feel. Easy access to Dublin city centre where there is lots to see and do. 7 BEDROOMS ALL EN SUITE.

38 DUBLIN 1
LYNDON GUEST HOUSE 26 Gardiner Place, Dublin 1.
Contact Mrs Measa Tel: 01 878 6950 Fax: 01 878 7420.
Luxurious Georgian period guest house situated in the city centre near all the major tourist attractions. Ensuite rooms are comfortably furnished and have many facilities. 9 BEDROOMS, ALL EN SUITE.

Prices from £30 to £60

39 DUBLIN 2
CLARION HOTEL & SUITES Earlsfort Centre, Lower Leeson Street, Dublin 2.
Tel: 00353 166 10585 Fax: 00353 163 81122.
Located Stephens Green-Merris Road-Pembroke St-Leeson Lower Street. Facilities include restaurant, cable TV and golf nearby. Situated in the heart of Georgian Dublin there is lots to see and do. Special package for bikers £26. per person inc. breakfast and dinner. Subject to availability. Must be booked through Central Reservations 0800 44 44 44. 37 SUITES.

40 DUBLIN 6
QUALITY CHARLEVILLE HOTEL & SUITES Lower Rathmines Road, Dublin 6.
Tel: 00353 140 66100 Fax: 00353 140 66200.
Take M50 to Tallaght, turn left at Tallaght onto N89 into Rathmines. Spacious and attractively decorated accommodation with stylish bar and restaurant. There is cable TV and entertainment. Golf nearby. Places of interest include Stephens Green, Rathmines Village only a few minutes walk, Trinity College, the Government buildings, art galleries, shops, pubs and theatres. Special package for bikers £26. per person inc. breakfast and dinner. Subject to availability. Must be booked through Central Reservations 0800 44 44 44. 52 BEDROOMS.

41 DUN LAOGHAIRE
WINDSOR LODGE 3 Ilsington Avenue, Sandycove, Dun Laoghaire.
Contact Mrs O' Farrell Tel: 01 284 6952 Fax: 01 284 6952.
Recently refurbished period home with views of Dublin Bay. Just a couple minutes walk from Dart and minutes from the ferry. Ensuite rooms are decorated to a high standard and offer comfortable surroundings in which to unwind and relax.

Prices from £25

42 DUNSHAUGHLIN
YE OLDE WORKHOUSE Ballinlough, Dunshaughlin.
Tel: 01 825 9251 Fax: 01 825 9251.
Guests can expect a warm welcome at this beautiful property restored and refurbished throughout. Antiques give a traditional feel to the property. Ideal for exploring the Boyne Valley heritage sites and award winning gardens. Excellent meals available. 5 BEDROOMS,
ALL EN SUITE.

Prices from £30 to £45

43 ENNIS
QUALITY HOTEL AUBURN LODGE Galway Road, Ennis, Co. Clare.
Tel: 00353 652 1247 Fax: 00353 652 1202.
Located on the N18. Centrally situated with access to attractions such as the Cliffs of Moher (25 miles), Bunratty Castle (15 miles), Ennis Abbey (2 miles) and Ballyalla lake (0.5 miles). Special package for bikers £26. per person inc. breakfast and dinner. Subject to availability. Must be booked through Central Reservations 0800 44 44 44. 100 BEDROOMS.

44 ENNISTYMON
GROVEMOUNT HOUSE Lahinch Road, Ennistymon, Co Clare.
Tel: 065 707 1431 Fax: 065 707 1823.
Located on the edges of Ennistymon with easy access to the Burren and Cliffs of Moher. Golfing, fishing and traditional music sessions can be arranged. 8 BEDROOMS, ALL EN SUITE.

Prices from £18 to £22.50

45 FEAKLE
SMYTH COUNTRY LODGE HOTEL Feakle, Co. Clare. Tel: 061 924000.
This hotel is located close to 36 beautiful lakes. Each of the 35 bedrooms have en suite facilities and TV. Restaurant open all day serving fresh sea food among many other fine dishes. Bar facilities with live traditional Irish music. Nearby activities include golf, watersports, fishing, pony trekking and walking. 35 BEDROOMS, ALL EN SUITE.

Prices from £70 to £94

46 GALWAY
QUALITY HOTEL & LEISURE CENTRE Oranmore, Galway.
Tel: 00353 917 92244 Fax: 00353 917 92246.
Located on the N6-main approach road to Galway. Good accommodation in central location. Rooms are well equipped and there is golfing and fishing nearby. Leisure centre with indoor swimming pool. Places of interest include Galway Crystal Heritage Centre, Druid Theatre, cinema, festivals, horseriding, walking and historic tours. Special package for bikers £26. per person inc. breakfast and dinner. Subject to availability. Must be booked through Central Reservations 0800 44 44 44. 93 BEDROOMS.

47 GLENDALOUGH
CARMEL'S Annamoe, Glendalough. Tel: 0404 45297 Fax: 0404 45297.
An attractive family run country home situated in a peaceful location in the heart of the Wicklow Mountains. Enjoy walks in the surrounding area. Ferry and airport are within easy reach. 4 BEDROOMS.

Prices from £34 to £36

48 KENMARE
ARDMORE HOUSE Killarney Road, Kenmare, Co. Kerry.
Tel: 064 41406 Fax: 064 41406.
Attractive property just a quarter of a mile from the city centre. Nearby activities include golf with three golf courses. Ideal for exploring the surrounding area. 6 BEDROOMS, ALL EN SUITE.

Prices from £18 to £28

49 KILKENNY
NEWLANDS COUNTRY HOUSE Seven Houses, Danesfort, Kilkenny, Co Kilkenny.
Tel: 056 29111 Fax: 056 29171.
Award winning accommodation with delicious breakfast. Bedrooms are wonderfully decorated and have whirlpool baths. Special weekend package includes 7 course dinner. 4 BEDROOMS, ALL EN SUITE.

Prices from £25 to £60

50 KILKENNY
SHILLOGHER Callan Road, Kilkenny, Co. Kilkenny.
Contact Mr Hennersey Tel: 056 63249 Fax: 056 64865.
Beautiful home in peaceful surroundings just 1km from the city and the castle. Unwind in the guest conservatory overlooking the scenic gardens. Varied breakfast menu. Open all year. 5 BEDROOMS, ALL EN SUITE.

Prices from £25 to £39

51 KILLARNEY
EARLS COURT HOUSE Woodlawn Junction, Muckcross Road, Killarney, Co Kerry.
Contact Mrs Mer Moynham Tel: 064 34009 Fax: 064 34366.
Guests can be assured of high standards of comfort and hospitality at this guest house. Luxurious bedrooms with bathrooms. Ideally situated within just a few minutes walk to the town centre. Good food available. 11 BEDROOMS, ALL EN SUITE.

🅾 Ⓢ   **Prices from £38 to £85**

52 KILLARNEY
GLEANN FIA COUNTRY HOUSE Old Deer Park, Killarney, Co Kerry.
Contact Nora Galvin Tel: 064 35035 Fax: 064 35000.
Spacious, attractive accommodation in 30 acres of mature woodlands. Cosy atmosphere with open peat fires. Enjoy private river walks. Imaginative breakfast menu. 17 BEDROOMS, ALL EN SUITE.

🅾 Ⓢ   **Prices from £25 to £60**

53 KILLARNEY
LOTHANS LODGE Tralee Road, Killarney, Co Kerry. Tel: 064 33871 Fax: 064 33871.
Modern bungalow conveniently located for touring lakes and gardens. Situated a few miles from Killarney where there are shops and other amenities. Closed 10 Nov-10 Feb. 5 BEDROOMS, ALL EN SUITE.

🅾 Ⓢ   **Prices from £34 to £35**

54 KILLARNEY
PURPLE HEATHER Gap of Dunloe, Beaufort, Killarney, Co Kerry.
Contact Mr Moriarty Tel & Fax: 064 44266.
Located in a superb area with wonderful views. Rooms have many facillties including electric blankets, hairdryers, tea/coffee and a pool room. Nearby activities include tennis, pony trekking and fishing. Restaurant just a short walk away. 6 BEDROOMS, 5 EN SUITE.

🅾 Ⓢ   ▇▾ VISA   **Prices from £17 to £34**

55 KILLARNEY
COUNTESS HOUSE Countess Road, Killarney, Co Kerry.
Contact Noreen Sheahan Tel: 064 34247.
Spacious and modern accommodation in peaceful location. Just 2 minutes walk from the town centre and bus and rail services. TV lounge and an extensive breakfast menu.

56 KILLARNEY
CLIMBERS INN Glencar, Killarney, Co Kerry. Contact John Walsh
Tel: 0161 4380222 Fax: 0161 4380185 E.mail: climbers@iol.ie.
A former rambling and hill walking centre, Climbers Inn is situated in the Kerry Highlands in a lovely woodland area. Good atmosphere and surroundings mean that visitors just cannot resist coming back. Excellent bar food. Closed 1 Dec-28 Feb. 10 BEDROOMS, ALL EN SUITE.

🅾 Ⓢ   **Prices from £23**

57 KILLARNEY
QUALITY HOTEL Tralee Road, Killarney. Tel: 00353 643 7070 Fax: 00353 643 7060.
Located on Tralee Road out of Killarney. Very high standards of accommodation and service. Guests have many facilities including restaurant and nearby golfing and fishing. Places of interest include the scenic walks around the Lakes of Killarney and Tralee and Killarney. Town centre. Special package for bikers £26. per person inc. breakfast and dinner. Subject to availability. Must be booked through Central Reservations 0800 44 44 44. 102 BEDROOMS.

S 🛉

58 KILLARNEY
CLARION HOTEL, RANDLES COURT Muckcross Road, Killarney, Co. Kerry.
Tel: 00353 643 5333 Fax: 00353 643 5206.
Located on the N22. Attractive building in good location. Restaurant and cocktail bar, cable TV and nearby fishing and horseriding. Places of interest include Killarney National Park 2 miles, Muckcross House and Gardens 3 miles and St Mary Cathedral 1 mile. Special package for bikers £26. per person inc. breakfast and dinner. Subject to availability. Must be booked through Central Reservations 0800 44 44 44. 49 BEDROOMS.

🍴 ∪ S

59 KILLINEY
QUALITY HOTEL, COURT Killiney Bay, Killiney, Co. Dublin.
Tel: 00353 128 51622 Fax: 00353 128 52085.
Located 30 mins from city centre, follow signs for Killiney Bay. Spacious and attractive accommodation in beautiful grounds. Facilities include restaurant, cocktail bar and there is golf and fishing nearby. Places of interest include Gardens and waterfalls (10 miles) and Dalkey Heritage Village 10 minutes by DART. Special package for bikers £26. per person inc. breakfast and dinner. Subject to availability. Must be booked through Central Reservations 0800 44 44 44. 86 BEDROOMS.

🍴 S

60 KILLORGLIN
DROMIN FARMHOUSE Miltown, Killorglin, Co. Kerry.
Contact Mrs Foley
Tel: 066 976 1867.
A friendly and warm welcome at this attractive home on a dairy/sheep farm with superb views of the mountains including McGillacuddy Reeks and Irelands highest mountain. Ideal base from which to tour. Closed Dec-Mid March. 4 BEDROOMS, 3 EN SUITE.

🖸 S   **Prices from £20 to £34**

61 KILLYLEAGH
THE DUFFERIN ARMS 35 High Street, Killyleagh, Co Down, BT30 9QF.
Tel: (028) 44 828 229.
Situated in the historic town of Killyleagh overlooking the shores of Strongford, The Dufferin Arms is a traditional country pub renowned throughout Ulster for its excellent, reasonably priced food and drink. Relax by the charming open fire and sample the wide range of wines and spirits available. Ensuite bedrooms have lovely four poster beds and there is also a residents lounge and a library. 7 BEDROOM ALL EN SUITE.

Price: £32.50

62 KILTEGAN
HUMEWOOD CASTLE Kiltegan, Co. Wicklow. Tel: 0508 73215 Fax: 0508 73382.
The most important Victorian Castle in Ireland is located in glorious countryside at the foot of the Wicklow Mountains. It has elegant accommodation and offers horse riding, fishing, shooting and delicous food prepared by the resident French Chef. Only 45 minutes south of Dubln.

63 KNOCK
BELMONT Knock, Co Mayo. Tel: 094 88122 Fax: 094 88532
E.mail: belmonthotel@tinet.ie
Spacious, comfortable accommodation with many facilities. Leisure club with gym and steam room and natural health therapy centre and jacuzzi. 64 BEDROOMS, ALL EN SUITE.

🖥 Ⓢ **Prices from £29 to £52**

64 LETTERKENNY
HILLCREST HOUSE Lurgy Brack, Sligo Road, Letterkenny, Co Donegal.
Contact Mr McGuire Tel: 074 22300 Fax: 074 25137.
Located on the N13 to Sligo, Hillcrest House is a modern bungalow overlooking the town and river. Rooms are comfortably furnished and offer a relaxing atmosphere in which to unwind after a busy day exploring the surrounding countryside. Closed Christmas. 6 BEDROOMS, 5 EN SUITE.

🖥 Ⓢ **Prices from £20 to £30**

65 LIFFORD
HAW LODGE The Haw, Lifford, Co Donegal. Contact Mrs Patterson
Tel: 074 41397 Fax: 074 41985 E.mail: hawlodgeb.b@internet.com.
Situated in beautiful countryside, Haw Lodge is a lovely farmhouse set in its own grounds. Ideal for an overnight stop and for exploring the surrounding area. Large family suite avilable. Leisure centre and good food places nearby. 2km from Lifford on Lifford/Sligo N15 road. 4 BEDROOMS, 2 EN SUITE.

🖥 Ⓢ **Prices from £17 to £36**

66 MACROOM
MILLS INN Macroom, Co Cork. Tel: 026 41074 Fax: 026 41505.
Accommodation with many facilities in ideal location. Rooms decorated to a high standard with TV available. Leisure club with pool, gym and solarium, steam room and jacuzzi. Closed 24-27 Dec.

📇 VISA **Prices from £32**

67 MOUNTSHANNON
MOUNTSHANNON Mountshannon, Co Clare. Tel: 061 927 162 Fax: 061 927 272.
Friendly guest house in superb location. Facilities include a restaurant preparing delicious meals and a function room. Enjoy walks around the nearby lake. Boat trips and pony trekking within walking distance. 14 BEDROOMS, ALL EN SUITE.

♨

68 NAAS
HARBOUR VIEW HOTEL Limerick Road, Naas, Co Kildare.
Tel: 045 879 145 Fax: 045 874 002.
Comfortable accommodation with TV, tea/coffee making facilities and fully licensed premises. Restaurant open all day serving a wide selection of quality food. Closed 25-27 Dec. 10 BEDROOMS, ALL EN SUITE.

69 NEW ROSS
WOODLANDS HOUSE Carrigbyrne, Newbawn, New Ross, Co. Wexford.
Contact Colin Campbell Tel & Fax: 051 428 287.
Tastefully decorated ensuite bedrooms with TV. Ideal base from which to explore Wexford, Waterford and Kilkenny. Located on Rosslare/New Ross road (N25), close to Chedar Lodge Hotel, just 30 minutes from the Rosslare ferries. Closed 1 Dec-1 Feb. 5 BEDROOMS, 4 EN SUITE.

🔒 [S]   **Prices from £18**

70 NEWCASTLE
THE BRIERS 39 Middle Tollymore Road, Newcastle, Co. Down, BT33 0JJ.
Contact Mary, David and Michelle Bowater Tel & Fax: (028) 437 24347.
Adjacent to Tollymore Forest Park and just a few miles from Newcastle, this hotel offers a warm welcome with comfortable rooms and a full Irish Breakfast. Local amenities include water sports, golf and pony trekking.

71 OMEATH
GRANVUE HOUSE Omeath, Co. Louth. Contact Mrs Brennan
Tel: 042 937 5109 Fax: 042 937 5415.
Recently refurbished spacious accommodation just 20 yards from the sea and ferry boat across Carlingford Lough to Warrenpoint. Rooms are decorated to a high standard. 9 BEDROOMS, ALL EN SUITE.

🔒 [S]   **Prices from £24 to £48**

72 ORANMORE
MOORINGS Main Street, Oranmore, Co. Galway. Contact Mrs Aneelynch
Tel & Fax: 091 790 462.
The Moorings welcomes business people and guests touring the local area. Burren and Connemara are within easy access. Nearby activities include golf, sailing and wind surfing. 6 BEDROOMS, ALL EN SUITE.

🔒 [S]   **Prices from £25 to £50**

73 ROSSLARE
ELMWOOD Station Road, Rosslare Harbour, Rosslare, Co. Wexford.
Contact Mrs Duggan Tel: 053 33321.
Beautiful location and accommodation just a couple of minutes drive from the ferry. Rooms have many facilities including TV, hairdryer and tea/coffee making facilities. Hearty breakfast that will set you up for the day. Travel agent vouchers accepted. Closed Nov-Feb. 3 BEDROOMS, ALL EN SUITE.

🔒 🔧 [S] ☕   **Prices from £36**

74 ROUNDSTONE
ELDONS Roundstone, Co. Galway. Contact Ann Connelly
Tel: 095 35933 Fax: 095 35871.
Situated in magnificent countryside, Eldons is an elegant property offering a friendly and cosy atmosphere. The restaurant has a varied menu including lobster and other catches from the harbour. 19 BEDROOMS, ALL EN SUITE.

ᚠ S   ▬ VISA   **Prices from £30 to £60**

75 SLANE
CONYNGHAM ARMS Slane, Co Meath. Tel: 041 982 4155 Fax: 041 982 4205.
Ideally located accommodation in attractive setting. Restaurant open in the evening and coffee shop open all day. Golf courses within walking distance. 14 BEDROOMS, ALL EN SUITE.

▬ VISA

76 STRABANE
THE FIR TREES HOTEL Dublin Road, Strabane, Tyrone, BT82 9JT.
Located right in the heart of magnificent countryside, The Fir Trees Hotel is just a mile from the market town of Stabane. Explore the wonderful Sperrin Mountains, Gortin Glen Country Park and the Donegal Mountains or try the angling rivers of Derg, Mourne and Finn. Excellent food at the hotels Meeting House Restaurant which has an extensive menu including local specialities and international dishes. Local bar with wonderful colonial feel and musical entertainment. 26 ROOMS ALL EN SUITE.

ᚠ S   **Prices from £35 to £55**

77 TIPPERARY
BANSHA CASTLE Bansha, Tipperary, Co Tipperary. Tel: 062 54187 Fax: 062 54294.
Attractive accommodation in well situated location. Lots of activities nearby including golf, fishing and pony trekking. Snooker room available for guests. 6 BEDROOMS, ALL EN SUITE.

78 TRAMORE
CLIFF HOUSE Cliff Road, Tramore, County Waterford. Contact Pat and Hilary O'Sullivan. Tel & Fax: 051 381 497.
This guest house enjoys beautiful, panoramic views and has its own private gardens. Activities available include walks and golf. Closed 20 Dec-7 Jan. 6 BEDROOMS, ALL EN SUITE.

ᚠ S   VISA   **Prices from £25 to £38**

79 TRALEE
QUALITY HOTEL Castle Street, Tralee. Tel: 00353 662 1877 Fax: 00353 662 2273.
Located in Tralee town centre. Facilities include restaurant, cocktail bar and cable TV. Local places of interest include Muckross House, the scenic Ring of Kerry and Tralee and Killarney town centres. Special package for bikers £26. per person inc. breakfast and dinner. Subject to availability. Must be booked through Central Reservations 0800 44 44 44. 40 BEDROOMS.

♈ S ☙

80 TRIM
BROGANS GUEST HOUSE High Street, Trim, Co. Meath.
Tel: 046 31237 Fax: 046 37648 E.mail: brogang@iol.ie.
Brogan's Guesthouse is located in the medieval town of Trim and offers a high standard of accommodation and service. Close to all amenities with golf and fishing also nearby. 14 BEDROOMS, ALL EN SUITE.

Prices from £25 to £40

81 WATERFORD
QUALITY HOTEL Canada Wharf, Waterford City, Waterford.
Tel: 00353 518 56600 Fax: 00353 518 56605.
City centre location, Dunmore Road 2nd right. A friendly welcome awaits guests at this comfortable hotel. Restaurant, cocktail bar, cable TV. Shops close by. Waterford Crystal Plant, South East Beach, Waterford Shopping Centre and Tramore seaside resort close at hand. Special package for bikers £2 per person inc. b/fst and dnr. Subject to availability. Book through Central Reservations 0800 44 44 44. 80 BEDROOMS.

82 WATERFORD
DIAMOND HILL Milepost, Slieverue, Waterford, Co. Waterford.
Contact Mrs Smith-Lehane Tel: 051 832 855 Fax: 051 832 254.
Set in award winning gardens, Diamond Hill is a country guest house with ensuite rooms, decorated to a high standard and offering a relaxing atmosphere. Closed 24-25 Dec. 12 BEDROOMS, ALL EN SUITE.

Prices from £20 to £27.50

83 WATERVILLE
KLONDYKE HOUSE New Line Road, Waterville, Co Kerry.
Tel: 066 947 4119 Fax: 066 947 4666.
Guests can expect a friendly welcome at this ideally located accommodation with many facilities. Well behaved pets are welcome by prior arrangement. 6 BEDROOMS, ALL EN SUITE.

84 YOUGHAL
AHERNE'S SEAFOOD RESTAURANT AND ACCOMMODATION 163 North Main Street, Youghal, Co. Cork. Contact The FitzGibbon Family
Tel: 00 353 24 92424 Fax: 00 353 24 93633 E.mail: ahe@iol.ie.
Aherne's Seafood Restaurant is an internationally renowned gourmet landmark specialising in the freshest locally caught seafood. Have a light meal in one of the 2 bars or enjoy a meal in the award winning restaurant. 10 luxurious bedrooms large and tastefully decorated with antique furniture, each having hairdryer, 6' beds, TV, trouser press and direct dial phone. Cosy drawing room with open turf fire. Deep Sea and River Angling, Equestrian facilities, 2 blue-flag beaches and 18-hole golf course close by. 10 ROOMS EN SUITE: DOUBLES £50PP (£60PP HIGH SEASON), SINGLES £70 (£80 HIGH SEASON).

Prices from £50 to £80

The basics of
motorcycle tyres

TYRES . . . SIMPLE THINGS, round, black, hole in the middle, you get the general idea. But put the wrong ones on your bike and you'll soon know about it.

There are two basic kinds of tyre, radials and crossply with a further side alley called bias-belted. Radials get their name from their casing angle; it lies at 90 degrees to the direction of tyre travel. The casing belts of crossplys cross at angles to each other and create a sturdier structure. Bias-belted tyres are a development of crossplys; they feature an extra belt or belts between the casing and tread compound. This belt could be used as added reinforcement or sometimes as an additional comfort layer.

Do not under any circumstances mix these different types of tyre unless the tyre manufacturer approves it. They have developed their tyres to work in matched pairs. One exception to this rule is that it is perfectly possible for a manufacturer to recommend a crossply front with a bias-ply rear, this is usually because the bias-ply tyre has been designed as an integral part of an existing range of crossply tyres. Neither will you get the best from your bike if you use a tyre from Brand A on the front and one from Brand X on the rear. In the UK it is illegal to fit the following combinations:

bias-belt front	crossply rear
radial front	crossply rear
radial front	bias-belt rear

There is a popular misconception that radial tyres are better than crossplys, this is simply not true. In recent years a couple of manufacturers have put a lot of development into bringing crossplys bang up to date and the best of these can sometimes outperform radials on bikes where manufacturers approve the use of both kinds of tyre. The simple rule of thumb is to only fit tyres in the matched pairs as recommended by the tyre manufacturer of your choice.

Selecting the type of tyre (super sports, sports, touring, etc) for use on your bike is more difficult. It will depend on the type of bike that you own, what sort of riding you do and what choices the tyre manufacturer recommends for your bike. Speak to people who understand tyres such as tyre specialists, manufacturers or their distributors, but definitely not the bloke you met down the pub last night! Fitting a different sort of tyre can change a bikes handling characteristics. If, for example, you own a VFR800 the steering can be made to feel a lot lighter by changing the original sports rubber for a pair of super sports tyres, but again, only if the tyre maker approves it. Don't be tempted to take this too far by fitting tyres intended for racing on street bikes. Pure racing tyres are not approved for road use, their casings are very light and can be easily damaged, and the profiles of these tyres is tuned towards hyper-quick steering and not the stability needed by road bikes. Road legal race tyres such as those used in super-sport racing do not always make good road tyres either. All out grip on the limit at the expense of all round handling ability on the road does not make for an easy life, besides any road orientated super-sport tyre will give you all the grip you can ever use.

Some machines require the use of specially constructed tyres. Outwardly these tyres appear identical to the standard version but they may have structural or compound changes that fine tune the handling of the bikes that they were designed for. The tyre makers then adjust one of their existing tyres until the handling characteristics that the bike manufacturer requires are achieved. In these cases it is obvious that you should only fit these specially constructed tyres.

After having a new tyre fitted you should always ride gently for about 100 miles, avoid sudden acceleration, maximum braking and hard cornering. This period is commonly known as scrubbing-in and

This is how the MEZ4 slices through a bend. Now try it without steel.

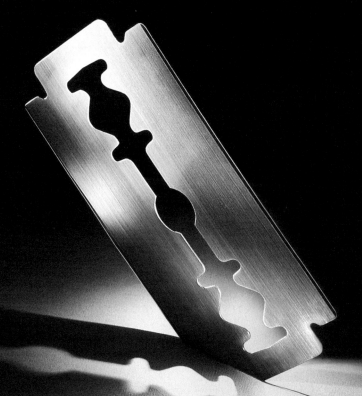

www.metzeler.com

Newly developed radial tyre with Zero degree steel belt for sport and sport touring machines from 600cc up. The tyres have the same construction and shape as MEZ3 sports tyres but feature a silica compound and deeper tread pattern for 25% longer life.

"These are great all-round tyres which are very hard to fault"....... MCN Tyre Test, May 1998.

After all, you want to get on.

METZELER
MOTORCYCLE TYRES

is necessary because when a tyre is new it still has some residue of the releasing agent on its surface. This agent prevents the tyre getting stuck in the mould during manufacture. It can also help to prolong the tyres life while it is in storage and this is the reason that the manufacturer does not clean the agent off the tread surface.

You should subject your tyres to a safety check regularly and often. It is unbelievable how many riders only look at their pressures every month or so. Tyres should be checked for damage and correct inflation pressure once a week, more often if you are covering high mileage, pressures should be checked only when the tyres are cold. Tyre pressures are very much a personal thing and no two riders will agree on what suits each best. Tyre manufacturers only recommend one inflation pressure, this is a pressure that will cope well with most riding conditions, whether you are riding solo or with a passenger, with or without luggage, commuting or scratching. It is obvious that by adjusting your tyre pressures you will be able to improve the handling in a given area. Generally speaking the higher the pressure the greater the stability and the longer the tyre will last. By reducing pressure you can increase grip, this is because the contact patch has been increased and the casing and tread can move around a little more and therefore heat up more. But remember, if you lower the pressure too far, instability can result. As a rule start with the tyre manufacturer's recommended pressure and reduce the rear by 2 psi and the front by 1 psi. Only adjust one tyre at a time so that you can analyse the results. When you feel that you are close, only make adjustments in 1 psi increments. This is a black art with no hard and fast guidelines and only you will be able to tell what suits you in different circumstances. Certain bikes, the Super Blackbird springs to mind, do not benefit from pressure adjustments, always check with your tyre expert first.

The marking on the sidewall of a tyre contains vital information, the main thing that you should concern yourself with though is the size and speed rating.

Let's take a typical size of **180/55 ZR17 (73W)**:

- **180** refers to the section width of the tyre in millimetres.
- **55** is the aspect (height) ratio expressed as a percentage of the width.
- **Z** is the speed rating (see chart below).
- **R** shows the tyre is of radial construction, a B would be bias-belted and a hyphen would be a crossply.
- **17** is the rim diameter, always shown in inches.
- **73** is the load index, it denotes the maximum load the tyre can carry at the designated speed rating and with maximum inflation pressure. This is to be used in conjunction with a chart, which converts the index into kg's.
- **W** is the maximum speed the tyre was designed for. W without brackets is up to 270 km/h, W with brackets is more than 270 km/h.

Some commonly used speed ratings are:

- **P** up to 93 mph/150 km/h
- **S** up to 112 mph/180 km/h
- **H** up to 130 mph/210 km/h
- **V** up to 150 mph/240 km/h
- **Z** over 150 mph/240 km/h

Remember, as long as you stick to the major manufacturers and their recommendations there is no such thing as a bad tyre these days, only tyres which are unsuitable for your bike or riding style.

WHEN YOU'VE WON AS MUCH AS WE HAVE, YOU DESERVE A LAP OF HONOUR.

DUNLOP ARE RUNNING RINGS ROUND THE COMPETITION. WE BUILT THIS RACE-WINNING TECHNOLOGY INTO OUR D207 ROAD TYRES AND THEY LAPPED UP THE ULTIMATE OFF-TRACK PRIZE, MCN'S 'PRODUCT OF THE YEAR'. CATCH DUNLOP D207s AT YOUR LOCAL DEALER NOW.

F.I.M. SUPERSPORT WORLD CUP · F.I.M. 250CC WORLD CHAMPIONSHIP · BRITISH SUPERBIKE CHAMPIONSHIP · BRITISH SUPERSPORT 600 CHAMPIONSHIP · AMERICAN AMA CHAMPIONSHIP · F.I.M. 125CC WORLD CHAMPIONSHIP

DUNLOP

D207

Social acceptance at last!

EVEN MOTORCYCLES WITH short memories can remember when pub owners hung out 'No Bikers' signs, and the media always assumed that any miscreant wearing a black leather jacket had to be a biker. At last, this attitude has (almost) disappeared and its refreshing to see this guide book welcoming the outcast of the past!

Part of the problem with leathers was that they had to be black, so that the oil stains wouldn't show! The perception of the rider as 'greasy' was, alas, often true due to the leaky bike. Of course, this was mostly down to obsolete and under-financed British products built by bitter old men in 1920's factories. A certain Birmingham bike was even nicknamed the 'Royal Oldfield'!

Now, superb oil-tight machines never leave their calling cards in car parks and their owners can relax that old dress code, but the oil inside those immaculate alloy castings has an even more demanding job to do. For years bike engine/transmission design has been diverging from the mainstream car approach. The most obvious difference is the combined engine/gearbox lubrication, yet up until now bike handbooks have recommended standard automotive oils. Particularly where low quality lubricants were used, this dependence on 'car oils' has not really suited the powerful, compact and high-revving bike where the highly stressed oil is also expected to survive in the transmission. At last, faced with global problems and increasing warranty claims, the Japaneses 'Big Four' (Honda, Yamaha, Kawasaki and Suzuki) got together four years ago and decided to ban one particular class of car oils known as 'API–SH'. They also, in the interests of reducing gear wear and noise, went against the 4-wheel trend towards very thin multigrades such as 5W/30 or OW/40, and recommended 10W/40 or heavier grades. Modern motorcycles have a number of design features not found in cars, such as wet clutches, back-torque limiters and one-way clutches on the starter motor. These all depend on friction yet they are awash with oil. But the point of oil is to reduce friction! In fact, conventional lubricants gave no serious trouble, the worst problems arise with thin 'friction modified' fuel – economy products common in the USA, which were really intended for big, lazy car engines idling along the freeway at 55mph. Anything less suited to a bike engine would be difficult to imagine.

So a year ago, the Japanese motorcycle standards outfit (JASO) finally split off from the car mainstream and issued their own specification called 'JASO MA' which became law in mid-1999. This covers all aspects of motorcycle engine/transmission lubricaton, but perhaps and the most significant test requirement is a 'clutch friction test'. This makes it easier for you to pick a genuine motorcycle oil for your bike – one that has been developed specially to suit motorcycle needs from day one.

Understanding motorcycle engine oil

RECENT RESEARCH BY Castrol has shown that most riders are uncertain about the right choice of oil for their bike. Some of us refer to the owners manual and try to make sense of all the different technical specifications, some of us ask a mechanic or a friend which oil we should use and some of us simply pick up a low, mid or higher specification oil because we believe without a great deal of reason that it's right for our type of bike.

Castrol is working towards easily understandable (non technical) product claims that will help bikers select the right oil for their bikes but in the meantime here is a brief guide to understanding motorcycle engine oils and their specifications.

Types of oil

Mineral Oil

Mineral means "of natural origin" and mineral oil is base oil extracted from underground refined once. Unfortunately, at this stage of processing, mineral oil still contains a number of undesirable components. Some of these components burn off at high temperatures and some form deposits. If the word synthetic does not appear in the product description then your oil is a mineral oil.

Semi-Synthetic/Synthetic based/Synthetically fortified

Semi-synthetic oils are mineral oils refined further to remove more of the undesirable components of mineral oil. This means there is less oil loss as less of the oil burns off at high temperatures and performance and efficiency are improved as fewer deposits are laid down.

Fully Synthetic

Fully synthetic oils are produced from a different, very pure part of the base oil. They are chemically synthetised to form oil molecules that are extremely difficult to break down providing the ultimate protection for an engine. As they do not contain any of the undesirable components of mineral or semi-synthetic oils they also provide outstanding performance and efficiency.

Additives

The other main component of motorcycle engine oils is additives that usually perform the following tasks: detergent (to breakdown deposits and keep the engine clean), anti-wear and, anti-corrosion agents, and dispersants. Generally the bigger brands have the most resource to develop the best additives.

Viscosity

The most common technical specification displayed on motorcycle oil packs are viscosity ratings. Viscosity measures the thickness of the oil at various temperatures and is usually displayed in the following way:

Blue R's Fly

Technomoto ADDITIVE SYSTEM

LET *THE* REVOLUTION BEGIN!

I.O.M. Production TT Lap Record Holder Ian Duffus on his Black's R1.

Powered by Putoline Syntec 4 *"The Ultimate Superbike Oil"*

PHOTO: DOUBLE RED

Putoline *Oil*

For more information or details of your nearest stockist telephone our hotline 01778 394909

10 W – 40

The "W" stands for winter and shows the thickness of the oil at cold temperatures. "10" is quite thin but "5 W" products like Castrol Superbike are very thin. The thinner the oil at cold temperatures the easier the bike will start from cold. Parts will also move more freely in the thinner oil making faster acceleration possible.

The second number shows the thickness of the oil at high temperatures. The thicker the oil at high temperatures the greater the protection it provides between moving parts. "40" is generally the maximum viscosity recommended by motorcycle manufacturers because oil thicker than this would be more difficult to spray around the engine as a lubricant. The letters SAE preceding the viscosity simply stand for the Society of Automobile Engineers who created viscosity scales.

Other technical specifications

JASO MA – is a Japanese specification intended to show that the oil in the pack is specially for motorcycles.

API stands for the American Petroleum Institute. Under their classification grades SE, SF, and SG are suitable for motorcycles. Do not forget to check your handbook for your bikes specific API grade.

A last bit of help

Q. Can I put different oils in my bike?

A. YES. Putting oil in your bike is similar to putting petrol in it. Just because you last filled up at Texaco does not mean you cannot fill up at TOTAL the next time you stop. As long as you are putting a well-respected brand of specialist motorcycle engine oil in your bike it will be fine.

You do need to understand however that adding semi-synthetic oil to a bike previously full of fully synthetic will down grade the overall protection and performance of the oil in your bike and vice versa.

THE RIGHT OL

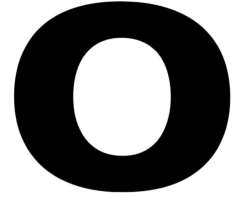

FOR YOUR BIKE

With no less than eight Silkolene four-stroke motorcycle oils, you can be sure there's one to suit your machine.
All Silkolene engine oils are JASO MA/MB certified which means we have a dedicated motorcycle lubricant to meet your needs.

Just remember that Silkolene is The Right Oil for you!

THE FUTURE IS ALREADY HERE
ASK FOR SILKOLENE BY NAME... DEMAND IT!

Fuchs Lubricants (UK) plc, Belper, Derbyshire. DE56 1WF
Technical Help Line. Tel: 0800 212542
Web: www.fuchs-oil.co.uk
E-mail: pippa.white@fuchs-oil.com

Bike Safe 2000

All too often the police and motorcyclists seem to be at odds with one another. Bikers feel they are singled out for minor violations of the law and feel that unpopular legislation, such as speed limits, is forced upon them. It may seem that the police are unsympathetic to bikers who want to have fun on their machines, but there is a darker side to motorcycling – the vulnerability of motorcyclists when involved in accidents. It is the police who have to pick up the pieces, often literally, and sort out the chaos and human misery accidents leave in their wake. This is where Bike Safe 2000 comes in.

Bike Safe 2000 is probably the most innovative initiative which has been introduced, by the police, in partnership with bikers, to reduce casualty rates and enhance riding enjoyment in a user friendly way.

The initiative was started in 1997 by biker David Short, a Superintendant with the North Yorkshire Police. Bike Safe 2000 is a radical break from traditional campaigns in that it focuses on EDUCATION and AWARENESS with enforcement being a secondary consideration.

Bike Safe 2000 works on a 10 point plan, compiled by rider groups and the Motorcycle Industry Association (MCI) working in partnership with the police.

The Bike Safe 2000 Ten Point Plan

1. Multi agency partnership
2. Industry involvement
3. Raising awareness of potential dangers
4. Encourage motorists to 'Think Bike'!
5. Target dangerous riding
6. Biker group involvement
7. Dealer involvement
8. Promoting voluntary post test training
9. Enforce speed limits
10. Target careless riding

The initiative has proved so successful in reducing biker casualties in North Yorkshire that it is now being adopted by police forces up and down the country. In 1998 it won a coveted Prince Michael of Kent Special Road Safety award for its innovative approach to reducing road casualties.

The message is very clear. Enjoy your motorcycling, IN SAFETY, that does not mean being boring! The real pleasure to be had from motorcycling is being in harmony with the machine and your surroundings, being aware of hazards and getting into the flow. Ask any TT rider about the key to successful mastery of the most demanding course in the world and they will describe the flow between bend to bend and of the synthesis of rider and machine working together as one.

Motorcycle touring is THE most enjoyable way of covering ground and visiting new places. Always ride to the Bike Safe 2000 ten point plan and you will add to that pleasure. For further information on Bike Safe 2000 contact the traffic department of your local police force and ask if they run the scheme. If they don't – ask why not!

Serious bikes deserve serious oil.

Castrol
SUPER BIKE
FULLY SYNTHETIC

COMP

4
STROKE

5W/40

Serious protection for your engine.

For details of your nearest Castrol stockist call 0645 123011

The Liquid Engineers

BIKERS RUNS

What to do and where to go

One of the greatest pleasures of motorcycling is riding on roads with a combination of gradual bends and long straights where you can open the throttle, lean the bike over, let the wind whistle by and enjoy the full experience of motorcycling at it's very best – all within the law of course! The following information features some of the best rides and meeting points in the UK.

SOUTH WEST

Bridgwater–Minehead–Exmoor–Ilfracombe–Taunton

Roads in the south west can be paradise for bikers – traffic congestion doesn't pose such a problem as it does for cars. Try the route from Bridgwater to Minehead and then over Exmoor to Lynton and on to Ilfracombe, returning via Blackmore Gate, Simonsbath and Weddon Cross, then on to Taunton.

This is a truly exhilarating ride, mixing good straight roads with twists and turns – but watch out for the sheep on Exmoor! Stop at Minehead where the preserved steam railway station has an excellent café in an old railway carriage – just the place for coffee and a chat, and there is ample free parking behind the station. Further down the road you can sample the delights of the pub at Porlock Weir before the climb up Porlock Hill.

Poole–Blandford Forum–Sturminster Newton–Dorchester–Wareham–Poole

If you want a run out from Poole try the A350 to Blandford Forum, then on to the A357 to Sturminster Newton. Take the A3030 out of Sturminster, and two miles after Lydlinch take the B3143 to Dorchester then the A352 to Wareham and A351 and A35 back to Poole.

Racing and track days

For racing and track days, try the Castle Combe circuit approximately three miles north-west of Chippenham on the B4039.

Motorcyclist Action Groups

Meetings take place most Thursday nights at the *Golden Lion*, Exeter.

Meeting places

Bikers meet on Friday nights at the *Bay Horse Inn*, Totnes, Devon, and on Wednesday nights at *The White Hart*, Wimborne Corn Market, Wimborne, Dorset. *Poole Quay* is a popular meeting place for bikers on Tuesdays. There is a wide selection of cafés, pubs, restaurants and cafés to choose from. Bikers congregate at *The Lord Nelson* or *The Sailor* on Tuesday nights.

CENTRAL SOUTHERN

Spectacular for road and off-road riding, Salisbury Plain and surrounding areas have lots to offer. You can spend all day riding off-road on Salisbury Plain quite legally, but you will need a large scale Ordnance Survey map of the area to ensure that you keep to the rights of way. These are public roads so your bike must comply with the Road Traffic Act. Any competent trail bike can tackle this terrain.

Salisbury Plain via Pewsey Valley

For riding on the road, why not try a ride across the north of Salisbury Plain and through the Pewsey Valley? Starting at Hungerford, ride south on the A338 to East Grafton, Collingbourne Kingston to North Tidworth and the A303. Travel along the A303 for around 7 miles towards Exeter then take the A360 to Shrewton. Stonehenge will be on your left. Carry on to Tilshead and then Devizes. Take the A361 to Beckhampton then the old A4 back to Hungerford.

Sammy Miller's Motorcycle Museum at New Milton, east of Bournemouth is well worth a visit. Give them a call for opening times 01425-620777. If tanks and other military equipment is your taste, a visit to the *Tank Museum* at Bovington is a must. You may be lucky and see the Army on manoeuvres or gunnery practice on the nearby ranges.

SOUTH EAST

Steyning–Winchester–Petersfield–Storrington–Steyning

Start at the picturesque village of Steyning, just outside Brighton. Crossing the bypass, head through Partridge Green before joining the A24 for a short while. Veer off west along the A272 (a well known bikers road). This sparsely populated area of the south east boasts some of the best biking roads in Britain – through sleepy villages and towns like Petworth and Midhurst that have changed little over the centuries.

Follow the short dual carriageway section around Petersfield and then back on the A272 over the hill to the ancient town of Winchester. Head for the town centre and Café Rouge is on your right. It opens at 10am on Sunday and when the sun shines you can sit at one of their tables outside (this has got to be one of the best breakfasts in the country too – butchers sausages and first rate poached eggs!)

Retrace your steps to Petersfield and follow signs for Chichester, then around historic Goodwood House which has motor-racing and motorcycle racing connections going back generations. The café here forms a gathering point for bikers. Looping around the back roads takes you up to Whiteways Lodge at the top of Bury Hill, then swoop down into the valley and head for home via Swinnington.

Meeting places

One of the largest meeting places for bikers in the south is *Box Hill* which is situated on the A24 towards Dorking, where up to a thousand bikers gather here on Sundays.
The Cricketers Arms at Sarratt in Hertfordshire is a lovely country pub with a great atmosphere. Hundreds of bikers congregate here on Sundays during the summer.
The Woodman at Black Fen in Kent is very welcoming to bikers, where they gather most Tuesday evenings, and *The Duke of Kent* in Faversham on Wednesday evenings is another gathering place.

Brands Hatch, possibly the premier bike racing circuit in the UK, is situated on the A20 in Kent, some three miles from Junction 3 on the M25.

MIDLANDS

Matlock Bath

A mecca for bikers is Matlock Bath, in Derbyshire, which is situated on the A6 approximately twelve miles north of Derby. Thousands of bikers gather here on fine summer Sundays where parking is provided for 'bikes only'. Beware, traffic wardens are on patrol and are enthusiastic in pursuit of their jobs so if you park illegally or overstay the time limit – expect a ticket. Facilities include pubs, cafés, chip shops and a motorcycle dealer.

The A6 from Derby to Matlock Bath is a favourite for bikers. Some bends are more severe than they first look and several fatalities have occurred on this road. It is now heavily policed by marked and unmarked bikes and cars, so ride carefully and enjoy the magnificent scenery of the Derwent Valley.

Matlock Bath—Castleton (Winnets Pass)–Sparrowpit–Bakewell–Matlock Bath

Leave Matlock Bath and head towards Derby on the A6. Take the A5012 at Cromford then turn on to the B5056 via Gellia Road. At the A6 turn right, stay on the A6 for approx. 1 mile then take the B6012 to Baslow. At Baslow take the A623 for approximately 8 miles. Then turn right on to the B6064 to Brough and left on to Castleton. Ride through the village and on to the narrow road known as Winnets Pass. Pause here to admire nature's work and the limestone formations. The Blue John Caves are here and you can visit for a small fee. The road up the Winnets Pass is narrow and very steep with some tight turns so be careful. Beware of sheep and falling stones. At the top of the pass turn left on the B6061 to Sparrowpit, then take the A623 to the crossroads with the B6049 and turn right. Follow this road to the A6 and turn right again. Stay on the A6 for about a mile, then turn left on to the A5270 down to the A515 and left again. Ride along the A515 to the B5055 and on to Bakewell. Finally, follow the A6 back to Matlock Bath for a cup of tea – you've earned it!

Meeting places

It is worth visiting *The Waterman* at Hatton on Wednesday nights, where several hundred bikers gather. Please be considerate and park your bike where indicated. On Mondays bikers meet at the *Grey Goose*, Arnold Road, Gedling, Notts. Around 200 bikers gather at this venue – watch your speed on the roads around here. On Tuesdays *The Wild Ox* on the Fosse Way A46, 10 miles north of Leicester is where several hundred bikers gather. Why not telephone to make a booking and stay overnight?

Visit *The Moon* at Spondon, Derbyshire, on Wednesday nights to experience a Derbyshire bike night. Live bands, discos, trade stands and a barbecue are usually a feature of this venue. *The Wheel*, Worfield, Shropshire is on the A454 approximately three miles east of Bridgnorth. This is a comparatively new meeting place for bikers on Wednesday nights and is fast becoming a favourite. *The Johnty Farmer*, Keddelstone Road, Derby is another new venue which has promise and is well worth a visit.

Quality Quality Quality Quality **Quality**

iability Reliability Reliability **Reliability**

gth Strength Strength Strength **Strength**

Coming on Strong!

For more information on different colours, specifications and the 15,000 mile guarantee please contact us on the number below

T01522 888444 **F**01522 888400 **E**lintektl@compuserve.com

BIRMINGHAM & WEST MIDLANDS

Meeting places for bikers tend to be outside Greater Birmingham. Try Stratford-upon-Avon on Sundays during the summer. Hundreds of bikers congregate at the *Waterside* in the town centre. *The Half-way House* on the A41 at Tettenhall, Wolverhampton, is another good venue on a Sunday evening, or if you want a bikers rock night, try *The Holly Bush*, Wolverhampton.

The Waterman pub is one of the largest venues for bikers on Wednesday nights, where the landlord has a field reserved for parking bikes. Take the A41 from central Birmingham, then the A4177 to Hatton.

If you haven't already been, a visit to the *National Motor Cycle Museum* is a must. Here you will find makes and models from the time when British bikes ruled the world plus many more overseas models on exhibit. The National Motor Cycle Museum is situated at Junc. 6 of the M42 and the A45, approximately five miles from the centre of Birmingham. There is an admission charge but there is a lot to see. Why not make it a winter's day out and visit the *Motor Cycle Show* at the NEC just across the A45 at the same time?

WALES

Oswestry–Llangollen–Betsw-y-coed–Blaenau Ffestiniog–Bala–Oswestry
Try the road from Oswestry on the A5 to Llangollen and on out to Betws-y-coed. Take the A470 down to Blaenau Ffestiniog. You can stop and see the steam trains here. Then take the B4391 across the mountains, join up with the A4212 to Bala and take the A494 to the A5. Then take the A5 back to Oswestry.

Brecon Beacons
A road worth riding in Wales is the main road triangle around the Brecon Beacons. Start at Brecon and go north up the B4520 to Builth Wells. Take the A483 all the way to Llandovery and then the A40 back to Brecon.

Mid Wales
Mid Wales has a network of brilliant biking roads, is relatively light on traffic and boasts some fabulous countryside. Maybe the best ride of all is the A44 straight across the middle.

Starting at Leominster, head west and enjoy the pretty black and white half-timbered villages leading to the roundabout at Kington just east of the Welsh border. This is where the ride starts for real, twisting and rising through the hills and winding down to the popular Sunday meeting point at Cross Gates. From here, down the mile-long straights gets you to Rhayader. There are pubs and cafes here which all welcome bikers and it's the centre for trail-riding, enduro and motocross in Wales. Refuel here – petrol stations are thin on the ground for the next 35 miles and you won't want to stop anyway. Turn right at the town clock and prepare yourself for another set of long straights leading to long sweeping bends and tight turns, all on well-surfaced roads with usually little traffic. This takes you all the way to the premenade at Aberystwyth where up to several hundred bikes gather on sunny Sundays.

Setting off east along the A44, ride up the long straights along the river valley before winding through a couple of villages and eventually above the line of trees past the lead mining museum and cafe to Ponterwyd – beware the tightening left-hand bend half a mile west of the village. Turn right after the bridge onto the A4120 signposted to Devils Bridge. This road starts narrow and twisty, then opens up into sweeping turns and brings you to the tourist spot centred around the three bridges stacked on top of each other. You now swoop twelve miles back to town which you can just see in the distance down the valley. If a full 33-mile lap is too long you can stop at the Halfway Inn at Pisgah where there is real ale, good food and a striking view. The last six mile section ends with tight turns overlooking the town. Check your watch and head out for another lap!

THE**ZING**

THE**SECTOR**

THE**STRYKER**TRAIL

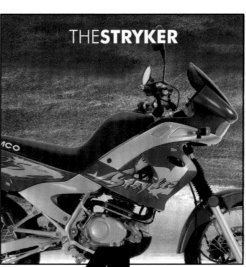

THE**STRYKER**

MOTORCYCLES**4**ALL!

Four beautifully engineered 125cc Motorcycles from KYMCO - to match your lifestyle (and your pocket) For everyday riding, weekend cruising or the best ON and OFF road experience, simply call the number below for your nearest KYMCO dealer - you won't be disappointed.

Call **01743 761107**

THE **PRICE** OF **FREEDOM** FROM **£1895** ON THE ROAD

www.kymco.co.uk

NORTH OF ENGLAND

Lake District
The Lake District boasts some of the finest scenery in the whole of England and the roads are fantastic for biking. Try the route north on the A683 to Sedbergh. Stay on the A683 to the A685 through Kirkby Stephen to Brough, then follow the A66 across to Penrith (Junction 40, M6).

Take the A592 south past Ullswater through the villages of Watermillock, Glenridding, Patterdale, Bridgend and Hartsop (watch your speed). Going in this direction you will descend the very steep Kirkstone Pass complete with hairpin bends. Stay on this road to the A591, cross over the main road and take the A5074 to Storrs. Then take the B5284 to Crook and join the A591 to Junction 36 of the motorway. Here take the A65 back to Devil's Bridge.

Meeting places
The Kent Tavern at Kendal, Cumbria, often have live bands and is a good meeting place for bikers, for more information, telephone them on 01539-722410. *Kirkstone Pass Inn*, Kirkstone Pass, is a favourite venue of the Morecoambe Harley-Davidson MCC. If it's Harleys you want, try here.

The Crown, Booth St, Manchester is a venue which holds rock nights, or try the *Hen & Chickens*, Prescot Road, Melling on Merseyside, a favourite with Merseyside bikers. Meetings take place on Wednesday evenings from 7.30pm.

Bikers often ride over to the *Scotch Piper* pub, Lydgate. Tuesday nights are bikers nights at the *Dog* pub in Rochdale. Go along! Who knows, Foggy may be there!

Racing circuits
Racing takes place at *Croft Circuit*, just south of Darlington, there are also track days held here. *Scarborough Race Circuit, a* bike festival, is held some years in the park of this Yorkshire seaside town. Check with the tourist office. *Oulton Park* in Cheshire, off the A54 Middlewich–Chester road, is a favourite bike racing circuit. Track days held here also.

SCOTLAND

If you want open roads, fantastic scenery and little traffic, then head for the Scottish Highlands, where you will meet touring motorcyclists from all over Europe.

Explore the islands of Mull, Skye or Arran, see the Highlands, lochs and visit historic Bannockburn and Glencoe or the Royal family's Estate at Braemar. Visit the beautiful City of Edinburgh, the shops on Princess Street or enjoy the hustle and bustle of Glasgow. Follow the world famous 'whisky trail' which begins in Aberdeen– see where some of the most famous brands of malt whiskies are distilled, or visit the home of golf at St Andrews, and play on some of the most wonderful courses in the world.

Visit Graham and Sue Larrington's Bridge of Brown Tea rooms where they cater especially for bikers. Graham and Sue are bikers themselves and they will give you all the information you want. See their entry in the Scotland section – they are located in the lovely area of Banffshire, in the village of Tomintoul.

Day One (Glasgow–Aberfoyle–Fort William–Dingwall)
Wherever you are starting from, get to Glasgow first then set off for the Trossachs on the A81. Arriving in the town centre at Aberfoyle, straight ahead is a no-through-road sign but turn right and over the hill to descend through woodland which is picturesque in any season. You now have to grab some quick

miles on wide undulating roads towards Crianlarich on the A84 and A85. You're now in the Grampians and the gentle scenery is left behind. The A82 now takes you down by way of the magnificent Glencoe then over the bridge and alongside the sea-loch into Fort William. Fuel up here. You can admire Ben Nevis but there is still a few miles left to do.

Still heading North bear left at Spean Bridge then turn on to the A87 heading for Kyle of Lochalsh. Once again the sheer scale of Scotland hits you, there are no more remote places in mainland Britain than this area. You can head for the bridge that links the Isle of Skye to the mainland or turn right onto the A890, look at this; an 'A' road that's single lane with passing places!

You now have a choice. Serious mile eaters turn left – Ullapool 35 miles, and then another sixty or so heading for the top left corner of Scotland but if you only have a long weekend then it's best to find a hotel in Dingwall (quite lively on Saturday nights) or the more touristy Strathpeffer.

Day Two (Dingwall–Tomintoul–Braemar–Edinburgh/Glasgow)

Southwards on the A9 or follow the A82 back down alongside Loch Ness. On the other hand you could make a real day of it by finding the A938 and A939 through Grantown-on-Spey and Tomintoul. At Garnshiel Lodge (you will know when you get there – it's the only building for miles) follow the sign for Balmoral down a tricky little 'B' road rejoining the A93 into Braemar. Famous for its Highland Games it also provides a focal point for bikers, fifty twisting undulating miles from Perth and about the same from Aberdeen.

Up and over Glenshee you now descend towards a more populated area but still Scotland has 'elbow room' you just don't get further south. The scenery calms down and now there's another choice to make. Edinburgh and down the East coast, or Glasgow and on to the Lake District. The Lakes win hands down and with a late afternoon stop in friendly Penrith an early start tomorrow morning could mean a couple of Lake District passes in the morning and still be home by early evening. Fifteen hundred miles in four days? Easy.

Racing

There is plenty of motorcycle racing at Knock Hill, which is situated North West of Dunfermline on the A823. The UK Superbike series visits here in mid summer – check the dates in the motorcycling press.

Knockhill is the race circuit for Scotland, north-west of Dunfermline on the A823. UK Superbike series visits here mid-summer. Check out the dates in Motor Cycle News. This circuit also provides very challenging track days.

<u>Not been to a race circuit before?</u>

Choose a major race meeting like the Grand Prix or one of the two World Superbike or British Superbike meetings held in the UK. The British Superbike series now attracts over 30,000 spectators with crowds of over 60,000 at Brands Hatch. Riding to the track with thousands of other bikers past the hundreds of cars queuing to get in creates the most wonderful atmosphere. Even if you are not interested in what critics say is the best domestic race scenes in the world, go along to experience the day. When the weather is good, this is a truly great experience on a motorcycle.

Haynes **Motorcycle** Manuals

Title	Book No.
BMW	
BMW 2-valve Twins (70 - 96)	0249
BMW K100 & 75 2-valve Models (83 - 96)	1373
BMW R850 & R1100 4-valve Twins (93 - 97)	3466
BSA	
BSA Bantam (48 - 71)	0117
BSA Unit Singles (58 - 72)	0127
BSA Pre-unit Singles (54 - 61)	0326
BSA A7 & A10 Twins (47 - 62)	0121
BSA A50 & A65 Twins (62 - 73)	0155
DUCATI	
Ducati 600, 750 & 900 2-valve V-Twins (91 - 96)	3290
HARLEY-DAVIDSON	
Harley-Davidson Sportsters (70 - 99)	0702
Harley-Davidson Big Twins (70 - 99)	0703
HONDA	
Honda NB, ND, NP & NS50 Melody (81 - 85)	◊ 0622
Honda NE/NB50 Vision & SA50 Vision Met-in (85 - 95)	◊ 1278
Honda MB, MBX, MT & MTX50 (80 - 93)	0731
Honda C50, C70 & C90 (67 - 99)	0324
Honda CR80R & CR125R (86 - 97)	2220
Honda XR80R & XR100R (85 - 96)	2218
Honda XL/XR 80, 100, 125, 185 & 200 2-valve Models (78 - 87)	0566
Honda CB100N & CB125N (78 - 86)	◊ 0569
Honda H100 & H100S Singles (80 - 92)	◊ 0734
Honda CB/CD125T & CM125C Twins (77 - 88)	◊ 0571
Honda CG125 (76 - 99)	◊ 0433
Honda NS125 (86 - 93)	◊ 3056
Honda MBX/MTX125 & MTX200 (83 - 93)	◊ 1132
Honda CD/CM185 200T & CM250C 2-valve Twins (77 - 85)	0572
Honda XL/XR 250 & 500 (78 - 84)	0567
Honda XR250L, XR250R & XR400R (86 - 97)	2219
Honda CB250 & CB400N Super Dreams (78 - 84)	◊ 0540
Honda CR250R & CR500R (86 - 97)	2222
Honda Elsinore 250 (73 - 75)	0217
Honda CBR400RR Fours (88 - 99)	3552
Honda VFR400 (NC30) & RVF400 (NC35) V-Fours (89 - 98)	3496
Honda CB400 & CB550 Fours (73 - 77)	0262
Honda CX/GL500 & 650 V-Twins (78 - 86)	0442
Honda CBX550 Four (82 - 86)	◊ 0940
Honda XL600R & XR600R (83 - 96)	2183
Honda CBR600F1 & 1000F Fours (87 - 96)	1730

Title	Book No.
HONDA (continued)	
Honda CBR600F2 & F3 Fours (91 - 98)	2070
Honda CB650 sohc Fours (78 - 84)	0665
Honda NTV600 & 650 V-Twins (88 - 96)	3243
Honda Shadow VT600 & 750 (USA) (88 - 99)	2312
Honda CB750 sohc Four (69 - 79)	0131
Honda V45/65 Sabre & Magna (82 - 88)	0820
Honda VFR750 & 700 V-Fours (86 - 97)	2101
Honda VFR800 V-Fours (97 - 00)	3703
Honda CB750 & CB900 dohc Fours (78 - 84)	0535
Honda CBR900RR FireBlade (92 - 99)	2161
Honda ST1100 Pan European V-Fours (90 - 97)	3384
Honda Shadow VT1100 (USA) (85 - 98)	2313
Honda GL1000 Gold Wing (75 - 79)	0309
Honda GL1100 Gold Wing (79 - 81)	0669
Honda Gold Wing 1200 (USA) (84 - 87)	2199
Honda Gold Wing 1500 (USA) (88 - 98)	2225
KAWASAKI	
Kawasaki AE/AR 50 & 80 (81 - 95)	1007
Kawasaki KC, KE & KH100 (75 - 99)	1371
Kawasaki KMX125 & 200 (86 - 96)	◊ 3046
Kawasaki 250, 350 & 400 Triples (72 - 79)	0134
Kawasaki 400 & 440 Twins (74 - 81)	0281
Kawasaki 400, 500 & 550 Fours (79 - 91)	0910
Kawasaki EN450 & 500 Twins (Ltd/Vulcan) (85 - 93)	2053
Kawasaki EX & ER500 (GPZ500S & ER-5) Twins (87 - 99)	2052
Kawasaki ZX600 (Ninja ZX-6, ZZ-R600) Fours (90 - 97)	2146
Kawasaki ZX-6R Ninja Fours (95 - 98)	3541
Kawasaki ZX600 (GPZ600R, GPX600R, Ninja 600R & RX) & ZX750 (GPX750R, Ninja 750R) Fours (85 - 97)	1780
Kawasaki 650 Four (76 - 78)	0373
Kawasaki 750 Air-cooled Fours (80 - 91)	0574
Kawasaki ZR550 & 750 Zephyr Fours (90 - 97)	3382
Kawasaki ZX750 (Ninja ZX-7 & ZXR750) Fours (89 - 96)	2054
Kawasaki 900 & 1000 Fours (73 - 77)	0222
Kawasaki ZX900, 1000 & 1100 Liquid-cooled Fours (83 - 97)	1681
MOTO GUZZI	
Moto Guzzi 750, 850 & 1000 V-Twins (74 - 78)	0339
MZ	
MZ ETZ Models (81 - 95)	◊ 1680
NORTON	
Norton 500, 600, 650 & 750 Twins (57 - 70)	0187
Norton Commando (68 - 77)	0125

The **Complete** List

Title	Book No.
PIAGGIO	
Piaggio (Vespa) Scooters (91 - 98)	3492
SUZUKI	
Suzuki GT, ZR & TS50 (77 - 90)	◊ 0799
Suzuki TS50X (83 - 99)	◊ 1599
Suzuki 100, 125, 185 & 250 Air-cooled Trail bikes (79 - 89)	0797
Suzuki GP100 & 125 Singles (78 - 93)	◊ 0576
Suzuki GS, GN, GZ & DR125 Singles (82 - 99)	◊ 0888
Suzuki 250 & 350 Twins (68 - 78)	0120
Suzuki GT250X7, GT200X5 & SB200 Twins (78 - 83)	◊ 0469
Suzuki GS/GSX250, 400 & 450 Twins (79 - 85)	0736
Suzuki GS500E Twin (89 - 97)	3238
Suzuki GS550 (77 - 82) & GS750 Fours (76 - 79)	0363
Suzuki GS/GSX550 4-valve Fours (83 - 88)	1133
Suzuki GSX-R600 & 750 (96 - 99)	3553
Suzuki GSF600 & 1200 Bandit Fours (95 - 97)	3367
Suzuki GS850 Fours (78 - 88)	0536
Suzuki GS1000 Four (77 - 79)	0484
Suzuki GSX-R750, GSX-R1100 (85 - 92), GSX600F, GSX750F, GSX1100F (Katana) Fours (88 - 96)	2055
Suzuki GS/GSX1000, 1100 & 1150 4-valve Fours (79 - 88)	0737
TRIUMPH	
Triumph Tiger Cub & Terrier (52 - 68)	0414
Triumph 350 & 500 Unit Twins (58 - 73)	0137
Triumph Pre-Unit Twins (47 - 62)	0251
Triumph 650 & 750 2-valve Unit Twins (63 - 83)	0122
Triumph Trident & BSA Rocket 3 (69 - 75)	0136
Triumph Triples & Fours (carburettor engines) (91 - 99)	2162
VESPA	
Vespa P/PX125, 150 & 200 Scooters (78 - 95)	0707
Vespa Scooters (59 - 78)	0126
YAMAHA	
Yamaha DT50 & 80 Trail Bikes (78 - 95)	◊ 0800
Yamaha T50 & 80 Townmate (83 - 95)	◊ 1247
Yamaha YB100 Singles (73 - 91)	◊ 0474
Yamaha RS/RXS100 & 125 Singles (74 - 95)	0331
Yamaha RD & DT125LC (82 - 87)	◊ 0887
Yamaha TZR125 (87 - 93) & DT125R (88 - 95)	◊ 1655
Yamaha TY50, 80, 125 & 175 (74 - 84)	◊ 0464
Yamaha XT & SR125 (82 - 96)	1021
Yamaha 250 & 350 Twins (70 - 79)	0040
Yamaha XS250, 360 & 400 sohc Twins (75 - 84)	0378
Yamaha RD250 & 350LC Twins (80 - 82)	0803

Title	Book No.
YAMAHA (continued)	
Yamaha RD350 YPVS Twins (83 - 95)	1158
Yamaha RD400 Twin (75 - 79)	0333
Yamaha XT, TT & SR500 Singles (75 - 83)	0342
Yamaha XZ550 Vision V-Twins (82 - 85)	0821
Yamaha FJ, FZ, XJ & YX600 Radian (84 - 92)	2100
Yamaha XJ600S (Diversion, Seca II) & XJ600N Fours (92 - 99)	2145
Yamaha YZF600R Thundercat & FZS600 Fazer (96 - 99)	3702
Yamaha 650 Twins (70 - 83)	0341
Yamaha XJ650 & 750 Fours (80 - 84)	0738
Yamaha XS750 & 850 Triples (76 - 85)	0340
Yamaha TDM850, TRX850 & XTZ750 (89 - 99)	3540
Yamaha FZR600, 750 & 1000 Fours (87 - 96)	2056
Yamaha XV V-Twins (81 - 96)	0802
Yamaha XJ900F Fours (83 - 94)	3239
Yamaha FJ1100 & 1200 Fours (84 - 96)	2057
ATVS	
Honda ATC70, 90, 110, 185 & 200 (71 - 85)	0565
Honda TRX300 Shaft Drive ATVs (88 - 95)	2125
Honda TRX300EX & TRX400EX ATVs (93 - 99)	2318
Polaris ATVs (85 to 97)	2302
Yamaha YT, YFM, YTM & YTZ ATVs (80 - 85)	1154
Yamaha YFS200 Blaster ATV (88 - 98)	2317
Yamaha YFB250 Timberwolf ATV (92 - 96)	2217
Yamaha YFM350 Big Bear and ER ATVs (87 - 95)	2126
Yamaha Warrior and Banshee ATVs (87 - 99)	2314
ATV Basics	10450
TECHNICAL TITLES	
Motorcycle Basics Manual	1083
MOTORCYCLE TECHBOOKS	
Motorcycle Electrical TechBook (3rd Edition)	3471
Motorcycle Fuel Systems TechBook	3514
Motorcycle Workshop Practice TechBook (2nd Edition)	3470

◊ = *not available in the USA*   **Bold type** = *Superbike*

Haynes motorcycle manuals are available from most motorcycle accessory dealers, mail order outlets and good bookshops.
If you have any difficulty finding a manual for your bike, call our Customer Care line:

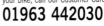

01963 442030

Haynes Publishing, Sparkford, Nr Yeovil, Somerset BA22 7JJ
Telephone: **01963 442030** • Fax: **01963 440001**
E-mail: **sales@haynes.co.uk** • Web site: **www.haynes.co.uk**

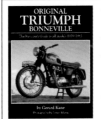

INSURANCE ■ INSURANCE ■ INSURANCE

CAROLE NASH INSURANCE CONSULTANTS LTD

For Award Winning Bike Insurance • For low cost Bike Insurance
Instant Cover
Free Breakdown Recovery on all policies
Open 8am-6.30pm Monday to Friday • Open 9am-12noon Saturday
Visa • Master Card

Call Freephone 0800 298 5500

Carole Nash Insurance Consultants Ltd

New Irish Policies now available

Visa • Master Card

For Northern Ireland Call 0800 5500
For Southern Ireland call Dublin 636 9191

VAUNTAGE

See how low our premiums are for learners, born again and direct access.
We are performance bike specialists

Instant quotes • Immediate cover • Instalments

Telephone 07000 828682 for freequote

YAMAHA LINK INSURANCE

For new and used Yamaha officially imported motorcycles.
Administered by Yamaha Motor UK or any Yamaha Dealer.
For further details or further information contact any Yamaha Dealer or Yamaha Motor UK on

Telephone 01932 358000

GO RACING!

MOTORCYCLE RACING IS probably the most exciting form of motorsport you will ever experience. You are likely to see more overtaking manoeuvres in just one lap than in a complete Formula One car race! The great thing about racing in the UK is that on any given weekend, there are more road racing, motocross, trials or enduro races here than in any other country in the world.

Unless you've been living in a cave, chances are you'll have heard about four times World Superbike Champion Carl Fogarty who has been largely responsible for the massive resurgence of interest in road racing in this country. His success, and that of other well known riders such as Jamie Whitham, Jeremy McWilliams and Chris Walker has helped elevate road racing in the eyes of the media and general public. The British Championships are now regarded by the major manufacturers as one of the most important domestic race series in the world – demonstrated by the fact that most of the top teams have the latest factory bikes. Of course what this means for British spectators is that we get to see the best riders competing on the best bikes on our famous British circuits. Maybe you were one of the 140,000 spectators at Brands Hatch for the World Superbikes – the largest sporting event in the country, bigger even than the British F1 Grand Prix at Silverstone.

Whoever is your favourite rider, whether its in World or British Superbikes, Grands Prix or the British Championships, there has never been a better time to go and see these modern day gladiators in action. The British Championships take place at circuits up and down the country from Thruxton in the South up to Knockhill in Scotland as well as the traditional circuits such as Brands Hatch, Silverstone and Donington Park, so there's always a circuit near you. Don't forget that the British Championships are more than just Superbikes, there's always a full action packed programme of events from the ultra competitive 125cc GP class right through to the big capacity production based bikes with all sorts of classes in-between. Of course you can always make a long weekend of these race meetings – most events have unofficial practice on the Friday, timed practice sessions on the Saturday and racing on the Sunday and you could always stay at one of the hotels or guest houses listed in this Guide where you'll be assured of a warm welcome. For details of the British Championship calendar, contact the MCRCB (Tel: 01327 876000 Fax: 01327 878114) or the ACU for other UK motorcycle racing events (Tel: 01788 540519 Fax: 01788 573585 www.acu.org.uk).

If you're looking further afield for a memorable weekend, why not travel to Europe and take in a race meeting abroad? With both the Channel Tunnel and ferries its never been easier to get to the continent. Popular events are the Assen World Superbike and Grand Prix races in Holland. Carl Fogarty has even remarked that with the huge number of British fans in Assen its almost like racing in England! With the Grand Prix and World Superbike Series both taking in most of the major European countries, there are plenty of world-class events all within easy riding distance of the UK and if you want to enjoy the local festivities, you can even leave your bike at home and travel by air or coach – just look in Motor Cycle News or the monthly magazines for details of organised trips. For information on Grands Prix contact Dorna (Tel: 003491 319 7878 www.dorna.com) and for World Superbike contact Superbike SBK International (Tel: 0171 4910995 Fax: 0171 4910997 www.superbike.it).

Don't forget that its not just road racing where the best action is – there are plenty of Off Road events taking place all over Europe. To whet your appetite, why not try the famous Le Touquet beach race which is on the northern coast of France? For further information on World Championship motorcycle racing in all disciplines contact the FIM (Tel: 004122 950 9500 Fax: 004122 950 950 www.fim.ch).

Of course, if you go and see all these fantastic events, be warned! You may want to try racing yourself! Fortunately, there's two great publications which provide all the information you'll need to get started in either road racing or off road sport or just have a try out on a track day or race school. Entitled "So you want to go Racing" and "Off Road Riders Guide", they are both available free from the Motorcycle Industry Association (Tel: 01203 227427 Fax: 01203 229175 www.mcia.co.uk).

Historic Racing

THE RACING SECTION of the Vintage Racing Motor Cycle Club has been organising Historic Road Race Meetings for over 25 years. All the household names of British Motor Cycling are involved, ranging in age from 1926 to 1972, including Norton, Rudge, Velocette, Vincent, Triumph, AJS, Matchless, Greeves, Sunbeam, Royal Enfield, Scott, BSA , Brough Superior, OK Supreme, AJW, Excelsior, Ariel and Morgan Three-Wheeler. In order for the club to move forward it introduced a specials class with a cut off year for machines of 1972, providing the machine was of European origin.

Historic Racing is a working museum, not a static display. Competitors ride to the limits of their own and their machines capabilities, whilst mechanics wring the last ounce of power from their engines.

Historic Racing provides a full day of family entertainment with not only superb competitive racing, but also full access to the paddock where you can meet the riders, and study and discuss their machinery at leisure.

We aim to promote yesterdays machines and recreate the atmosphere of over 30 years ago and race at most circuits across the country like Mallory Park, Cadwell Park, Snetterton, Lydden, Three Sisters, Darley Moor and The Anglesey Race Circuit.

For more information on racing, becoming a marshall or training or if you would like to become an official, please contact Racing Section Secretary Lesley Reaney, 318 Osmaston Park Road, Allenton, Derby, DE24 8FB Tel: 01332 368699 Fax: 01332 726435, or Email: racesec@adyx.co.uk

Major Road Race Venues in the UK

Brands Hatch – Off the A20 between Swanley and Wrotham in Kent
(Tel: 01474 872331 Fax: 01474 874766).
Cadwell Park – Off the A153 between Horncastle and Louth in Lincolnshire
(Tel: 01507 343248 Fax: 01507 343519)
Donington Park – Wight miles south east of Derby close to East Midlands airport
(Tel: 01332 810048 Fax: 01332 850422)
Knockhill – Five miles north of Dunfermline on the A823 in Fife, Scotland
(Tel: 01383 723337 Fax: 01383 620167)
Mallory Park – Off the A47 and A447 between Hinckley and Leicester
(Tel: 01455 842931 Fax: 01455 848289)
Oulton Park – Off the A54 near Tarporley in Cheshire (Tel: 01829 760301 Fax: 01829 760378)
Silverstone – Off the A43 between Brackley and Towcester in Northants
(Tel: 01327 857271 Fax: 01327 857663)
Snetterton – Off the A11 London to Norwich road between Thetford and Attleborough in Norfolk
(Tel: 01953 887303 Fax: 01953 888220)
Thruxton – Off the A303 two miles west of Andover on the Hampshire Wiltshire border
(Tel: 01264 772696 Fax: 01264 773794)

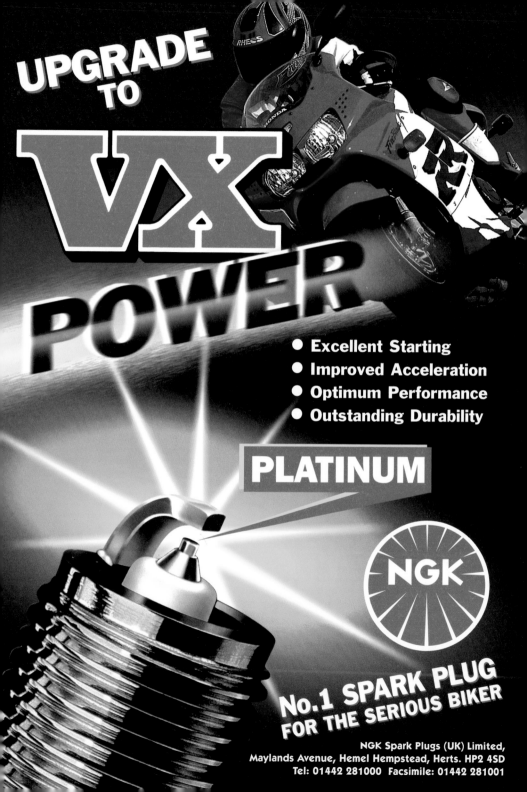

Bike Trader TO ADVERTISE CALL **0121 683 2662**

SELLING YOUR BIKE? CALL Bike Trader NOW!

www.biketrader.co.uk

Advertise your bike to over 365,000✦ bikers, with full colour photograph. Simply follow the instructions below.

To advertise in the next issue 0f Bike Trader :

WITHOUT A PHOTOGRAPH - BY TELEPHONE:

1. Prepare your ad before you call, including make, model name and number, brief description, asking price and your phone number/s, using a maximum of 30 words. Choose from 7 classified sections Sports, Learner legal, Classics, Trails & Off Road, Cruisers & Customs, All Rounders & Tourers or Scooter Buyer...
2. The cost for 30 words is **£22***, and your advert will appear in a colour coded box...
3. Have your credit or debit card to hand.

WITH A FREE PHOTOGRAPH - BY POST:

Write out your ad, **as step 1**, including desired section. Enclose your name address & telephone number, and payment of **£22*** by cheque/postal order made payable to Bike Trader, **OR** enclose your debit/credit card details (16-20 digits) including the 'valid from' & 'expiry' dates. The issue number must be given if Switch. Now send your written ad, payment and photograph to:
BIKE TRADER, 12 Phoenix Park, Avenue Close, Nechells, Birmingham B7 4NU.

* Rate may be subject to change after March 2000.
✦ (Source NRS)

Your advert will also appear on the internet FREE!

(you must provide your postcode)

0121 683 2662

Lines are open 9am - 5.30pm Mon-Fri

Bike Trader TO ADVERTISE CALL **0121 683 2662**

Auto Trader interactive

Interactive www.biketrader.co.uk

Britain's Biggest Showroom

In the UK over 10 million people are using the internet and this is growing every day. Britain is fast becoming a nation of net shoppers with over £50m of transactions taking place every day.

Bike Trader Interactive is the top bike site on the web with over 14,000 bikes for sale each week, many with colour photos. Stock is updated every two weeks.

Consumers can find a vehicle by Marque, Model, Price, Age - and even by how far they want to travel. So to further the chance of selling your bike to a wider audience, we place your bike **FREE** on the internet.

Welcome to Bike Trader

Search the best choice of bikes throughout the UK. Use the Basic Search to specify minimum requirements or the Advanced Search to specify more features, including mileage, bodytype and colour.

Plan your Finance options with the AA and get an Insurane quote from an insurer in our dealer directory.

Things to do today

- Get a pair of boots
- Buy a helmet
- Secure your bike
- Look for leathers
- Buy tyres
- Shop till you drop
- News & Reviews
- Get traffic news
- Touring cars 99
- Insure your bike
- Link to bike web sites
- Learn to ride

Get the best advice on buying on selling your bike from the leading industry brands in Helping Hand.

Check out Features for the latest Touring Car news, plan your journey with RAC Traffic News and find the best bike web sites in Links.

Visit Bike Store for all your bike parts and accessories, from helmets to tyres, search our directories for suppliers and bid on-line in our auction store. Check out our Shopping Centre and buy on-line.

Accessories	**Insure your bike**	**Find your bike breaker**
Best of bike accessories	Best information and quotes on-line	Parts for your bike

JUST BIKERS

 CAROLE NASH
INSURANCE CONSULTANTS LTD

Basic Search

Suppliers

The following helmet companies have been found in your area

Company	Address	Postcode	Telephone	Email	WWW
A R D Racing	Walsall Rd Springhill Lichfield	WS14 0BX	01543 378893		
Alf England (Bedworth) Ltd	Leicester Road Bedworth Nuneaton	CY12 8AH	01203 312184		
Ancher Kawasaki Centre	97-99 Wellingborough Road Finedon Wellingborough	NN9 5LG	01933 680274		

 **For the best in biking...**

Hints and Tips

Buying a Bike

Bike Trader

Background

Find out general details about your preferred bike - engine size, insurance cost, etc. Ring the insurance companies that advertise in Bike Trader. Good research will make the task of choosing a bike much easier. The colour photo ads in Bike Trader are the actual bike for sale and of course help immensely in your choice. Look through Bike Trader and Auto Trader paper and on-line editions to get a feel for current prices.

Arranging a meeting with the seller

- Always check a bike in daylight - darkness may hide faults.
- If you're not mechanically minded, have the vehicle inspected by an expert, a service provided by motoring organisations. It could save you money.
- Beware of 'between 5pm and 6pm' adverts which could mean a phone box is being used. Try calling out side this time.
- If you meet the owner away from their home, make sure the meeting point is public and check proof of ownership.
- Beware of mobile telephone numbers which may not be traceable.
- Is the seller familiar with the vehicle and its controls?
- Check all the documentation for **PROOF OF OWNERSHIP** If you buy a stolen bike, you have no right to keep it.
- It's also worth checking the vehicle's background with **HPI Autodata**, quoting **Auto Trader 01722 435 500 for a £3.50 discount .**
- Registration plates may be false if they appear newer than the bike, have too many screw holes or appear to have been removed.
- Check all the parts of the bike well. Take your time.
- If the bike has a security system, does it work?
- Has the locking petrol cap been forced and replaced?

Bike Trader

Dealers

Bike Trader checks the dealers advertising in the magazines thoroughly. However, if you do ever have a problem with a dealer you have four options :

1. Most dealers provide warranties with bike sales. Check the small print before you buy. The warranty is the dealer guarantee. Remember, being good natured initially always helps.
2. If the dealer is a member of the Motorcycle Retailers Association he has to comply with the MRA's arbitration service. The MRA are contactable on 0171 580 9122.
3. Contact your local Trading Standards office.
4. Contact a solicitor. Check costs. You have rights under the Sale of Goods Act.

Bike Trader

Final Advice

- Never feel pressured into buying.
- Obtain proof of identity from the seller. They should hold the vehicle registration document, MOT certificate, and a log book. If you have doubts **WALK AWAY!**
- A banker's draft is safer than cash. Always ask for a receipt.

You will have no right in law to ownership of a stolen vehicle. You will **LOSE BOTH THE BIKE AND YOUR MONEY!**
We try to ensure that motor trade advertisers state 'Trade', but some still break the rules. If you're suspicious that a private seller is really a trader, inform your local Trading Standards Authority.

Hints and Tips

Selling Your Bike

Bike Trader
Advertising your vehicle

Include age, make, model, mileage, enhancements, colour and service history. Look through the online and paper versions of Auto Trader and/or Bike Trader to define a fair price.

Bike Trader
Potential buyers

- A clean vehicle is more attractive to buyers !
- Be there to answer telephone enquiries. Leave daytime and evening/weekend numbers.
- Show documentation for proof of ownership - bills and service history confirm you have cared for your bike.

ALWAYS be careful over potential buyers test driving your bike. We suggest that you ride the bike and the potential buyer goes pillion. There are fools out there who have pushed people off and driven off into the sunset. If you do let them ride then check they have at least third party insurance and make sure they recognise that they will pay for any damage. It can be advantageous if they have brought someone with them. There are people who will see your bike to case your security. Its advantageous to take their home and work no's and give them a ring back to check.

Bike Trader
Price & Payment

- Be pleasant and don't let derogatory remarks lure you into price reductions.
- Unless the potential buyer leaves a substantial deposit, keep other enquirer's numbers in case the transaction falls through.
- After cash, a deposit followed by a banker's draft is best. Ensure the payment has cleared before releasing your bike.

Bike Trader is published Tuesday fortnightly. Our advice is to wait until the magazine is on sale or online to the public where a better price can be obtained.

Bike Trader
Important Notice

When your advertisement is published, it is possible that you will be telephoned by organisations offering to sell your bike.
We believe that Bike Trader and Auto Trader is the most effective means of selling bikes and suggest that you ignore any other offer until your advertisement takes effect.
If, however, you follow up any proposal, we strongly advise that you:-
DO NOT release credit card details or particulars of your bike unless you are dealing with an established and reputable company.
ARE SURE of exactly what you are getting for your money.

- Is the fee only paid if a sale is made?
- Where will your advertisement be published?
- How many people will see it?

IF IN DOUBT , don't commit yourself on the telephone. Ask them to post a proposal including their terms and conditions for you to consider.
Of course, Bike Trader is not connected with or responsible for the activities of any such organisation, but in the interests of our readers, please notify us of any problems and we shall pass details on to the relevant Trading Standards departments.

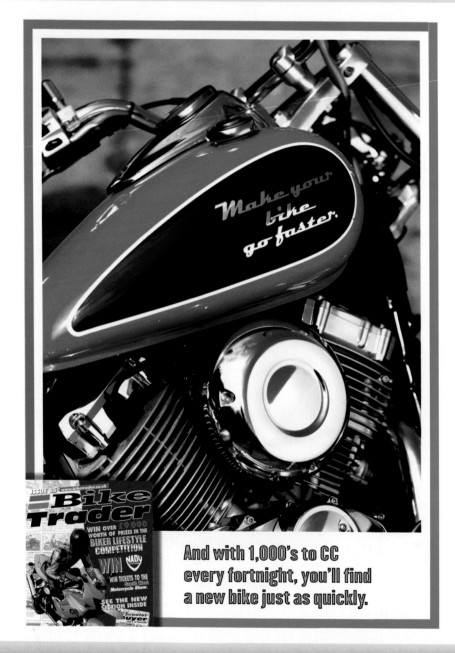

FINANCE ■ FINANCE ■ FINANCE ■ FINANCE

CHARTERED TRUST PLC

24-26 Newport Road, Cardiff CF2 1SR
Telephone 0870 901 9024
Fax: 0645 100246
Sales Manager: Mr Dave Macey

Chartered Trust plc have been engaged in the finance industry in excess of 40 years. They provide finance for motorcycle dealers and their customers and their services are available virtually every day of the year. Chartered Trust have a dedicated motorcycle sales team, headed by Dave Macey.

Deutsche Financial Services

1 Station View, Guildford, Surrey GU1 4JY
Managing Director Mr P Underhill
Sales Director: Mr L Pocket
Telephone: 01483 458045

DFS provide finace by way of stocking finance plans for motorcycle dealers.

Newcourt Financial Ltd

66 Buckinghamgate, London SW1E 6AU
Managing Director Peter Johnstone

Newcourt is a subsidiary of Newcourt Credit Group. Newcourt is a non-bank owned commercial finance company. They have offices in 15 European countries and provides leasing, inventory, finance, capital loans, retail credit and asset based lending. Newcourt can tailor credit solutions.

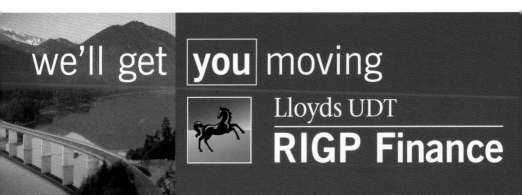
we'll get **you** moving
Lloyds UDT
RIGP Finance

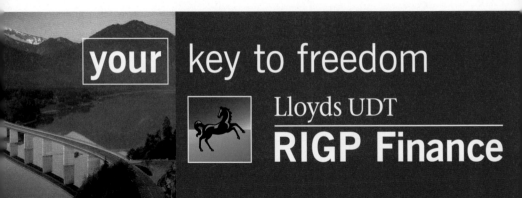

TOURIST BOARDS

Following is a list of the main tourist boards in England, Scotland, Wales, Isle of Man, Northern Ireland and Southern Ireland.

Most local tourist areas, eg The Peak District or the Cotswolds, will have their own regional offices, and will be able to supply information relevant to that area. If you contact the main office nearest to the region you want, they will then refer you to the local office.

Cumbria Tourist Board
Ashleigh
Holly Road
Windermere
Cumbria
LA23 2AQ
Telephone: 015394 44444
Fax: 015394 44061
Covers Cumbria and The Lake District

Northumbria Tourist Board
Aykley Heads
Durham
DH1 5UX
Telephone: 0191 375 3000
Fax: 0191 386 0899
Covers Durham, Northumberland, The Tees Valley and Tyne and Wear

North West Tourist Board
Swan House
Swan Meadow Road
Wigan Pier
Wigan
Telephone: 01942 81222
Fax: 01942 820002
Covers, Cheshire, Greater Manchester, Lancashire and Derbyshire.

Yorkshire Tourist Board
312 Tadcaster Road
York
YO2 2HF
Telephone: 01904 707961
Fax: 01904 701414
Covering Yorkshire and North East Lincolnshire

Heart of England Tourist Board
Woodside
Larkhill Road
Worcester
WR5 2EF
Telephone: 01905 763436
Fax: 01905 763450
Covering Parts of Derbyshire, Gloucestershire, Hertfordshire, Leicester, Northamptonshire, Nottinghamshire, Rutland, Shropshire, Staffordshire, Warwickshire, Worcestershire, The West Midlands, and representing the districts of Cherwell and West Oxfordshire.

East of England Tourist Board
Topplesfield Hall
Hadleigh
Suffolk
P7 5DN
Telephone: 01473 822922
Fax: 01473 823063
Covering Cambridgeshire, Essex, Hertfordshire, Bedfordshire, Norfolk, Suffolk and Lincolnshire.

The London Tourist Board
6th Floor,
Glen House
Stag Place
London
SW1E 5LT
Telephone: 0171 932 2000
Fax: 0171 932 0222
Covering London and Greater London

West Country Tourist Board
60 St Davids Hill
Exeter,
Devon
EX4 4SY
Telephone: 01932 425426
Fax: 01932 420891
*Covering Bath, Bristol, Cornwall, and the
Isles of Scilly, Devon, Dorset, Somerset
and Wiltshire.*

Southern Tourist Board
40 Chamberlayne Road
Eastleigh
Hampshire
SO5 5LH
Telephone: 01703 620006
Fax: 01703 620010
*Covering Berkshire, East and North
Dorset, Hampshire, Isle of Wight
Buckinghamshire and Oxfordshire*

South East Tourist Board
The Old Brew House
Warwick Park
Tunbridge Wells
Kent
TN2 5TU
Telephone: 01892 540766
Fax: 01892 511008
*Covering East aand West Sussex, Kent
and Surrey.*

Northern IrelandTourist Board
St Ann's Court
59 North Street
Belfast
B11 1ND
Tel: 01232 231221
Fax: 01232 240960

Scottish Tourist Board
23 Ravelston Terrace
Edinburgh
EH4 3EU
Telephone: 0131 332 2433
Fax: 0131 343 1513

Wales Tourist Board
Brunel House
2 Fitzalan House
Cardiff
C F2 1UY
Telephone: 01222 499909
Fax: 01222 498076

Southern Ireland Tourist Board
Baggot Street Bridge
Dublin 2
Southern Ireland
Telephone: Dublin 676 5871
(From UK precede with 00353 1)
Fax: Dublin 602 4100
(From UK precede with 00353 1)

Jersey Tourism
Liberation Square
St Helier
Jersey
Channel Islands
JE1 1BB
Telephone: 01534 500700
Fax: 01534 500899

States of Guernsey Tourist Board
P O Box 23
White Rock
Guernsey
Channel Islands
Telephone: 01481 726611
Fax: 01481 721246

Isle of Man Dept of Tourism
Sea Terminal Building
Peveril Square
Douglas
Isle of Man
IM1 2RG
Telephone: 01624 686766
Fax: 01624 686800

Where Legends Live On!

Hundreds of perfectly restored British motorcycles from the turn of the century to the 1990's. From everyday machines to the extraordinary. They're all at the National Motorcycle Museum.

Open 10am to 6pm everyday. Near Birmingham International Airport and opposite the National Exhibition Centre.

NATIONAL MOTORCYCLE MUSEUM

Coventry Road, Bickenhill, Solihull,
Tel: Hampton-in-Arden (01675) 443311

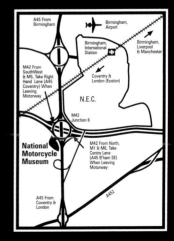

PROTECTING YOUR BIKE

Bike theft in the UK is big business. Every year 28,000 bikes are stolen – one every 19 minutes and 86% are never recovered. Of course nobody wants their bike to be stolen because it's not just the loss of the bike, but also the increased insurance premiums, the hassle and time it takes to get things sorted. However, you can help to keep your bike safe by choosing the right security.

Basically, the more layers of security you can put around your bike, the less attractive it will be to thieves. No single product can cover all eventualities but if you invest in both hard and electronic security, you will stand less chance of becoming a victim of theft. Always look for "Thatcham" or "Sold Secure" approved products as these have been attack tested to stringent industry standards and will usually qualify you for insurance discounts (up to 10 % for systems with immobilisers) .

■ Combined alarm immobilisers are an extremely good deterrent. They activate if someone is tampering with your bike and will prevent thieves from riding the vehicle away. Alternatively, you can buy basic alarm or immobiliser systems to suit your own preference. Things to look for are low current drain and comprehensive warranty support. Some systems even come with free roadside assistance.

■ A good disc lock will act as a deterrent to casual thieves, but that's all – most will only delay the professional for a matter of seconds. Don't rely on a disc lock alone.

■ U-locks are better, but make sure they are long enough to secure the bike to railings or other immovable features.

■ Chain and padlocks are the most versatile hard security. They're difficult to carry around but some come with carrying bags to go on the pillion seat.

■ Whatever type of lock you choose, always try and secure your bike to something solid and immovable because the most common method of stealing bikes is to simply lift them into the back of a van. Also, try to keep the lock off the ground as this makes it harder to overcome.

■ For protecting your bike at home, ground anchors are a good bet. If you have a garage, fit stronger locks too. Some alarm immobiliser systems can extend their protection to include garage entry points or you could even invest in a pager to alert you if someone is attempting to steal your bike.

■ Another option to consider is marking/tagging systems. These will deter thieves and can help you to get your bike back if it's been stolen.

Security Tips

- During the day, park in a busy, public place
- At night, park in a well lit area
- Try to vary the parking place
- Wherever possible, use custom built parking places especially ones with fixed stands or security loops
- Keep a look out for car parks displaying a "Secured Bike Park" sign
- Cover the machine if possible
- Always engage the steering lock
- Don't leave your helmet or other possessions on the motorcycle or in luggage/panniers

IS YOUR BIKE STILL WHERE YOU LEFT IT?

The Datatool Veto Evo Alarm Immobiliser System is the bike thief's least favourite accessory.

It will help prevent your motorcycle becoming part of the UK's stolen bike statistics. But it's not just thieves who recognise the performance of the Datatool Veto Evo System, most insurance companies recognise its protective effect and allow a reduced premium (normally 10%) if the motorcycle has a Veto Evo System professionally installed. Whilst the reduction is unlikely to pay for the System in full, the yearly premium reduction can make Veto Evo an attractive proposition. In addition to protecting your bike, you will also enjoy the following advantages of Veto Evo ownership

- ✔ Attack tested and approved to the highest available standards, Thatcham category MC1
- ✔ 3 Year System Guarantee.*
- ✔ Free Roadside Assistance.*
- ✔ Low Current Consumption - **under 3mA.**
- ✔ Programmable Movement Detection
- ✔ Model Specific Systems available for selected motorcycles.
- ✔ **From only £269 plus installation.**
- ✔ Optional Security Accessories, including Radio Pager.

For details of your nearest Datatool dealer call 01420 541444, or visit our website www.datatool.co.uk

Also available from Datatool:
Insurance approved (Thatcham/Sold Secure) Uno and Duo immobilisers, from £85.50 (plus installation) and a comprehensive range of other electronic motorcycle security items.

THATCHAM
THE MOTOR INSURANCE REPAIR RESEARCH CENTRE

Complies with The British Insurance Industry's Criteria for Motorcycle Security

DATATOOL ®
S E R I O U S   P R O T E C T I O N

3 YEAR WARRANTY

5 PASS

TÜV AUTOMOTIVE

*Written details of the Datatool Roadside Assistance and Three Year Warranty are included with each product and are also available by contacting Datatool direct.

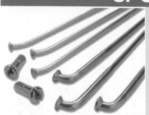

DEALER LISTINGS

SOUTH WEST

			Aprillia	Benelli	BMW	Buell	Cagiva	CCM	Derbi	Ducati	Gilera	Harley	Honda	Kymco	Kawasaki	Laverda	M-Guzzi	MV Agusta	Peugeot	Piaggio	Suzuki	Triumph	Yamaha
Barnstaple	IRELAND SERVICES, Unit 6, Two Rivers Industrial Estate, Braunton Road, EX31 1JX.	01271 374243							•		•									•			
	TRUSCOTTS (BARNSTAPLE) LTD., Old Station Road, Whiddon Valley Industrial Estate, EX32 8PB.	01271 326622																	•				
Bodmin	MAC SERVICES MOTORCYCLES, 56 Higher Bore Street, PL31 1JW.	01208 73246																	•				
Bridgewater	ANDERSON & WALL, Church Street, TA6 5AS.	01278 423089												•						•			
	PAT WATTS MOTORCYCLES, 40 St. Mary's Street, TA6 3LY.	01278 447165							•										•				
Bridgwater	RIDERS OF BRIDGWATER, Riders House, Wylds Road, TA6 5BH.	01278 457652	•			•				•		•			•							•	
	V & J HONDA, Wyldes Road, TA6 4BH.	01278 410110											•										
Bristol	ARRIVA KAWASAKI, 64 Avon Street.	0117 977 2272													•								
	BATH ROAD MOTORCYCLES, 379-385 Bath Road, Brislington.	0117 971 1447			•																		
	BRISTOL M/CYCLE CENTRE, Bristol Motorcycle training Centre, Old Gloucester Road, Hambrook.	01454 776333												•									
	BRISTOL SCOOTER CENTRE, Long Ashton Road, Flax Bourton, BS48 3QR.	01275 463666	•	•					•														
	EASY WHEELS 2000, 24 North Road, Yate, BS17 5DA.	01454 320196	•	•																			
	PORTISHEAD SCOOTER CENTRE, 120 High Street, Portishead, BS20 6PR.	01275 843444																		•			
	ROB TAYLOR MOTORCYCLES LTD, 59-63 Pembroke Road, Shirehampton, BS11 9SA.	01179 823042											•										
	T T MOTORCYCLES, High Street, Staplehill, BS16 5HE.	0117 908 9970		•																			
Cambourne	ANTON PARRIS MOTORCYCLES, 14 Pendarves Street, Tucking Mill, TR14 8RF.	01209 719767											•								•		
Clevedon	CLEVEDON MOTORCYCLES, 135 Old Street, BS21 6BW.	01275 340909												•									
Crewkerne	E. A. TAYLOR & SON, Mosterton Road, Misterton, T18 8NT.	01460 72318													•				•				
	TAYLOR'S MOTORCYCLES, Mosterton Road, Misterton, TA18 8NT.	01460 72318							•														•
Cullompton	R.T. MOTORCYCLE CENTRE, Willand Industial Estate, Willand, EX15 2QW.	01409 241380																	•				
	RON EDWARDS MOTORCYCLES, 11 Alexandria Industrial Estate, Station Road.	01884 32314							•														
Exeter	BRIDGE MOTORCYCLES LTD, Alphinbrook Road, Marsh Barton, EX2 8RG.	01392 260200									•		•		•					•	•	•	•
	D. J. MOTORCYCLES (SALES) LTD., 19a Church Road, St. Thomas, EX2 9AZ.	01392 424234							•					•					•				
	ITALIAN MOTORCYCLE CENTRE, Unit 4, Oak Units,, Lords Meadow Trading Estate, Crediton.	01363 774499														•	•						
	MOTORCYCLES UNLIMITED, 1-3 Verney Street, EX1 2AW.	01392 424234	•				•												•				
Exmouth	ALBION MOTORCYCLES, 33 Exeter Road, EX8 1PT.	01395 272491											•						•				
Helston	CARRS OF HELSTON, 85 Meneage Street, TR13 8RD.	01326 573001																	•				
Holsworthy	D.F.M. MOTORS, Langdon Road Industrial Estate, Bradworthy, EX22 7SF.	01409 241380																	•				
Minehead	WEST COAST MOTORCYCLES, Unit 4, Hawkesworth Road, TA24 5BZ.	01643 702511																	•				
Newquay	NEWQUAY MOTORCYCLES, 38b Cliff Road, TR7 2ND.	01637 873761							•										•				
Newton Abbot	GRAND PRIX MOTORCYLES, Unit 5/6 Rydon Estate, Canal Way, TQ12 3SJ.	01626 335000	•						•										•				
	MOTORCYCLE CITY (SALES) LTD, Pottery Road Ind Estate, Kingssteinton, TQ12 3BN.	01626 331020	•	•						•	•												•
	TORBAY MOTORCYCLES, 87 Queen Street, TQ12 2BG.	01626 352527											•										
Ottery St. Mary	BROWNS MOTORCYCLES, 89 Mill Street, EX11 1AJ.	01404 813853																		•			
Paignton	G.T. MOTORCYCLES TORBAY, 79 Torquay Road, TQ3 2SE.	01803 559949									•								•		•		•
Penzance	BLEWETT & PENDER, Albert Street, TR18 2LR.	01736 333224					•		•		•			•		•			•	•	•		
Plymouth	DAMERELLS MOTORCYCLES LTD, 99 Mutley Plain, Mutley, PL4 6JJ.	01752 667806																		•			

SOUTH WEST continued

	Dealer	Phone	Aprilia	Benelli	BMW	Buell	Cagiva	CCM	Derbi	Ducati	Gilera	Harley	Honda	Kymco	Kawasaki	Laverda	M-Guzzi	MV Agusta	Peugeot	Piaggio	Suzuki	Triumph	Yamaha
Plymouth	G.T. MOTORCYCLES, 152-158 Albert Road, Devonport, PL2 1AG.	01752 559063	•		•						•		•		•				•	•	•		•
	OCEAN PLYMOUTH, St Mowden House, Longbridge ROad, Marsh Mills, PL6 8LH.	01753 202828			•								•		•							•	•
	R.S. DAMERELL & SON LTD, 99 Mutley Plain, PL4 6JL.	01752 667806																			•		
Redruth	KEITH PARNELL MOTORCYCLES LTD., Lanner, TL16 6AS.	01209 821045																	•	•			
St Austell	R.S. DAMERELL & SON LTD, Whitemoor, Nanpean Street, PL26 7XN.	01726 822402																					
ST. Austell	DAMERELL MOTORCYCLES LTD., Whitemoor, PL26 7XN.	01726 822402																					
St. Ives	ST. ERTH SERVICES, Rose-aw-Grouse, St Erith, Hayle, TR27 8SW.	01736 752 028	•																				
Taunton	ATKINS MOTORS (SKOOTERS), 90 Wellington New Road, TA1 5LA.	01823 254555																					
	GERRY INGRAM MOTORCYCLES, 46 Wood Street, TA1 1UW.	01823 331397											•										
	SKOOTERS, 90 Wellington Road, TA1 5LA.	01823 254555																					
	TAYLOR'S MOTORCYCLES, Unit 1, Venture 11, Priorswood Industrial Estate, TA2 8DG.	01823 274247																					•
	V & J SUPERBIKES, 43-45 East Reach, TA1 3EJ.	01823 272378								•													
	VINCENT & JERROM, 43-45 East Reach, TA1 3ES.	01823 272378	•																				
Tauton	GRAHAMS MOTORCYCLES, 46 Wood Street, TA1 1UW.	01823 331397											•										
Templecombe	KEN DOYLE MOTORCYCLES LTD, 2 Throop Road, BA8 0HR.	01963 370368											•										
Torquay	P G H MOTORCYCLE CENTRE, Broomhill Way, TQ7 7QR.	01803 616164	•																				
	TORRE MOTORCYCLES LTD, 246 Union Street, TQ2 5QU.	01803 294184																					•
Truro	FERRIS GARAGE LTD, FEOCK, TR3 6RE.	01872 511100																					
Weston-S-Mare-	MORSE MOTORCYCLES, 13-15 Locking Road, BS23 3BY.	01934 621187							•														
	WYVERNS, 5 Locking Road, BS23 3DA.	01934 624201															•						
Yeovil	BRANSONS OF YEOVIL LTD, 7 Oxford Road Pen Mill Trading Estate.	01935 474 998								•				•						•	•		•
	G.T. MOTORCYCLES LIMITED, Main Street, Mudford, BA21 5TE.	01935 850 505								•	•										•		•
	PAUL BRANSON MOTORCYCLES, 22 Oxford Rd, Pen Mill Trade Est., BA21 5HR.	01935 474998										•											

CENTRAL SOUTHERN

	Dealer	Phone	Aprilia	Benelli	BMW	Buell	Cagiva	CCM	Derbi	Ducati	Gilera	Harley	Honda	Kymco	Kawasaki	Laverda	M-Guzzi	MV Agusta	Peugeot	Piaggio	Suzuki	Triumph	Yamaha
Addlestone	SURREY CYCLE COMPANY LTD., 75 Station Road, KT15 2AR.	01932 820716																			•		
Alton	SPC MOTORCYCLES LTD, Lower Farrington.	01420 588691																		•			
	W. M. SNELL, Station Road, GU34 2PZ.	01420 84480																					
Andover	BRIDGE MOTORCYCLES LTD, Station Approach, SP10 3HN.	01264 354 200								•			•										•
	R D MOTORCYCLES, 101 Commercial Centre, Picket Place.	01264 363712							•	•			•										
Aylesbury	ON YER BIKE, A41 Bicester Road, Wescott, HP18 0JQ.	01296 655999																					
	STREET MACHINE, 119 Bicester Road, HP19 3BA.	01296 433266		•																			
Basingstoke	MOTT MOTORCYCLES LTD, Kempshott Hill, Kempshott, RG23 7LL.	01256 321989													•				•			•	•
Bath	BISHOPS OF BATH, 42 Third Avenue, Oldfield Park, BA2 3NZ.	01255 421805										•	•					•	•		•		
	GT PARSONS & SONS, Old Pit Garage, Coombend, Radstock, BA3 3AT.	01761 433522											•									•	•
Bedford	BOB KING MOTORCYCLES, 14-16 Ashburnham Road, MK40 1DS.	01234 359684										•	•		•			•	•	•	•	•	•
	RICK STRINGER MOTORCYCLES, 20 London Road, MK42 0NS.	01234 352951																		•			

Bournemouth	CRESCENT MOTORCYCLE COMPANY. 324 Charminster Road, BH8 9RT.	01202 512923
	KINSON MOTORCYCLES, 1448 Wimborne Road, Kinson, BH10 7AS.	01202 591133
	MOORDOWN SCOOTERS, 918 Wimborne Road, Moordown, BH9 2DH.	01202 514700
	POWERHOUSE SOUTHWEST LTD., 1483 Wimborne Road, Kinson, BH10 7BQ.	01202 591711
	ROGER BARRETT, 24-26 Seabourne Rd, Southbourne, BH5 2HT.	01202 426244
	SK00T, 26 Poole Hill, BH2 5PS.	01202 555005
Bristol	BIKE MART, 190-192 West Street, Bedminster, BS3 3NB.	0117 966 1112
	BRISTOL 6 SCOOTERS, 65 - 69 Cotham Hill, Redland, BS6 6JR.	0179 734807
	CHIPPING SODBURY MOTOR CO., Hatters Lane, Chipping Sodbury.	01454 310136
	F B MOTORCYCLES, 2A Downend Road, Fishponds, BS16 5UJ.	0179 659690
	FOWLERS MOTORCYCLES, 2-12 Bath Road, Pylle Hill, BS4 3DR.	0117 977 0466
	MOTORCYCLE CITY (SALES) LTD, 15-19 Stokes Croft, BS1 3PY	0117 942 0500
	PETE ROBINSON, 1 Gloucester Road North, Filton, BS7 0SG.	0117 969 8040
	WHEELTORQUE, 200 Church Road, Redfield Bristol, BS5 9HW.	0117 941 1014
Brockenhurst	HAYTER BROS., Waters Green, SO42 7RG.	01590 624000
Calne	P.R. TAYLOR & SONS, The Square, 4 Wood Street, SN11 0BZ.	01249 812259
Camberley	HYPERBLADE, Unit 1 c Bridge Works, GU15 2QR.	01276 686571
	LUCKY RACING, 465-467 London Road, GU15 3JA.	01276 282208
Carrisbrook	DAVE DEATH MOTORCYCLES, Priory Garage, 9, Priory Road, PO30 5JS.	01983 522160
Chesham	FORD & ELLIS MOTORCYCLES LIMITED, 132-152 Broad Street, HP5 3ED.	01494 772343
Chichester	CMW MOTORCYCLES LTD, 20 The Hornet, PO19 4JG.	01243 782544
	COLIN STRUDWICK, 13 The Square, Barnham, Bognor Regis, PO22 0HP.	01243 544 577
Chippenham	D M A RACING, Brinkworth Garage, The Street, Brinkworth, SN15 5DJ.	01666 510456
	P. R. TAYLOR & SONS, 23-25 Station Hill, SN15 1EG.	01249 657575
Christchurch	POWERSPORT MOTORCYCLES, 189 Barrack Road, BH23 2AR.	01202 485645
Cirencester	PETER HAMMOND MOTORCYCLES LIMITED, 40-44 Watermoor Road, GL7 1LD.	01285 652467
Consett	MOTECH MOTORCYCLES, Knitsley Lane, DH8 7NN.	01207 591912
Coulsdon	DOBLE MOTORCYCLES, 86-88 Brighton Road, CR3 2NA.	0181 668 8851
Cowley	HARPERS OF COWLEY LTD, 208 Garsington Road, OX4 5NG.	01865 772960
Crawley	P & H MOTORCYCLES LIMITED, 61-63 Gatwick Road, RH10 2RD.	01293 413300
Crowthorne	HATFIELDS OF CROWTHORNE LTD, Hight Street, RG11 7AD.	01344 772674
Devizes	RICHARD STEVENS MOTORCYCLES, 14 Estcourt Street, SN10 1LQ.	01380 725467
Didcot	CROWMARSH CLASSIC MOTORCYCLES, 34 Wantage Road, OX11 0BT.	01235 212727
	T. GOODALL MOTORCYCLES, 76a Lower Broadway, OX11 8AE.	01235 812766
	TREVOR GOODALL MOTORCYCLES, Lower Broadway, OX11 8AE.	01235 812766
Dorchester	CW MOTORCYCLES, Great Western Industrial Centre.	01305 269370
	DORCHESTER COLLECTION, London Road, DT1 1NE.	01305 264491
	POWERHOUSE SOUTHWEST LTD., Unit 3, Pomeroy Buildings, The Grove Industrial Estate.	01305 266797
Dorking	SURREY HARLEY-DAVIDSON, 258 High Street, RH4 1RL.	01306 883825
Fareham	RAFFERTY NEWMAN (FAREHAM), 242 West Street, PO16 0HD.	01329 232424

CENTRAL SOUTHERN continued

Town	Dealer	Phone	Aprilia	Benelli	BMW	Buell	Cagiva	CCM	Derbi	Ducati	Gilera	Harley	Honda	Kymco	Kawasaki	Laverda	M-Guzzi	MV Agusta	Peugeot	Piaggio	Suzuki	Triumph	Yamaha
Farnborough	MOTORCYCLE CITY (SALES) LTD, 149-151 Lynchford Road, GU14 6HD.	01252 400000	•	•	•	•	•	•	•	•	•	•	•	•	•	•	•	•	•	•	•	•	•
Gerrards Cross	PROPHETS (GERRARDS CROSS) LTD, 10 Packhorse Raoad.	01753 888388		•	•																		
Guernsey	MILLARD & CO. LTD, 9 - 11 Victoria Road, St. Peters Port, GY1 1HU.	01481 720777																		•			
Godalming	G D BROWN MOTORCYCLES, 12 Meadrow.	01483 427979									•												
	STAG HILL MOTORS, Hurtmore Road, GU7 2RO.	01483 414311																					
Gosport	DIMONS OF GOSPORT, 150 Forton Road, PO12 3HJ.	01705 583494	•				•																
	TREVOR POPE MOTORCYCLES, 57 Forton Road, PO12 4TD.	01705 521 111																					
Great Bookham	BECKLEY'S OF BOOKHAM LTD, Leatherhead Road, KT23 4RQ.	01372 450033							•										•				
Guernsey	CHICKS MOTORS LTD, Collings Road, Peter Port, GY1 1FL.	01481 723716																	•				
	C.I. SUZUKI LIMITED, Airport Garage, La Planque Lane, GY8 0DR.	01481 66332																			•		
	JACKSONS GARAGE LTD, Airport Forecourt, Forest.	01481 35441																					
	MAC'S MOTORCYCLES PREMIUM, Lef Banques Street, St Petersport.	01481 730635						•							•								
	PANCHOS MOTORCYCLES, Church Road, St Sampsons, GY2 4NU.	01481 48550																					
	TREV'S MOTORCYCLES, P O Box 377, Route Du Passeur, Vale, GY1 3YX.	01481 46463															•						
Guildford	COOMBES OF GUILDFORD LTD, Slyfield Estate, Woking Road.	01483 207000																	•				
	GORDON FARLEY M/C LTD T/A GUILDFORD HONDA CENTRE, 15 Barrack Road, GU3 6RV.	01483 538485											•										
	PORTMAN MOTORCYCLES, 23 Woolbridge Hill, GU2 6AA.	01483 560945													•						•	•	
Haslemere	HASLEMERE MOTORCYCLES (WHEELSPORT), Weyhill, GU27 1BZ.	01428 651580																					•
Haywoods Heath	MR. SCOOTER, 42 - 46 Queens Road, RH16 1EE.	01444 414848									•								•				
Hemel Hempstead	BIKE SHACK, 28 Lawn Lane, HP3 9HL.	01442 211567																					
	MOORES (HEMEL HEMPSTEAD) LTD, London Road, HP3 9SX.	01442 252601							•														
High Wycombe	BRIAN GRAY MOTORCYCLES, Station Road, HP13 6AD.	01494 438615		•					•														
	BROWNS FORD CENTRE, London Road, Wooburn Moor, HP10 0NJ.	01494 678881																					
	GODDARDS, The Desborough Cycle Works Ltd, Bridge Street.	01494 532104																	•				
	MOTORCYCLES PLUS, 210 Micklefield Road, HP13 7HB.	01494 464000											•										
	THE DESBOROUGH CYCLE WORKS LTD, Bridge Street, HP11 2GL.	01494 532104																					
Hockliffe	WHEELS INTERNATIONAL, Watling Street (A5), LU7 2AH.	01525 210130												•									
Horley	T NORTHEAST LTD, 4 Station Road, RH6 9HL.	01293 783229																	•				•
Jersey	BIKERS, 16 Cheapside, St Helier, JE2 3PG.	01534 36531	•									•				•	•						
	G & B MOTORAMA LTD, 9 Great Union Road, JE2 4QY.	01534 22819																					•
Knebworth	SAUNDERS MOTORCYCLES, 17 Station Road, SG3 6AP.	01438 811524	•						•											•			
Littlehampton	LITTLEHAMPTON MOTORCYCLES, 23-25 Beach Road, BN17 5TN.	01903 713102										•											
Luton	DAVE BLISS MOTORCYCLES, 123 - 125 Castle Street, LU1 3AL.	01582 452452																			•	•	
Lymington	A J BARTLET, 3 Gosport Street.	01590 676968							•														
	H. E. FIGGURES, 122-124 High Street, SO41 9AQ.	01590 672002																	•		•		•
Maidenhead	THAMES VALLEY HARLEY DAVIDSON, 84 Attwood Road, SL6 4QB.	01628 788188										•											
Melksham	BOB MISSEN, 15-17 Church Street, SN12 6LS.	01225 702325																					

Town	Dealer	Phone
	MELKSHAM MOTORCYCLES, Units 3&4 Indus Acre, Avro Way, Bowerhill Industrial Estate.	01225 351122
Mitcham	HARTGATE LTD, 24-28 Upper Green East, CR4 2F.	0181 648 5395
New Milton	BURSEY ENGINEERING, 24 Old Milton Road, BH25 6DX.	01425 612 436
Newbury	BEST OF BIKES, 4 Oxford Street, RG13 1JB.	01635 30004
	PRO-BIKE SERVICES, 11 Newton Road, RG14 7BL	01635 581500
Petersfield	RAFFERTY NEWMAN, Unit 4, Bedford Road, GU32 3LJ	01730 264484
Poole	BRIAN WHITESIDE, The Quay, BH15 1HB.	01202 679980
	POOLE MOTORCYCLES, 138a Stanley Green Road, Sterte, BH15 3AH.	01202 670023
	ROGER BARRETTS, 149-151 Ashley Road, Parkstone, BH14 9DL.	01202 718990
	VILLAGE MOTORCYCLES, Gables Garage, 59 High Street, Lychett Matravers, BH16 6BL.	01202 632615
Portsmouth	BIKE BUSINESS, 49 Fratton Road.	01705 832575
	MOTORCYCLE CITY (SALES) LTD, 153 Fratton Road, PO1 5EP.	01705 828425
	NELSON'S MOTOR, 2 & 4 Kingston Road, Fratton, PO1 5RZ.	01705 825515
	RAFFERTY NEWMAN, 271 London Road, PO2 9HA.	01705 665000
Pulborough	POPLAR CAR CITY, Codmore Hill, RH20 1BQ.	01798 873400
Reading	C J M, P O Box 2748, RG30 2FT.	01189 500055
	COOPER READING, BMW Centre, Kingsmeadow Road.	0118 956 3707
	MOTORCYCLE CITY (SALES) LTD, 470-478 Oxford Road, RG3 1EF.	0118 957 4044
	PEGASUS KAWASAKI, 324 Oxford Road, RG30 1AF.	0118 957 1977
Redhill	FINNS MOTORCYCLES, Unit 6, Hockley Industrial Estate, Hooley Lane, RH1 6ET.	01737 768129
Ringwood	THREE CROSS MOTORCYCLES LTD, Woolsbridge Industrial Estate, Three Legged Cross, BH21 6SP	01202 824531
Salisbury	HAYBALL MOTORCYCLES LTD, Brunel Road, Churchfields, SP2 7PS.	01722 322796
Salisbury	HONDA OF SALISBURY LTD, Churchfields Industrial Estate, Newton Road, SP2 7QA.	01722 341200
	MAXIMUM MOTORCYCLE SALES, The headlands, Downton, SP5 3HH.	01725 510288
	RANGERS GARAGE, Bulford Road, Durrington, SP4 8DL.	01980 652246
Shaftesbury	JUST BIKES, Unit 6, Plot 25C, Longmead Industrial Estate, SP7 8PL.	01747 851005
Slough	SID MORAM LTD, Wexham Road Corner, High Street, SL1 1UA.	01753 522720
	SUPERBIKING, 351 Bath Road, Cippenham, SL1 5PR.	01753 811122
South Godstone	PRO TWINS, Lambs Business Park, Tilburstow Road, RH9 8LJ.	01342 892888
Southampton	BIKERS LTD, 92 Botley Road, North Baddesley, SO52 9DU	01703 741 234
	BRIDGE MOTORCYCLES LTD, West Quay Road, SO15 1GZ.	01703 321321
	DOCKGATE 20, Second Avenue, Millbrook, SO15 0LP.	01703 571200
	DOUG DEARDEN MOTORCYCLES, 207 Long Lane, Holbury, SO4 1PD.	01703 891110
	PARKROAD POWERBIKES, 160 Shirley Road, Shirley, SO15 3FP.	01703 228718
	PRO-SPORT MOTORCYCLES, 46-50 Dean Road, Bitterne, SO18 6AP.	01703 440595
	ROB WILLSHER MOTORCYCLES, Victoria Garage, Portsmouth Road, Bursledon, SO31 8ES.	01703 403203
	STRIDES CYCLES, 150 Commercial Road, Totton, SO40 3AA.	01703 862 011
Spennymoor	NELSON'S OF SPENNYMOOR, Cambridge Street, DL16 6DF.	01388 818511
St Helier	GORDON BISSON M/C LTD, 21-1/2 New St. Johns Rd, JE2 3LD.	01534 27897
St Helier	BOB'S MOTORCYCLE CENTRE, 21 Gloucester Street, JE2 3QR.	01534 58255
St Peter Port	ST PETER PORT GARAGES, Trinity Square, GY1 1PL	01481 725777

CENTRAL SOUTHERN continued

Town	Dealer	Phone	Aprilia	Benelli	BMW	Buell	Cagiva	CCM	Derbi	Ducati	Gilera	Harley	Honda	Kymco	Kawasaki	Laverda	M-Guzzi	MV Agusta	Peugeot	Piaggio	Suzuki	Triumph	Yamaha
St. Helier	CROSS MOTORCYCLES, 9 Great Union Road, JE2 3YA.	01534 33911			•		•		•		•				•					•	•		•
St. Saviour	JACKSONS GARAGE LTD, Rue Des Pres Trading Estate, Longueville.	01534 20281					•				•												
Steyning	STEYNING MOTORCYCLES, Tanyard Lane, BN44 3RJ.	01903 814980																		•	•	•	
Swindon	FOWLERS MOTORCYCLES, 207 Rodbourne Road, SN2 2AA.	01793 534985									•		•								•	•	
	GEORGE WHITE MOTORS LTD, 1-8 Manchester Road, SN1 2AB.	01793 522786											•								•		
	GEORGE WHITE MOTORS LTD, 42-44 Manchester Road.	01793 616638											•										
	LOVETT SPORTING, Ashworth Road, Bridgemead, SN5 7YH.	01793 615222									•												
	P R TAYLOR & SONS, 136 Cricklade Road, Gorse Hill.	01793 480770												•	•								
	THE CYCLING CENTRE, 233 Ferndale Road, SN2 1DD.	01793 536657											•										
Tadley	DES HELYAR MOTORCYCLES, 5 Pamber Heath Road, RG26 3TH.	01189 700665								•													
Taplow	SOLO MOTORCYCLES, The Leisure Track Centre, 94 Bath Road, SL6 0NX.	01628 664433									•		•		•					•	•		
Tidworth	TIDWORTH, 1 Station Road.	01264 363712											•	•						•	•		
Totton	BERNIE LEIGH MOTORCYCLES, 26-28 Rumbridge Street, SO4 4DP.	01703 863295											•						•				
Tring	MARKET MOTORCYCLES, 4 Misswell Lane, HP23 4BX.	01422 822599																	•				
Trowbridge	PHOENIX MOTORCYCLES, 18c Bradley Road, BA14 0QX.	01225 775171							•				•		•		•	•	•				
Ventnor	CHURCH STREET, Church Street, PO38 1SW.	01983 852232											•										
Waterlooville	RAY DENITH MOTORCYCLES, 6 London Road, Purbrook, PO7 5LJ.	01705 230746							•				•	•					•				
Wells	MOTORCYCLE CITY (SALES) LTD, Westfield Road, BA5 2HS.	01749 673462								•			•	•									
Weymouth	POWERHOUSE MOTORCYCLES, Grove Trading Estate, Dorchester, DT1 1ST.	01305 266 797	•																				
	TILLEY'S AUTO CENTRE, 9 Fredrick Place, St Thomas Street, DT4 8HQ.	01305 785672											•										
Winchester	HUSKEY SPORT, The Green, Cheriton, SO24 0QA.	01962 771122																					
	T F ENGINEERING MOTORCYCLE, 6 Hopkins Court, Bennetts Field Trading Estate.	01963 33589																	•				
Woking	CONTINENTAL MOTORCYCLES LTD, 77 Goldsworth Road, GU21 1LU.	01483 756050					•			•	•		•					•	•		•		
	POCKET ROCKETS LTD, 107 Goldsworth Road, GU21 1LJ.																						
Worthing	SCOOTERIFIC, Central Works, Bridge Road, BN14 7BU.	01903 823880																	•				
	WORTHING M.O.T. STATION, 89 Chapel Road.	01903 238287																	•				•

SOUTH EAST

Town	Dealer	Phone	Aprilia	Benelli	BMW	Buell	Cagiva	CCM	Derbi	Ducati	Gilera	Harley	Honda	Kymco	Kawasaki	Laverda	M-Guzzi	MV Agusta	Peugeot	Piaggio	Suzuki	Triumph	Yamaha
Ashford	POWERHOUSE MOTORCYCLES, Unit 6 George's Business Centre, Brunswick Road, TN23 1ED.	01233 665520	•																				
	SIGNPOST CORNER, Kingsnorth Garage, Ashford Road, Kingsnorth.	01233 636699																	•				
Beckenham	FRANK DUNSTALL MOTORCYCLES, 1 Goodwood Parade, Upper Elmers End Road, BR3 3QZ.												•										
Brighton	BIKES OF BRIGHTON, 30 Preston Road.	01273 607635																					
	CASTLE STREET MOTORCYCLES, 29-30 Castle Street, BN1 2HD.	01273 733180							•									•					
	P & H MOTORCYCLES (BRIGHTON) LTD, 112/113 Lewes Road, BN2 3QB.	01273 669 944											•		•						•	•	•
	SCOOT-TECH, 39 Beaconsfield Road, BN 4QH.	01273 626 909	•								•								•				
Canterbury	KENT MOTORCYCLES, Dover Road (A2), Barham, CT4 0AS.	01227 832601											•										•
	STANLEY SCOOTERS, 53-54 Castle Street, CT1 2PY.	01227 453196																		•			

It's going to be a whole new

world

Don't miss it!

BIRMINGHAM

10th - 19th November 2000 - NEC Birmingham

The International Motor Cycle Show

www.motorcycleshow.co.uk

SOUTH EAST continued

Town	Dealer	Phone	Aprilia	Benelli	BMW	Buell	Cagiva	CCM	Derbi	Ducati	Gilera	Harley	Honda	Kymco	Kawasaki	Laverda	M-Guzzi	MV Agusta	Peugeot	Piaggio	Suzuki	Triumph	Yamaha
Canterbury	THE FOUNDRY, Broad Oak Road, CT2 7QG.	01227 766267				•						•										•	
Chatham	BARNEY'S BIKES, 272 Luton Road, ME4 5BU.	01634 826386																					
Crayford	JOHN RILEY MOTORCYCLES, 5-6 The Parade, Crayford Way, DA1 4JA.	01322 526111																					
Crowborough	JOHN HARRIS MOTORCYCLES, Blair House, Whitehill Road, TN6 1JU.	01892 652380												•						•			
Dartford	AUTOWHEELS OF DARTFORD, 68d East Hill, DA1 1RZ.	01322 223165																					
Dartford	E.C. BATE, Bates Yard, 52 West Hill, DA1 2EU.	01322 220748																					
Dover	D P LEAD & SONS, Kearnsey Garage, London Road, CT16 3AB.	01304 824155												•									
Eastbourne	J.S. GEDGE MOTORCYCLES, 3-4 Pevensey Court, Eastbourne Road, Pevensey Bay, BN24 6EX.	01323 765515												•									
Eastbourne	MOTOPORT EASTBOURNE, 110 Longstone Road, BN21 3SJ.	01323 730026																		•			
Eastbourne	PARK MOTORCYCLES, 17-19 Mountfield Road, BN22 9BJ.	01323 502187																					
Faversham	THE BIKE SHOP (FAVERSHAM) LTD, The Mall, ME13 8JN.	01795 532365																					
Folkestone	ALFORD BROS, 20 Cheriton Road, CT20 1BU.	01303 254057																					
Folkestone	ALL BIKES, units 19 & 20, Highfield Industrial Estate, CT19 6DD.	01303 248444												•									
Folkestone	CHERITON MOTORCYCLES, 293 Cheriton Road, CT19 4AZ.	01303 278550																					
Gillingham	JD SCOOTER CLASSIC, 164 Grange Road, ME7 2QT.	01634 855765																					
Gillingham	MAGNUM MOTORCYCLES, 43-45 Canterbury Street, ME7 5TH.	01634 851200																					
Gravesend	MILTON MOTORCYCLES, 20 Milton Road, DA12 2RF.	01474 326428																					
Hastings	J.S. GEDGE MOTORCYCLES, 10 Silchester Road, St. Leonards-on-sea, TN38 0JB.	01424 423520																		•	•		
Hastings	J.S. GEDGE MOTORCYCLES, 406 Old London Road, TN35 5BB.	01424 423708																					
Heathfield	JOHN W. GROOMBRIDGE, Mayfield Road Garage, Cross-in-Hand, TN21 0SP.	01435 862466																					
Herne Bay	EXPRESS GARAGE, 227 Sea Street, CT6 8LF.	01227 364 077																					
Herne Bay	STANLEYS, 10 Stanley Road, CT6 5SH.	01227 374015																					
Hornchurch	MATCHLESS RIDER TRAINING, The Cardrome, Upper Rainham Road, RM12 4PH.	01708 449797																					
Horsham	AUTOSHORE SCOOTER CENTRE, Hurst Court Garage, Hurst Court, RH12 2EN.	01403 261952		•																			
Maidstone	INTA MOTORCYCLE SERVICES LTD, 99-107 Upperstone Street, ME15 6HE.	01622 688727								•											•		
Maidstone	LAGUNA MOTORCYCLES LIMITED, Hart Street, ME16 6RD.	01622 681765																					
Margate	ALEXANDER MOTORCYCLES, 123 Canterbury Road, Westbrook, CT9 5BD.	01843 223610																					
Margate	KENT MOTORCYCLES, 250-252 Northdown Parade, Cliftonville, CT9 2PX.	01843 223585																					
Margate	THANET AREA SCOOTER SERVICES, 114 Northdown Road, CT9 2RE.	01843 292440																					
Paddock Wood	MOTORCYCLE CITY (SALES) LTD, 62 Maidstone Road, TN12 6AF.	01892 835353								•										•		•	
Ramsgate	DAVE FOX MOTORCYCLES, 146 - 152 King Street, CT11 8PJ.	01843 591113																		•			
Ramsgate	DAVE WOOD MOTORCYCLES, 146 King Street.	01843 591113																					
Rochester	CHAMBERS OF ROCHESTER, George Lane, High St, ME1 1QB.	01634 845512																					
Rochester	MARK BOWEN MOTORCYCLES, Unit 6 Central Business Park, Medway City Estate, Frinsbury.	01634 721906																					
Sidcup	GAROZZO MOTORCYCLES, 19 Wellington Parade, Blackfen Road, DA15 9NB.	0181 303 1811																	•	•			
Sittingbourne	SITTINGBOURNE SERVICE STATION, 88-100 West Street, ME10 1AS.	01795 424124																		•			
Thurso	ALTERMOTIVE ENGINEERING, Unit 7a, Ormlie Industrial Estate, KW14 7QU.	01847 892762																					

Tonbridge	MICHAEL CASS GARAGES LTD, 111 Commercial Road, Paddock Wood, TN12 6DS.	01892 836388
	STURDEY MOTORCYCLES, 94A-94C Shipbourne Road, TN10 3EG.	01732 354082
Tunbridge Wells	BREAK-AWAY MOTORCYCLES, 153 Camden Road, TN1 2RF.	01892 542350
	L & C AUTO SERVICES LTD, St Johns Road.	01892 548877
Welling	AYE GEE MOTORCYCLES, 211-219 Bellegrove Road, DA16 3RQ.	0181 856 4273
West Kingsdown	STEVENS TRIAL CENTRE, Unit 43, Blue Chalet Industrial Park, London Road, TN15 6BQ.	01474 854265
West Wickham	PLANET MOTORCYCLES, 10 Kingsway, BR4 9JF.	0181 462 1816
	PREMIER MOTORCYCLES LTD, 131-133 High Street, BR4 0UL.	0181 777 8040
Whitstable	FREEWAY SCOOTERS, Ubit 6a, 3 Belmont Road, CT5 1QJ.	01227 277865
Worthing	ALF'S MOTORCYCLES, 100 Dominion Road, BN14 8JP.	01903 200948
	KEYS BROS, 142a Montague Street, BN113HQ.	01903 236842

LONDON

Acton	MOTORCYCLE ACTION, 273-279 High Street, W3 9BT.	0181 993 0336
Arnos Grove	FIRSTLINE MOTORCYCLES LTD, 464-466 Bowes Road, N11 1NL.	0181 361 5151
Barnet	NLM LTD, 3 Greenhill Parade, EN5 1ES.	0181 441 4191
	NORTH LONDON MOTORCYCLES, 12 Western Parade, EN5 1AD.	0181 441 4191
Bedfont	MOTORCYCLE CITY (SALES) LTD, 533 Staines Road, TW14 8BP.	0181 751 8888
Bromley	S. G. SMITH, 2 Tylney Road, BR1 2RP.	0181 464 7070
Carshalton	LAMBA MOTORCYCLES, 120-132 High Street, SM5 3AE.	0181 647 4851
Catford	RON COMPTON MOTORCYCLES, 109 Brownhill Road, SE6 2HF.	0181 697 2779
Cheam	SUTTON MOTORCYCLES, 43 The Broadway, SM3 8BL.	0181 643 2916
Chiswick	CULT SCOOTER, 132 Chiswick High Road, W4 3EA.	0181 995 1339
Croydon	CARL ROSNER, Station Approach, Off Sanderson Road, CR2 0PL.	0181 657 0121
	PLANET MOTORCYCLES, 44/45 Tamworth Road, CR0 1XU.	0181 686 5650
Ealing	BILL BUNN MOTORCYCLES LTD, 194 South Ealing Road, W5 4RJ.	0181 560 6396
	M.L.&S. BIKESMART LTD, 140-142 Northfield Avenue, W13 9SB.	0181 566 0000
	METOPOLIS MOTORCYCLES, 272-274 Northfield Avenue, W5 4UB.	0181 567 8885
East Ham	EAST LONDON MOTORCYCLES LTD, 249 Barking Road, E6 1LB.	0181 472 8301
East Moseley	WALTON ROAD GARAGE, 34 Walton Road, KT8 0DF.	0181 941 1600
Edgeware	REX JUDD LTD, Brooklands House, 415 Burnt Oak, Broadway, HA8 5AH.	0181 952 6911
Edmonton	J.A. LOCK LTD, 333-335 Fore Street, N9 0PD.	0181 807 5269
Enfield	CARNELL MOTORCYCLES LTD, 2 Lockfield Avenue, Brimsdown, EN3 7UU.	0181 443 1333
Fulham	BULLET MOTORCYCLES LTD, 51 New Kings Road, SW6 4SE.	0171 736 3811
	CHELSEA SCOOTERS LIMITED, 334-336 Wandsworth Bridge Road, SW6 2TZ.	0171 736 6670
Greenford	MOTORCYCLE CITY (SALES) LTD, 300-304 Ruislip Road East, UB6 9BH.	0181 578 3218
Hammersmith	HARRY NASH SCOOTERS, 391 King Street, W6 9NJ.	0181 748 2837
	WORLDS END MOTORCYCLES, 238 Trussley Road, W6 7PP.	0181 746 3595
Harold Park	MAYLANDS MOTORCYCLES, 4 The Parade, Colchester Road, RM3 0AQ.	01708 374500
Harrow Weald	H.G.B. MOTORCYCLES LTD, 215-219 High Road, HA3 5EE.	0181 427 5575
Hayes	H. G. B. BIKE STUDIO, 13 Broadway Parade, Cold Harbour Lane, UB3 3HF.	0181 573 5995

LONDON continued

Location	Dealer	Phone	Yamaha	Triumph	Suzuki	Piaggio	Peugeot	MV Agusta	M-Guzzi	Laverda	Kawasaki	Kymco	Honda	Harley	Gilera	Ducati	Derbi	CCM	Cagiva	Buell	BMW	Benelli	Aprilia
Hillingdon	STREETFIGHTER & CLASSIC MOTORCYCLES, 4 Lees Parade, Uxbridge Road, UB10 0PQ.	01895 235805										•											
Hitchin	FIRSTLINE MOTORCYCLES LTD, 66 Bancroft, SG5 1LL.	01462 434443		•																			
Ilford	BACONS MOTOR CYCLES, 730 Eastern Avenue, IG2 7RT.	0181 252 6020			•								•										
Ilford	EDDY GRIMSTEAD LTD, 741-755 Eastern Avenue, Newbury Park, IG2 7RT.	0181 590 6615				•																	
	SCOOTERS UNLIMITED, 948 Eastern Avenue, Newbury Park, IG2 7JD.	0181 597 1177																					
Kenley	COLIN HILL RACING, 197 Godstone Road, CR8 5BN.	0181 660 3728																					•
Kingston	SCOOTAROUND, 23 High Street, Hampton Wick, KT1 4DA.	0181 977 7758					•					•											
Lewisham	PARKS OF LEWISHAM (SALES), 404 High Street, SE13 6LJ.	0181 690 8666					•						•										
Leytonstone	DOUBLE R MOTORCYCLES, 311 High Road, E11 4JT.	0181 558 4819			•										•								
London	ASHAN SCOOTERS, 59 East Hill, Wandsworth, SW18 2QE.	0181 874 4043																					•
	B M G SCOOTERS, 416 Upper Richmond Road West, SW14 7JX.	0181 878 8121																					
	BIKEADELIC, 1A Howley Road, Camden, NW1 8RP.	0171 267 1557				•				•					•								
	BIKERAMA, 42 - 50 High Street, Hornsey, N8 7NX.	0171 348 1771																					
	BLACKWATER, 126 Wadsworth High Street, Wandsworth, SW18 4JP.	0181 970 9007					•						•		•								
	BOYER RACING, 151 Plumstead Road, SE18 7DY	0181 854 8133																					
	BURWIN MOTORCYCLES, 378-380 Essex Road, N1 3PD.	0171 359 3050																					
	CARNELL MOTORCYCLES LTD, 73-75 Camberwell Road, SE5 0EZ.	0171 703 2271		•							•		•				•						
	COMMUTER WORLD LTD, 216 Great Portland Street, W1N 5HG.	0171 388 8458					•						•										
	DAYTONA MOTORCYCLES, Angel House, Pentonville Road, N1 9HJ.	0171 833 2411														•						•	
	EXAN COACHWORKS, 392 Camden Road, Holloway	0171 609 1600															•						
	F H WARR & SONS, 611 Kings Road, SW6 3EL	0171 736 2934												•									
	GORGEOUS BIKES, 496 Kings Road, Chelsea, SW10 0LE.	0171 351 1191																	•				
	HGB SCOOTABOUT, 1-3 Leeke Street, WC1X 9HZ.	0171 833 5995																					
	HOOTER SCOOTER, 345 Lee High Road, Lee Green, SE12 8RU.	0181 355 8020																					•
	H R OWEN, 125 Old Brompton Road, SW7 3RP	0171 341 6300																					
	J. C. G. BARNES, 4 Castelnau Barnes, SW13 9RU.	0181 741 1578		•				•															•
	JON'S SCOOTERS, D M Smither Motorcycles, 62 Dalston Lane, Dalston, E8 3AH.	0171 254 0260					•																
	LAZER MOTORCYCLES, 1 Belmont Street, Chalk Farm, NW1 8HJ.	0171 267 3321																					
	LIGHTNING MOTORCYCLES, Arch 454, Robeson Street, Bow, E3 4JA.	0181 980 7999					•																
	MACH MOTORCYCLES, 97 Kenton Road, Harrow, HA3 0AN.	0181 907 6705																					•
	METROPOLIS MOTORCYCLES, 23 Dowgate Hill, EC4R 2YB.	0171 236 1913					•								•								
	METROPOLIS MOTORCYCLES, 59-62 Albert Embankment, SE1 7TP.	0171 793 9313					•								•								
	MOTORCYCLE CITY (SALES) LTD, 165 Seven Sisters Road, ., N4 3NS.	0171 561 9500	•																			•	•
	MOTORCYCLE CITY (SALES) LTD, 24-26 Clapham High Street, Clapham, SW4 7UR.	0171 720 6072			•																		
	MOTORCYCLE CITY (SALES) LTD, Service Centre only, 137a Wandsworth Road, Vauxhall, SW8.	0171 501 3434																					
	MOTORCYCLE SERVICE CENTRE, 541 Harrow Road, W10 4RH.	0181 960 6434					•																•
	MOTTINGHAM, 282-284 Court Road, SE9 4TU.	0181 857 7777					•																•

	NEIL HARRIS MOTORCYCLES, 28 Chingford Mount Road, Chingford.	0181 527 7330
	PARK LANE LTD, 70 Park Lane, Mayfair.	0171 409 3355
	PLATINUM MOTORCYCLES LTD, 658 Tottenham High Road, N17 0AB.	0181 855 2000
	PRESTIGE MOTORCYCLES LTD, 300 Broadway, Bexleyheath.	0181 303 3030
	R. AGIUS LTD, 363 Edgware Rd, W2 1BS.	0171 723 0995
	R. G. S. MOTORCYCLES LTD, 134-142 Tooting High Street, Tooting, SW17 0SQ.	0181 767 8408
	SCOOTER MANIA, 246 Church Lane, Kingsbury, NW9 8SL.	0181 205 3476
	SCOOT ABOUT, 1-3 Leeke Street, WC1X 9HZ.	0171 833 4609
	SCOOTAROUND, 61 Sheen Lane, SW14 8AR.	0181 876 9888
	SCOOTECH, 425-427 Roman Road, E3 5LU.	0181 983 4111
	SCOOTER STORE INTERNATIONAL, 48 Shepherds Bush Road, Shepherds Bush, W6 7PH.	0171 610 4131
	SCOOTER WORLD LTD, 105 Westbourne Grove, W2 3ST.	0171 243 1100
	SCOOTERS LTD, 296 Fulham Road, SW10 9EN.	0171 351 7400
	SCOOTERS OF ENFIELD, 228 Baker Street, Enfield, EN1 3JY.	0181 292 2003
	SCOOTERZONE, 1a Drysdale Street, N1 6ND.	0171 613 5323
	SMITH AND HUNTER LTD, 17-19 Edge Street, Kensington Church Street, W8 7PN.	0171 221 0441
	SNOBS ULITMATE CUSTOMS, 12 Norbeck Parade, NW10 7HR.	0181 566 8881
	STADIUM, 2 Loxham Road, Chingford, E4 8SE.	0181 531 9026
	STRAWBERRY HILL CARS, 45 Hampton Road, Twickenham, TW2 5QE.	0181 893 8711
	STREAMLINE, 517-533 Lordship Lane, East Dulwich, SE22 8LA.	0181 693 6024
	SUNRISE MOTORS, 42 Station Road, Willesden Green, NW2 4NX.	0181 830 5600
	THE YAMAHA SERVICE CENTRE, 347 New Kings Road, Fulham, SW6 4RJ.	0171 3701 9700
	TWICKENHAN SCOOTERS, 45 Hampton Road, Twickenham, TW2 5QE.	0181893 8711
London Colney	MOTORCYCLES AND MOORE, 166 High Street, AL2 1QF.	01727 824248
Morden	SUNAMI MOTORCYCLES, 14 - 15 Morden Court Parade, London Road, SM4 5HJ.	0181 646 1554
North Cheam	CHURCHILLS OF CHEAM, 126 Abbotts Road, SM3 9SX.	0181 644 1928
North Harrow	COLIN COLLINS MOTORCYCLES, 90-100 Pinner Road, HA1 4JD.	0181 861 1666
Purley	MOTORCYCLE CITY (SALES) LTD, Russell Hill Road, CR8 2LA.	0181 763 5700
Raynes Park	WHEELPOWER BIKE CENTRE LTD, 264 Grand Drive, SW20 9NE.	0181 543 0321
Richmond	RICHMOND MOTOR CO, Dundas Street, DL10 7AB.	01748 823 956
Romford	HYSIDE MOTORCYCLES, 98 Collier Row Road, RM5 2BA.	01708 763 360
	JOHNS OF ROMFORD LIMITED, 162 Rush Green Road, RM7 0JU.	01708 761047
	JOHNS OF ROMFORD LIMITED, 46-52 London Road, RM7 9QX.	01708 726048
	PERPETUAL MOTION, 1065 High Road, Chadwell Heath.	0181 590 3000
	KENISTONS, 5-6 Station Chambers, Victoria Road, RM1 2HS.	01708 746283
	STEAD'S SCOOTERS, 181 South Street, RM1 1PS.	01708 740040
Ruislip Manor	DAYTONA MOTORCYCLES, 42 Windmill Hill, HA4 8PT.	01895 675511
	H.G.B. MOTORCYCLES LTD, 69-71 Parkway, HA4 8NS.	01895 676451
Shepperton	JACK LILLEY MOTORCYCLES, 109 High Street, TW17 9BL.	01932 224574
South Woodford	WOODFORD MOTORCYCLES, 51-53 George Lane, E18 1LN.	0181 989 3157
Southwark	BRAVEN, 330 St James Road, Bermondsey SE1 5JX.	0171 232 1814

LONDON continued

		Aprilia	Benelli	BMW	Buell	Cagiva	CCM	Derbi	Ducati	Gilera	Harley	Honda	Kymco	Kawasaki	Laverda	M-Guzzi	MV Agusta	Peugeot	Piaggio	Suzuki	Triumph	Yamaha
Staines	G. T. MOTORCYCLES, 139 Kingston Road, TW18 1PD. — 01784 452489	•				•				•								•				
Stratford	STRATFORD MOTORCYCLES, 38 Romford Road, E15 4BZ. — 0181 555 4346											•		•						•		•
Streatham	HAMILTONS POWERSPORTS, 420 - 446 Streatham High Road, SW16 3PX. — 0181 764 0101																		•	•		
Surbiton	RAEBURN GARAGE, 118 Raeburn Avenue, KT5 9EA. — 0181 390 6388											•						•				
	TIPPETTS MOTORS (SURBITON) LTD, 312-320 Ewell Road, Tolworth, KT6 7AW. — 0181 399 2417											•						•				
Surrey Quays	RACEWAYS, 201-203 Lower Road, SE16 2LW. — 0171 237 6494																	•				
Twickenham	BLAYS OF TWICKENHAM LTD, 32-34 The Green, TW2 5AB. — 0181 894 1397									•								•				
	C.B.S. (WHITTON) LTD, 136 Kneller Rd, Whitton, TW2 7DX. — 0181 898 5492											•										
Walthamstow	JACK NICE MOTORCYCLES, 129-133 Grove Road, E17 9BU. — 0181 520 1920					•						•							•			
Wandsworth	AHSAN SCOOTERS, 59 East Hill, SW18 2QE. — 0181 874 4043									•								•				
Watford	COLIN COLLINS MOTORCYCLES, 81 Queens Road, WD1 2QN. — 01923 235346	•										•										
	LLOYD COOPER MOTORCYCLES, 61 Queens Road, WD1 2QN. — 01923 221125											•		•				•			•	
West Croydon	GREYHOUND MOTORS LTD, 258-264 London Road, CR10 2TH. — 0181 688 8447																	•				
West Drayton	MOTORCYCLE HQ LTD, 9 High Street, Yiewsley, UB7 7QG. — 01895 442595								•													
West Hampstead	SCOOTER POWER, 56 Fortune Green Road, NW6 1DT. — 0171 625 1200																					
Willesden	SLOCOMBES MOTORCYCLES, 46-52 Dudden Hill Lane, Dollis Hill, NW10 1DG. — 0181 830 1000			•																		
Wimbledon Chase	FRONTIERS MOTORCYCLES LIMITED, 363 Kingston Road, SW20 8JX. — 0181 540 7774								•	•								•	•	•	•	

WALES

		Aprilia	Benelli	BMW	Buell	Cagiva	CCM	Derbi	Ducati	Gilera	Harley	Honda	Kymco	Kawasaki	Laverda	M-Guzzi	MV Agusta	Peugeot	Piaggio	Suzuki	Triumph	Yamaha
Aberaeron	D & L DAVIES, The Bont, South Road, SA46 0DY. — 01545 570286																					
Aberbargoed	JEFF SMITH MOTORCYCLES LTD, 66 Commercial Street, CF81 9BU. — 01443 838900						•															
Abergavenny	BLACK MOUNTAIN YAMAHA, Llanwenarth Citra, Crickhowell, NP8 1EP. — 01873 811776																					•
Abergele	THREEWAYS OF ABERGELE LTD, Faenol Avenue, LL22 7HT. — 01745 825847								•			•										
	WOODS MOTORCYCLES, Units A1 - A4, Peel Street, LL22 7HF. — 01745 822922	•										•										•
Bangor	BILL SMITH MOTORS (GWYNEDD) LIMITED, Cyttir Lane, LL57 4DA. — 01248 352085											•		•						•	•	•
Bridgend	THUNDER ROAD MOTORCYCLES LTD, Tremains Road, CF31 1UA. — 01656 661131/2																				•	
Brigend	M & P MOTORCYCLES (2 WHEEL SERVICES), 79 Nolton Road, CF31 3AE. — 01656 657887																			•		
Camarthen	D L MOTORCYCLES, Unit 6C, Crosshands Business Park, Crosshands, SA14 6RB. — 01269 832750									•				•					•			
Cardiff	EDWARDS MOTORCYCLES, 82 Cowbridge Road East. — 01222 396500	•										•						•	•			
	FOWLERS CITY CENTRE YAMAHA, 82 Cowbridge Road East, Canton, CF1 9DX. — 01222 396500																					•
	FOWLERS MOTORCYCLES, 218 Penarth Road, CF1 7NN. — 01222 390100																				•	
	MERLIN DUCATI, Cambria House, North Road, CF4 3BH. — 01222 614622								•													
	ROBERT BEVAN & SON, Hadfield Road, CF1 8AQ. — 01222 227477																				•	
	ROBERT BEVAN & SON, Hadfield Road, CF1 8AW. — 01222 227477														•	•		•				•
Colwyn Bay	COLWYN BAY MOTORCYCLES, 4 Groes Road, LL29 8PU. — 01492 535959																•					
Crosshands	SHADDOW SUPERBIKES, The Square, 2 Llandeilo Road, SA14 6NR. — 01269 832 211													•				•	•	•	•	
Denbigh	A & D MOTORCYCLES, Unit 1a Spencer Industrial Estate, Colomendy, LL16 5TQ. — 01745 815105																		•			

Town	Dealer	Phone	1	2	3	4	5	6	7	8	9	10	11	12	13	14	15	16	17	18
Haverfordwest	GARLAND & GRIFFITHS (M & P) MOTORCYCLES, Old Hakin Road, Merlins Bridge, SA61 1XE.	01437 768434			•		•	•					•	•	•			•		•
	MASON MOTORCYCLES, Fountain Row, Barn Street, SA61 1SX.	01437 765651																		•
Hollywell	S K SCOOTERS, Lixwm Road, CH8 8AD.	01352 710001												•						
Lampeter	RODY REES MOTORS, 56 Bridge Street, SA48 7AB.	01570 422327									•									
Llanelly	ASHLEY AUTO REPAIRS, Ysbitty Service Station, Bynea, SA14 9ST.	01554 778800														•				
Llantrisant	MOTORCYCLE WORLD, Talbot Green, CF7 8AW.	01443 227903															•			
Merthyr Tydfil	BOB WILDING MOTORCYCLES, 20-22 Pontmorlais, CF47 8UB.	01685 385201						•												
	GREG THOMAS RACING, Pentrebach Road.	01685 722773						•												
Mold	E.R. WILLIAMS MOTORCYCLES, Bromfield Trading Est, Gas Lane, CH7 1UT.	01352 753619												•						
Monmouth	FULL THROTTLE, 6 St James Street.	01600 715447						•												
Nant Y Glo	KEN FINNEY MOTORCYCLES, 37-39 Queen Street, NP3 4JN.	01495 290099									•									
Newcastle Emlyn	G C MOTORFACTORS, Rear of Cawdor Garage, Tanyard Lane, SA38 9AJ.	01239 710791								•										
Newport	ISLE OF WIGHT MOTORCYCLES, 7-9 Hunny Hill, PO30 5HJ.	01983 522675							•								•	•		
	K W & SONS, 33a Wharf Road.	01633 514401						•												
	KEN ROBERTS MOTORCYCLES, 133a Caerleon Road, NP7 7BZ.	01633 252803							•								•	•		
	SOUTH WALES SUPERBIKES LTD, Meadows Estate, 10-11 Estuary Road, Queensway Meadows.	01633 277970								•		•					•	•	•	•
Newtown	DAVID JONES MOTORCYCLES, Poole Road, SY16 1DD.	01686 625010									•						•			•
Pontypool	PAVILION GARAGE, Osborne Road, NP4 6NR.	01495 751375												•						
Pontypridd	W MOUNTER CYCLES, 46 Pentrebach Road, Glyntaff, CF37 4BW.	01443 400960												•						
Port Talbot	KICKSTART MOTORCYCLES, 51 Talbot Road, SA13 1HU.	01639 881585	•						•						•					
	MOUNT MOTORCYCLES LIMITED, 57-61 Commercial Road, Taibach, SA13 1LP.	01639 883936						•								•		•		
	THE CYCLE SHACK, 51 Talbot Road, SA13 1HU.	01639 881585												•						
Portmadog	E D S, Unit 18, Penamser Industrial Estate.	01766 513826						•												
Pwlheli	GPI MOTORCYCLES, The Cynfil Centre, The Maes, LL53 5HB.	01758 613087							•											
Swansea	J.T.'S MOTORCYCLES, Unit 2 Heol-Y-Gors, Cwmbwrla, SA5 8LD.	01792 461776													•			•		
	M & P ACCESSORIES LTD, Phoenix Way, Garngoch Industrial Estate, Gorseinon, SA4 1GZ.	01792 224451											•		•					
	MOUNT MOTORCYCLES LIMITED, 9-13 Wyndham Street, SA1 3HZ.	01792 645708															•			
Treorchy	WAYNE BOWEN MOTORCYCLES, 164 Bute Street, CF42 6BY.	01443 776060							•		•				•					
Wrexham	WREXHAM SCOOTERS, 62 Smithfield Road, LL13 3ES.	01978 265795												•						

CENTRAL MIDLANDS

Town	Dealer	Phone	1	2	3	4	5	6	7	8	9	10	11	12	13	14	15	16	17	18
Abingdon	ABINGDON MOTORCYCLES, Marcham Road, OX14 1TZ.	01235 550055												•						
	BIKEWISE MOTORCYCLES, Unit 8, Radley Road Industrial Estate, OX14 3SB.	01235 535037														•				
Aldridges	STEVE GOODE MOTORCYCLES, 33 Empire Industrial Park, Brickyard Road, WS9 8SR.																			•
Banbury	BANBURY SCOOTER CENTRE, 2 Bridge Street, OX16 8PH.	01295 272757														•				
	MAX MOTORCYCLES LTD, 18 Southam Road, OX16 7EG.	01295 252 506	•					•										•		
Bicester	NEIL WHITING MOTORCYCLES LTD, 43 London Road, OX6 7BU.	01869 243034								•										
Birmingham	CARNELL MOTORCYCLES LTD, 137-148 Digbeth High Street, B12 0JU.	0121 604 4111					•				•	•					•	•		•
	GRAN SPORT AUTOSCOOTERS LTD, 596 Pershore Road, Selly Park, B29 7HQ.	0121 471 4555							•											
	IDEAL GARAGE, 321 Bromford Lane, Ward End, B8 2SH.	0121 327 4559						•											•	
	J C MOTORCYCLES LTD, 367 Stockfield Road, Yardley, B25 8JP.	0121 707 4879							•			•				•				

CENTRAL MIDLANDS continued

Town	Dealer	Phone	Yamaha	Triumph	Suzuki	Piaggio	Peugeot	MV Agusta	M-Guzzi	Laverda	Kawasaki	Kymco	Honda	Harley	Gilera	Ducati	Derbi	CCM	Cagiva	Buell	BMW	Benelli	Aprilia
	PACE MOTORCYCLES, 978 Tyburn Road, Erdington, B24 0TL.	0121 373 0084					•																•
	SELLY OAK MOTOR COMPANY, 520 Bristol Road, Selly Oak, B29 6BD.	0121 472 0670					•																
	SIXWAYS MOTORCYCLES, 5 Wood End Road, Erdington, B24 8AA.	0121 350 8129			•																		
	SPEEDAWAY MOTOR CYCLES, 78a Oldbury Road, Blackheath, B65 0JS.	0121 589 1270			•		•										•						•
	TEAM CENTRAL LIMITED, College Auto Centre, Kingstanding Road, Perry Barr, B44 8AA.	0121 344 3400		•									•			•							
Bishops Stortford	HUNTS MOTOR GARAGE LTD, 26 Northgate End, CM23 2EV	01279 653494											•										
Brackley	SLIDERS, Shires Road Off Buckingham Road, NN13 7E2.	01280 700769									•							•					
Brierley Hill	Q.B. MOTORCYCLES (QUARRY BANK), 91 High Street, Quarry Bank, DY5 2AD.	01384 637168				•			•				•		•		•	•					
Bromsgrove	WILDMORE COMP SHOP, Sandy Lane.	0121 457 9040/30																					
Buckley	MOTORCYCLE & SCOOTER WARE, 53 Brunswick Road.	01244 541111					•																
Burton-on-Trent	JACKSON'S MOTORCYCLES LIMITED, 22-23 Borough Road, DE14 2DA.	01283 565154	•		•		•						•		•		•						•
Cannock	FOWLERS MOTORCYCLES, Unit 16, Brindley's Business Park, Chaseside Drive, WS11 2GD.	01543 428528		•		•	•				•		•		•		•						•
	HEDNESFORD MOTORCYCLES, 3-7 Market Street, Hednesford, WS12 5AY.	01543 426143																					
Cheltenham	AMS MOTORCYCLES, 25 Wellington Street, GL50 1XZ.	01242 583985											•										
	DAVE PARRY MOTORCYCLES, Elim Works, Dunalley Parade, GL50 4LS.	01285 230403									•												
	FOWLERS MOTORCYCLES, 84 Fairview Road, GL52 6LR.	01242 262555								•						•							
	PITVILLE MOTORCYCLES LTD, 11-15 Prestbury Road, GL52 2PN.	01242 513782	•																				
Cheshunt	WALTHAM CROSS MOTORCYCLES LTD, 50-54 Crossbrook Street, EN8 8OJ.	01992 625173									•						•						
Cinderford	HAINES & CO LTD, 125 High Street, GL14 2TB.	01594 822202																					
Congleton	RICHARDSONS OF CONGLETON, 47 Mill Street, CW12 1AG.	01260 279425			•								•				•						
Corby	CORBY KAWASAKI CENTRE, Courier Road, Phoenix Parkway, NN17 1DY.	01536 410010									•												
Coventry	DRAYTON CROFT MOTORCYCLES, 323-325 Foleshill Road, CV1 4JS.	01203 665433											•				•						
	J H PERFORMANCE, Rear of White Lodge, Watery Lane, Corley Moor, CV7 8AV.	01676 542991														•							
	LUMLEY INSURANCE CONSULTANTS, Lumley House, Waters Court Salt Lane.	01203 527820																					
	SCOOTER JUNCTION, 328 Radford Road, CV6 3AA.	01203 594464				•																•	
Cradley Heath	CRADLEY HEATH KAWASAKI, St Anns road.	01384 633455									•												
Crewe	A.R. MORRIS (CREWE) LTD, 146 West Street, CW1 3HO.	01270 213575											•										
	CREWE MOTORCYCLES, 92 Mill Street, CW2 7AS.	01270 212268															•						
	SINGLE TRACKER, 20-28 Flag Lane, CW1 3BG.	01270 212965			•										•								
Derby	CLARKES MOTORCYCLES, 63 Osmaston Road.	01332 293760	•																				
	DERBY POWERSPORTS, Sir Frank Whittle Road, Pentagon Island, DE21 4EE.	01332 206092											•			•							
	DON AMMOTT LEISURE LTD, Hilton, DE65 5FJ.	01283 732193									•												
	ROY PIDCOCK MOTORCYCLES, 277 Osmaston Road.	01332 349673																					
Droitwich	C.J. MOTORCYCLES, 10-12 Colman Road, WR9 8OU.	01905 774333				•	•																
Dudley	STREETBIKE (DUDLEY), 73 King Street, DY2 8QE.	01384 253464	•		•	•	•																
Dursley	DURSLEY MOTORCYCLES CENTRE, Prospect Place, May Lane, GL11 4JH.	01453 544757					•						•										
Evesham	DAVE LOUDOUN CARS, Davies Road, Four Pools, WR11 6XJ.	01386 412222			•		•																

Power release

Let it fly. Release the full power potential of your bike. All you need is a pack of Mobil 1 Racing 4T. Developed to withstand the extreme speeds of today's high-revving machines, it maximises power output from the moment you fire up your engine. Helping you take your bike to the limit.

For details of your nearest stockist, call 0800 040 111. www.mobil.co.uk/automotive

Mobil 1 Feel the difference

CENTRAL MIDLANDS continued

Evesham	MIKE TAYLOR MOTORCYCLES, Unit 2, Northwick Road.	0386 443387
	RAWLEY MOTORCYCLES, 27 Weston Industrial Estate, Honey Bourne, WR11 5QB.	0386 840588
Flitwick	FLITWICK MOTORCYCLES, Station Road, MK45 1ED.	01525 712197
Gainsborough	RAY HAMBLIN LIMITED, 47 North Street.	01427 612887
Gloucester	CLAREMONT MOTORCYCLES LTD, Unit 14, Spinnaker Park, GL2 5FD.	01452 525903
	FRASER'S OF GLOUCESTER, 261 Bristol Road, GL2 6EY.	01452 306485
	TREDWORTH MOTORCYCLES LTD, 64 High Street, GL1 4SR.	01452 301513
Grantham	GRANTHAM CARAVANS LTD, Spittlegate Level, NG31 7UH.	01476 560 599
	HARBOROUGH BIKE CENTRE, 44 Watergate, NG31 6TR.	01476 564126
	R. A. WILSON MOTORCYCLES, Inner Street, NG31 6HN.	01476 593793
Halesowen	BLACKCOUNTRY MOTORCYCLES, 1 Clarage House, Long Lane, B62 9LA.	0121 604 4111
Hall Green	SHERWOOD MOTORCYCLES, 192 & 194 Robin Hood Lane, B28 0LG.	0121 777 1311
Harlow	HARLOW MOTORCYCLE CENTRE, 18 Wych Elm, CM20 1QR.	01279 425262
Hatfield	WATERS & SONS LTD, Comet Way, AL10 9TE.	01707 264521
Heanor	COLIN LOMAX MOTORCYCLES, 3 Ray Street, DE7 7GE.	01773 713475
Hereford	BOB GALLIER, 22 - 23 Berrington Street.	01432 268 813
	MOTORCYCLE CENTRE (HEREFORD) LIMITED, Belmont Roundabout, 7-9 Ross Road. HR2 7RH.	01432 272341
Hertford	BOB HILL MOTORCYCLES, 7 Cowbridge, SG14 1PQ.	01992 551711
	SAWBRIDGEWORTH MOTORCYCLES, 33-37 Chaber Street.	01992 583135
Hinckley	DRAYTON CROFT MOTORCYCLES, Stockwell Head, LE10 1RE.	01455 637654
Huntingdon	HUNTINGDON MOTORCYCLES, 7 George Street, PE18 6BD.	01480 453790
Kettering	APE ACCESSORIES, 178 Regent Street, NN16 8QII.	01536 516078
Kidderminster	MOTORCYCLE MART (KIDDERMINSTER) LTD, Stourport Road, DY11 7QP.	01562 824259
Kidlington	T. W. MOTORCYCLES, 139 Oxford Road, OX5 2NP.	01865 375702
Leamington Spa	ARCH MOTORCYCLES, 111 Warwick Street, CV32 4QZ.	01926 330102
	DENNIS COOPER CARS LTD., Tachbrook Park Drive, CV34 6RH.	01926 740010
	FRETTONS OF LEAMINGTON LIMITED, 15-17 Clemens Street, CV31 2DW.	01926 429214
Ledbury	LEE MOTORCYCLES, Homend Trading Estate, HR8 1AR.	01531 634475
Leek	ROLY CAPPER MOTORCYCLES, Russel Street, ST13 5JF.	01538 382861
Leicester	ARNOLDS MOTORCYCLES, 106 Belgrave Gate, LE1 3GR.	0116 253 0272
	CLIVE CASTLEDINE MOTORCYCLES, 141-143 Humberstone Road, LE5 3AP.	0116 262 0966
	LEICESTER HONDA 2000, 3 Blaby Road, Wigston, LE18 4PA.	0116 2782544
	PLANET BIKES, Goose Island, 401 Aylestone Road, LE2 8TB.	0116 224 2000
	REDCAR MOTORCYCLES, 2 Redcar Road, LE4 6PD.	0116 266 1637
	REV & GO SCOOTERING, 279 Aylestone Road, LE2 7OJ.	0116 283 6020
Letchworth	A & M MOTORCYCLES, Unit 7/8, Glebe Road, SG6 1DR.	01462 483211
	COLIN COLLINS MOTORCYCLES, The Pavilion, Campus 5, Third Avenue, SG6 2JF.	01462 483399

322

Lincoln	BROCKLESBY MCS (B & B MCS LIMITED), 429 High Street, LN5 8HZ.	01522 545879
	FRANCIS MOTORS, 173a Burton Road, LN1 3LW.	01522 537324
	ITALIA CLASSICS, 7 Bargate, High Street, LN5 5BU.	01522 511851
	JACK MACHIN MOTORCYCLES, 128 Carholme Road, LN1 1RU.	01522 512887
	THE OTHER BIKE SHOP, 111 Portland Street, LN5 7LG.	01522 511584
	WEBBS OF LINCOLN, 117 Portland Street, LN5 7LG.	01552 528951
Long Eaton	THE BIKE SHOP, 68-72 Tamworth Road, NG10 3LH.	01159 732862
Loughborough	ARNOLDS TWO WHEELERS, 66-68 Leicester Road, LE11 2AG.	01509 212988
	CRM SCOOTER COMMUTER CENTRE, Astry Road, Shepshed, LE12 9EE.	01509 651181
	JOHN MONK MOTORCYCLES, 35 Pinfold Gate, LE11 2LL.	01509 232875
	REDLINE MOTORCYCLES (LEICESTER), 10 High Street, Sileby, LE12 7RX.	01509 816177
	TWIGGERS MOTORCYCLES, 30 Nottingham Road, LE11 1EU.	01509 263967
Louth	MARTIN WILSON MOTORCYCLES, 16 Queen Street.	01507 603416
Ludlow	HONDA EQUIPE (LUDLOW), Coronation Avenue, SY8 1DL.	01584 874738
	LUDLOW BIKE CENTRE, Raven Lane Garage, Raven Lane, SY8 1BW.	01584 876505
Luton	COBURN & HUGHES, 6-7 Moor Street, LU1 1HA.	01582 410666
Macclesfield	THE BIKE CONNECTION LTD, 58-60 Dallow Road, SK11 7SP.	01582 731488
	REDLINE SUPERBIKES, 151 London Road, SK11 7SP.	01625 617278
Malvern	JOHN JENKINS MOTORCYCLES LTD, 72 Worcester Road, WR14 1NU.	01684 572257
Mansfield	PLEASLEY MOTORCYCLES, 520 Chesterfield Road North, Pleasley, NG19 7SR.	01623 810133
	TWO WHEELED ENGINEERING, 50 Ratcliffe Gate, NG18 2JR.	01623 427232
	UNIQUE AUTOS 2, 32 Church Street.	01623 646661
Market Drayton	WYLIE & HOLLAND MOTORCYCLES, 63-73 Shrewsbury Road, TF9 3DN.	01630 657121
Melton Mowbray	LEN MANCHESTER MOTORCYCLES, 17 Burton Street, LE13 1AE.	01664 562302
Milton Keynes	CARNELL MOTORCYCLES LTD, Roebuck Way, Knowlhill, MK5 8HT.	01908 325700
	GRAFTON MOTORCYCLES, 14 Stratford Road, Wolverton, MK12 5JL.	01908 313290
	MISSION MOTORCYCLES, 13 Victoria Rd, Bletchley, MK2 2NG.	01908 372211
Newcastle-u-Lyme	D & K MOTORCYCLES, Swift House, Liverpool Road, ST5 9JL.	01782 861100
Northampton	FOWLERS MOTORCYCLES, 53-54 Barrack Road, NN1 3RL.	01604 622411
	M & P ACCESSORIES LTD, 2 Museum Way, Riverside Park, NN3 9HW.	01604 417000
	MICK BERRILL MOTORCYCLES, 1-3 Henry Street, NN1 4JD.	01604 636760
	WOOLASTON MOTORS LTD, St Peters Way.	01604 232000
Northampton	MIDLAND MOTORCYCLE CENTRE, 30 - 40 Campbell Street, NN1 3DT.	01604 37551
Nottingham	BIG ROCK HARLEY-DAVIDSON, Church Street, Stapleford, NG9 8DA.	0115 949 9800
	CENTRAL SCOOTERS, 303 - 321 Main Street, Bulwell, NG6 8E7.	0115 927 1234
	D C MOTORCYCLES, 35 Annersley Road, Hucknall, NG15 7AD.	0115 953 2104
	PIDCOCK MOTORCYCLES LTD, 701 Woodborough Road, Mapperley, NG3 5QG.	0115 9692200
Nuneaton	ALF ENGLAND (BEDWORTH) LTD, 65 Leicester Road, Bedworth, CV12 8AH.	01203 312184
	DIAMOND MOTOR CYCLES, Unit A5 Greenford Court, Veasey Close, Attenborough Fields, CV11 6RT.	01203 341382
Oxford	FAULKNER & SON LTD, 165-167 Botley Road, OX2 0PB.	01865 250147/8
	GEORGE WHITE SUPERBIKE CENTRE, 379 Cowley Road, OX4 2BS.	01865 773333

CENTRAL MIDLANDS continued

Location	Dealer	Phone	Yamaha	Triumph	Suzuki	Piaggio	Peugeot	MV-Agusta	M-Guzzi	Laverda	Kawasaki	Kymco	Honda	Harley	Gilera	Ducati	Derbi	CCM	Cagiva	Buell	BMW	Benelli	Aprilia
Oxford	HUGHENDEN M 40, Milton Common, OX9 2NU	01844 279701		•																			
	OXFORD MOTORCYCLE ENGINEERS LTD, 10 Hythe Bridge Street, OX1 2EW.	01865 250570				•															•		
Pinxton	DETROIT SOLAR, 25 Lambcroft Road.	01773 860030			•																		
Redditch	KNOTTS OF REDDITCH, 189 Evesham Road, Headless Cross, B97 5EN.	01527 404391			•								•										
Rednal	CLARKS, 472 Lickey Road.	0121 453 3117																					
Retford	RETFORD MOTORCYCLES, 4 Bridge Mews.	01777 708828					•										•						
Ross on Wye	LUCAS MOTORCYCLES, 34 Brookend Street, HR9 7EE.	01989 563261					•																
Rugby	NIGHTINGALES LTD, 58-60 Lawford Road, CV21 2EA.	01788 573257					•						•										
Saffron Walden	F C MOORE, Jet Garage, Thaxted Road.	01799 508003															•						
Shrewsbury	INTASPEED CARS, New Street Garage, Copthorne Road, SY3 8NW.	01743 232168					•						•										
	PETE JONES MOTORCYCLES, Coleham Road, SY3 7BJ.	01743 236529	•																				
	SHREWSBURY HONDA CENTRE LTD, Harlescott Lane, SY1 3AD.	01743 440770											•										
Silverstone	BAINES RACING, Unit 34, Silverstone Circuit, N12 8TN.	01327 858916																	•				
Solihull	DORRIDGE CYCLES, 488 Station Road, Dorridge, B93 8HP.	01564 779996										•	•										
St Albans	J D THOMPSON MOTORS LTD, 260-264 Hatfield Road, AL1 4UN.	01432 272341					•																
St. Albans	KINSBOURNE CARS, 26-32 High Street, Sandridge, AL4 9DA.	01727 855866					•								•								
St. Neots	ST. NEOTS MOTORCYCLE CO. LIMITED, 29-39 St. Marys Street, Eynsbury, PE19 2TA.	01480 212024											•										•
Stafford	C.G. CHELL MOTORCYCLES, 25-27 Marston Road, ST16 3BS.	01785 242356											•			•							
	WALTON'S OF STAFFORD LTD, Walton on the Hill, ST17 0JX.	01785 661293											•				•					•	
Stamford	MOTOMOVE, 36A Broad Street, PE9 1PJ.	01780 763232											•										
Stanstead Abbotts	D.C. BUTLER MOTORCYCLES, 8 High Street, SG12 8AB.	01920 870566										•	•										
Stevenage	TONY GRANT MOTORCYCLES, 25 Orchard Road, SG1 3HE.	01438 315562											•										
Stoke on Trent	FOWLERS MOTORCYCLES, 81- 83 Stoke Road, Shelton, ST4 2QH.	01782 415768	•		•		•						•										
	FRED HOLDCROFT LTD, 95-97 Upper Normacot Road, Longton, ST3 4QG.	01782 319123		•								•				•							
Stoke-On-Trent	FOWLERS HONDA, 243-245 City Road, Fenton, ST4 2PX.	01782 847245											•										
Stoke-on-Trent	GREENS OF LONGTON, Bridgewood Street, Longton, ST3 1HW.	01782 319932	•		•						•												
Stratford on Avon	YARNOLDS, Birmingham Road, CV37 0HR.	01789 414866					•								•								
Stratford-U-Avon	KNOTTS OF STRATFORD LIMITED, 15 Western Road, CV37 0AH.	01789 205149											•										
Stroud	BMW MOTO, London Road, GL5 2DA.	01453 762743																			•		
	ROADRUNNER MOTORCYCLES, 223 Bath Road, GL5 3TA.	01453 757942																					•
Studley	D. C. EDGINTON, 109 Alcester Road, CV34 6RH.	01926 740010					•																
Sutton Coldfield	SUTTON MOTORCYCLES, 49 Boldmere Road, B73 5UY.	0121 354 6901	•	•	•								•										
Telford	AUTOMOTIVE COMPONENTS LTD, Holyhead Road, Ketley, TF1 4DY.	01952 610371				•	•																
	WYLIE & HOLLAND MOTORCYCLES, 146 Watling Road, Wellington, TF1 2NH.	01952 248868		•									•										
Walsall	EXPLORER MOTORCYCLES, 114 Wolverhampton Road, WS2 8PR.	01922 636633	•		•	•						•	•										
	MOTORCYCLE MART, 12 Ablewell Street, WS1 2EQ.	01922 23363			•																		
Watford Gap	BROADLANE LEISURE, Toll House, A5 Watling Street, NN6 7YL.	01327 703371		•			•						•										

Wednesbury	ADAM JAMES PERFORMANCE CARS LTD., 75 Bridge Street, WS10 0AH.	0121 556 0100
Wellesbourne	BRIDGE GARAGE, 7 Bridge Street, CY35 9QP.	01789 840 328
Wellingborough	ANCHOR KAWASAKI CENTRE, 99 Wellington Road, Finedon.	01933 682234
	JOHN LEE MOTORCYCLES, 8 Market Sq, Higham Ferrers, NN9 8BP.	01933 312827
Welwyn Garden City	DUCATI LONDON LTD, 57 Great North Road, Lemsford, AL8 7TZ.	0707 378210
Wem	TONY MOSS MOTORCYCLES, 56 Aston Street, SY4 5AU.	01939 232223
West Bromwich	BOB JOYNER & SON, 361 High Street, B70 9QJ.	0121 553 2239
Wolverhampton	CHAPEL-ASH HARLEY-DAVIDSON, WV3 0UF.	01902 371600
	GEO. DUGMORE LTD, 247 Bilston Road, WV2 2JW.	01902 452313
	HIGHWAY MOTORCYCLES, Moseley Street off Stafford Road, WV10 6HL.	01902 773608
	SCOOTER COMMUTER, C/O Castlecroft Garage, Finchfield Hill, WV3 9EN.	01902 763030
	WOODS OF WEDNESFIELD LTD, 21 Rookery St., Wednesfield, WV11 1UN.	01902 731390
Worcester	CHAPMAN-TYRRELL RACING (EVESHAM), 25 Worcester Road, Evesham, WR11 4JU.	01386 40951
	JIM STREFFORD GARAGE, Gregory's Mill Street, WR3 8AR.	01905 23532
	MOTEX, Shire Business Park, Warndon, WR4 9FD.	01905 756683
	PHIL'S MOTORCYCLES, 14b Lowesmoor Trading Estate WR1 2SF.	01905 21616
	RP MORTIMER LTD, Four Pools Road, Evesham. (Opening March 2000)	01905 641069
	SKELLERNS MOTORCYCLES, 52 Sidbury, WR1 2JA.	01905 20580

EAST ANGLIA

Basildon	CHUCK CUSTOMISED (NELSON & FORD), 90 Whitmore Way, SS14 3JT.	01268 521822
	CHUCKS MOTORCYCLES, 90 Whitmore Way, SS14 3JT.	01268 521822
Beccles	L C GREEN & SON LTD, Pedders Lane, NR34 9UE.	01502 712370
Borehamwood	LEE RANKIN MOTORCYCLES, 13 Shenley Road, WD6 1AD.	0181 953 3404
Braintree	JOHN PEASE MOTORCYCLES, 37-43 Railway Street, CM7 3JD.	01376 321819
Brandon	BRECKLAND GARAGES LTD, Weeting.	01842 810 387
Brentwood	BRENTWOOD CYCLE CO. LTD, 5 Crown Street, CM14 4BA.	01277 212423
Bury St Edmonds	FASTLANE MOTORCYCLES, 1 Out Northgate.	01284 760916
Bury St. Edmunds	C. J. BOWERS & SON LIMITED, 11-13 Risbygate Street, IP33 3AA.	01284 705726
Cambridge	GRAHAM JENKINS MOTORCYCLES, 29 Cromwell Road, CB1 3EB.	01223 243074
	H DRAKE, 56-60 Hills Road, CB2 1LA.	01223 363468
	HALLENS MOTORCYCLES LIMITED, The Maltings, 41 High Street, Chesterton, CB4 1NQ.	01223 356225
	M & P ACCESSSORIES LTD, 184 Histon Road, CB4 3JS.	01223 311611
Chelmsford	BITS & PIECES, 45 Baddow Road, CM2 0DD.	01245 351196
	CANNON MOTORCYCLES, Unit Three Kingsdale Industrial Estate, REgina ROad.	01245 496444
	HADLERS GARAGE LTD, 198-200 Baddow Road, CM2 9QP.	01245 354844
	JOHN PEASE MOTORCYCLES, 91 Wood Street, CM2 8BH.	01245 264350
	NEWCOMBE BROTHER'S MOTORCYCLES, New Street, CM1 1PP.	01245 352635
Clacton on Sea	MANLEYS MOTORCYCLES, 6 Ford Road, CO15 3DS.	01255 421528
Colchester	G. H. MOTORCYCLES, 23 Barrack Street, CO1 2LL.	01206 793605
	KENDALL & PITT, 36-42 Barrack Street, CO1 2LR.	01206 794849

EAST ANGLIA continued

Location	Dealer	Phone	Aprilia	Benelli	BMW	Buell	Cagiva	CCM	Derbi	Ducati	Gilera	Harley	Honda	Kymco	Kawasaki	Laverda	M-Guzzi	MV Agusta	Peugeot	Piaggio	Suzuki	Triumph	Yamaha
Colchester	MOTORCYCLES UK, 5a Military Road.	01206 545277	•						•				•										
	REDLINE HONDA, 40 Nayland Road, CO4 5EN.	01206 842226	•												•								
	RON PARKINSON MOTORCYCLES, 35 London Road, Marks Tey, CO5 1DZ.	01206 21467																	•				
	SUPPLYMOTORS LTD., 35-37 London Road, Marks Tey, CO6 1DZ.	01206 210467																					
Colchester	T. K. COPE MOTORCYCLES, 38 Military Road, CO1 2AJ.	01206 574765											•										
Dagenham	CASTLE SPORTS LTD, 290-292 Heathway, RM10 8LU	0181 592 1066								•													
	LEN WADE MOTORCYCLES, 448 Beacontree Avenue, RM8 3UB.	0181 590 2761																					
Dereham	THE CONTAINER COMPANY LTD, 12-14 Bertie Ward Way, Rush's Green Industrial Estate.	01362 698147							•														
Diss	MIKE BAVIN MOTORCYCLES, 101 Victoria Road, IP22 3JG.	01379 642631							•														
	PAT LEWIS & SON LTD, Rose Lane Garage, Rose Lane, Palgrave, IP22 1AP.	01379 643745													•								
Downham Market	DENVER GARAGE, 1 Sluice Road, Denver, PE38 0DY.	01366 386510									•					•	•	•	•				
Ely	PRIORY GARAGE, Church Street, Isleham.	01638 780625																					
Felixstowe	THE FELIXSTOWE MOTORCYCLE CENTRE, 20 Bridge Road, IP11 7SL.	01394 672005											•							•			
Grays	CHADWELL MOTORCYCLES, 101 River View Road, Chadwell St. Mary's, RM16 4BD.	01375 842601						•															
	GRAYS MOTORCYCLE CENTRE LTD, 63 Southend Road, RM17 5NL.	01375 370066																					
	SOUTH ESSEX MOTORCYCLES, 15-17 Southend Road, RM17 5NH.	01375 375653							•														
Great Dunmow	ONGAR MOTORCYCLES, Unit 1 Oak Industrial Park, Chelmsford Road, CM6 1XN.	01371 875252																	•				
	SKIDROW, Unit 9, Zone D, Chelmsford Road Industrial Estate, CM6 1XG.	01371 879774																					
Harleston	P.F.K. LING LTD, 22 Redenhall Road, IP20 9ER.	01379 852405											•						•				
Harwich	FERRY MOTORS (HARWICH) LTD., 66 West Street, CO12 3DB.	01255 421528																					
Haverhill	G. J. MOTORCYCLES, Unit 8 Spring Rise, Falconer Road, CB9 7XU.	01440 708700																		•			
Hoddesdon	GLR, Unit 1, Essex Road, EN11 0AT.	01992 471154																					
Huntington	A & D VERITY MOTORCYCLES, 7 East Street, St Ives.	01480 463637							•														
Ipswich	DAVEY BROS. MOTORCYCLES LTD, 98 Alan Road, IP3 8EZ.	01473 254488											•										
	LEGEND MOTORCYCLES, Washbank Service Station, Old London Road, Copdock, IP3 3LA.	01473 730282									•												
	ORWELL MOTORCYCLES LIMITED, Barrack Corner, IP1 2NB.	01473 257401											•										
	P.F.K. LING LTD, 713 Foxhall Road, IP4 5TH.	01473 272289																	•				
	REVETT'S LTD, 53 Norwich Road, IP1 2ER.	01473 253726																			•		•
King's Lynn	EDEN MOTORCYCLES, 123 Wootton Road, PE30 4DJ.	01553 679 070													•					•		•	•
	SWAN ST. MOTORS LTD, Scania Way, PE30 4LP.	01553 772644																					
	THE TWO WHEEL CENTRE (KINGS LYNN), 102/103 London Road, Setchey, PE30 5ES.	01553 772116																			•		•
Leigh-on-Sea	ALPHA MOTORCYCLES, 944-946 London Road, SS9 3NF.	01702 476260																	•	•			
	BIKEWISE MOTORCYCLES, 1339 London Road, SSG 2AB.	01702 710 123																		•			•
	JOHN E. VINES LTD, 39 Elm Road, SS9 1SW.	01702 472034												•									•
	The CAR COMPANY, 1763 London Road, SS9 2ST.	01702 480325																		•			•
Lowestoft	A R MOTORCYCLES, 79 St. Peters Street, NR32 1QE.	01502 516055													•						•		
	BAYCOVER PERFORMANCE CARS & MOTORCYCLES, 25a Wapload Road.	01502 583352																			•	•	•

	P.F.K. LING LTD, 136 St. Peters Street, NR32 1UD.	01502 573758
Newmarket	BLACK BEAR, Black Bear Lane, CB8 0JT.	01638 664455
Newton Flotman	SEASTAR SUPERBIKES, The Garage, Ipswich Road, NR15 1PN.	01508 471919
Norwich	C.J. BALL & SON, Yarmouth Road, Hales, NR14 6SP.	01508 548681/2
	LIND LTD, 120 Ber Street.	01603 620222
	MOONRAKER MOTORCYCLES, 125-129 Oak Street, NR3 3BP.	01603 623601
	R. O. CLARK LIMITED, 93-101 Ber Street, NR1 3EY.	01603 628805
	TINKLERS (MOTORCYCLES) LTD, 182-190 Northumberland Street, NR2 4EE.	01603 627786
Peterborough	BALDERSTON MOTORCYCLES, 260 Lincoln Road, Millfield, PE1 2PF.	01733 312311
	BALDERSTONE, 339 Lincoln Road.	01733 565470
	BERNARD'S MOTORCYCLES, 27 Lincoln Road, PE7 2RH.	01733 561062
	I D LEISURE, Unit B C Mancetter Square, Lincoln Road.	01733 579555
	PETERBOROUGH HONDA CENTRE, 27 Lincoln Road, PE1 2RH.	01733 561062
	PETERBOROUGH KAWASAKI, 740 Lincoln Road.	01733 341003
	RICHARD MARSON MOTORCYCLES, 25 Market Street, Whittlesey.	01733 203519
Royston	RIGHT TRACK, Bridge Garage A10, Shepreth, SG8 6RA.	01763 262 112
Southend	KEGRA RACING, 91 Prince Avenue, SS2 6RL.	01702 331686
Southend on Sea	BELLE VUE MOTORS, 460 Southchurch Road, SS1 2QA.	01702 464945
Spalding	BROADGATE SCOOTER CENTRE, Swapcoat Lane, Long Sutton, PE12 9HD.	01406 364 474
	C. H. BIGGADIKE, 23-27 Westlodge Street, PE11 2AF.	01775 723037
Stanford-Le-Hope	B WYBROW MOTORCYCLES LTD, 26 Corringham Road, SS17 0AH.	01375 672823/53
Stowmarket	MOTORCYCLES TECHNICS, Unit 18 Tomo Business Park, Creeting Road, IP14 5AY.	01449 775775
Thetford	MACRO'S MOTORCYCLE SALES, 711 Castle Street, IP24 2DL.	01842 762848
	P.F.K. LING LTD, 90-94 High Street, Watton, IP25 6AH.	01953 881285
Westcliff	COSTINS LTD, 233-237 London Road, SS0 7BP.	01702 242215
Wisbech	GILDO'S MOTORCYCLE CENTRE, Weasenham Lane.	01945 474315
Witham	BRIDGE STREET GARAGE, 30 / 38 Bridge Street.	01376 513302
Wyndmondham	CHRIS CLARKE MOTORCYCLES, 36 Norwich Road, NR18 0NS.	01953 605120

NORTH MIDLANDS

Beeston	NOTTINGHAM POWERSPORTS, 216 Queens Road, NG9 2DG.	0115 967 7369
Boston	LAUNCHBURY MOTORCYCLES, H Launchbury & Son, Pump Square.	01205 363820
	NOEL CRAFT CYCLES, Mountain Tames House, Nelson Way, PE21 8TS.	01205 311888
	R. A. WILSON MOTORCYCLES, 200 London Road, P21 7HH.	01205 356070
Burton on Trent	MELBOURNE MOTORCYCLES, 243 Horninglow Road, DE14 2PZ.	01283 536874
Chester	BILL SMITH MOTORS LTD, 30/36 Tarvin Road, Boughton, CH3 5DH.	01244 323845
	CHESTER HONDA CENTRE, 11-11A Liverpool Road, CH2 1AA.	01244 378365
	SCOOTER SCENE, 43 St. James Street, CH1 3EY.	01244 348527
Chesterfield	CHESTERFIELD MOTORCYCLE CENTRE, Top Road, Calow, S44 5AE.	01246 555900
	CLAY CROSS POWERSPORTS LTD, Derwent Buildings, High Street, Clay Cross, S45 9DP.	01246 250128
Crewe	BLUE BELL, Fourth Avenue, Weston Road.	01270 212525

NORTH MIDLANDS continued

Town	Dealer	Phone	Aprilia	Benelli	BMW	Buell	Cagiva	CCM	Derbi	Ducati	Gilera	Harley	Honda	Kymco	Kawasaki	Laverda	M-Guzzi	MV Agusta	Peugeot	Piaggio	Suzuki	Triumph	Yamaha
Crewe	D. H. GROCOTT, 613 Crewe Road, Wistaston, CW2 6PR.	01270 664111																	•				
Derby	BOB MINION LTD, 156-160 London Road, DE1 2ST.	01332 342064											•						•	•			
	SMALLEY CROSS SCOOTER CENTRE, Smalley Cross Road, Morley, DE7 6QG.	01332 881882																				•	
	TOP MARQUES, 247 Chellaston Road, Shelton Lock.	01332 703 007							•										•				
Eccles	CLAYBANK MOTOR COMPANY, 718 Liverpool Road, Peel Green, M30 7LW.	0161 788 0471									•								•	•			
	MONTON MOTORCYCLES, 159 Monton Road, Monton, M30 9GS.	0161 789 3774	•																•				
Horncastle	J. T. FRISKNEY LTD, 17-29 West Street, LN9 5JE.	01507 523233	•																•				
Ilkeston	SPEEDLINE MOTORCYCLES, 107 Park Road, DE7 5DN.	0115 932 4528							•		•								•	•	•		
Kirby in Ashfield	B & S MOTORCYCLES, 19a Urban Road, NG17 8AH.	01623 758601									•								•				
Leicester	MARCOL, 52 Fosse Road North, LE3 5EQ.	0116 2623554	•	•				•	•	•													
	WINDY CORNER, 8 Moat Way, Barwell, LE9 8EY.	01455 842922															•		•			•	
Mansfield W/hse	TWO WHEEL (PETER SCOTT), Anvil Garage, Warsop Road, NG19 9LF.	01623 627600																	•	•			
Market Harborough	HARBOROUGH BIKE CENTRE, 26 St. Mary's Road, LE16 7DU.	01858 466163									•												
Matlock	STANLEY FEARN & SON, 19 Bakewell Road, DE4 3AU.	01629 582089																	•				
Newark	PRATT & GELSTHORPE, Bolderton Gate, NG24 1UF.	01636 673888								•													
Newark-on-Trent	NORTH NOTTS MOTOR CO, 5 Farndon Road, GG24 4SF.	01636 704 131	•																				
Northwich	NORTHWICH MOTORCYCLES LTD, 129-133 Witton Street, CW9 5DY.	01606 42720											•										
	SCOOT 'N' COMMUTE, 263-265 Manchester Road, CW9 7NE.	01606 350251																		•			
Nottingham	FOWLERS MOTORCYCLES, Daybrook Square, Mansfield Road, Arnold, NG5 6AA.	0115 926 7720							•		•								•	•			
	MARCOL, 17 Huntingdon Street, NG3 1JH.	0115 950 7912	•						•										•	•			
	ROY PIDOCK MOTORCYCLES LTD, Fields Farm Road, Long Eaton.	0115 9462233																			•		•
Peterborough	CARNELL MOTORCYCLES LTD, High Street, Eye, PE6 7UR.	01733 223444							•														
Pontefract	PETER SMITH, Unit 2, North Baily Gate, WF8 1ES.	01977 701064																	•				
Ripley	ROY JERVIS & CO. LTD, 8-10 Chapel Street, DE5 3DL.	01773 743358							•												•		
Rugeley	MOTOR COMPONENTS (UTTOXETER) LTD, Sheepfair, WS25 2AT.	01889 586278																					
Skegness	A. J. MOTORCYCLES, T/A Slipstream, 117 Roman Bank.	01754 767879																	•				
	SLIPSTREAM MOTORCYCLES, 117 Roman Bank, PE25 2SW.	01754 760925																	•	•			
Southport	C & D CARS, 174 Liverpool Road, Birkdale, PR8 4NY.	01704 565953																					
	SOUTHPORT SUPERBIKES, 80-90 Eastbank Street.	01704 536192			•																		
Stapleford	MIDLAND SCOOTER CENTRE, Pasture Road, NG9 8GG.	0115 939 2713									•								•	•			
Stoke-On-Trent	C.R. MOTORCYCLES, 89 Tape Street, Cheadle, ST10 1ER.	01538 752145																					
Stoke-on-Trent	NORMAN & BIRCH LIMITED, 25-27 Marsh Street South, Hanley, ST1 1JA.	01782 202467																	•	•			
Tamworth	MOTORCYCLE CITY (SALES) LTD, 361 Watling Street, Wilnecote, B77 5AD.	01827 280 905		•												•					•	•	
Whitchurch	BIKE SPARES MOTORCYCLES, Bridgewater Garage, Bridgewater Street.	01948 667976		•												•					•	•	
	WHARF MOTORCYCLES DEPOT, 36 Greenend, SY13 1AA.	01948 662151																	•				
Worksop	BIKE DEPOT, 10a Carlton Road, S80 1PH.	01909 482614																					
	UNIQUE AUTOS, 26 Gateford Road.	01909 484448																			•	•	

NORTH OF ENGLAND

Town	Dealer	Phone	1	2	3	4	5	6	7	8	9	10	11	12	13
Accrington	GEORGE CLARKE & SON MOTORCYCLES LTD, Peel Garage, Whalley Road, BB5 1AR.	01254 385025													
	KEITH DIXON MOTORCYCLES, 392-396 Blackburn Rd, BB5 1SA.	01254 231221		•						•					
	PHILIP YOULES MOTORCYCLES, Belgarth Road, BB5 6AH.	01254 234051				•									
	RIBBLE VALLEY MOTORCYCLES, 54 Whalley Road, BB7 1EE.	01200 425093									•				
Altrincham	ALEXANDERS, 3A Wicker Lane, Hale Barns, WA15 0HG.	0161 980 1933					•								
	MORETONS OF ALTRINCHAM LTD, 74 Manchester Road, WA14 4PJ.	0161 928 2639		•					•						
Ashton-under-Lyne	CLAREMONT MOTORCYCLES LIMITED, 275-277 Stamford Street, OL6 7QU.	0161 303418			•				•						
	L M MOTORCYCLES LTD, 145 Stamford Street.	0161 344 5606													
Barnsley	B & B MOTORCYCLES, 155 Midland Road, Royston, S70 1TL.	01226 72500			•				•						
	DIRT WORLD, 18 Fallbank Industrial Estate, Dodworth, S75 3LS.	01226 244770											•		
	GEORGE WARD & CO., 42 Doncaster Road, S70 1TL.	01226 203982				•									
	RON DALEY LTD, 46 - 52 Doncaster Road, S70 1TL.	01226 203377					•		•						
Barrow-in-Furness	CROOKS SUZUKI LIMITED, 36-44 Crellin Street, LA14 1DY.	01229 822342		•						•					
	JOHN STEWART MOTORCYCLES LTD, Bridgegate Garage, Flass Lane, LA13 0BZ.	01229 824757						•	•						
	JOHN WREN MOTORCYCLE SERVICES, 162 Rawlinson Street, LA14 1DQ.	01229 836038									•				
Batley	EXCEL SCOOTERS, Kickstart (UK), Leeds Road, Birstall, WF17 0EW.	01924 475242													
	KAWASAKI AUTORAMA, Bradford Road.	01924 461112					•								
	PADGETTS (BATLEY) LIMITED, 234 Bradford Road, WF17 5JO.	01924 478491			•				•						
Bedale	GEORGE DAWKINS & SON, Bridge Garage, 36 Emgate, DL8 1AL.	01677 422491							•					•	
Bedlington	IAN BELL MOTORCYCLES LTD, 62 Rothesay Terrace, NE22 5PT.	01670 822311										•			
Berwick U Tweed	BORDER BIKES, 2 Fowl Ford, TD15 1HQ.	01289 305768					•								
	T I MOTORCYCLES, Albert Hall, West Street Corner, Spittal, TD15 1SB.	01289 331603						•	•						
Birkenhead	MARRIOTT MOTORCYCLES, 72-76 Oxton Road, L41 2TW.	0151 653 8704			•			•		•					
Bishop Auckland	SOUTH DURHAM, 59 North Bondgate.	01388 601221													
Blackpool	JOHN HALL & SON (BLACKPOOL), 108 Devonshire Road, FY3 8AW.	01253 300478							•						•
	STEWART LONGTON CARAVANS, 228 Common Edge Road, FY4 5DH.	01253 763 133						•	•						
	SAM TAYLOR, 5/21 Vicarage Lane, FY4 4EF.	01253 868018													
	VIN DUCKETT MOTORCYCLE CENTRE, Archersholme Lane East, Cleveleys, FY5 3QY.	01253 826142								•					
Blyth	FERGUSONS MOTOR & CYCLES, 16 Union Street, NE24 2DX.	01670 352218						•							
Bolton	DAISY HILL DIY, 477 leigh Road, Westhaughton, BL5 2JH.	01942 813145													
	DOUG HACKING MOTORCYCLES, Ivy Garage, Ivy Road, BL1 6DJ.	01204 491511							•						
	E S B MOTORCYCLES, 3 Marsden Road, BL1 4AA.	01204 535443							•						
	FULL THROTTLE, Cleggs Buildings, Back Chorley Street.	01204 396524													
	LYTHGOE MOTORS, Thynne Street, BL3 6BD.	01204 388 000						•							
	PARK MOTORCYCLE COMPANY, 190 Chorley New Road, Horwich, BL6 5NP.	01204 699377										•			
Bowness-on-Windermere	S B MOTORS, Unit 3 Stopes Garage, Stopes Road, Little Lever, BL3 1NP.	01204 861941	•						•						
	SCOOTERAMA, Lake Road, Bowness, LA23 3AJ.	01539 444 994	•												
Bradford	BRADFORD M/C CENTRE LTD, 216-222 Manningham Lane, BD8 7BZ.	01274 734248							•						

NORTH OF ENGLAND continued

Location	Dealer	Aprilia	Benelli	BMW	Buell	Cagiva	CCM	Derbi	Ducati	Gilera	Harley	Honda	Kymco	Kawasaki	Laverda	M-Guzzi	MV Agusta	Peugeot	Piaggio	Suzuki	Triumph	Yamaha	Phone
Bradford	J.K. HIRST LTD, 436 Thornton Road, BD8 9BS.									●									●				01274 480388
	POWERSPORT MOTORCYCLE CENTRE, 221 Sunbridge Road, BD1 2HB.																			●			01274 727496
	ST. ENOCH'S GARAGE, St Enoch's Road, Wibsey, BD6 3BU.																						01274 678 272
	THE CARNATION LTD, Carnation House, Mill Lane, BD5 0HG.																						01274 202020
Bramley	ACORN OF BRAMLEY LTD, The Old Fire Station, German Road, Off Campbell Road.																	●					01256 882322
Bridlington	MCS, Hamilton Road, YO15 3HP.							●															01262 675336
	RO-JO MOTORCYCLES, 48 St. Johns Avenue, YO16 4NL.							●				●											01262 600321/2
Broughton-in-Frns	NIGEL BIRKETT MOTORCYCLES, The Old Wood Yard, Foxfield Road.																	●					01229 716806
Bury	ITALSPORT, Unit 1, Yanwood Street, Bury, BL9 7AU.											●						●					0161 797 6124
Carlisle	ALAN REAY CAR SALES LTD, Currock Road, CA2 5RE.												●										01228 590000
	JACK HORSEMAN MOTORCYCLES, 39 London Road, CA1 2JZ.							●				●											01228 545333
	JOHN STEWART MOTORCYCLES LTD, 3 Citadel Parade, Viaduct Estate, CA2 5BN.								●														01228 596826
	K C SUPERBIKES, 30-32 Bridge Street, Caldewgate, CA2 5SX.																	●					01228 525024
	KAWASAKI CENTRE, 30 Bridge Street.													●									01288 525024
Carnforth	BIKE SPARES, Lower North Raod, LA5 9LJ					●																	01524 720727
	C. A. STEPHENSON MOTORCYCLES, Melling Mill, Melling, LA6 2RA.							●															01524 221188
Castleford	CASTLE MOTORCYCLES, 3-7 Bridge St, WF10 1JL.											●						●					01977 553523
Choppington	LIDDELLS OF STAKEFORD LTD, Milburn Terrace, Stakeford, NE62 5UN.									●			●										01670 523343
Chorley	CHORLEY YAMAHA CENTRE, Eaves Lane, PR6 0TB.																					●	01257 230300
	STEWART LONGTON CARAVANS, Friday Street, PR6 0AH.																						01257 279 921
	YARROW BRIDGE GARAGE, Bolton Road, PR7 4AB.							●															01257 263186
Chorlton	A. P. HYNES & CO, 245 Barlow Moor Road, M21 7DL.											●		●				●		●			0161 861 9390
Clifton	YORK SUZUKI CENTRE, 179-181 Burton Stone Lane, YO3 6DG.																			●	●		01904 625404
Colne	JUMBOSTATE LTD, North Valley Road Garage, North Valley Road, BB8 9LJ							●															01282 863896
Darlington	THE SCOOTER PLACE, Haughton Road Garage, 215 Haughton Road, DL1 2LD.									●		●	●					●	●				01325 465045
	WHITE BROS (DARLINGTON) LTD, Corporation Road, DL3 6AE.											●						●		●			01325 483121
Darwen	VIN CUNNINGHAM MOTORCYCLES, 51 Blackburn Road, BB3 1EJ.											●						●			●		01254 702032
Dewsbury	MANNING MOTORCYCLES, Mill Street West.																	●					01924 460669
Doncaster	CARNELL MOTORCYCLES LTD, The Showroom Marshgate Industrial Estate, Marshgate, DN5 8AF.									●						●	●	●	●		●		01302 327722
	CUSWORTH DISTRIBUTORS LTD, Princegate, DN1 3EN.																	●					01302 814444
	CUSWORTHS, 8 Wood Street, DN1 5EN.							●	●										●				01302 814444
	PREMIER BIKES LIMITED, Premier House, Selby Road, Askerny.							●															01302 703100
Doncater	TEAM ROBERTS LTD, 30 Doncater Road, Cornisborough, DN12 4ET.											●						●		●		●	01709 860001
Durham	M&S MOTORCYCLES LTD, Finchale Road, Newton Hall, DH1 5HL.											●						●		●			0191 384 1582
East Heslerton	RAYSPEED LTD, Five Acres, YO17 8BN.																	●					01944 710693
Ellesmere Port	REBEKA CARS DIRECT, Phoenix House, Rossmore Road East, L65 3BR.																	●		●	●	●	0151 355 5535
Farnworth	CONCORDE MOTOR CYCLES, Frederick Street, BL4 9AL.																		●				01204 573717

Fleetwood	RACEWAYS MOTORCYCLES, 190-192 Dock Street, FY7 6NU.	01253 872037
Goole	RICHWOOD GARAGE, 3 Rawcliffe Road, DN14 8JQ.	01405 720990
Grimsby	CARNELL MOTORCYCLES LTD, Victoria Street, DN31 1DJ.	01472 357573
	HARVEY'S, Grimsby Road, Laceby.	01472 276666
	JAMBUSTER, 11 Brighowgate, DN32 0Q9.	01472 354 402
	OAKLEIGH LEISURE, Laceby cross road.	01472 230212
	ROBSPEED MOTORCYCLES, 174-176 Cleethorpes Road, DN31 3HW.	01472 268714
	WHEELS (GRIMSBY) LTD T/A GEORGE PET, 13/15 Brighowgate, DN32 0QL.	01472 354402
Halifax	M J MOTOR CYCLES LTD, 169 Kings Cross Road, HX1 3LN.	01422 351 569
	NORTH DEAN GARAGE, Stainland Road, Greetland, HX4 8LS.	01422 379796
	RON LEE LTD, Keighley Road, Oxendon, HX3 5TJ.	01422 361 108
Harrogate	G.W. JOHNSON MOTORCYCLES, 5 Cheltenham Parade, HG1 1DD.	01423 569251
	H ACKLAM, 11 Bower Road, HG1 1BB.	01423 565125
	HARROGATE KAWASAKI, 6 Mayfield Grove.	01423 508823
	STAIANO MOTORCYCLES LIMITED, 8 Knaresborough Road, HG2 7DE.	01423 887985
	STARBECK MOTORCYCLES, 2a Camwal Road, Starback, HG1 4PT.	01423 889916
	WHEELS OF HARROGATE, 302 Skipton Road, HG1 3HE.	01423 504777
Heywood	WARWICKS MOTORCYCLES, 14 - 18 Rochdale Road East.	01706 620707
Heckmondwhike	FIRTH'S GARAGE, 158 Leeds Road, WF16 9BJ.	01924 472605
Hexham	A V TAYLOR LTD, Tyne Mills Industrial Estate, NE46 1XL.	0191 265 0028
Hornsea	APC (ASHTON PERFORMANCE CENTRE), Merehead Service Station, Southgate.	01964 537575
Huddersfield	G A EARNSHAWS, Huddersfield Superbikes, Manchester Road, HD1 3LE.	01484 421232
	LOCKWOOD ROAD MOTORCYCLES, 234 Lockwood Road, HD1 3TG.	
	TERRY SILVESTER MOTORCYCLES, Spring Lane Mills, Woodhead Road, Holmfirth, HD7 1PR.	01484 683665
Hull	BIKETECH MOTORCYCLE CENTRE, 453 Holderness Road, HU8 8JT.	01482 374400
	FIVEWAYS MOTORCYCLES, 17 Walton Street, HU3 6JB.	01482 355023
	MILES KINGSPORT LIMITED, 104 Whitham, HU9 1AT.	01482 323529
	RON STOREY MOTORCYCLES, 13 Hessle Road, HU3 2AA.	01482 323393
Hyde	ROAD & RACING, 71-73 Manchester Road, SK14 2BT.	0161 366 5167
Keighley	COLIN APPLEYARD MOTORCYCLES, Wellington Road, Worth Way, BD21 5AL.	01535 606311
Kendal	PPM SCOOTERS, 5-7 Lowther Street, LA9 4DH.	01539 737373
	SAPPHIRE MOTORCYCLES, Station Road, Staveley, LA8 9NB.	01539 821401
Lancaster	FRANK SHEPHERD MOTORCYCLES, 32 North Road.	01524 65627
	WALL & SAGAR LTD, 51 North Road, LA1 1NS.	01524 63817
Lanchester	RUSSELL CLOSE MOTORS, Whitbank Garage, DH7 0QH.	01207 520336
Leeds	CHISELSPED TUNING, Unit 6, Enterprise Estate, Barwick in Elmet, LS15 4EF.	01943 462 427
	COLIN APPLEYARD MOTORCYCLES, Unit 1 North Leeds Centre, 9 Roseville Road, LS8 5DR.	0113 248 5000
	DYRONS MOTORCYCLES, 410-412 York Road, LS9 9EE.	0113 249 9208
	EDDY WRIGHT FOR HARLEY-DAVIDSON, 217 Kirkstall Road, LS2 2AH.	0113 234 0717
	EDDY'S MOTORCYCLES, Wright's Auto Corner, Barwick Roundabout, York Road, LS14 6HR.	0113 232 6665
	K P MOTORCYCLES, 37 Compton Road, LS9 7BJ.	0113 235 1232

NORTH OF ENGLAND continued

Location	Dealer	Phone	Franchises (• = stocked)
Leeds	WOOSTERS MOTORCYCLES, York Road, Whinmoor, LS15 4NE.	0113 273 3556	Kymco, Honda, Derbi
Leigh	E.S.B. MOTORCYCLES, 5 Queen Street, WN7 4NQ.	01942 671822	Honda, Derbi
Liverpool	BRIDGE ROAD MOTORCYCLES, 37 Bridge Road, Blundellsands.	0151 924 2369	Peugeot, Suzuki, Kawasaki, Honda, Gilera, Derbi
	CARNELL MOTORCYCLES LTD, Sandhills Lane, Off Derby Road, L5 9XJ.	0151 955 6222	Aprilia
Liverpool	HOYLAKE CYCLES, 2 Market Street, Hoylake, CH47 2AE.	0151 632 1419	
	SCOOTER CENTRE, 452 Longmoor Lane, Aintree, L9 9BY.	0151 525 6733	
	THE SCOOTER CENTRE, 452 Longmoor Lane, L9 9BY.	0151 525 6733	Cagiva
Malton	AUSTINS MOTORCYCLES, 92 Commercial Street, YO17 9JQ.	01653 692473	
Manchester	B.J. WEST MOTORCYCLES LIMITED, 336-340 Deansgate, M3 4LY.	0161 834 1520	Piaggio, MV Agusta, Honda
	BAUR MILLET LTD, 325 Deangate, M3 4LQ.	0161 839 1000	
	CHORLTON SCOOTER CENTRE, 245 Barlow Moor Road, Chorlton, M21 7QL.	0161 861 9390	Peugeot, Suzuki, Kawasaki, Gilera, Derbi
	HUNTS MOTORCYCLES LTD, 255 Kingsway, M19 1AN.	0161 432 1303	Honda
	MOTO-TECHNIQUE, Arches 1&2, Millgate, Dantzic, M4 4BS.	0161 833 4136	Ducati
	MA MOTORCYCLE CITY (SALES) LTD, 620 Chester Road, M16 0HP	0161 737 6000	Suzuki, Honda, Ducati, Aprilia
Maryport	LONG & SMALL GARAGE, Flimby, CA15 8RP	01900 602742	
Mexborough	CRYSTAL DERBI, Wath Road.	01709 578186	
Middlesborough	W.M. ARMSTRONG LTD, 379-381 Linthorpe Road, TS5 6AE.	01642 818007	Peugeot
Nevilles Cross	NORTH EAST MOTORCYCLES, Darlington Road, DH1 4PE.	01913 869212	Kawasaki, Gilera
Newcastle u Tyne	F1 SPORT, South Sheilds.	0191 536 0011	Peugeot, Aprilia
	JUST HARLEYS, Thunder Alley, 3 Dinsdale Place, Warwick Street, NE2 1BD.	0191 232 7174	Harley, Buell
	KAWASAKI NEWCASTLE LTD, 195 Scotswood Road.	0191 272 3335	Kawasaki, Peugeot
	KEN'S MOTORCYCLES LIMITED, 246-250 Westgate Road, NE4 6AQ.	0191 232 1793	Suzuki, Piaggio, Kymco, Honda, Benelli
	M & S MOTORCYCLES LTD, 195 Westgate Road, NE4 6DN.	0191 261 0121	Piaggio, Gilera, Derbi, Benelli
	MOTECH SCOOTERS, 23a Sheilds Road, West Byker, NE6 1JN.	0191 265 9793	Ducati
	SCOOTER WORLD, 2 Sheilds Road, Byker, NE6 1DR.	0191 224 4224	Peugeot
Normanton	K & K SCOOTERS, 26 Altofts Road.	01924 220361	
	KB SCOOTERS, 26 Altofts Road, WF6 2AY.	01924 220361	
Oldham	HIGHBARN MOTORCYCLES, 177 Broadway, Chadderton, OL9 0JX.	0161 678 8990	Suzuki, Honda
	MOTOCROSS MOTORS, Primrose Bank, 27/31 Ashton Road, OL8 1JX.	0161 624 2313	
Ormskirk	BLACK'S BIKE SHOP 3 Ring Tail Place, L40 8JY.	01704 897 551	Peugeot, Honda
	ORMSKIRK MOTORCYCLE CENTRE, 22 Wigan Road, L39 2AU.	01695 572991	
Otley	KITCHINGS OF OTLEY Station Road, LS21 3HX.	01924 462427	Peugeot, Honda
Penrith	PENRITH MOTORCYCLES, Unit 9, Cowper Road, Gilwilly Industrial Estate, CA11 9BN.	01768 891300	Suzuki, Honda
Peterlee	DAVID SYKES SUPERBIKES, Cotsford Lane, Horden, SR8 4JJ.	0191 586 4589	Peugeot, Honda
Preston	BILL HEAD (PRESTON) LTD, Southgate, PR1 1NP.	01772 252066	Peugeot, Piaggio, Gilera
	FAST LINE M/CYCLES, 127 Church Street, PR1 3BT	01772 902600	Benelli
	NORTHWEST SUPERBIKES, 26 New Hall Lane, PR1 4DV.	01772 798882	

	SHORROCK MOTORCYCLES, 84-86 Leyland Road, Penworthan, PR1 9XS.	01772 744392
	SLINGER MOTORCYCLES LIMITED, Waterloo Garage, 40 Waterloo Road, PR2 1BQ.	01772 727213
	WILLIAM KELLETT & SONS LTD, Factory Lane Trading Esate, Penwortham, PR1 9TE.	01772 744544
Prudhoe	BEWICK MOTORCYCLES, Bank Top, Station Road, NE42 5PY.	01661 833913
Pudsey	RAY DELL MOTORCYCLES, 49 Chapeltown, LS28 7RZ.	0113 257 7256
Radcliffe	SPEEDWELL MOTORCYCLES, 75 Church Street, M26 2SX.	0161 723 4774
Redcar	PETITE & FRANCE MOTORCYCLES, The Motorcycle Centre, 93-101 Station Road, TS10 1RD.	01642 476927
Ripon	SUPA SCOOTERS, Ripon Business Park, Dallamires Lane, HG4 1TT.	01765 690590
Rochdale	ALL BIKES, 48 Milnrow Road, OL16 1UD.	01706 713680
	H ROBINSON & SONS LTD, Central Garage, Water Street, OL16 1UH.	01706 716666
	NEWHEY SCOOTERS, Unit 1 Newhey Garage, Huddersfield Road, OL16 3RU.	01706 290066
	P MERCHANT SCOOTER SERVICE, Church Buildings, Water Street, OL16 1UH.	01706 355339
Rossendale	ROSSENDALE KAWASAKI, 801 Burnley Road, Crawshawbooth, BB4 8BW.	01706 226910
Sale	JOHN BOLTON (AUTO SALES) LTD, 156 Cross Street, M33 1AQ.	0161 973 5688
	SALE YAMAHA CENTRE, 156 Cross Street, M33 1AQ.	0161 973 5688
Scarborough	ANDREWS OF SCARBOROUGH LTD, Roscoe Street, YO12 7BY.	01723 366083
	ANDY NOBLE, 5-7 Hoxton Road, YO12 7ST.	01723 367660
Scunthorpe	PRO BYKE, 149-153 Frodingham Road, DN15 7JR.	01724 844878
	SCOOTERTYME LTD, 212 Ashby High Street, DN16 2JR.	01724 844409
Settle	F. H. ELLIS, The West Yorkshire Garage, 47 Duke Street, BD24 9AL.	01729 822592
Sheffield	CHARLES FREEMAN M/CS LTD, 4-6 High Street, Eckington, S31 9DN.	01246 432258
	DRONFIELD MOTORCYCLE CENTRE, 132 Sheffield Road, Dronfield, S18 6GE.	01293 413300
	EMPIRE GARAGE, 148 Machon Bank, S7 1GR.	01246 410911
	HILLSBOROUGH APRILIA, 32 Penistone Road Industrial Estate, S6 2FL.	0142 855 580
	JACK WOODS MOTORCYCLES LTD, 369 Abbeydale Road.	0114 258 4200
	JEFF HALL (M/C) LTD, 130-142 Langsett Road, S6 2UB.	0142 333116
	JEFF HALL MOTORCYCLES, 130-142 Langsett Road, S6 2VG.	0114 233 3116
	MANHATTAN MOTORCYCLES, 643 London Road, Heeley, S6 2UB.	0114 258 2161
	RAINBOW MOTORCYCLES, Broad Oaks Garage, 160 Broad Oaks.	0114 244 1211
	SHEFFIELD SCOOTERS, 246 Moorfields, Shalesmoor, S3 8UH.	0114 275 2444
Shipley	ALLEN JEFFERIRES BMW, Otley Road.	01274 776077
	COBB & JAGGER MOTORCYCLES, 3-7 Saltaire Road, BD18 3HH.	01274 591017
	MOTORCYCLE CITY (SALES) LTD, 206 Saltaire Road, BD18 3JQ.	01274 771122
Skipton	PETER WATSON(SKIPTON)LTD, Otley Road, BD23 1EY.	01756 792911
South Shields	SCOT KEITH, Fowlers Street, NE33 1PF.	0191 455 4708
South Wirral	SCOOTERS DIRECT, Boathouse Lane, Parkgate.	0151 336 3965
St. Helens	JUST SCOOTERS, 7a Cooper Lane, Haydock, WA11 0JA.	01744 45295
	MILLIUM MOTOR CYCLE CENTRE, Aspinal Place WA9 5PE.	01744 755 333
Stockport	APRILLIA STOCKPORT CENTRE, 309 Manchester Road, Heaton Chapel, SK4 5EA.	0161 442 5805
	BLACKBROOK SCOOTER CENTRE, Weybrook Road, Wellington Road, M19 2QD.	0161 442 6466
	CARNELL MOTORCYCLES LTD. St Marys Way, Hempshaw Lane, SK1 4LL.	0161 429 5500

NORTH OF ENGLAND continued

Location	Dealer	Address	Phone	Aprilia	Benelli	BMW	Buell	Cagiva	CCM	Derbi	Ducati	Gilera	Harley	Honda	Kymco	Kawasaki	Laverda	M-Guzzi	MV Agusta	Peugeot	Piaggio	Suzuki	Triumph	Yamaha
Stockport	MOTOR CYCLE CENTRE	2 Carrington Road, SK1 2QE.	0161 480 3346	•	•					•		•								•				
	THE PEUGEOT SCOOTER CENTRE	116 Wellington Street, Churchgate, SK1 1YW.	0161 477 0001											•						•			•	
Stockton	W.J. TILLSTON LTD	49-50 Brunswick Street, TS18 1DU.	01642 611138												•									
Stockton	MILLENNIUM MOTORCYCLES	Mandale Road, Thornaby, TS17 6AW.	01642 612000																	•				
Sunderland	HARBOUR VIEW MOTORS	Dame Dorothy Street, Roker Seafront, SR6 0NL.	0191 567 3878			•																		
	MILL GARAGES LTD	Ryhope Road, Toll Bar.	0191 523 7373																					
	SUNDERLAND SCOOTERS	Pallion Road, SR4 6ND.	0191 514 1200							•		•												
Thirsk	DENNIS TEASDALE SCOOTERS	Water Coy, Norby.	01845 523310												•									
Wakefield	HARRY THOMAS LTD	Jaguar House, Calder Island Way, Denby Dale Road, WF2 7AW.	01924 381111											•						•				
	IAN KEMP SCOOTERS	5 Cross Lane, WF2 8DA.	01924 366386																					
	P&D AUTOS LTD	184 Leeds Road, Newtown Hill, WF1 2QA.	01924 372907																				•	
Warrington	BILL POPE (MOTORS) LIMITED	51-59 Winwick Road, WA2 7DG.	01925 634131	•	•																			
	FOWLERS MOTORCYCLES	240 Manchester Road, WA1 3BE.	01925 656628											•						•	•			
	REVOLUTION SCOOTERS	17 Kingsway North, WA1 3NU.	01925 828787																		•			
	WARRINGTON SCOOTERS	752 Knutsford Road, Letchford, WA4 1JS.	01925 414521																					
Whitehaven	CENTRAL MOTORCYCLES	Bus Station, New Road, CA28 6DL.	01946 599500																					
Widnes	SCOOT 'N' COMMUTE	Ditton Road, Off Ashley Road West, WA8 0PJ.	0151 420 5251					•																
Wigan	J.K. MOTORCYCLES	60 Hallgate, WN1 1HP.	01942 241889																					
	KIM	2a Toogood Lane, Wrightington, WN6 9PL.	0125 745 1656													•				•	•			
	RIVERWAY MOTORCYCLES	1a Westbridge Mews, WN1 1XN.	01942 242392																	•				
Wirral	TURNER SCOOTERS	23 Station Road, Little Sutton, L66 1NT.	0151 348 0900																	•				
	WALLASEY MOTORCYCLES	7 Martins Lane, Wallasey, L44 1BA.	0151 637 2225											•						•				
York	A1 MOTO SERVICE	73 Market Place, Market Weighton, YO4 3AN.	01430 873030					•																
	BARRIE ROBSON MOTORCYCLES	Unit 17, Auster Road, North Yorks Trading Estate, Clifton.	01904 691470											•										
	GREENSIDE GARAGE LTD	The Green, Acomb, YO2 5LL.	01904 798150												•					•				
	MILES KINGSPORT LTD	82-86 Holgate Road, YO2 4AB.	01904 655124	•						•						•				•				
	TRANSIT MOTORCYCLES	20 Toft Green, YO1 1JT.	01904 637169																	•	•			
	YORK YAMAHA CENTRE	Heworth Village Garage, YO3 0AP.	01904 424597																					•

SCOTLAND

Location	Dealer	Address	Phone	Aprilia	Benelli	BMW	Buell	Cagiva	CCM	Derbi	Ducati	Gilera	Harley	Honda	Kymco	Kawasaki	Laverda	M-Guzzi	MV Agusta	Peugeot	Piaggio	Suzuki	Triumph	Yamaha
Aberdeen	BROADFOLD GARAGE	Bridge of Don, AB23 8EE.	01224 826170		•									•										
	MCGOWAN MOTORCYCLES LTD	72 Hutcheon Street, AB25 3TB.	01224 638894							•						•				•				
	SCOTT SIMPSON MOTORCYCLES	Craigshaw Place, Tullos, AB12 3AH.	01224 878222			•															•	•	•	•
	SHIRLAWS MOTORCYCLES	92 Crown Street, AB1 2HU.	01224 584855								•			•						•				
Argyll	MILLFORD MOTORS	99 Mill Lane, Oban, PA34 4PL.	01631 566476	•		•				•				•						•	•		•	
Ayr	AYR MOTORCYCLE CENTRE	38 Waggon Road, KA8 8BA.	01292 286313													•					•	•	•	
	NORTH HARBOUR MOTORCYCLES	14-18 North Harbour Street, KA8 8AA.	01292 281933	•						•		•								•				•

SCOTLAND continued

Town	Dealer	Phone	Yamaha	Triumph	Suzuki	Piaggio	Peugeot	MV Agusta	M-Guzzi	Laverda	Kawasaki	Kymco	Honda	Harley	Gilera	Ducati	Derbi	CCM	Cagiva	Buell	BMW	Benelli	Aprilia
Ayr	SP MOTORCYCLES, 19 - 21 Green Street, KA8 8AD.	01292 289628	•			•							•										
Bathgate	JIM ALLAN MOTORCYCLES, 20 North Bridge St, EH48 4EU.	01324 6201111	•		•								•										
Bongate	BORDER CAR CLINIC, Oakvale, TD8 6DU.	01835 863181					•																
Coatbridge	BIKES AT SCOTCAST, 5 Palacecraig Street, Rosehall Industrial Estate, Shawhead, ML5 4NP.	01236 436112					•																
Cupar	CUPAR MOTORCYCLES, Water End Road, KY15 5HP.	01334 655707			•		•				•												
Dumfries	SCOTSPEED MOTORCYCLES LTD, 2-6 Nith Place, DG1 2PN.	01387 265050				•	•						•	•								•	•
Dundee	ALAN DUFFUS MOTORCYCLES, 304-308 Strathmore Avenue, DD3 6RX.	01382 817051	•		•												•					•	•
Dundee	ANDREW HART, 23 Milnbank Road, DD1 5QD.	01382 667281/2				•																	
Dundee	JOHN CLARK (TAYSIDE) LTD, Rutherford Roas, Dryburgh.	01382 815993		•																			
Dunfermline	DUNFERMLINE MOTORCYCLES, 161 Chalmers Street, KY12 8DG.	01383 732952															•						•
Edinburgh	ALAN DUFFUS MOTORCYCLES, 187 Dundee Street, EH11 1DH.	0131 622 6220			•						•				•				•			•	•
Edinburgh	ALVINS MOTORCYCLES, 9B Springfield Street, EH6 5EF.	0131 551039									•												
Edinburgh	CARRICK MOTORCYCLES, 62 Queen Charlotte Street, EH6 7ET.	0131 555 2575				•									•	•							
Edinburgh	EDINBURGH KAWASAKI, 195 Slateford Road, EH14 10A.	0131 443 913/15									•												
Edinburgh	J B SCOTT & SON LTD, Kingsknowe Garage, Lanark Road, EH14 2LR.	0131 443 2936											•										
Edinburgh	THE SCOOTER SHOP, 24 Rodney Street, EH7 4EA.	0131 566 2800				•	•																
Edinburgh	TWO WHEELS, 36 Peffermill Road, EH16 5LL.	0131 667 7305		•	•																		
Elgin	WILLIE YOUNG MOTORCYCLE SALES, 5 Parade Spur South, Pinefield Industrial Estate, IV30 3AL.	01343 540355			•							•	•										
Falkirk	JIM ALLAN MOTORCYCLES LIMITED, 208 Graham's Road, FK2 7BX.	01324 620111	•		•																		
Forfar	ARDUTHIE MOTORS LTD, Lockside Road, DD8 1BW.	01307 462676	•								•												
Fort William	P J'S SCOOTERS, North Road, PH33 6TQ.	01397 706133					•																
Forth	J.M.T MANUFACTURING LTD, Combfoot Garage, Main Street, ML11 8AU.	01555 811645					•										•						
Glasgow	BIKELINE, Clarkston Cycle Centre, 681 Clarkston Road, G44 3SE.	0141 225 8100				•	•						•										
Glasgow	BIKERITE, Unit 10 Dalmarnoch Trading Estate, Dalmarnoch Road, Rutherglen, G73 1AB.	0141 643 2200			•																		
Glasgow	POWERHOUSE, Enterprise Building, 243 Glasgow Road, Shawfield, G73 1SU.	0141 647 5878					•				•		•										
Glasgow	RIDE ON MOTORCYCLES LTD, 19-21 Nithsdale Street, G41 2QA.	0141 424 0404	•		•																		
Glasgow	SCOTBIKE LIMITED, Hyde Park Street, G3 8PW.	0141 226 8100			•						•												
Glasgow	TOYSHOP POWERHOUSE LTD, Enterprise Building, 243 Glasgow Road, Shawfield, G73 1SU.	0141 647 5878				•	•																
Glasgow	VICTOR DEVINE & CO LTD, 234-236 Gt Western Rd, G49 9EI.	0141 332 6264		•									•								•		
Glasgow	WEST COAST HARLEY-DAVIDSON, 147 North Street, G3 7DE.	0141 883 1340												•						•			
Greenock	MOTORCYCLE SALES AND SERVICCS, 9 Bruce Street, PA15 4LL.	01475 724 372					•										•						•
Greenock	WILLIAM MUSTARD LTD, 10/12 Eldon Street, PA16 7UE.	01475 786022											•		•				•				
Huntly	HUNTLY MOTORCYCLES, 8 Macdonald Street, AB54 8EW.	01466 792070	•										•								•		
Inverness	CALTERDON LTD, Harbour Road.	01463 236566	•				•						•										
Inverness	MACINTOSH MOTORCYCLES, 23 Grant Street, IV3 6PN.	01463 243099			•	•	•										•						
Inverness	MITCHELL'S MOTORCYCLES, 38 Greig Street.	01463 233478	•								•		•										
Inverness	PRO-BIKE, 42 Millburn Road, IV2 3OX.	01463 714515	•		•																		•

Inverurie	TWO WHEEL CENTRE, Port Elphinstone, AB51 9UT	01294 273 731
Irvine	WEST COAST RIDERS, Third Avenue, Heathermouse Industrial Estate, KA12 8LT	01360 550696
Killearn	KILLEARN GARAGE LTD, The Square, G63 9NF	01592 264135
Kirkcaldy	ALAN DUFFUS MOTORCYCLES LTD, 19-21 Cairie street, KY1 2QF	01595 692709
Lerwick	GRANTFIELD GARAGE LIMITED, North Road, ZE1 0NT	01592 712697
Leven	DAVE GRIEVE MOTORCYCLES, 19 Sandywell Street, Buckhaven, KY8 1BY	01631 564176
Oban	STODDART'S MOTORCYCLES, 4 Soroba Road, PA34 4HU	0413 327374
P.Dundas	MICKEY OATES MOTORCYCLES, North Canal Bank Street, G4 9XP	0141 889 1600
Paisley	MCS SCOOTERWORLD, 14 - 16 Abercorn Street, PA1 3PN	0141 887 5846
	TWIST 'N GO SCOOTERS, 80 Glasgow Road, PA1 3PN	01738 622020
Perth	BUCHAN MOTORCYCLES, Ranoch Road, PH1 2DP	01738 630550
	DICKSONS OF PERTH LTD, 172 Dunkeld Road, PH1 3XZ	01738 451050
	DRYSDALE MOTORCYCLES, 1 St Leonard Bank, PH2 8EB	0141 561 7521
Renfrew	WILLAIM THOMAS T/A MOTORCYCLE SERVICES, 18-20 Fulbar Street, PA4 8PD	01595 693192
Shetland	THULECRAFT LTD, Commercial Road, Lerwick, ZE1 0HX	01786 451616
Stirling	HARDIE OF STIRLING, Kerse Road, FK7 7RT	01786 465292
	STEWART WILSON CYCLES, 44 Barnton Street, FK8 1NA	
Tranent	ECLIPSE MOTORCYCLES, 5 - 7 Elphinstone Road, EH33 2LG	01875 611400
Uphall	C & J WILSON, 25 West Main Street, EH52 5DN	01506 856751
	C &J WILSON, 23 - 25 West Mian Street, EH52 5DN	01506 856751

IRELAND

Antrim	ADAM H ERWIN, 23 Ballymena Road, BT41 4JG	01849 463364
Armagh	ROADSIDE ARMAGH LTD, 2 Barrack Hill, BT60 1BL	01861 522912
Ballymena	PROVINCEWIDE HARLEY-DAVIDSON, 16 George Street, BT43 5AP	01266 44488
	R.F. LINTON & SONS, 31-33 Springwell Street, BT43 6AT	01266 652516
	RAY'S MOTORCYCLES, Unit 16, Mena Business Centre, Calgorm Ind. Estate, Cullybacky, BT42 1FL	01266 632888
Belfast	CHARLES HURST LTD, 62 Boucher Road, BT12 6LR	01232 381721
	EAST END MOTORCYCLES, 224 Newtonards Road, BT4 1HB	01232 731 454
	G.S. MOTORCYCLES, 23 Lisburn Road, Hillsborough, BT26 6AA	01846 689777
	HURST MOTORCYCLES LTD, Boucher Road, Balmoral, BT12 6LR	01232 381721
	OWENS BROS. (BELFAST), 206 Albertbridge Street, BT5 4GJ	01232 458230
	RACE BASE, 76 Donegal Pass.	01232 232376
	SCOOTER SERVICES LTD, 27 Donegal Pass, BT7 1DQ	01232 321509
Carrickfergus	H. WILSON & SON, 85 Belfast Road, BT38 8BX	01960 351025
Co Armagh	ALLENS HONDA, Armagh Road, Portadown, BT26 4EJ	01762 332525
Coleraine	WRIGHT'S MOTORCYCLES, Longuestown Industrial Estate, Bushmills Road, BT52 2NS.	01265 53745
Dublin	KAWASAKI DISTRIBUTORS (IRELAND), 17 Wood Street, Balmoral, BT12 6TR.	01232 381721
Dublin 24	CCM RACING, Unit 52, Cookstown Industrial Estate, Tallaught.	00353 1452 5866
Dublin 7	DUBLIN HARLEY-DAVIDSON, 24 Blessington Street.	00 35316794062
Londonderry	RIDE ON, Unit 6, Glendermott Business Park, Glendermott Road, BT47 1BJ.	01504 345984

IRELAND continued

			Aprilia	Benelli	BMW	Buell	Cagiva	CCM	Derbi	Ducati	Gilera	Harley	Honda	Kymco	Kawasaki	Laverda	M-Guzzi	MV Agusta	Peugeot	Piaggio	Suzuki	Triumph	Yamaha	
Lurgan	ROADSIDE MOTORS, 71 Belfast Road, Dollings Town, BT66 7JP.	01762 327423												●					●					
Moira	CELCO TRADING COMPANY, Trummary House, 9 Lisburn Road, BT67 0JP.	01846 613390													●						●		●	
Newry	CROSSAN MOTORCYCLES, 14 Trevor Hill, BT34 1DN.	01693 694 58	●																					
Newton Stewart	GEORGE MILLER MOTORCYCLES, Ardstraw, BT78 4LN.	01662 661571																						
Newtownards	REGENCY CARS, 39 Church Road, BT23.	01247 814581																	●					
Omagh	M & N MOTORS, Gortin Road, BT79 7DH.	01602 252623																	●					
Omagh	MOTORWORLD (OMAGH) LTD, Great Northern Retail Park, James Street, BT78 1QX.	01662 252623																	●					

FOWLERS

Discover a two-wheeled society you only dreamed of...

No more wondering who you can ask to come for a spin, no more staring blankly at a map for inspiration - just join Fowlers Riders Club...!

Life will never be the same again - yours that is!

It's Fun!

- **Evening Ride Outs**
- **Sunday Breakfast Runs**
- **Ride Outs to Britain's top race meetings**
  Including the British Superbikes Championships and the British Grand Prix
- **Factory Visits** - Visit the Triumph factory
- **Weekend Ride Away Trips**

It's Fantastic!

- **Track Days** - Special prices for FRC members at Castle Combe and Mallory Park
- **Advanced Rider Training**
  10% reduction available for FRC members
- **Theme Park Weekends**
  Big thrills at Alton Towers at reduced prices
- **Genuine Motorcycle Parts** - 10% reduction on production of a FRC card at Fowlers branches
- **Big Rock Intercontinental Bike Tours**
  10% discount available to FRC members

& It's Free!

- **No Membership Fees** • **Introductory Goody Bag**
- **Free Quarterly magazine, 'The Flying F'**
- **FRC Information Hotline**
- **Promotion Evenings & Barbecues**

To join Fowlers Riders Club, call Barry Maunders at Fowlers on 0117 977 0466

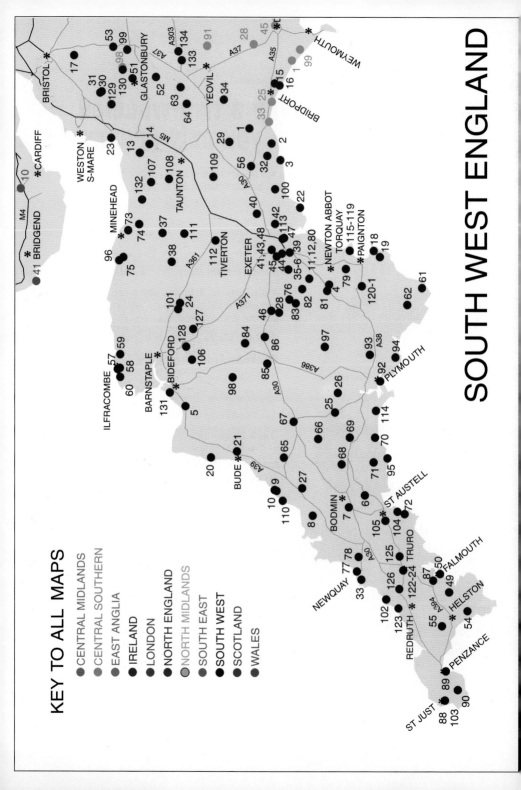

SOUTH WEST ENGLAND

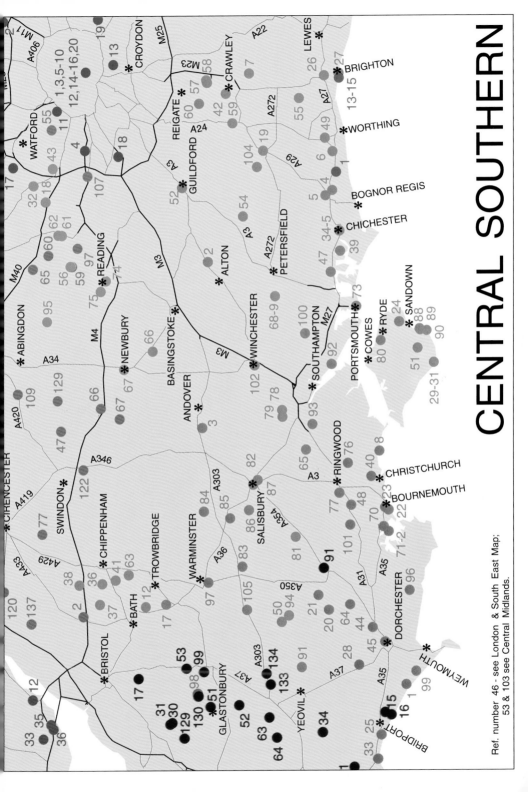

CENTRAL SOUTHERN

Ref. number 46 - see London & South East Map;
53 & 103 see Central Midlands.

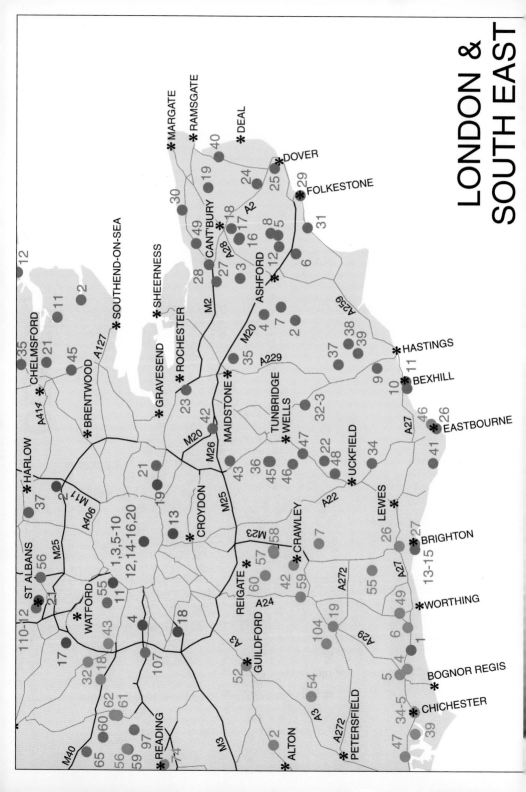

LONDON &
SOUTH EAST

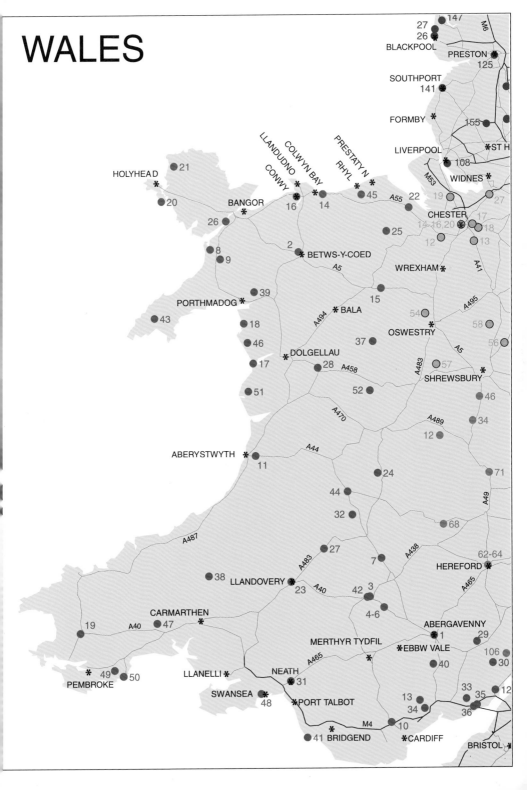

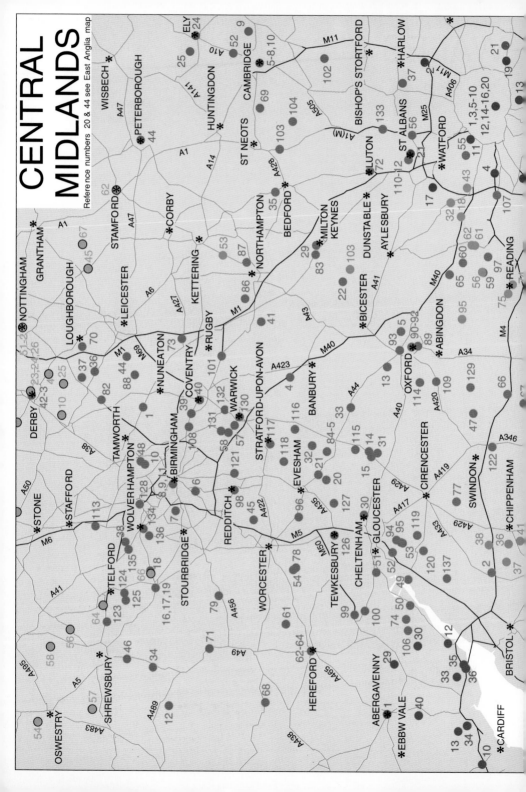

EAST ANGLIA

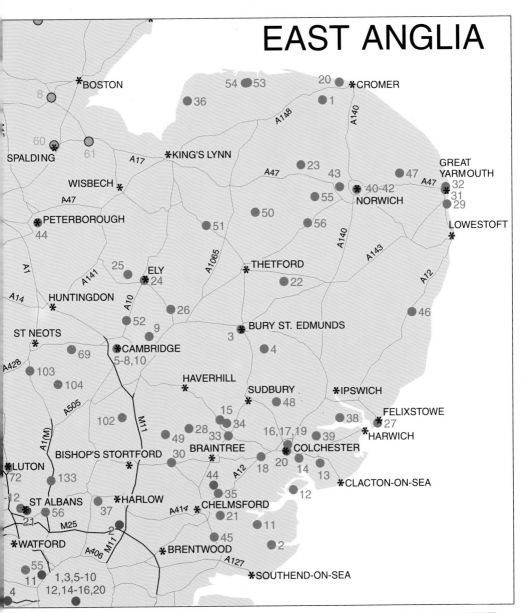

* BOSTON
8
54 ● 53
● 36
20 ●
● 1
* CROMER
A148
A140
60 ●
SPALDING
61
A17
* KING'S LYNN
23
● 43
● 47
A47
GREAT
YARMOUTH
WISBECH *
A47
55
● 40-42
NORWICH
● 32
● 31
● 29
PETERBOROUGH
44
● 51
● 50
● 56
A140
LOWESTOFT
25
A141
ELY
24
● 26
A1065
* THETFORD
● 22
A143
A12
A1
A14
HUNTINGDON
A10
52
9
3
● 46
ST NEOTS
● 69
CAMBRIDGE
5-8,10
* BURY ST. EDMUNDS
● 4
A428
● 103
● 104
A505
HAVERHILL
SUDBURY
● 48
* IPSWICH
102
15
● 38
FELIXSTOWE
27
A1(M)
M11
● 49
28
33
34
16,17,19
39
* HARWICH
30
BRAINTREE
COLCHESTER
BISHOP'S STORTFORD
* LUTON
72
133
44
A12
18
20
14
13
* CLACTON-ON-SEA
12
ST ALBANS
56
21
M25
37
35
HARLOW
A414
CHELMSFORD
21
● 11
2
* WATFORD
55
11
4
A406
M11
A127
* BRENTWOOD
45
● 2
1,3,5-10
12,14-16,20
* SOUTHEND-ON-SEA

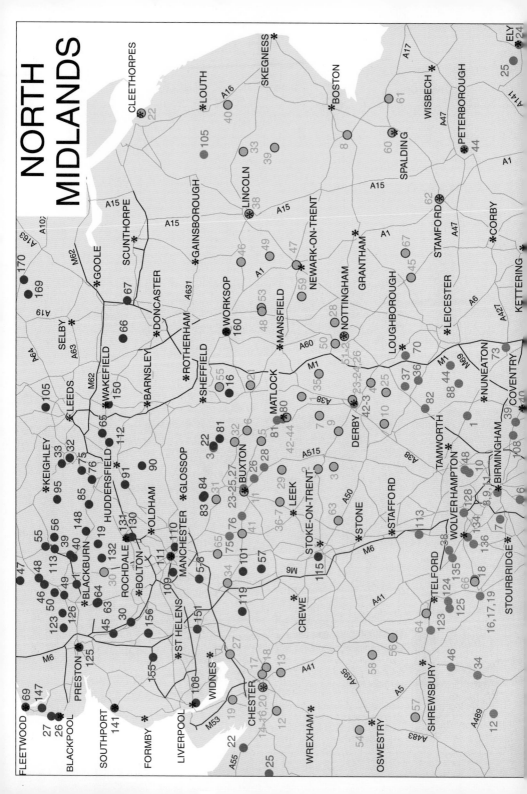

NORTH
MIDLANDS

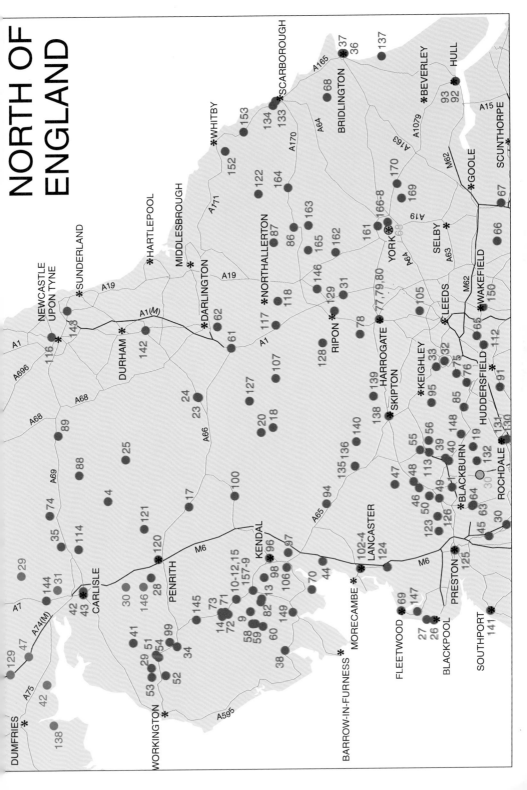

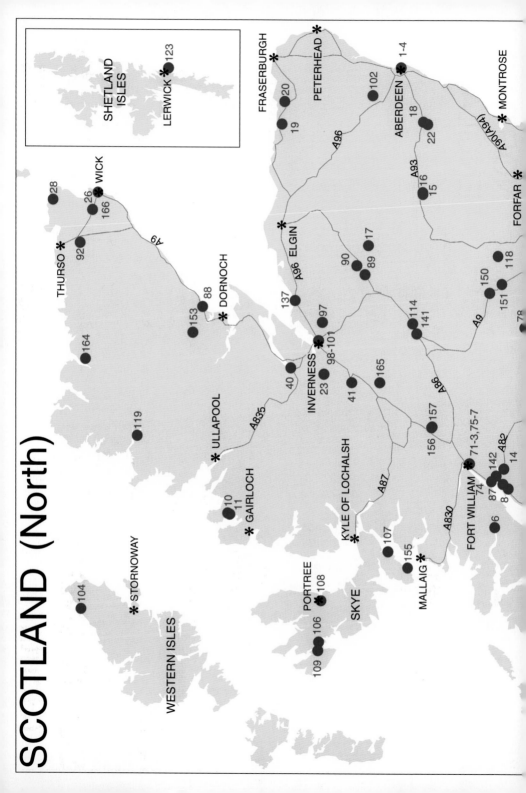

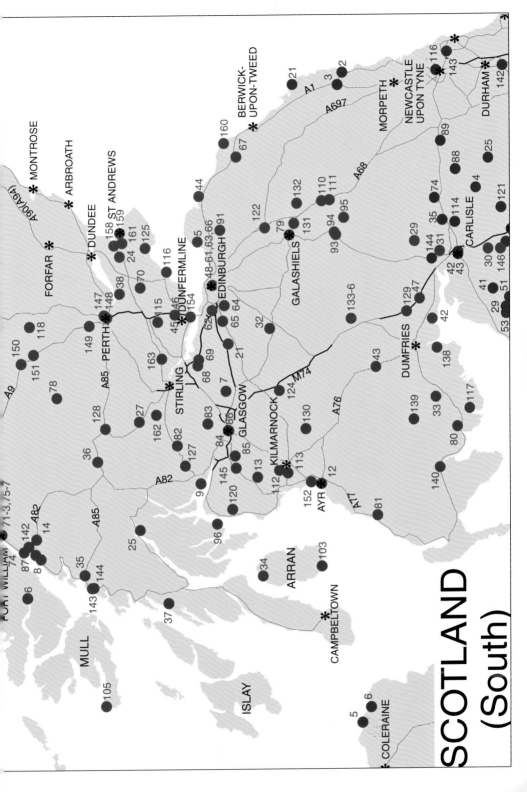

SCOTLAND
(South)

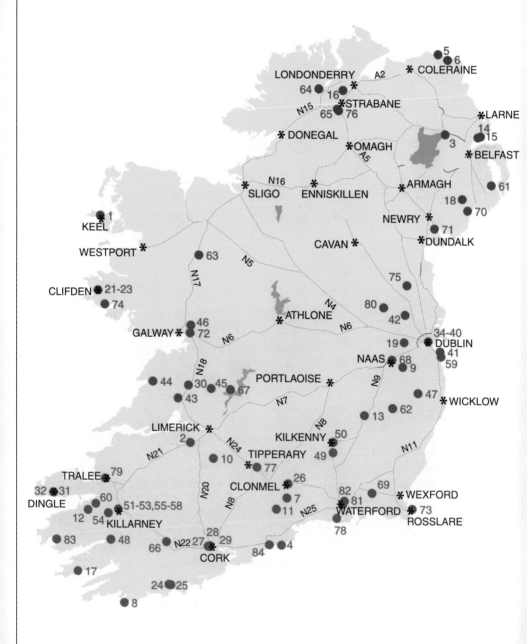

IRELAND

INDEX OF ADVERTISERS

AA Insurance Services *279*
Akito *41, 267*
Baglux *13, 79*
Belstaff *104*
Bennetts Insurance *280*
Bickers Telecom *187*
Bike Trader *290–294*
British Motorcyclists Federation (BMF) *74*
BMW Motorcycles *53, 55*
Bull I th Thorn Pub, nr Buxton *99*
Butley Ash Pub, nr Macclesfield *110*
Carole Nash Insurance *278*
Castrol Oils *263*
Cavendish View *99*
Central Wheels *306*
Chartered Trust *297*
Datatool *305*
DID Chains *209*
Devitt DA Insurance *268, 284*
Duke of York Pub, Buxton *97*
Dunlop Tyres *255*
EBC Brakes *65, 129, 103, 140, 145, 165, 285*
EK Chains *269*
Ellen House B & B, Matlock *112*
Ferodo Brakes *141*
FM Helmets *67, 225*
Frank Thomas *17*
Fowlers Rider Club *191, 339*
Givi *33*
Graham Arms Hotel, Cumbria *193*

Haynes Publishing *162-163, 276-277*
HJC Helmets *125, 247*
International Motorcycle Show *313*
Knox Body Armour *265*
Lazer Helmets *173*
Lloyds UDT RIGP Finance *105, 195, 286, 195, 196, 256, 338*
Metzeler Tyres *253*
Michelin Tyres *251*
Micron Exhausts *197*
Mobil Oils *321*
Morris Oils *273*
Motad International *167*
Motorcycle Action Group (MAG) *298-299*
Motorcycle Museum (The) *303*
Motorex Oils *275*
NGK Spark Plugs *289*
Nonfango Luggage *275*
Oxford Lifetime Luggage *125, 247*
Oxford Locks *125, 247*
Pirelli Tyres *257*
Putoline Oils *259*
Rev'it! *116-117*
Richa Clothing *133, 217*
RIGP Finance (see Lloyds UDT)
Scorpion Exhausts *47*
Sebring Exhausts *209*
Shoei Helmets *95*
Sidi Boots *233*
Silkolene Oils *261*
Spada Clothing *221*

Staden Grange *98*
Shad Luggage *137*
Spyball Alarms *213*
Suomy Helmets *9*
Swift Clothing *71*
Texport *87*
V E Scooter Parts *335*
Vemar Helmets *inside front cover, 23*
Weise Clothing *159*

Motorcycle Manufacturers
Aprilia *111*
Benelli (see Dealer Listings)
BMW *53, 55*
Buell (see Dealer Listings)
Cagiva *179*
CCM (see Dealer Listings)
Derbi UK *281*
Ducati (see Dealer Listings)
Gilera (see Dealer Listings)
Harley-Davidson *148-149*
Honda *26-27*
Kawasaki *301*
Kymco *271*
Laverda *179*
Moto-Guzzi *179*
M V Agusta *179*
Peugeot *179*
Piaggio (see Dealer Listings)
Suzuki *201, 203*
Triumph *58, 59, 127*
Yamaha *352–353*

ACKNOWLEDGEMENTS

This Guide was produced as a result of extensive and detailed research requiring substantial commitment from friends and family and I would like to offer my thanks for all their effort and tireless work.

My thanks go to Haynes Publishing and their staff who have worked so hard in order to meet deadlines, which have all been achieved. Also:

My wife Vivienne; my sister Pauline and brother-in-law Lawrence; Inspector David Short (Bike Safe 2000); Pippa White and Trevor Kemp (Silkolene Oils); David Foster (Castrol Limited); Frank Finch (Motoport, Eastbourne) and David Pinder (Lintek Gleave) for articles written; Andrew Riseam (my computer boffin); Andrew Banfield (Lloyd Lifestyle); Adrian Roberts (Datatool); Bryn Phillips (Cambrian Tyres) and all my friends of many years standing in the motorcycle industry, who have been so kind and helpful.

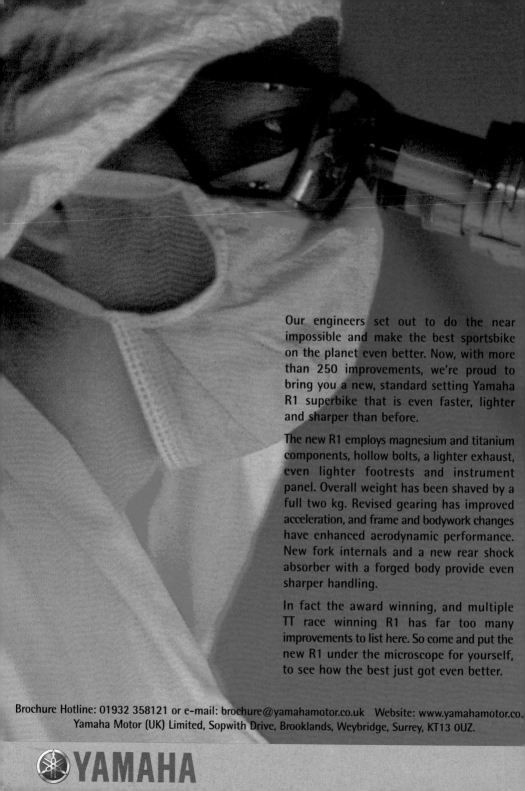

Our engineers set out to do the near impossible and make the best sportsbike on the planet even better. Now, with more than 250 improvements, we're proud to bring you a new, standard setting Yamaha R1 superbike that is even faster, lighter and sharper than before.

The new R1 employs magnesium and titanium components, hollow bolts, a lighter exhaust, even lighter footrests and instrument panel. Overall weight has been shaved by a full two kg. Revised gearing has improved acceleration, and frame and bodywork changes have enhanced aerodynamic performance. New fork internals and a new rear shock absorber with a forged body provide even sharper handling.

In fact the award winning, and multiple TT race winning R1 has far too many improvements to list here. So come and put the new R1 under the microscope for yourself, to see how the best just got even better.

Brochure Hotline: 01932 358121 or e-mail: brochure@yamahamotor.co.uk   Website: www.yamahamotor.co.
Yamaha Motor (UK) Limited, Sopwith Drive, Brooklands, Weybridge, Surrey, KT13 0UZ.

YAMAHA